Beginning Visual Basic 2005 Express Edition

From Novice to Professional

Peter Wright

Apress®

Beginning Visual Basic 2005 Express Edition: From Novice to Professional

Copyright © 2006 by Peter Wright

ISBN-13 (pbk): 978-1-59059-622-7

ISBN-10 (pbk): 1-59059-622-6

Printed and bound in the United States of America 9 8 7 6 5 4 3 2 1

Trademarked names may appear in this book. Rather than use a trademark symbol with every occurrence of a trademarked name, we use the names only in an editorial fashion and to the benefit of the trademark owner, with no intention of infringement of the trademark.

Lead Editor: Jim Sumser
Technical Reviewer: Jason Bock
Editorial Board: Steve Anglin, Ewan Buckingham, Gary Cornell, Jason Gilmore, Jonathan Gennick, Jonathan Hassell, James Huddleston, Chris Mills, Matthew Moodie, Dominic Shakeshaft, Jim Sumser, Keir Thomas, Matt Wade
Associate Publisher, Production Director, and Project Manager: Grace Wong
Copy Edit Manager: Nicole LeClerc
Copy Editors: Sharon Wilkey, Ami Knox
Assistant Production Director: Kari Brooks-Copony
Senior Production Editor: Laura Cheu
Compositor: Pat Christenson
Proofreader: Nancy Riddiough
Indexer: Broccoli Information Management
Cover Designer: Kurt Krames
Manufacturing Director: Tom Debolski

Distributed to the book trade worldwide by Springer-Verlag New York, Inc., 233 Spring Street, 6th Floor, New York, NY 10013. Phone 1-800-SPRINGER, fax 201-348-4505, e-mail orders-ny@springer-sbm.com, or visit http://www.springeronline.com.

For information on translations, please contact Apress directly at 2560 Ninth Street, Suite 219, Berkeley, CA 94710. Phone 510-549-5930, fax 510-549-5939, e-mail info@apress.com, or visit http://www.apress.com.

The information in this book is distributed on an "as is" basis, without warranty. Although every precaution has been taken in the preparation of this work, neither the author(s) nor Apress shall have any liability to any person or entity with respect to any loss or damage caused or alleged to be caused directly or indirectly by the information contained in this work.

The source code for this book is available to readers at http://www.apress.com in the Source Code section. You will need to answer questions pertaining to this book in order to successfully download the code.

Contents at a Glance

Contents

About the Author

PETER WRIGHT has been programming with, and writing about, Microsoft development tools since 1992. He is the author of about a dozen books, including the international best-selling series *Beginning Visual Basic*, and has written numerous articles for the both the print and online press worldwide. Born in England, Peter now lives in Florida, along with his wife, two kids, and two fluffy attack spaniels called Mac and Tosh.

About the Technical Reviewer

JASON BOCK is a senior consultant for Magenic Technologies (http://www.magenic.com). He has worked on a number of business applications using a diverse set of substrates and languages such as C#, .NET, and Java. He is the author of *Applied .NET Attributes, CIL Programming: Under the Hood of .NET, .NET Security,* and *Visual Basic 6 Win32 API Tutorial.* He has written numerous articles on software development and has presented at a number of conferences and user groups. Jason holds a master's degree in electrical engineering from Marquette University. Outside of his professional life, he enjoys spending time with his wife Liz, his son Hayden, and his three cats, along with writing music, playing golf, and wasting too much time with his Xbox 360. Visit his website at http://www.jasonbock.net.

Acknowledgments

I moved to Florida in August 2005. As I write this it's one year later, and this is the second book that I've had published since stepping off the plane. The weather's great, the scenery beautiful, and the way of life simply outstanding. But the one thing that has changed that has led so much to me being able to do this is my social environment: the circle of friends and family around me. So, it makes sense that I should thank them first of all.

Lew and Sara—the best in-laws in the world—thanks for all the babysitting help and for putting up with a moody son-in-law when he was in the middle of tight book-writing schedules. Laura, Donald, Zack, Cody, Phoebe, and Joshua—you guys are awesome and so wonderfully encouraging. With you guys around, anything seems possible.

Over at Apress, the same team that stuck with me through the last book endured this one too. So, a *huge* thanks to Grace, Jim, Sharon, Laura, and Amy. As usual, you guys turned a few hundred pages of idle meanderings into a veritable work of art. Thank you so much for all your help and support.

My reviewer on this book was Jason Bock. Now, I've known Jason through email, Xbox Live, and MSN Messenger for a couple of years now, and I'm honored that he managed to make time to review this book. He was a tough reviewer, and his take-no-prisoners approach to reviewing means the book you hold in your hands is so much better than it would have been without his help. As if that's not enough, he managed to fit all this in between caring for his newborn son and making preparations for the one his wife has in Beta. All the best to you both, and thanks a million for the help, Jason.

Finally, *my* family. olmHeather, Ethan and Eloise, and the attack spaniels Mac and Tosh—I love you guys! Without you, this would all be so very pointless.

Introduction

It was in Amsterdam, in 2004, that I first discovered the Express tools from Microsoft. During the keynote at Microsoft's huge developer event, TechEd, various personas from inside the company were getting extremely animated about the possibilities these tools gave to the development community. At a time when most of us thought Microsoft was quietly beavering away on Visual Studio 2005 and nothing else, the boys and girls from Redmond did a massive turnabout and announced that they would be, at last, introducing a set of extremely well-priced reduced-functionality development tools aimed specifically at students and hobbyists.

I saw something different, though. With a very cheap price (they're actually free at the time of this printing), the Express tools are the ideal way for anyone to get up to speed in .NET development. Ignoring the obvious benefits these tools have for students, there's a whole raft of people out there coding like demons in Java, classic Visual Basic, and even the Linux tools that prior to the release of the Express family may never have had a chance to experience the power and versatility of .NET.

I sat down at lunch to discuss the book ideas with Gary Cornell, Apress's venerable publisher, and something else occurred to me. The Express family of tools probably represents the most groundbreaking move in development tools Microsoft has made since the release of Visual Basic way back in the early 90s. Visual Basic opened up a previously locked world, enabling practically anyone to sit down and write computer programs that would run on the Windows operating system. It was a paradigm shift away from the traditional crusty world of C++ compilers, huge technical reference books, and headaches, and into a world where developing a program was as simple as dragging and dropping components with a mouse and then gluing them all together with code.

Visual Basic was also very keenly priced. In fact, it was so keenly priced and so easy to use that within a decade it had grown to become the world's single most popular programming tool, and I believe almost certainly helped propel the popularity of Windows itself (after all, what good is an operating system without software, and what better way to get software than to make it easy for people to develop it).

As the popularity of Visual Basic grew, so too did its features, and along with them the price of the package. By the end of its life, Visual Basic was most commonly bought as part of the Visual Studio suite of tools, a phenomenally powerful collection of programming gems that commanded a staggering price (from a mere man-on-the-street's point of view). Visual Studio .NET followed with a similar price, and so too did Visual Studio .NET 2003. When Visual Studio 2005 was announced, the world pretty much assumed that Microsoft was now totally committed to delivering development tools that only the big companies could afford. Similarly, the features in that tool were focused totally on solving the sorts of problems the big boys faced every day.

Express was a radical U-turn. Once again Microsoft was returning to its roots by making available easy-to-use programming tools that sacrificed nothing in terms of power and that would be available to all budgets.

Since the first ever release of .NET, Visual Basic has matured into a wonderfully elegant object-oriented language. Despite what the press would have you believe, Visual Basic is still way more popular than C#, and that owes a lot to the verbosity and almost English-like syntax of the language. After spending my days writing C# code, it was a surprising joy to come home at night to write Visual Basic once again.

This book is designed for anyone who has ever wanted to learn .NET programming with Visual Basic but who has never been able to, probably because they couldn't legally get the tools to do so. Perhaps you've never programmed a computer before in your life. If that's the case, the early chapters of the book will lead you gracefully into the world of code. On the other hand, perhaps you're an old hand at classic Visual Basic or even Java and have come here to learn just what all the fuss is about in .NET land. Great, welcome aboard! You'll find plenty to cut your teeth on, and hopefully at the end of this book you'll be able to find plenty of reasons to jump ship completely!

So, what exactly do I cover?

Chapter 1: Welcome to Visual Basic Express

Firing up Visual Basic 2005 Express for the first time can be a little daunting. There are a myriad of buttons, menus, and options to twiddle with, and no obvious best place to start. In this chapter I'll walk you through just what it's like to use the Visual Basic 2005 Express environment, and by the end of the chapter we'll even write our own full-blown Windows application together. What better way to get your head wet than to just dive straight in?

Chapter 2: The Basics of Visual Basic

In Chapter 2 you'll start exploring the Visual Basic language itself. There are two aspects to the package: the Visual Basic 2005 Express integrated development environment (IDE) and the Visual Basic language. In this chapter we'll turn away from the pretty bells and whistles for a whistle-stop tour of the features of what is rapidly becoming one of the world's most popular programming languages.

Chapter 3: Working with Variables

If you've programmed before, you know that it's pretty much impossible to achieve anything without variables. Variables are the placeholders in your code where you'll store data your program works with, the items that you'll use in code to make decisions while the program is running. In this chapter you'll find out all there is to know about variables in Visual Basic.

Chapter 4: Classes and Object Orientation in Visual Basic 2005

Visual Basic is (now) an object-oriented programming language. In this chapter you'll get a good look at just what that means as you explore the fundamental object-oriented facilities that Visual Basic provides.

Chapter 5: More-Advanced Object Orientation

It's a big subject and gets two chapters. In this one you'll go beyond the basic syntax of working with objects and classes and dive into the mysteries of inheritance, virtual methods, abstract classes, and interfaces.

Chapter 6: Handling Exceptions

Inevitably sometimes things just don't go to plan. When that happens in code, you get exceptions. In this chapter you'll explore all of Visual Basic's tools for processing and dealing with exceptions.

Chapter 7: How Visual Basic 2005 Express Helps You Code

Now we get to return to the IDE. Visual Basic 2005 Express has a ton of features designed to help you write programs. In fact, features such as IntelliSense can actually write some of the code for you, while features in the graphical designer tools let you build standards-conforming user interfaces effortlessly. This is the chapter where you'll explore all these toys.

Chapter 8: Building Windows Applications

Visual Basic 2005 Express is designed to help you write programs for Windows. In this chapter you'll explore just how as we dive into the world of building user interfaces, handling user interface events, and much more user interface goodness.

Chapter 9: Windows and Dialogs

Now that you know how to build a user interface, it's time to explore the different kinds of windows most Windows applications have. In this chapter you'll take a look at dialog boxes, both creating your own and using the built-in ones, as well as taking a peek at just how to customize the appearance of a window itself.

Chapter 10: Lists

Lots of Windows programs these days have lists: lists of employees, lists of high scores, grids containing details of those people you must not forget during the holidays. This chapter explores how to create them and work with them, diving into the details of the powerful List controls that every Windows program contains.

Chapter 11: Menus and Toolbars

What's a Windows application without a menu to let you get at its features? In this chapter you'll explore just how those menus are created, how to work with them in code, and of course how to supplement them with cool-looking toolbars.

Chapter 12: Events

Everything in a Windows application revolves around events. When the user clicks a button, moves a slider, or selects an item in a list, an event gets fired off that it's your job to handle. In this chapter you'll look at Visual Basic's events, and .NET delegates, the inner workings of .NET's event handling.

Chapter 13: Lists and Generics

I know, we already covered lists back in Chapter 10. In this chapter, though, you'll look at how to create lists internally, in code, without graphical user interfaces. You'll explore one of the cool new features of Visual Basic that makes working with lists of information so painless: generics.

Chapter 14: Files and Streams

Displaying information in your program is one thing, but where did that information come from? In this chapter you'll look at how to work with files and streams as I show you how to seamlessly stream information in and out of your program to both files and the Internet.

Chapter 15: Working with XML

XML data is everywhere these days, and .NET has some fantastic support for working with what has rapidly become the lingua franca of the Internet. In this chapter I'll show you just how .NET lets you manipulate and work with XML with ease.

Chapter 16: Database Programming

Visual Basic 2005 Express ships with a very powerful database engine based on Microsoft's SQL Server system. In this chapter you'll explore just how to create databases and work with them in your programs.

Chapter 17: The Internet and Visual Basic

Who hasn't heard of the Internet these days? Visual Basic 2005 Express makes working with the Internet in your programs trivial. You'll see how to write your own browser, how to use web services out there on the Net, and how to download information you find on websites around the globe.

Chapter 18: Threading

We close out our look at the language and tools of Visual Basic 2005 Express with threading. Threading is all about making your program do two (or more) things at once. It used to be a topic that scared off even seasoned programming vets, but VB Express makes this once-fearsome land as warm and inviting as a tropical island paradise.

Chapter 19: Where to Now?

When you reach this point in the book you'll have no trouble writing your own programs, and writing code that talks to the Internet and databases. You'll know how to build the next killer user interface. But, as Douglas Adams once observed about space, .NET is big. In fact, it's so big that no book could ever cover every single class in the framework or every use someone would want to put those classes to. In this chapter I'll send you on your way with some pointers to resources that can help take you to the next level in your .NET adventures.

CHAPTER 1

■■■

Welcome to Visual Basic Express

Visual Basic is the original Microsoft Windows Rapid Application Development (RAD) tool. When it first hit the market way back in '91, it started a revolution in how people write computer programs.

Prior to Visual Basic (VB) arriving, writing a program to run on Windows—complete with all the bells and whistles of the Windows graphical user interface—was an exercise in pain. Windows is, after all, a hideously complex beast to work with in code. Visual Basic, though, simplified the whole thing. If you wanted a window with a button in it, all you had to do was drag and drop controls from a Toolbox onto a window the program gave you, and you were finished.

Visual Basic 2005 Express carries this tradition forward. It's just as easy today to write programs for the very latest versions of Windows as it was back then to create programs for Windows 3.0. Visual Basic 2005, though, while strikingly similar to classic Visual Basic in many areas, is radically different in others. The language has evolved and is now a truly *object-oriented* language. Because Visual Basic is now also a .NET-enabled language, when you sit down to write your Visual Basic masterpieces today, you have the full backing and power of Microsoft's legendary .NET Framework at your disposal. Of all the Express tools, I still feel happiest in Visual Basic 2005 Express (or VB Express—I use the names interchangeably). It's the most descriptive language to use in many cases, bearing more than a passing resemblance to English in terms of its syntax and structure.

In this chapter I'm going to set the stage a little. If you've never programmed before and you've already installed and taken a look at VB Express, you may feel a little daunted by all the strange icons, words, and images that the user interface has plastered all over it. I'll demystify it all for you in this chapter.

If you're an old hand, perhaps an accomplished Visual Basic or Java developer, or perhaps a .NET developer looking to learn new things with Express, this is the chapter where you'll see some of the most obvious and stunning changes that Microsoft has made to its development environments in the Express tools. A lot of the functionality in Visual Basic 2005 Express comes from Visual Studio .NET 2005, so you'll get a glimpse into just what that product can provide, if perhaps you are viewing it as a target for the future.

Whoever, and whatever, you are though, this is the chapter where I hope I can show you just some of why VB Express is, in my mind, one of the most significant product releases Microsoft has ever made.

Visual Basic has had a bad rap since the release of .NET, with many people calling classic Visual Basic a toy, an amateur programming environment that's great for prototyping ideas, but not really that great when it comes to producing high-performance, easy-to-maintain applications of any complexity. That's ignoring something vital, though. Visual Basic was designed to make Windows programming accessible to everyone. It didn't matter whether you were a professional programmer, a graduate, a high-school dropout, or a retired garbage collector, Visual Basic was designed to put everyone on an even playing field when it came to making great-looking, functional software.

In addition, Visual Basic was an extremely focused piece of software. Visual Basic let you do one thing (create Windows applications) and do it very well indeed. It was only later in Visual Basic's life that it was integrated into "Visual Studio," and as a result had access to facilities for creating server-side components and web applications.

Because of its easy-to-use features and its inherent goal of focusing on doing just one thing, and doing it very well, Visual Basic brought a few million new developers to the world of Windows, and helped not only propel Windows even further into the hearts and minds of millions of people all over the world, but also set the benchmark for just what writing a computer program should really be like. You only have to look around the market today at products such as Delphi, JBuilder, C#Builder, and of course Visual Studio .NET to instantly spot similarities between those tools and good old-fashioned classic Visual Basic.

You can see the warm welcoming UI of Visual Basic 2005 Express in Figure 1-1.

Visual Basic 2005 Express is the result of the years of experience Microsoft has had with VB as a whole. Everything that made Visual Basic great is still there. You can still rapidly build user interfaces for your applications just by dragging and dropping controls. The programming language is still beautifully descriptive and easy to read (if not fully understood) by all. Therefore, Visual Basic 2005 (the language) is perhaps the least error prone of all the languages Microsoft supports, particularly for beginners.

Conversely, all the arguments that were ever leveled at Visual Basic have been addressed. Visual Basic 2005 is a .NET language. You write code in VB and then compile it. When it's compiled, the compiler spits out Microsoft Intermediate Language (MSIL), an intermediary language that *all* the .NET compilers (yes, including the C++ and C# ones) produce. The net result is that Visual Basic programs now run at pretty much exactly the same speed as their C++ .NET and C# counterparts. In fact, a common selling point of .NET (which applies to VB now) is that .NET programs in general can be faster than pure C or C++ written ones because at runtime the .NET system will optimize the code for the processor in your machine. Most classic C and C++ compilers, on the other hand, will target a base processor compatible with all machines to let the programs run on the widest possible range of hardware.

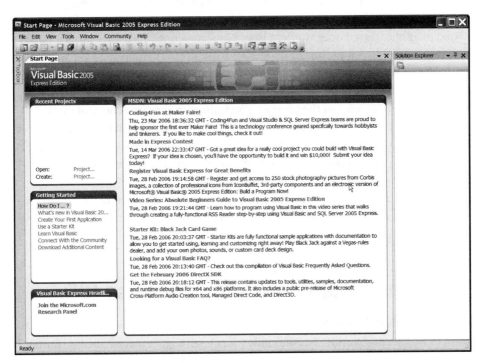

Figure 1-1. *The clean, welcoming user interface of Visual Basic 2005 Express*

Visual Basic 2005 is also a fully object-oriented (OO) language now. If that means nothing at all to you, don't worry. We'll go into the full details of object-oriented programming starting in Chapter 4. There is nothing that C# and the other OO languages can do now that VB can't. In fact, in some instances Visual Basic makes life easier. For example, if you are writing a Microsoft Office automation program, VB is the best choice. Why? Well, many of the components of Office still expect variable-length parameter lists to be passed to them, and VB is still the best language on the planet for doing that. I'm getting a little ahead of myself here, but the time will come when a friend or colleague will denigrate Visual Basic and you for learning it. When that time comes, you'll remember this paragraph.

In short, Visual Basic is now a completely modern, high-performance language. In Microsoftspeak it's also a first-class .NET language and fully able to use and take advantage of all that the .NET Framework has to offer.

Just What Is Express?

Express is the name given by Microsoft to a range of entry-level .NET 2.0 development tools. Each tool (there are six in all) is focused on allowing you to learn how to develop one specific kind of application. For example, Visual Web Developer 2005 Express is focused on developing web applications. Visual Basic 2005 Express and Visual C# 2005 Express are both focused on producing standard Windows-style applications, either with the Visual Basic or C# programming language.

Each tool also includes a lot of the tools and technologies that you can find in the full Visual Studio 2005 package. Visual C# Express, for example, includes some fantastic tools for restructuring the code in your programs (a process called *refactoring*). The user interface of all the Express products also have a lot in common with all previous versions of Visual Studio .NET, as well as the new Visual Studio 2005.

The best way to learn everything the package can do, and to get comfortable with it, is to use it. So, if you haven't installed Visual Basic 2005 Express already, now is the time to do so.

Exploring the Visual Basic 2005 Express IDE

It's a tired tradition that the first program you write when learning a new programming language or tool is "Hello, World!" Traditionally it has been a great way to become familiar with how to write your program's code, figure out how to display something on the screen, compile the code, and then run the resulting program. Visual Basic 2005 Express makes programming so easy that this little exercise is almost a no-brainer. In fact, in Charles Petzold's book *Programming Windows* (Microsoft Press, 1998), Charles had us write a program that displays a window, puts "Hello, World" in the center of it, and then made the text always stay in the center of the window no matter where the user moved it or resized it. The resulting code was around 80 lines. Let's do the same thing in VB Express.

Try It Out: Hello, World, VB Express Style

First, open Visual Basic 2005 Express. When the welcome screen appears (you saw what this looked like in Figure 1-1), click File ➤ New Project on the menu bar. The New Project dialog box appears, just as in Figure 1-2.

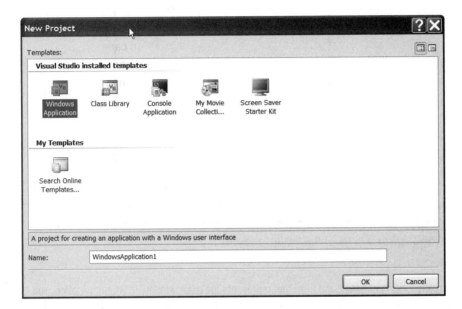

Figure 1-2. *The New Project dialog box*

If you've used Visual Studio .NET before, you'll probably be surprised by just how few options appear. As I said earlier, VB Express is focused on doing just one thing, very well.

For now, just click Windows Application and then click the OK button.

After a bit of a pause (how long you wait depends on how powerful your machine is), you'll be dropped into Visual Basic's form-editing mode. You can see this in Figure 1-3.

Don't panic if your screen looks a little different from mine. The user interface of the IDE (integrated development environment—the thing you should be looking at right now) is highly customizable, so chances are that if you've already been playing around with it, it may look slightly different.

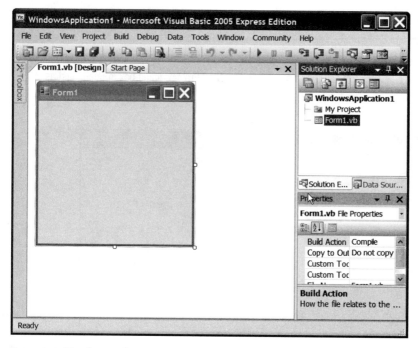

Figure 1-3. *The form editor in Visual Basic 2005 Express*

What you are actually looking at here is the form that represents the main window of your application. You candrag and drop controls from the Toolbox on the left onto the surface of the window to build up a nice professional-looking user interface for your application. The Properties window on the right lets you customize those controls to give your application a unique look and feel, and also provides options that relate to the code that you'll need to write to get a more complex application off the ground.

If your Toolbox is not showing (mine isn't in Figure 1-3), the first thing you'll need to do is display it. Move the mouse over the word *Toolbox* on the left side of the IDE and you'll see the Toolbox slide out, as in Figure 1-4.

When you move the mouse out of the Toolbox area, the pane will slide shut again. To prevent this from happening (some people like it that way, some don't), click the pushpin at the top of the pane, to the left of the Close icon (the X), to lock the Toolbox open. Finally, click on the plus symbol (+) next to the words "Common Controls" to display the list of the most common controls. The Toolbox will look like Figure 1-5 when you do this.

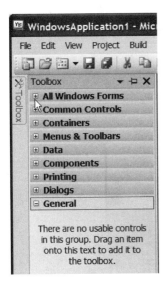

Figure 1-4. *If the Toolbox is not showing, just hover the mouse over the Toolbox tab on the left of the IDE.*

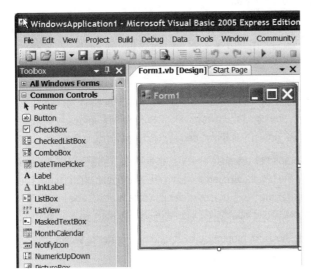

Figure 1-5. *The controls in the Toolbox are grouped. Clicking the + sign next to each group's name expands the group to show the controls it contains.*

Move your mouse over the Label control in the Toolbox, and then drag and drop it onto the form (a window in design mode is called a *form*). Your form should look a lot like Figure 1-6 when you're finished.

Figure 1-6. *Your form with the label on*

Looking good so far; you've created a form that at runtime will become a window, and it has some text in it. Best of all, you haven't written any code yet, so let's carry on.

The Properties window on the right of the IDE allows you to customize pretty much anything in your application. Click on the label you just dropped onto the form and you'll see the text at the top of the Properties window change to show that you are now looking at the properties of the Label control that you just added, as in Figure 1-7.

Properties are easy to understand, and in fact bear a lot in common with the real world. Take me, for example. I'm a pale and pasty Englishman with black hair. You could say that my SkinColor property (property names don't have spaces in them) is White, my HairColor property is Black, and my Name property is Pete.

In the case of our Label control, a couple of its properties are quite obvious. Its name is `label1` (you can see this at the top of the Properties list), because it's the first Label control that you have dropped on the form. The text that you can see inside the label on the form is the `Text` property, and its value is also `label1`. You'll need this text to show the message "Hello, World," so obviously you'll need to change that `Text` property.

Scroll the Properties list down until you can see the `Text` property, click it, and type in **Hello, World**. The property should look like Figure 1-8 when you're finished.

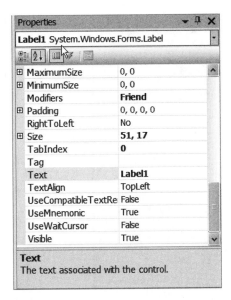

Figure 1-7. *The top of the Properties window always shows you the object that you are working with.*

Figure 1-8. *Change the Text property from label1 to Hello, World.*

So far, so good. Now, Charles Petzold's application had the text always centered in the window, but you'll find that what you've done so far won't achieve that. To demonstrate, click the Run button on the toolbar at the top of the IDE (it looks like the Play symbol on a VCR or DVD player), or press F5 on your keyboard to do the same thing. A flurry of activity takes place while VB Express compiles the application and then runs it. You should now see a brand new window on screen, probably overlapping VB Express itself as mine did in Figure 1-9.

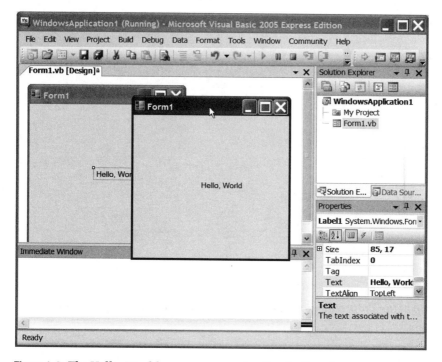

Figure 1-9. *The Hello, World program, running for the first time*

If you try making the window smaller or larger, you'll find that the text always remains in the same position and could even vanish if you made the window small enough. That needs to change. Close the window (by clicking its Close icon—the X) and you'll be returned to the VB Express IDE.

At this point, even in classic Visual Basic, you'd have to do a bunch of typing to get that text to stay centered on the form. Not so anymore. Click on the label once to make sure it's selected and then take another look at the Properties window.

First, scroll up to find the property called AutoSize. This is set to True, which means that the label will always be just big enough to hold all the text inside. No bigger, no smaller. Double-click the word True next to the property name to set it to False.

Now find the Dock property. Dock lets you lock a control, like our label, to a specific position on the form. You want the label to always be the same size as the form. If you click on the word None next to the Dock property name, you'll see a down arrow appear. Click it, and you'll see a Dock property editor appear as in Figure 1-10.

Each box in the editor represents a position inside the form. Click on the middle one to make the label fill the entire form. You should see the Dock property value change to the word Fill, and the label will grow to take up the entire form. You can see this in Figure 1-11.

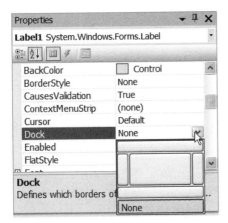

Figure 1-10. *The Dock property editor*

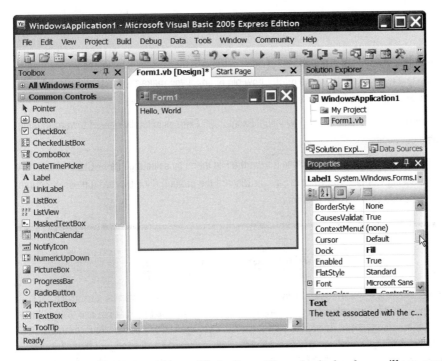

Figure 1-11. *The label should now fill the form (if you look closely, you'll see a subtle border inside the form itself).*

Now all that remains is to align the text properly within the now massive Label control. This is achieved in much the same way as setting up the Dock property. Find the TextAlign property, and just as you did with the Dock property, click the property value and then click the arrow that appears, as in Figure 1-12.

Figure 1-12. *The TextAlign property editor works in a similar way to the Dock property editor.*

Again, click the middlemost button to center the text in the control, and then press F5 to run the program once again. This time the text remains centered, no matter how big or small you make the form. You just did, with a few mouse clicks, what traditionally would have taken quite some code to achieve.

It's a very simple example, but it does show how Visual Basic 2005 Express is totally geared toward making your life easier as a developer.

When you're finished exploring the example, close it from the File menu by selecting File ➤ Close Solution. A dialog box appears, asking whether you want to Save or Discard the project. Click Discard (unless of course you really want to save it to your disk for posterity).

ALREADY USED .NET?

If you've used .NET before, you'll know that creating simple projects to try things out was something of a pain. You'd create a new Windows application, for example, and call it WindowsApplication1, and Visual Studio would save that to your hard disk. This meant of course that if you created a bunch of simple example programs to test things out, you'd end up with a bunch of unused directories and files on your hard disk.

The Express tools and Visual Studio 2005 get around that problem with *temporary* projects. Any project you create is classed as a temporary project and will be discarded when you close it or shut down the IDE, unless you explicitly save it.

When using temporary projects, you can create as many test programs as you like without worrying about cluttering up your hard disk.

FOR THE VISUAL BASIC DEVELOPERS

If you did press Save instead of Discard at the end of the preceding "Try It Out," you would have noticed that you were asked just two things: what you want to call the project, and where you want it stored. This is completely different from Visual Basic, in which saving a project resulted in a series of dialog boxes appearing and asking you to name every file in the project and the project itself.

The reason for this can be found in the Solution Explorer. When you first create a project, you are asked to give it a name. This name appears in the Solution Explorer. Similarly, each file you create is also assigned a name, which you can change by right-clicking the file in the Solution Explorer and choosing Rename. For example, our form from the earlier "Try It Out" is a file called `Form1.vb`.

When you save a project in Express, a directory is created for the project based on its name, and all the files in the project are saved into that directory by using the names shown in the Solution Explorer. Isn't that so much easier?

Exploring the IDE a Little More

I've just scratched the surface of what the Visual Basic 2005 Express IDE can do for you. This is only Chapter 1, after all. So, let's take a minute to look at some of the other cool features it has before you dive into a much bigger "Try It Out" example.

At the start of this section I mentioned that your IDE might look a little different from mine. Let me show you why (even if you have used Visual Studio before, keep watching—this is pretty cool).

Each of the things around the form editor (the Properties window, the Toolbox, and so on) is actually a docked window. You can make them hide and appear on demand, you can undock them and leave them floating around on the desktop, and you can even stick them to different edges of the IDE.

Try it—grab the title of the Properties window and drag it left. The screen changes to look like the one in Figure 1-13.

Notice all the arrow shapes. These let you tell VB Express exactly where you want the window that you're dragging around docked. Simply drag over the appropriate arrow, and hey, presto, the window docks. Prior to this marvelous invention, I always found docking and moving windows to be a real pain in the neck; I could never position the floating window in just the right place for it to dock to where I really wanted it to end up.

You've probably already noticed that there are more windows docked around the edges of the IDE than just the Solution Explorer and the Properties window. In fact, if you tell the IDE to display every possible window, you soon end up with a huge mess of tabs everywhere. VB Express, like its big brother Visual Studio, has a ton of windows that you can use to gain different views into your application and the things going on with it.

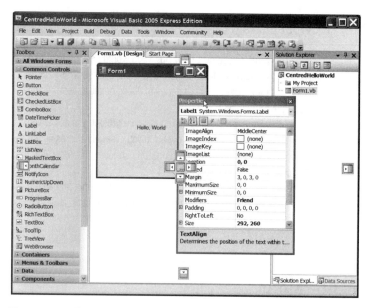

Figure 1-13. *The new docking arrows make it simple to put a floating window exactly where you want it.*

You can see the full list of windows by clicking the View menu at the top of the IDE, as shown in Figure 1-14.

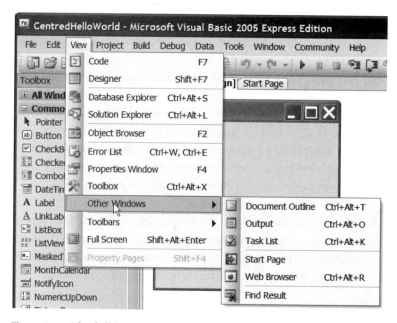

Figure 1-14. *The full list of windows in Visual Basic 2005 Express*

Rather than bore you to tears explaining each one in excruciating detail, Table 1-1 summarizes what each window does. You'll look in more detail at each of them as you come across them throughout the book.

Table 1-1. *The Full List of Standard Windows Available in Visual Basic 2005 Express*

Window Name	Description
Code	Shows you the actual Visual Basic code behind a form. When writing programs in VB Express, you'll find yourself switching between the form designer and the code behind the form a lot.
Designer	You've seen the designer already. The designer is the view you'll use to drag controls from the Toolbox onto your forms to build up your application's user interface.
Database Explorer	When you start programming database-aware applications, the Database Explorer comes into play, showing you the tables, stored procedures, and other artifacts inside the database you're working with.
Solution Explorer	The Solution Explorer, as you've seen, shows you all the files in your project. A solution, though, can contain more than one project, and in that case the Solution Explorer will show you every single project in the solution, and all the files in each project.
Object Browser	As you'll see throughout the rest of this book (and in the "Try It Out" shortly), everything you do when creating programs in VB Express revolves around using objects. The Object Browser shows you just which ones are available to you (think of it as a glimpse into the .NET LEGO box)
Error List	Inevitably as you start to work on your own programs (and even when working through some of the examples in this book), you'll make mistakes that will show up as errors when you try to run the program. When that happens, the Error List automatically comes into view, letting you double-click on each error to automatically jump to the corresponding problem in the code.
Properties	The Properties window gives you a way to customize the look and feel, and behavior, of the various components of your program and its user interface.
Toolbox	The Toolbox is a dynamic window in that its contents change based on what you are doing. If you are designing a form for your application's user interface, for example, the Toolbox shows you all the various user interface controls that you can drop onto the form to customize it.
Document Outline	The Document Outline window gives you a great way to keep track of everything on your forms as you build them. For example, if you add a group box to the form, and then a button inside the group box, the Document Outline window will show a nice hierarchical tree indicating exactly which controls and UI elements contain which other UI elements.
Output	When you compile and run a program, this window shows you the output of the Visual Basic compiler. It can also be used by your own program to output debugging information while it's running.

Continued

Table 1-1. *Continued*

Window Name	Description
Task List	The Task List is a flexible window, showing you the errors that occurred at compile time, as well as tasks that you have added yourself. You can actually write little notes into your application to remind you to do things, and these appear in the Task List window.
Start Page	This window displays the start page, the view that you see when you first start VB Express. The Start Page window shows you news and other interesting tidbits from the Microsoft Express communities.
Web Browser	VB Express includes a built-in web browser, and that is just what the Web Browser window is. This is a great tool for quickly looking something up on the Internet if you come across some problems in your code. It's also the window that's used to display the online help system.
Find Results	Your programs can get huge. If VB Express had a search tool like that in Microsoft Word, finding things would be a nightmare (you'd have to keep repeatedly clicking through a Find dialog box to get to just the thing you really need). Instead then, VB Express has a Find Results window that shows you every match that a Find finds. Just double-click an entry in the Find Results window to jump right to the located element.

As you work through the next "Try It Out," use the View menu to display some of the windows in Table 1-1 and watch how they update as you work through the example.

The main toolbar of the IDE also provides you quick access to some of the most common windows. The View icons are at the right-hand end of the toolbar, as shown in Figure 1-15.

Figure 1-15. *Icons on the main toolbar provide quick access to some of the most common windows.*

Simply hover the mouse over an icon to see a ToolTip appear, explaining what the button does.

Working with the Editors

You already experienced working with the form designer in the previous "Try It Out." Let's take a more detailed look before you dive into the next "Try It Out."

Most of the nontrivial programs you'll work on will have more than one form and definitely more than one source code file. It's not uncommon, therefore, to have many editors open at once. VB Express shows each currently open "document" as a tab across the top of the main editor window, as in Figure 1-16.

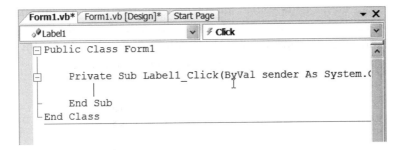

Figure 1-16. *When the editor has more than one document open, tabs at the top of the editor window let you quickly select which document to jump to.*

You can switch between the various open documents either by clicking the tab you want or by holding down the Ctrl key and pressing Tab. When you do that, a dialog box appears, as in Figure 1-17, showing you all the open documents and windows in the IDE.

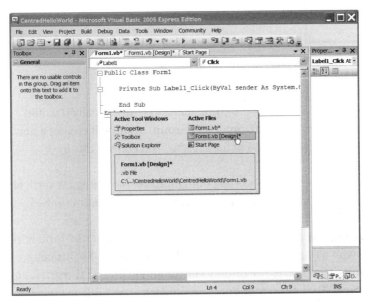

Figure 1-17. *Holding down the Ctrl key and then pressing Tab shows you which documents and windows are currently open in the IDE.*

If you keep tapping the Tab key while holding down the Ctrl key, you'll find that the highlight moves between each document in the Open Files list. Alternatively, while still holding down the Ctrl key, you can click the document or window that you want to activate, or even use the arrow keys on the keyboard.

VB Express also offers you a stunning amount of flexibility in how you can configure the editors (form editor, code editor, and so on) to suit you best. For example, I develop on a machine with two monitors, and I like to have a form or source code displayed on one monitor, and another source file on a separate monitor. This is really easy to set up in VB Express. Just right-click one of the editor tabs, and a context menu appears, as you can see in Figure 1-18.

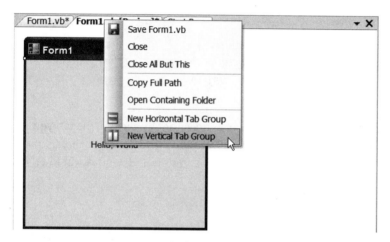

Figure 1-18. *Right-clicking an editor tab pops up a context menu.*

If you then select New Vertical Tab Group, the editor splits in two vertically (I would have preferred Microsoft to call this New Horizontal Tab Group, because it creates a new group of tabs listed horizontally across the top of the screen). You can see this in Figure 1-19.

So, on my machine I simply make VB Express span both monitors, create a new vertical tab group, and then click and drag the divider bar that splits the editor window in two until I have each half of the editor taking up exactly one monitor.

If you really wanted to go crazy with this, you could keep creating new vertical and horizontal groups and end up with a bunch of source files on display at once. Realistically though, even on two monitors, that makes the display very cramped indeed (I yearn for a couple of Apple Cinema 23-inch flat screen monitors, but until I get them, I'll just relegate this feature to the "neat to have" box).

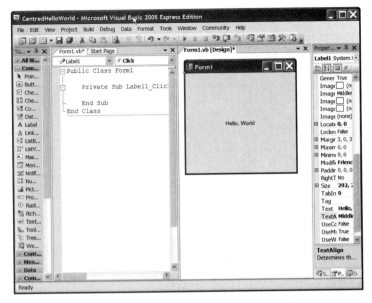

Figure 1-19. *Creating a new vertical tab group splits the current editor view in half, vertically.*

As I said, this is a "neat to have" feature, but it doesn't really offer developers like you that much in the way of productivity benefits. IntelliSense on the other hand does.

All versions of Microsoft's "Visual" development tools have had IntelliSense for years. In fact, even Microsoft's Office tools now have IntelliSense, but that's really only because office workers using Excel and Word get jealous when they see all the cool toys that we developers have to play with.

IntelliSense basically is a way for Visual Basic 2005 Express to guess what it is you're trying to do and offer assistance as you write your program code. It's awesome. In fact, in VB Express it's beyond awesome thanks to another neat technology called code snippets, which you'll look at shortly.

Try It Out : Using IntelliSense

Create a new project in Visual Basic 2005 Express by selecting File ➤ New Project from the menu bar, or by pressing Ctrl+N.

When asked what kind of project to create, select Console Application and click the OK button in the dialog box. A console application has no windows-based user interface and simply runs in a text window. This interface is ideal for giving you a flavor of how IntelliSense and the other code development features of the IDE work.

After a short pause, the project will be created and your IDE will look very similar to the one in Figure 1-20.

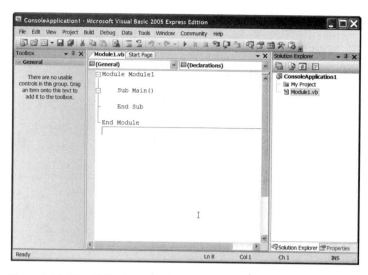

Figure 1-20. *The IDE after starting up a new console application*

Because a console application has no real graphical user interface in the traditional Windows application sense, the IDE automatically drops you into the code editor. If you have never written any Visual Basic applications before, don't worry if the text on the screen looks worryingly cryptic. You'll work through just how a Visual Basic program looks and what it all means, in detail, in the next chapter.

When you write a program in Visual Basic, you actually spend most of your time either creating or using objects and classes (think of a *class* as a blueprint for an object). Visual Basic also provides you with something called *modules*. These are just containers for short snippets of code. Take a look at the code on-screen and you'll see that we're already working with a module:

```
Module Module1

    Sub Main()

    End Sub

End Module
```

As you can see, your program consists of a single module called Module1. Inside that module is an empty *subroutine* called Main. This is the subroutine that will run when you hit F5 to start the program. It all looks pretty simple, doesn't it. The complexity comes in when you consider what it means to work with the .NET Framework.

The .NET Framework consists of hundreds of classes that each contain a bunch of subroutines that you can call. That all adds up to a lot of things to remember, which is exactly what IntelliSense is designed to help you with.

Position your cursor on the blank line between `Sub Main()` and `End Sub` and then hit Ctrl+spacebar. The IntelliSense window appears just beneath the cursor, as shown in Figure 1-21.

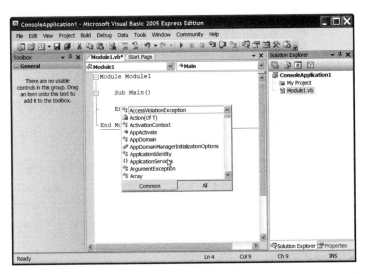

Figure 1-21. *The IntelliSense window appears when you press Ctrl+spacebar.*

Here you'll find all the classes that are available for you to use, as well as namespaces. Because there are so many classes in the framework, .NET uses *namespaces* to group them. For example, if you were about to write code to talk to the Internet, you'd need the classes in the `System.Net` namespace. We'll look more at IntelliSense and namespaces in the next chapter.

If you were to run the program at this point, all you'd see is a text window (called the console window—this is a console application after all) appear briefly and disappear. Because this is a console application, running it causes the console to appear, and because you don't have any code in your application, the console window immediately disappears. There's a way to stop that from happening.

The `System` namespace contains a class called `Console`. This has lumps of code in it (methods) to do various tasks, such as display text in the console window and other such console-related goodies. There's also a method in there called `ReadLine()` that waits for the user to enter some text and press Enter before continuing. Let's use IntelliSense to add a line of code into your `Main ()` subroutine to do just that.

If the IntelliSense window is not currently displayed, press Ctrl+spacebar once again to show it, and then type the letters **Sys**. The IntelliSense window automatically jumps to the first entry it can find that begins with those letters—the `System` namespace (as shown in Figure 1-22).

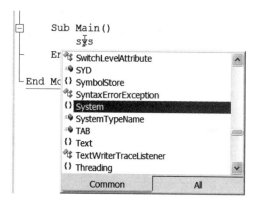

Figure 1-22. *Typing while the IntelliSense window is open causes it to automatically jump to the first match closest to whatever you typed.*

You can select the entry shown in the list by clicking it with the mouse, pressing Enter, typing **.**, or **(**, or by pressing Tab. Why so many choices? Well, to use a method in the System namespace's Console class, you'll need to list the namespace followed by a period, followed by the name of the class, followed by a period, followed by the method name. So, try it out. Erase the text you just typed and press Ctrl+spacebar once again. This time, type exactly this: **Sys.Cons.ReadL**. Your editor will look like the one in Figure 1-23.

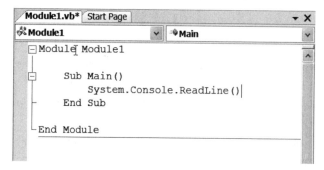

Figure 1-23. *Notice how IntelliSense automatically fills in the rest of the text for you.*

As you can see, IntelliSense can save you an awful lot of typing. More to the point though, it can save you an awful lot of grief by avoiding spelling mistakes. Notice also that IntelliSense changes when you start to call a method on a class by showing you a description of that method.

Finish the line of code, and your program should look like this:

```
Module Module1

    Sub Main()
        System.Console.ReadLine()
    End Sub

End Module
```

If you run the program now (F5), you'll see the console window appear, and it will stay visible until you click in it and press Enter. `System.Console.ReadLine()` is waiting for you to do just that, and until you do, the program won't end. When it does end, the console is closed down and you are returned to the normal IDE view.

IntelliSense does far more than this, though, and can actually help you add structure to your program. For example, let's get this program to count from 1 to 10 and display those numbers in the console.

Now, just to play dumb here, say I know that the Visual Basic command I need to use to count is the `For` command, but I can't remember how to use it. I do know that IntelliSense can help me.

Place the cursor on the `S` of `System` on the line of code you just typed in, and press Enter to insert a blank line.

Click in that blank line and right click with the mouse. A menu appears, as in Figure 1-24.

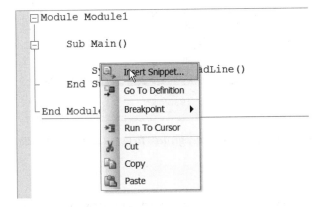

Figure 1-24. *The context menu in the code editor*

Now go ahead and select Insert Snippet. Another list appears, showing you a list of expansions. These are actually code snippets, lumps of code written by Microsoft (you can add your own to the list as well) that you can insert into your own projects as you need them. You can see the snippets list in Figure 1-25.

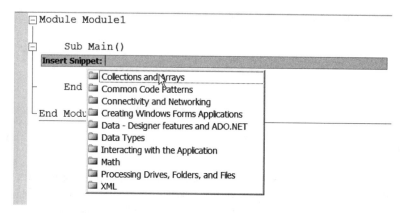

Figure 1-25. *The list of code snippets*

Click on the code snippet group called Common Code Patterns. The list will change to show you more snippet categories. Click Conditionals and Loops, and the list will change once again, this time showing you actual code snippets, as in Figure 1-26.

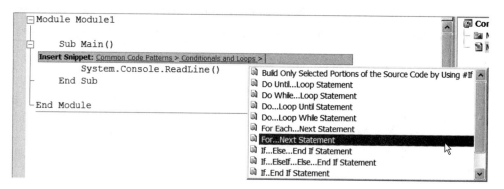

Figure 1-26. *You need to click through numerous code snippet groups to get at the actual code snippets themselves.*

Select the snippet called For...Next Statement and you'll see the code window suddenly change, as in Figure 1-27.

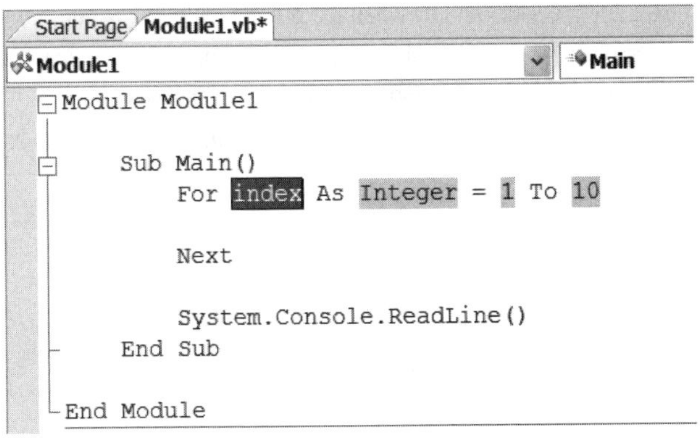

```
Start Page / Module1.vb*
Module1                                    Main
Module Module1

    Sub Main()
        For index As Integer = 1 To 10

        Next

        System.Console.ReadLine()
    End Sub

End Module
```

Figure 1-27. *The selected code snippet is inserted into your own code.*

Notice that there are two elements in the new code highlighted in green. These are called *replacements* and are meant for you to, umm, replace. For now, ignore the highlighted "index" thing—it's called a *variable*, and if you've never come across them before, then you'll be introduced to them in the next chapter.

You want your loop to count from 1 to 10, and that's exactly what this snippet does. If you wanted to count from 10 to 100, you would just change the numbers on that first line of code accordingly.

All that remains is to put some code in to display the numbers. You can use IntelliSense for this as well. Click so that your cursor is on the blank line inside the new code snippet block. Press Ctrl+spacebar to bring up the IntelliSense window and type **Sys.Cons.WriteL(**. Your code window will look like Figure 1-28.

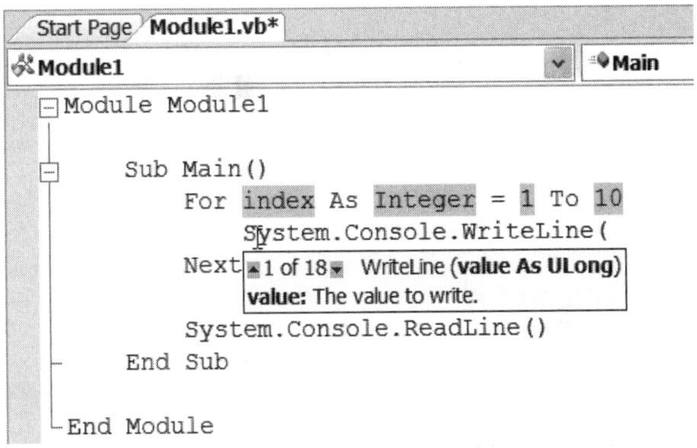

```
Start Page / Module1.vb*
Module1                                    Main
Module Module1

    Sub Main()
        For index As Integer = 1 To 10
            System.Console.WriteLine(
        Next ▲1 of 18▼  WriteLine (value As ULong)
             value: The value to write.
        System.Console.ReadLine()
    End Sub

End Module
```

Figure 1-28. *Use IntelliSense to make your code window look like this.*

System.Console.WriteLine displays text in the console window when the program is running. You simply put the item that you want displayed inside the parentheses at the end of the command. Now, your code snippet uses something called Index to count from 1 to 10. Inside your loop then (The For...Next thing is called a *loop*), you'll just have WriteLine display Index. Change the code so that it looks like this:

```
Module Module1

    Sub Main()
        For index As Integer = 1 To 10
            System.Console.WriteLine(index)
        Next

        System.Console.ReadLine()
    End Sub

End Module
```

Run the application now, and your console window will display the numbers 1 to 10 and wait for you to press Enter before closing down. You can see this in Figure 1-29.

Figure 1-29. *When you run the program, it will visibly count from 1 to 10 and then wait for you to press Enter on your keyboard before shutting down.*

Writing Your Own Web Browser

I'm going to close out this chapter with a nice big "Try It Out" that not only shows you even more about the IDE and what it can do, but also focuses on what Visual Basic is best at: writing great applications.

In this example you're going to produce a really simple but functional web browser, something that took Microsoft many years to produce. You're going to do it in about 15 minutes.

Try It Out: Writing a Web Browser

Start a new Windows application project in the usual way (click File ➤ New Project and then choose Windows Application from the Project Type dialog box when it appears).

After the form appears in the editing area, take a look at the Toolbox, shown in Figure 1-30.

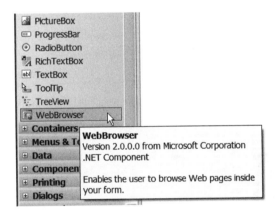

Figure 1-30. *The Toolbox contains a ready-made WebBrowser control.*

Scroll down the Toolbox. Near the bottom you'll see a WebBrowser control. Double-click it to add it to the form.

The form will appear to change color, but other than that, there's no obvious sign that the form is now a web browser. By default, when you drop the WebBrowser control onto a form, it just shows a blank white page and docks itself to the entire form area. Let's fix that.

Many of the controls in VB Express support something called *smart tags*, a technology originally developed to make people's lives in the Office applications more productive. The WebBrowser control has a smart tag attached, and you can access it by clicking its icon (a small left-pointing arrow at the top right of the browser). Figure 1-31 shows this.

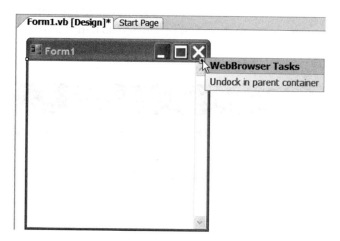

Figure 1-31. *Clicking the smart tag icon on a control pops up an additional menu.*

Select Undock in Parent Container (the only menu item that appears), and the web browser will undock itself to take up a lot less of the form, as shown in Figure 1-32.

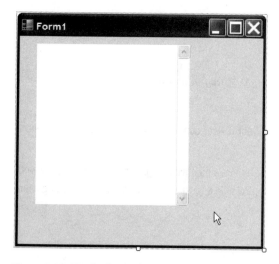

Figure 1-32. *Undocking the web browser makes it take up less room and allows you to move and resize it.*

Go ahead now and drop some labels, a text box, and a few buttons onto the form so that it looks like mine in Figure 1-33. If you can't remember how to do this or to set properties on a control, refer to the first "Try It Out" in this chapter.

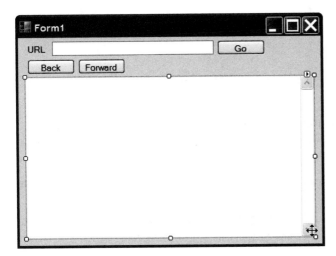

Figure 1-33. *Your web browser form should look like this.*

The next thing that you need to do is to set up anchor points for the various controls. If you were to resize the form right now (please don't), you would find that the form would grow or shrink in size but the controls would remain exactly where they are. What you really want to happen is that when the user resizes the form, the controls move to match the new form size. This is achieved by setting up the Anchor property of a control.

In the case of our web browser form, set the Anchor property for the text box holding the URL to Top, Left, and Right. This will make the URL stay in the same place on the form, but grow in width as the form is resized. Set the Anchor property for the Go button to Top Right, which means it will always appear at its current location, in relation to the top-right corner of the form.

Finally, set the Anchor property for the browser control to Top, Left, Right, and Bottom. This means that the web browser will never move, but as the form changes in width, so too will the browser. Similarly, as the form changes in height, so too will the browser.

Try resizing the form now and you should see the effects of the Anchor property changes, like mine in Figure 1-34.

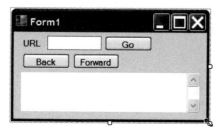

Figure 1-34. *Anchoring controls lets you move and/or resize them as the form changes in size.*

So far you've managed to set up a pretty neat-looking user interface for the web browser that will actually respond to users changing the size of the form. The next step is to add some functionality to this, to make the program useable.

However, before diving into writing some code, you first need to rename some of those controls. The reason for this is that you will be writing code that tells the controls what to do by name. Having a button called Button1 is okay for just messing around and trying things out, but your code will be a whole lot clearer and easier to follow if you give everything a decent name. So with that in mind, set the Name properties as shown in Table 1-2.

Table 1-2. *Name Properties*

Control	Name Property
URL text box (not the label)	urlBox
Go button	goButton
Back button	backButton
Forward button	forwardButton
The WebBrowser control	browser

Perhaps the most important bit of code you need to write is the code that responds to the user hitting that Go button. When the user clicks it, you want the web browser to navigate straight to the URL that the user entered into the text box.

Double-click the Go button, and the code window appears.

The way to make a WebBrowser control navigate to a new page is a method called Navigate. All you need to do is tell that Navigate method where to go.

Type in code so that your goButton_Click code looks like this:

```
Public Class Form1

    Private Sub goButton_Click(ByVal sender As System.Object, _
        ByVal e As System.EventArgs) Handles goButton.Click
        browser.Navigate(urlBox.Text)
    End Sub

End Class
```

What's happening here? Well, when you double-clicked the button on the form, you told VB Express that you wanted to write some code to deal with the button's default event. An *event* is something that happens in response to something else. For example, when a user clicks a button, a Click event happens, and you can write code to deal with that.

The code that's most interesting here is the bit that you have to write. You're simply using the "browser's" Navigate function to navigate to the text entered into the text box. Text is a property of the TextBox control that you can look at in the Properties window. You can refer to it in code as shown.

Go ahead and run the application now. Type in a URL, click the Go button, and watch what happens—see Figure 1-35.

Figure 1-35. *The Go button's Click event brings the web browser to life, telling it exactly where to navigate.*

To stop the application, just close the form as you would any other window.

All that remains now is to get those Back and Forward buttons working.

Double-click the Back button to edit its Click event (you'll be looking at the code window, so to get back to the form in order to double-click the Back button, click the tab labeled Form1.vb [Design] at the top of the code editor).

To get the browser to go back a page (assuming there is a page to go back to), you just need to tell it GoBack(). Type in code so that the Back button's Click event looks like this:

```
Private Sub backButton_Click(ByVal sender As System.Object, _
    ByVal e As System.EventArgs) Handles backButton.Click
        browser.GoBack()
    End Sub
```

Do the same thing for the Forward button, but set its code to look like this:

```
    Private Sub forwardButton_Click(ByVal sender As System.Object, _
      ByVal e As System.EventArgs) Handles forwardButton.Click
        browser.GoForward()
    End Sub
```

Voilà – you're done. Run the program, navigate to a web page, click some links, and then start using those Back and Forward buttons.

Those of you who have never written a program before in your life are probably quite worried by the typing that went on. Aside from that, what this example demonstrates is the very essence of Visual Basic 2005 Express. Express makes application development easy. In fact, the .NET Framework 2.0 makes application development easy, and VB Express just adds even more to the mix to make the whole deal so much more satisfying.

Summary

You covered a lot of ground in this introduction to Visual Basic 2005 Express. You saw how to change the look and feel of the IDE, how to create projects, and how to write code. You also took a look at IntelliSense, and hopefully I managed to give you a sense of just what a great time-saver that feature is in VB Express. Finally, we wrapped everything up by developing a simple but fully functioning web browser application.

After this whirlwind tour of the IDE, you'll be pleased to know that in the next chapter I slow things down a bit so you can take a long hard look at just what a Visual Basic program is and what it all means. Those of you who have never written code will soon understand all the things that may have worried you in the earlier examples. Those of you coming here from other languages are about to wonder just how on earth you ever got along before Visual Basic 2005 Express came along.

See you in Chapter 2.

■■■

CHAPTER 2

The Basics of Visual Basic

This chapter in the C# version of this book begins with a description of how C# can be quite a difficult, bewildering language to read. It's an intentionally terse language, with its commands succinct to the point of obscurity in some cases.

Thankfully, Visual Basic 2005 doesn't suffer from that problem. Visual Basic is an extremely descriptive language. This can lead to other problems, though. Because the language is so descriptive, it's easy for new programmers to find the language running away with them as they pound on the keyboard hour after hour. Without care, a Visual Basic program can soon become an immense list of seemingly unrelated instructions. To be fair, this is more a carryover of its non-object-oriented legacy. With a little effort and focus, Visual Basic programs these days can appear almost artistic.

In this chapter you'll take a brief whirlwind tour of the Visual Basic language, its features, and how to use it. If you've never programmed before, you will no doubt find some of the concepts in this chapter confusing. Stick with it, though. This chapter gives you a foundation to build on as you dive deeper into Visual Basic through the rest of the book.

Don't be put off reading this chapter if you've done some programming in some other language, even classic Visual Basic; I'll be dropping pointers throughout to put the new Visual Basic 2005 programming language into a context that you old hands should appreciate.

The Basic Structure

The focus of Visual Basic 2005 is to keep things as simple as possible. It's a productive programming language, and the designers were keen to make sure that your attention is always where it should be—on writing new features for your application. For this reason, the Solution Explorer is quite uncluttered, as shown in Figure 2-1.

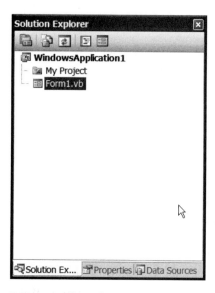

Figure 2-1. *The Solution Explorer in Visual Basic 2005 Express is always clean and uncluttered.*

When you create a new project in Visual Basic 2005 Express, you usually see just two items in the Solution Explorer. The first, My Project, provides quick access to the project options. Double-clicking it replaces the form designer, or code view, with a neat view into the project's main properties, as shown in Figure 2-2.

The tabs down the side of the options display let you drill down into specialist settings for tasks such as debugging and compiling. You don't need to know about these just yet. The vast majority of the time, you'll never even change any of these option settings. The common things that you would want to change, such as the project's name, can be done by other means.

The other item that you'll see in the Solution Explorer is your main form file, usually named Form1.vb. Double-clicking this brings up the form in the form designer mode. This is the mode that we used in the walk-throughs in Chapter 1. As you add new forms and classes (more on those in Chapter 4) to the project, you'll see the Solution Explorer start to fill up with more items whose names end in .vb.

Forms, as you saw in the previous chapter, consist of two elements. On the one hand, there are the visual elements of the forms, controls that build up your application's user interface. On the other hand, there is the actual Visual Basic code that you'll need to write to respond to events on the user interface. This is known as your program's *source*, and it's this that we'll be focusing on in the rest of this chapter.

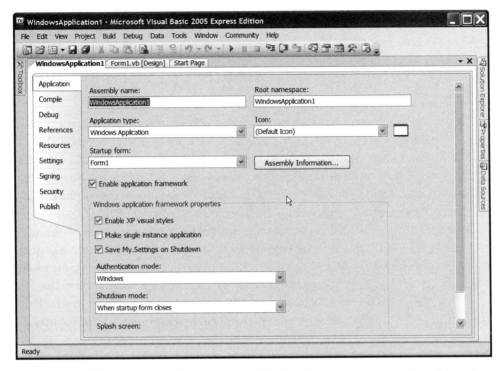

Figure 2-2. *Double-clicking My Project in the Solution Explorer takes you into the project properties view.*

Source Code and the Two Project Types

Every project you create in Visual Basic 2005 Express will start with a single source file. In a console application project, this is a *module*. In a Windows application project, it's a *form*. (There is another type of project you can create called a *class library*, but its source file, on the surface at least, looks the same as the form you get with a Windows application.) Let's look at the differences between them.

The module that you get with a console-type application looks like this:

```
Module Module1

    Sub Main()

    End Sub

End Module
```

The form you get with a Windows application looks like this:

```
Public Class Form1

End Class
```

There are two obvious differences between the two files.

First, a console application starts off with a module. You can see this because the first line of code in the source file actually has the word Module, followed by the module's name. A Windows application, on the other hand, starts out with a class, called Form1. The most basic (excuse the pun) type of source file you can create in VB Express is a module. It's just a container of code. Classes, on the other hand, are the root of everything that is object oriented and hence they get a chapter all of their very own in Chapter 4.

The second difference is that in a console application, the module starts out with a sub-routine that is always called Main(). When you run the program, the .NET runtime system looks for the subroutine called Main() and runs it. Actually the same thing happens when you start up a Windows application, but VB Express hides the implementation of the Main() method away from you. All it does in a Windows application is set up the .NET runtime and then fire up the first window of the application before waiting for the user to do something.

That's the reason a console application has a subroutine waiting for you to add code, and a Windows application doesn't. A console application can't do anything unless you give it some code inside that Main() subroutine. A Windows application on the other hand can do a bunch of stuff, including starting up a form as a window. The window comes pre-equipped with a bunch of functionality of its own, such as the ability to show and hide, change its size, shut down when its Close icon is clicked, and so on. If you want or need the program to do anything else, it's up to you to add controls to the form and then write code to respond to events on those controls. If I added a button to the form, for example, and double-clicked it to get at its Click event, the code in my form would change, like this:

```
Public Class Form1

    Private Sub Button1_Click(ByVal sender As System.Object, _
        ByVal e As System.EventArgs) Handles Button1.Click

    End Sub

End Class
```

Now it looks a little similar to the module, doesn't it. At the very least you may have noticed that this event handler is a Sub just like Main (albeit with a bunch of things inside parentheses following the name of the Sub).

These are *subroutines*. Inside a class, as the preceding event handler is, they are more commonly referred to as *methods*. Basically a Sub is a small unit of code with a name. In our console application, we add code to the subroutine called Main(), and that code (anything between the Sub Main() line and the End Sub line) is what gets run when the program starts. Similarly, in our preceding event handler, any code that lives between the Sub Button1_Click line and the End Sub line is run whenever the user clicks on a button.

You may also have noticed by now that there's a slight difference between some of the code printed on these pages and what you're seeing on-screen. Take a look at the following code and then compare it with Figure 2-3:

```
Private Sub Button1_Click(ByVal sender As System.Object, _
    ByVal e As System.EventArgs) Handles Button1.Click


End Sub
```

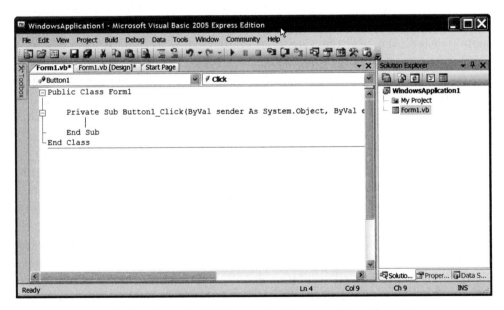

Figure 2-3. *Notice the long line of code that marks the start of the subroutine.*

The Sub line in the screen shot is so long that it extends off the right-hand side of the editor. To view the whole line of code, you would need to scroll the editor to the right by using the scrollbar at the bottom. However, the code before the screen shot splits that long line of text in two, and if you look closely you'll notice that the first line ends with an underscore symbol.

In Visual Basic each line is treated as a command. When you are finished entering a command, you hit the Enter key. The Visual Basic compiler is smart enough to know that when it reaches the end of a line, that command is finished and the next physical line in the code starts something new. Sometimes this is a pain. For example, if you do have a long line of code such as the one at the start of the preceding subroutine, splitting the code over two lines can be handy. The underscore symbol is used for that purpose. By placing an underscore at the end of the line, you are telling the Visual Basic compiler "I'm not finished yet—the next line continues this one." I have used the underscore throughout the book because the width of the book's pages places a limitation on the length of the code lines.

Subroutines and their cousins, functions, are the lifeblood of your programs. Let's dive in and take a closer look at what they do and how they work.

There used to be a time when if you wanted to write a computer program, you'd just sit down and key in reams of code with little to no structure to it. Today things are different. Program code is broken down into classes, and within those classes into functions and subroutines (collectively known as methods).

Subroutines let us group blocks of code into a common place, a subroutine. Instead of performing each individual step each time we need to do something, we can just call the subroutine. Think of it as making coffee. You don't go to your favorite coffee house and tell the guy at the counter, "Grab some milk, make it really hot and fluffy, grab some beans…" Instead you just say, "One skinny decaf semi-skinned latte and a doughnut please," and they know exactly what to do. The guy at the counter knows how to perform the *function* "one skinny decaf semi-skinned latte with a doughnut." That subroutine has a bunch of steps to it, but in our coarsely grained world, we the customers don't really care what they are. That's how programmers like to think too.

Strictly speaking, ordering a cup of coffee is actually a function. Think of subroutines as orders you give at a coffee shop, expecting no result. For example, telling the guy at the counter you will be using a credit card is a subroutine. He might take some steps to prepare for receiving your credit card, but you don't get anything out of him other than that. Functions *return* something to you. Ordering a cup of coffee and doughnut is a function because when all the steps are complete, the guy behind the counter will hand over the goods along with a cheesy smile.

The distinction is typically so subtle that when subroutines and functions live inside of a class, we call both of them *methods*.

Try It Out: Creating Methods

Start up a new console application, by choosing New Project from the File menu. When the New Project dialog box appears, choose Console Application and click OK. You can see the New Project dialog box in Figure 2-4.

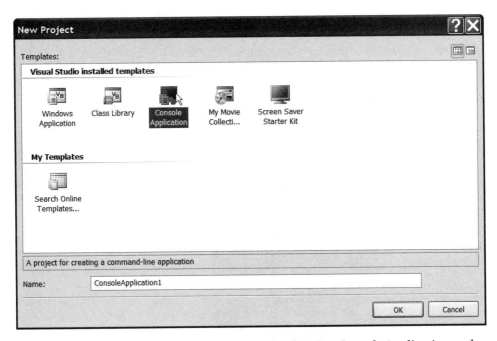

Figure 2-4. *You can create a console application by choosing Console Application as the project type when starting up a new project.*

When the code editor appears, type in code so that the Main() subroutine looks like this:

```
Sub Main()
    For x As Integer = 1 To 10
        Console.WriteLine("Counting up : {0}", x)
    Next

    For y As Integer = 10 To 1 Step -1
        Console.WriteLine("Counting down: {0}", y)
    Next

    Console.ReadLine()
End Sub
```

It's not too hard a program to read, even if you're not totally comfortable with Visual Basic. But subroutines could make it even easier to follow.

Run the program and you'll see a console window appear that simply shows the numbers from 1 to 10, then from 10 to 1. Finally, the program waits for you to hit the Enter key on the keyboard before it finishes (whenever the Main() subroutine finishes, so too does your program). You can see the program's output in Figure 2-5.

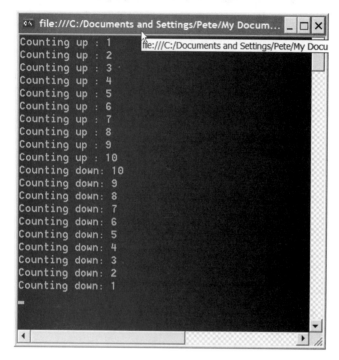

Figure 2-5. *The console window shows the output of a console application.*

Given what the program does (counts up, counts down, and waits for input), it would be a lot easier to read and understand if you broke those three operations out into separate subroutines. Let's go ahead and do that now.

The first block of code you'll tackle is the bit that counts up. So, you'll create a new subroutine called CountUpwards(). Make the highlighted changes to the source code:

```
Module Module1

    Sub Main()
        For x As Integer = 1 To 10
            Console.WriteLine("Counting up : {0}", x)
        Next

        For y As Integer = 10 To 1 Step -1
            Console.WriteLine("Counting down: {0}", y)
        Next

        Console.ReadLine()
    End Sub

    Sub CountUpwards()

    End Sub

End Module
```

Next, cut and paste (not copy and paste) the first For...Next block down into the new subroutine:

```
    Sub Main()

        For y As Integer = 10 To 1 Step -1
            Console.WriteLine("Counting down: {0}", y)
        Next

        Console.ReadLine()
    End Sub

    Sub CountUpwards()
        For x As Integer = 1 To 10
            Console.WriteLine("Counting up : {0}", x)
        Next
    End Sub
```

So, now you have a new subroutine that counts up from 1 to 10. You need to *call* it though. You need a new line of code in the Main() subroutine that can actually hand over control to the new subroutine. This is easy. When you wrote Console.ReadLine(), for example, you were calling a subroutine (method) called ReadLine. So, all you need to do to call a new subroutine is type its name on a line in your code. Our new subroutine is called CountUpwards(), so the change you need to make is fairly straightforward:

```
Sub Main()
    CountUpwards()

    For y As Integer = 10 To 1 Step -1
        Console.WriteLine("Counting down: {0}", y)
    Next

    Console.ReadLine()
End Sub

Sub CountUpwards()
    For x As Integer = 1 To 10
        Console.WriteLine("Counting up : {0}", x)
    Next
End Sub
```

It's customary, though not required, to suffix the name of the subroutine you are calling with parentheses. When you get used to reading code, you'll find that doing this makes it obvious where you are calling subroutines, and where you are dealing with something else.

Go ahead repeat what you just did, creating a new subroutine called CountDownwards(), and move the second For...Next block into that new subroutine. When you're finished, your code will look like this (I've highlighted the changes for you):

```
Module Module1

    Sub Main()
        CountUpwards()
        CountDownwards()
        Console.ReadLine()
    End Sub

    Sub CountUpwards()
        For x As Integer = 1 To 10
            Console.WriteLine("Counting up : {0}", x)
        Next
    End Sub
```

```
Sub CountDownwards()
    For y As Integer = 10 To 1 Step -1
        Console.WriteLine("Counting down: {0}", y)
    Next
End Sub

End Module
```

If you run the program now, you'll find that it works just the same as before. The only difference is in how you have structured the code. Rather than having one long `Main()` subroutine, you broke it into three subroutines. Why? Well, other than the benefit of getting some experience under your belt in writing your own subroutines, this process made the `Main()` subroutine a lot easier to understand. Rather than having a bunch of technical code in there, the `Main()` function looks like this now:

```
Sub Main()
    CountUpwards()
    CountDownwards()
    Console.ReadLine()
End Sub
```

It's dead easy to look at that and know what the program is going to do, even if you are new to Visual Basic. There are other benefits to refactoring the code like this. If there is a bug in the program, perhaps in how it counts upward, it's easy to identify quickly just which subroutine is likely to have the error. You can even easily rearrange the order that the program does things, perhaps to make it count down first, and then up. Go ahead and try moving the lines of code in the Main subroutine around to see what I mean. Now imagine if you had tried to do the same things when the Main subroutine contained all that longhand code for the two loops.

Obviously this is a contrived example, just so that I can get my point across, but you should recognize just how useful subroutines can be if you were writing a much larger and far more complex program.

Take a look at the source for a brand new console application once again:

```
Module Module1

    Sub Main()

    End Sub

End Module
```

Whenever you run a program, the computer needs to know just where to start; if you have a bunch of forms in your application, each with a selection of event handlers and other functions, the computer has no real way of knowing the starting point. That's where the `Main()` subroutine comes into play (whenever you see me name a function from now on, you'll notice me put ( ) after it–this shows that I'm talking about a function as opposed to something else).

All .NET programs contain a single `Main()` function, and this is where the program starts. When you create a Windows Forms application, you don't get to see the `Main()` subroutine yourself. Instead, VB Express creates it for you and hides it behind the scenes. You then tell VB Express which form you want to start your application with, and it amends the hidden `Main()` subroutine accordingly.

So, when you run a program you are effectively saying "Do everything that the `Main()` subroutine tells you to do". Of course, `Main()` is just one function, and with any nontrivial program it makes sense to have a few others—doing so simplifies the structure of the code, makes it easier for you to read, and decreases the likelihood of making quite so many mistakes.

Types

Now take a look at the source for a brand new form in a Windows application again. If you want to follow along, you can see this for yourself by creating a new Windows application, clicking in the form, and then pressing F7 to show the source code for it:

```
Public Class Form1

End Class
```

Notice how there is no `Main()` subroutine, but there is something called a class, in this case a class called `Form1`.

Visual Basic is an object-oriented language, and types, like the preceding class, are absolutely vital to everything you do in any serious VB program. So you'll be working with classes a lot, almost exclusively in fact, throughout the rest of the book.

Instead of focusing on what a program is supposed to do and how it is supposed to do it, object-oriented programming lets you focus on the *objects* that your program needs to work with. You then add methods to the objects to essentially turn them into self-contained black boxes of functionality. A class is the *type* from which an object is created.

Okay, that's as clear as mud. Think of it this way. A billionaire is someone who has far too much money for their own good. A billionaire, then, is a type, or class, of person. Bill Gates is an object of that class. So, *class* defines the characteristics of something (a dog hasfour legs, a car has four wheels, a billionaire has a small continent for a vacation home), and an *object* is an instance of that class (Mac, my attack spaniel, is an object of the dog class).

As you've probably figured out from the preceding code, you define a class simply with the Visual Basic keyword Class followed by a name for the class (Dog, Cat, Billionaire, InsanelyJealousAuthor, and so on). Everything that is a part of the class then goes inside the class block (the stuff between the line with the word Class on it and the line that says End Class).

But that doesn't really explain how to actually create an object from a class, does it. Let's take a look at some code.

Try It Out: Creating and Using a Class

Create a new console application, just as before. If you don't want to save the project, don't worry about giving it a name, just accept the standard one.

What you'll do in this program is hold some information about my two dogs and be able to display that information in the console window. Without classes and objects, this program would have taken one of two forms. You'd either create a whole bunch of variables (don't worry, I'll get into what variables are shortly), or create a couple of arrays (lists of variables, which I'll cover later as well). The code would get pretty long and messy.

With an object-oriented programming language such as Visual Basic, you can tackle the program by defining a Dog class. Let's go ahead and add code into the code editor. The first thing you need to do is create the class itself:

```
Module Module1

    Sub Main()

    End Sub

End Module

Class Dog

End Class
```

As you can see, defining a class is really pretty easy stuff. In a much bigger application than this, you'd define the class in its own .vb file within the project, just to keep things simple and easy to navigate, rather than having a mass of code all bunched into a single source file.

The next thing you're going to need to do is add some fields to the Dog class. Fields on classes are similar to the properties you've already seen on controls when creating an application's Windows-based user interface. The big difference of course is that you need to create those fields yourself. It's quite painless, though. Go ahead and add a couple of fields to store information about the dog's name and breed in the class, like this:

```
Class Dog
    Public Name As String
    Public Breed As String
End Class
```

Okay, now I can talk about variables a little bit (much more to come later—they're quite an important deal). The fields you've added here are really just variables. The Public part simply says that this is a "*visible*", or public, field of the Dog class. The two fields are both string fields, which means that they are going to hold text and alphanumeric data as opposed to numbers. The final part of the field declarations just gives the two fields names; in the first case, Name, and in the second case, Breed.

So, you have a Dog class that can store data about the dog (the dog's name and breed), but no functionality that actually does anything. Time to write a method (remember what I said earlier—subroutines inside classes are usually called methods):

```
Class Dog
    Public Name As String
    Public Breed As String

    Public Sub ShowInfo()
        Console.WriteLine("{0} is a {1}", Name, Breed)
    End Sub
End Class
```

This is a pretty simple method. It makes a call out to Console.Writeline() and outputs the contents of our two fields. That's really where the {0} and {1} symbols come in. You can pass a list of things to WriteLine(), and it will replace those {} symbols with the items from the list, in this case Name and Breed.

Now that you have a Dog class, all that remains is to create a couple of dog objects from it.

Creating an object from a class is straightforward. Let's add a line of code to the Main() subroutine to do just that:

```
Sub Main()
    Dim mac As New Dog()

End Sub
```

To create an *instance* of a class (when you make an object, we say that you are creating an instance of a class), you use the Dim keyword. Back in ancient times (the late 60s) when BASIC was first invented, Dim meant "dimension." You were asking the BASIC system to dimension a block of memory to store your new data. It doesn't really mean that these days, but it's accepted that Dim means make something new. In our case we're making an object called mac that is a New Dog.

After you've created an object, you can start working with its methods and properties, just as if you were working with properties on a control in a Windows Forms application. Add some more lines to set the object's name and breed:

```
Sub Main()
    Dim mac As New Dog()
    mac.Name = "Mac"
    mac.Breed = "Fluffy attack spaniel"
End Sub
```

Remember how you set up the Name and Breed fields to hold strings? That's why the values that you put into those fields in our code here are contained within double quotation marks.

Let's create a second dog object, and then get them both to show some information about themselves by calling the ShowInfo() method you defined inside the Dog class:

```
Sub Main()
    Dim mac As New Dog()
    mac.Name = "Mac"
    mac.Breed = "Fluffy attack spaniel"

    Dim tosh As New Dog()
    tosh.Name = "Tosh"
    tosh.Breed = "Uber dumb muppet spaniel"

    mac.ShowInfo()
    tosh.ShowInfo()

    Console.ReadLine()
End Sub
```

The program is complete. If you run it now, you'll see a console window like the one in Figure 2-6.

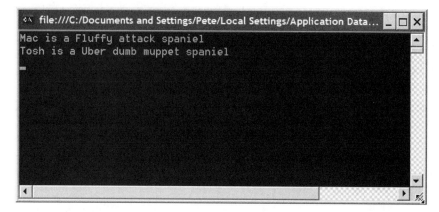

Figure 2-6. *When the program runs, the two dog objects output information about themselves into the console window.*

There are a couple of interesting things to note about the code before we move on. First, I added an extra line to the end of the program, the same line that you saw in earlier console applications, to make the program wait until the user presses the Enter key. Without this, the console window would vanish from view as soon as the program finished running and you wouldn't be able to see the application do anything. What I'm doing here is calling a method called ReadLine() on the Console class.

Now, pay attention here. I'm calling a method on a class. I didn't create a Console object in the same way that we'd already created Dog objects. The reason for this is that Microsoft defined the ReadLine() method on the Console class as a *shared* method. This makes it a method that you can call without actually having to create an object. You'll see a lot more uses of Shared in Chapter 4.

Calling the ShowInfo() methods on our two Dog objects takes exactly the same form as calling ReadLine() on the Console class. You simply specify the name of the object followed by a period, followed by the name of the method to run.

Inheritance and Polymorphism

The real power of object-oriented programming starts to make itself known when you learn about subclassing and overloading. We have a whole chapter on that and some of the other more in-depth features of object-oriented programming in Chapter 4, but let's whet your appetites.

In the previous example you created a Dog class and then two dog objects. If you were going to write a serious application to keep track of a number of dogs, you'd structure it a little differently. For example, some dogs can jump really well, others make good guard dogs, and others still (my two in particular) excel at drooling.

Try It Out: Subclassing

Fire up another console application (or just delete all the code out of the one you already have). Get your `Main()` subroutine looking like this one:

```
Module Module1

    Sub Main()
        Dim butch As Dog = New Rottweiler("Butch")
        Dim mac As Dog = New spaniel("Mac", "yips")

        butch.Bark()
        mac.Bark()

        butch.DoYourThing()
        mac.DoYourThing()
        Console.ReadLine()
    End Sub

End Module
```

Obviously, this program won't do much yet—it's not complete. Pop quiz: how many classes do you need to write to get this program running? It's a trick question. You could do it with two, but as the program grows more complex (perhaps actually drawing the dogs, getting them to do other dogly things like sleeping and so on), the code would grow significantly. The idea behind programming is to keep things simple, and so the correct answer is three classes. I'll explain why in a second.

First, take a look at the two lines of code where you're actually creating the dog objects. They look a little different from the last time you created an object. In fact, they look more like method calls:

```
Dim butch As Dog = New Rottweiler("Butch")
Dim mac As Dog = New spaniel("Mac", "yips")
```

In fact, they are method calls. There's a special kind of method called a *constructor* that you can put into a class. When you create an object from the class, you can pass values to the constructor. In both cases here, you are passing in the name of the dog. In Mac's case you're also passing in the sound he makes. That's called *polymorphism*, or overloading—more on that in a second.

Back to the three classes concept. The reason the correct number of classes to have in this application is three is really quite simple, if you stop thinking about computers for a second. Both Butch and Mac are specialized versions of a dog. So, the three classes you'll need are Dog (which does all the basic stuff that dogs do), Rottweiler (does all the things normal dogs can do, but with very large teeth), and Spaniel (does all the things normal dogs do, when it feels like it). You can see this in the code already. You're creating two Dogs here, but each is a specific breed of dog. They are breeds that "inherit" everything a dog can do, and then some.

Let's go ahead and get the Dog class built first—I'll explain exactly what all the weird new stuff is after you've finished typing it in:

```
MustInherit Class Dog
    Protected _name As String
    Protected _sound As String

    Public Sub New()
        '
    End Sub

    Public Sub New(ByVal name As String)
        _name = name
        _sound = "barks"
    End Sub

    Public Sub New(ByVal name As String, ByVal sound As String)
        _name = name
        _sound = sound
    End Sub

    Public Sub Bark()
        Console.WriteLine("{0} {1}", _name, _sound)
    End Sub

    Public MustOverride Sub DoYourThing()
End Class
```

The first thing you'll notice is the word `MustInherit` in front of the usual class declaration. Why? Well, you don't typically go to a pet shop and ask for a dog. You go to the pet shop and ask for a specific breed. `MustInherit`, then, makes sure that no one ever creates just a plain old dog. You can't create objects from this class; you must inherit the class into another. Don't panic, all will become clear in a second.

The next thing you'll notice is that the variables that were declared public in the preceding example (to make them properties) now have the word `Protected` in front of them:

```
Protected _name As String
Protected _sound As String
```

When you set up a variable inside a class as public, it can be treated as a property when you create an object. Adding `Private` or `Protected` instead hides them. So, you can't now say `mydog.Name` = something. The difference between private and protected will become clear in a very short while.

Directly after the two variables come the constructors I mentioned earlier:

```
Public Sub New()
    '
End Sub

Public Sub New(ByVal name As String)
    _name = name
    _sound = "barks"
End Sub

Public Sub New(ByVal name As String, ByVal sound As String)
    _name = name
    _sound = sound
End Sub
```

When you create a `Dog` object, one of these methods will run. Which method runs depends on whether you pass in one or two strings. In the case of our `Rottweiler` in the `Main()` subroutine, you just pass in one string, so you're saying "When the class becomes an object, set up its name." When the Spaniel gets created you pass in two strings, effectively saying, "When the Spaniel comes to life, set up its name and the sound it makes." The third constructor—the `New()` subroutine with no code in it—is simply required. We'll never use it. In fact, in a real application there would be code in here to make the program throw an error to effectively tell whoever called it, "You need to tell me a name, or a name and a sound to make."

The `Bark()` method should be fairly obvious to you now. It writes out the dog's name, followed by the sound it makes.

The DoYourThing() method, though, is very weird. Take a look:

```
Public MustOverride Sub DoYourThing()
```

This method has absolutely no code in it and uses the Visual Basic keyword MustOverride. What this is telling Visual Basic is that this method must be replaced with something else before it's called. What do I mean by that? Well, to see that, you're going to have to key in the other two classes. Pay special attention to the code editor as soon as you type in each Inherits line. You'll see Visual Basic instantly kick in and write some code for you:

```
Class Rottweiler
    Inherits Dog

    Public Sub New(ByVal name As String)
        MyBase.New(name)
    End Sub

    Public Overrides Sub DoYourThing()
        Console.WriteLine( _
            "{0} snarls at you in a menacing fashion.", _
            _name)
    End Sub
End Class

Class spaniel
    Inherits Dog

    Public Sub New(ByVal name As String, ByVal sound As String)
        MyBase.New(name, sound)
    End Sub

    Public Overrides Sub DoYourThing()
        Console.WriteLine( _
            "{0} licks you all over, then drools on you.", _
            _name)
    End Sub
End Class
```

You could run the program now and you'd see a console window just like the one in Figure 2-7.

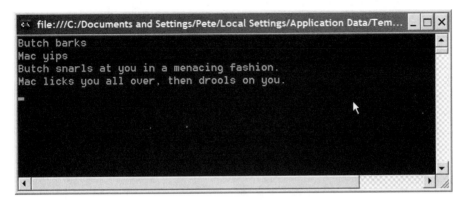

Figure 2-7. *When the program runs, even though you have two "dog" objects, they behave differently, thanks to inheritance.*

Both these classes use inheritance. To put it another technical and confusing way, they *subclass* the Dog class. Take a look at how the Rottweiler class starts out:

```
Class Rottweiler
    Inherits Dog
```

What this code is saying is that Rottweiler, although it's a whole new class, is based on Dog. Everything a Dog can do, the Rottweiler can automatically do too. Hopefully you noticed that as soon as you entered Inherits Dog on the line of its own, the VB Express editor provided you with an empty DoYourThing() method. Why? Because it spotted that in Dog we had marked DoYourThing() as MustOverride, so it knew you were going to have to write your own method for that. Handy, isn't it. More on this in a second.

Now, you set up a couple of constructors in the Dog class to set the name and/or the sound the dog makes. Visual Basic requires that you also write matching constructors in any subclass. The reason for this is that it lets you perform any specific operations in the subclass when it gets created, which may be different from the base class (the one you inherited—Dog). In this case you don't want to do anything different, so the Rottweiler's constructor looks quite strange:

```
    Public Sub New(ByVal name As String)
        MyBase.New(name)
    End Sub
```

NEW TO .NET?

Classes, objects, and object-oriented programming (OOP) play an important role in the .NET Framework. Everything you work with in the .NET Framework class library itself is an object (well, it's actually a type, and types include classes, objects, and a bunch of other stuff you'll get into soon enough). This provides you with a great deal of power after you start to understand just what OOP lets you do.

For example, you could subclass a standard user interface control, and override some of the methods it contains to quickly and easily develop your own custom control. You could develop a form that acts as a base class for a whole bunch of other forms, in a wide range of applications, but which itself subclasses the standard form class in the framework.

Aside from OOP being a cool and productive way to develop code, you really can't make full use of .NET itself without a good understanding of OOP concepts. It's for that reason you'll be spending a lot of time looking at OOP from Chapter 4 onward.

This just says that when a Rottweiler object is created, do what the base class (Dog) did, and nothing else.

Now, remember that MustOverride empty DoYourThing() method in the Dog class? In the Rottweiler class (and in the Spaniel class), you can actually put in some code to show this specific breed of dog (subclass of dog) doing what it does best:

```
Public Overrides Sub DoYourThing()
    Console.WriteLine( _
        "{0} snarls at you in a menacing fashion.", _
        _name)
End Sub
```

It's just the same as writing any other method in a class, but the use of the word Overrides tells Visual Basic that when this object is asked to DoYourThing(), the object will completely ignore what a generic dog would do, and do this instead.

That, in a nutshell, is inheritance, polymorphism, and object-oriented programming for you. I know that a lot of you reading this may be quite confused. Don't panic. It's such an important part of Visual Basic that I had to cover it in this overview, but you'll spend a lot of time going much deeper and slower through the various concepts in later chapters in the book.

Control Structures

The last thing I need to cover in this whirlwind look at Visual Basic is control structures. So far you've seen how to group your code into subroutines, and how to group those subroutines into classes. I've also touched on variables and storing data (by the end of the next chapter you'll be eating sleeping, and breathing variables). What you haven't seen yet is how to actually do anything. How do you breathe life into your programs to make them seem to "think" for themselves? That's where control structures come in.

Visual Basic's *control structures* provide you with a way to make your programs repeatedly do things (loop), do things for a set number of times (another loop), or decide to do something *if* some condition is met (conditional statements).

Conditional statements give your program life. They enable the program to make decisions. For example, if the dog is a Rottweiler, run away; otherwise, pet the dog. The format for a conditional statement looks like this:

```
If somecondition Then

Else

End If
```

`If` and `Else` are Visual Basic keywords that enable you to build up your conditional statements.

Do you remember back in school when the computer science teacher would drone on about binary and all that supremely tedious stuff? Well, it's come back to haunt you, but it's a lot simpler to understand than he made out. That `somecondition` thing is a statement (it could call a subroutine, it could compare two or more values) that must only result in `True` or `False` (it stems from binary, which has only two digits, 1 or 0). For example, you could write a condition that compares an object's name to, say, `Apress`. If the object's name is `Apress`, you could say that the result is `True`. On the other hand, if the object's name were `Joe Schmo Publishing`, the condition would be `False`. Easy, isn't it.

Let's take a look at a simple example—a Windows login form.

Try It Out: Writing Conditional Statements

Start up a new project in Visual Basic 2005 Express, but unlike last time, choose to create a Windows Application project, as shown in Figure 2-8.

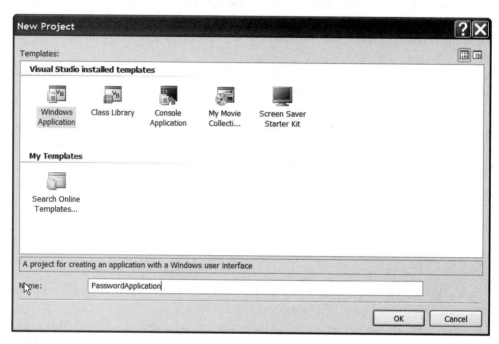

Figure 2-8. *Choose a Windows Application project from the New Project dialog box as shown.*

When the form editor appears, click on the form and set its text property to `Password`.

Now add some controls to the form so that it looks roughly like the one in Figure 2-9. Remember, you can use the positioning guides when you drop controls onto the form to align the controls consistently with one another and to conform to Windows standards.

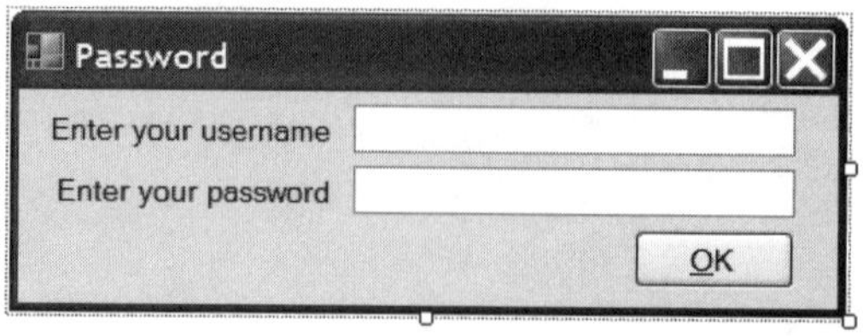

Figure 2-9. *Drop some controls onto the form, and perhaps even resize it, so that yours looks like this one.*

To make sure that the code you're going to type in shortly is the same on your machine as on mine, set up the controls' properties shown in Table 2-1 by using the Properties window (press F4 if you can't see it for some reason).

Table 2-1. *Properties of the Controls on Your Password Form*

Control	Property	Value
First label control	Text	Enter your username
Second label control	Text	Enter your password
First text box	Name	usernameBox
Second text box	Name PasswordChar	passwordBox *
Button	Text Name	&OK okButton

What you're going to do here is check the username and password when the user clicks the OK button, and then display a message to the user indicating whether they managed to log in. So, go ahead and double-click the OK button in the form designer to pop open the code editor, shown in Figure 2-10.

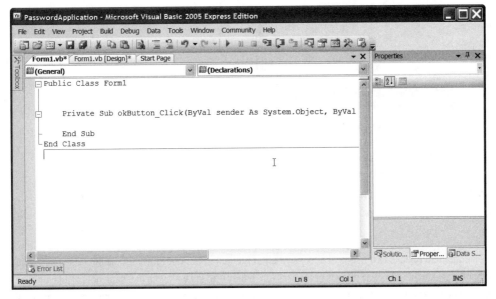

Figure 2-10. *Double-clicking a control drops you into the code editor to work on the standard/ most common event for that control.*

Now you'll see why I made you go to all the trouble of properly naming the controls. Type in code so that the okButton_click function looks just like this—I'll explain what it all means when you are finished:

```
    Private Sub okButton_Click(ByVal sender As System.Object, _
      ByVal e As System.EventArgs) Handles okButton.Click
        If usernameBox.Text = "apress" And _
            passwordBox.Text = "noidea" Then

            MessageBox.Show("Welcome! You're logged in")
        Else
            MessageBox.Show("Sorry, try again")
        End If
    End Sub
```

I've intentionally formatted the code in this rather obscure way to make it easier to explain and understand.

Take a look at the code and you should already be able to figure out what it's going to do. That's one of the beauties of using a highly descriptive and communicative language like Visual Basic.

Go ahead and run the application. Type in anything for the username and password, and then click the OK button to see the login failed message. Then try again but type **apress** for the username, and **noidea** for the password. You'll see a message like the one in Figure 2-11

Figure 2-11. *Enter the username and password correctly, and the condition statement displays the right message.*

The If statement checks two things. It checks whether the text in the usernameBox is set to apress, and whether the text in the passwordBox is set to noidea. If they are, the welcome message gets displayed. The keyword And makes sure that both parts of the condition are satisfied before the welcome message appears.

If statements are not the only place that conditions are used. Visual Basic supports a number of *looping* keywords to allow you to run blocks of code over and over. For example, in a business application you may need to run over a set of numbers repeatedly until a specific condition is met.

The loops that Visual Basic supports are `While` loops (which run *while* a condition is met), `Do...Until` loops (which run *until* a condition is met) and `For` loops (which run a specific number of times). I won't go into a detailed example here, but just to give you the inside track, a `While` loop might look like this:

```
While passwordBox.Text <> "noidea"
    TryAgain()
End While
```

The `<>` symbol means "is not equal to." Obviously, `TryAgain()` in this example would probably be some subroutine that prompts the user to reenter the password, with the loop running over and over until the password is correctly entered. `For` loops are a little more complex:

```
For index As Integer = 1 To 10

Next
```

Here the loop runs 10 times. It starts out by declaring a variable (`index`) to keep track of the number of times the loop has run, and then runs, setting `index` to every number from 1 to 10 inclusive. When it's done, any line of code following `Next` is run.

Summary

I wanted in this chapter to give you a quick tour of the Visual Basic language and the kinds of things you can do with it. The programmers among you will by now have had a lot of your questions answered, but also a lot more will have come up. For example, what about interfaces and structures, abstract classes, reference types and value types, scoping, and so on?

The newcomers among you will also have a lot of questions, I'm sure. This chapter covered a lot of the very basics of Visual Basic, but I intentionally avoided a great many details. It would take an entire book to cover the language and what you can do with it (this book in fact), but Visual Basic is one of those languages where it can be tricky to explain any one thing without introducing a whole bunch of others.

So, in in Chapter 3 you'll dig a lot deeper, starting out with working with data in your programs, revisiting control structures, and looking at some of the nuances and trip wires Visual Basic brings with it when working with these things. So consider what you just read as a video walk-through of just what the theme park holds. In the next chapter you'll get to go on some of the rides.

CHAPTER 3

■■■

Working with Variables

Now that the whirlwind tours are out of the way, it's time to drill into the details of Visual Basic 2005 Express. The fundamental thing that every single line of code you write will ever do is work with data—not the big scary database kind of data, but small lumps of data. If you're adding a screen to your program to handle logging in, for example, you'll want to work with the username and password that the user enters. That's the kind of data I'm talking about.

The proper name for this kind of stuff is variables. *Variables* are places in your program code that you create to store and work with data while your program is running (as opposed to databases, which store data for as long as you need them to). In this chapter you'll take a look at just how to set up and use variables. Instead of getting too technical, I'm going to focus on the stuff that you'll want to do every day. For example, how do you store a number and work on it? What about text? How do you convert one type of data to another (numbers to text and vice versa, for example)?

The topics we'll cover in this chapter are the fundamentals of Visual Basic, the foundations, if you like, on which you'll build your future magnificent applications.

The Basic Basics

In the whirlwind tour in Chapter 2 I touched on the concept of object-oriented programming. It rears its head even here, but in a good way. You see, every type of data you work with has a class defined for it in the .NET class library, and as you saw in the previous chapter, classes come with handy methods that let you do things.

Every class in the .NET Framework is based on, directly or indirectly, one specific class called System.Object. It all comes back to the topic of inheritance, which I touched on briefly in the preceding chapter. You are a unique individual, as am I, but we are both human. You could say then that we *inherit* all the traits every other human being has, and then add to those our own unique properties and abilities. I could also say that I *indirectly* inherit the traits of any other human because there's a lot between me and the basic definition of a human. Given that I'm a dark-haired English guy with a penchant for technology, you could say that my *inheritance chain* looks like this:

Human ➤ Man ➤ EnglishMan ➤ DarkHaired ➤ Nerd ➤ Pete

I am thus indirectly based on a human. Every other object in that chain is also based on a human, but at each stage of the chain more and more unique attributes are added, finally ending up with little old me.

In the .NET Framework every class has at its very core the System.Object class. What this means is that everything System.Object can do, every single class in the .NET Framework can also do. It's kind of like saying that because humans can walk on two legs, see with two eyes, hear with two ears, and hug with two arms, so can pretty much every other human subclass (like me).

Why is this important, I hear you scream. Well, System.Object brings with it a couple of handy functions, such as ToString(). Take a look at this.

Try It Out: System.Object Stuff

Start up a new console application and then key in some code to set up variables to hold a bunch of different types of data. Because I haven't covered just how to do that in any real amount of detail just yet, go ahead and copy the following code so that your Main() subroutine looks like mine:

```
Sub Main()
    Dim anInteger As Integer = 12
    Dim aDouble As Double = 12.34
    Dim name As String = "Pete"
    Dim theTime As DateTime = DateTime.Now()
End Sub
```

Don't worry too much about what some of the code means at this point. All will become clear a little later in this chapter.

Next, define a new subroutine called ShowMe() that looks like this (add it beneath the Main() subroutine):

```
Sub ShowMe(ByVal anObject As Object)
    Console.WriteLine(anObject.ToString())
End Sub
```

Can you see where this is going yet? ShowMe() takes a single object as a parameter. Because every type of data you work with in VB Express derives from Object, you can pass literally any kind of data to this. In addition, every type in VB Express has a ToString() method (because the base System.Object class has one), so ShowMe() can get any object to convert itself to a string (lump of text) and write it out to the console.

It gets even better than that. In the call to Console.WriteLine() in the preceding code, you didn't actually have to put ToString() on the end of the object you passed in. System.Object has a ToString()

method, which in turn means every class you'll ever use or create has one too. This in turn allows the .NET Framework developers at Microsoft to make handy assumptions. If you don't pass a string to the WriteLine() method, the code inside that method will call ToString() on whatever you pass to it. For example Console.WriteLine(myObject) produces the same result at runtime as Console.WriteLine(myObject.ToString()). I like to put ToString() on code like this because it makes it clear to me and anyone else reading the code that I am actually after the string version of my object.

Go ahead and add the missing lines of code to the Main() subroutine to call the ShowMe() function:

```
Sub Main()
    Dim anInteger As Integer = 12
    Dim aDouble As Double = 12.34
    Dim name As String = "Pete"
    Dim theTime As DateTime = DateTime.Now()

    ShowMe(anInteger)
    ShowMe(aDouble)
    ShowMe(name)
    ShowMe(theTime)

    Console.ReadLine()
End Sub

Sub ShowMe(ByVal anObject As Object)
    Console.WriteLine(anObject.ToString())
End Sub
```

Run the program now and you'll see the console window in Figure 3-1.

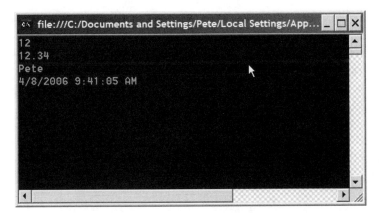

Figure 3-1. *All variables can be treated as objects—handy, isn't it.*

This is just shown to demonstrate the fundamental concept that everything is an object. I wouldn't recommend you go around writing a bunch of methods like ShowMe(), though, that take Objects as parameters. There's quite a performance hit when you do this, and it all has to do with something called boxing and unboxing, which I'll cover in Chapter 4 when I discuss classes and objects in more detail.

For now, let's look at the most common specific data types that you'll be working with.

Numbers

When I was a kid, a number was a number. Simple as that. When I went to college, they melted my brain with terms like "integer," "real and complex numbers," and "floating point." I didn't pay attention of course, but soon wished I had.

VB Express has two categories of numbers that it can deal with, and no less than 10 variations of them. You won't need to memorize exactly how they all work, and so I'm not going to go into excruciating detail on all 10. It's handy to get an overview of the most common ones in each category, though.

Integers

Integers are whole numbers. They have nothing after the decimal point, and no fractional bits: 1; 2; 3; 50,000,000; 123,878,127; –6687—those are all integers. You'll find that unless you write code for a bank, integers are probably the most common type of number variable you'll ever work with in your code.

Declaring and using an integer is simple. For example:

```
Dim anInteger As Integer = 12
```

That's really all there is to it.

Integer Types

In VB Express, there are several integer types, and the only real difference between them is the range of numbers that each can hold. They are (from smallest to biggest) Sbyte, Byte, Char, Short, Integer, Uinteger, Long, Ulong, Single, Double, and Decimal. The Sbyte, Ushort, Uinteger, and Ulong types can hold only positive numbers (the U prefix stands for "unsigned"). Rather than having me regurgitate the Microsoft documentation, take a look at the online help and search for "Data Type Summary" to see a complete list of the sizes and ranges of numbers these can hold (see Figure 3-2).

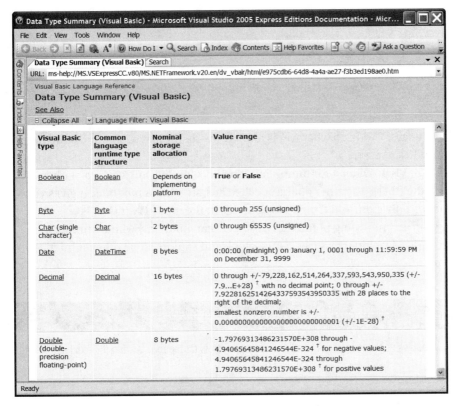

Figure 3-2. *Search the online help for "Data Type Summary" to get a complete list of the types and the kinds of data each can hold.*

Operators

Of course, simply having a variable to store data in is no good if you can't do anything with that data. To operate on data in a variable, you need to use an *operator*. On the whole these are pretty straightforward: + adds, - subtracts, / divides, and * multiplies. There are a couple of odd ones, though, and a few things to be careful of.

First the odd ones. You can add and subtract two numbers in a quite simple way:

```
Dim a As Integer = 1
Dim b As Integer = 2
Dim c As Integer = a + b
```

You can of course just use the numbers in your code if you so desire:

```
Dim result = 1000 - 457
```

A lot of times you'll just want to add a value to something already inside in a variable. You could do so like this :

```
loginAttempts = loginAttempts + 1
```

But a much cleaner way to write this is by using the VB += operator:

```
loginAttempts += 1
```

This basically says, "Add 1 to whatever is already inside loginAttempts and store the result back into loginAttempts."

Now, although VB provides * for multiplication and / for division, you may be surprised to learn that there's another operator called Mod, which is a *modulus*. It gives you the remainder of a division. You'll take a look at this in the next "Try It Out."

This brings up an interesting point. Since integers can hold only whole numbers, what happens with division? Let's take a quick look and explore some other subtleties along the way.

Try It Out: Math with Integers

Start up a new Windows application project and drop some controls on the form so that it looks like the one in Figure 3-3.

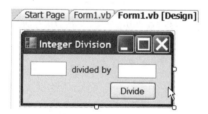

Figure 3-3. *Make your "division" form look like this with some judicial waving of the mouse.*

Set the name of the first text box (by using the Name property in the Properties window) to divisorBox. Set the Name of the second textbox to dividendBox. Don't worry about setting a name for the button.

The first thing you're going to want to do is put whatever the user enters into some integer variables. Double-click the button to open up the code editor for its Click event, and type in just two lines of code to make it look like this (I've highlighted the lines you have to add):

```
Private Sub Button1_Click(ByVal sender As System.Object, _
    ByVal e As System.EventArgs) Handles Button1.Click
        Dim divisor As Integer = divisorBox.Text
        Dim dividend As Integer = dividendBox.Text
    End Sub
```

The old hands among you may have expected to see a bug here. After all, a text box holds text, and an integer is a number. So, how can we possibly copy the contents of a text box into an integer variable? Really, you can't. Visual Basic is a smart enough language, though, that it will do the conversion from text to an integer for you. Personally, I prefer to actually write the code to do the conversion; that way I can be sure that I know what's going on.

Change your code to look like this:

```
Private Sub Button1_Click(ByVal sender As System.Object, _
    ByVal e As System.EventArgs) Handles Button1.Click
    Dim divisor As Integer
    Dim dividend As Integer

    divisor = Integer.Parse(divisorBox.Text)
    dividend = Integer.Parse(dividendBox.Text)
End Sub
```

Everything in .NET is an object, and objects come with methods that you can use. In the case of an integer, one very handy method is Parse(). Simply pass this method a piece of text, and if that text contains nothing but an integer number, the result will be an integer number, which in this case you can store in your variables.

Let's keep going and add a new integer variable to store the result of the division:

```
Private Sub Button1_Click(ByVal sender As System.Object, _
    ByVal e As System.EventArgs) Handles Button1.Click
    Dim divisor As Integer
    Dim dividend As Integer

    divisor = Integer.Parse(divisorBox.Text)
    dividend = Integer.Parse(dividendBox.Text)

    Dim result As Integer

    result = divisor / dividend

End Sub
```

Finally, display the result in a message box:

```
MessageBox.Show(result)
```

Now you can run the application without any problems. Go ahead and press F5 to run it. Then enter **5** in the first box and **3** in the second before clicking the Divide button to see the result, shown in Figure 3-4.

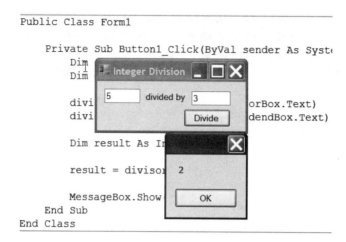

```
Public Class Form1

    Private Sub Button1_Click(ByVal sender As Syst
        Dim
        Dim

        divi                                    orBox.Text)
        divi                                    dendBox.Text)

        Dim result As I

        result = diviso       2

        MessageBox.Show
    End Sub
End Class
```

Figure 3-4. *Dividing integers can produce some very strange results.*

Obviously, that answer is wrong; 5 divided by 3 is 1.666666667, or less depending on the precision of your calculator.

When you divide two integers, or store the result of a division as an integer, VB rounds the answer. So, if the answer were really 1.1, VB would round the answer down to 1. On the other hand, if the answer were 1.666666667 as it is here, VB would round the result up to 2. That's definitely something to be aware of.

Let's extend the program a bit more and calculate the modulus to see a different answer:

```
Private Sub Button1_Click(ByVal sender As System.Object, _
        ByVal e As System.EventArgs) Handles Button1.Click
    Dim divisor As Integer
    Dim dividend As Integer

    divisor = Integer.Parse(divisorBox.Text)
    dividend = Integer.Parse(dividendBox.Text)

    Dim result As Integer
    Dim modulus As Integer

    result = divisor / dividend
    modulus = divisor Mod dividend

    MessageBox.Show("The answer is " + result.ToString() + _
            " with " + modulus.ToString() + " left over")
End Sub
```

Notice how you can add strings together by using the + sign (technically, it's called concatenating strings). Because modulus and result are both integers, we need to call their ToString() methods to turn them into strings.

This code also uses the modulus operator Mod to calculate the remainder of the division.

If you run the program now, you'll see a result like that in Figure 3-5.

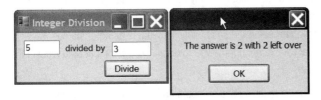

Figure 3-5. *Modulus can be used to show the remainder result of a division.*

Well, that's not really any better at all. The Mod operator is working just fine. It tells us that 5 divided by 3 doesn't work out cleanly, and that there would be 2 left over. But that rounding problem is still giving us issues; 5 divided by 3 should be 1 with 2 left over.

The solution to this is incredibly subtle. Take a look:

```
Private Sub Button1_Click(ByVal sender As System.Object,_
   ByVal e As System.EventArgs) Handles Button1.Click
      Dim divisor As Integer
      Dim dividend As Integer

      divisor = Integer.Parse(divisorBox.Text)
      dividend = Integer.Parse(dividendBox.Text)

      Dim result As Integer
      Dim modulus As Integer

      result = divisor \ dividend
      modulus = divisor Mod dividend

      MessageBox.Show("The answer is " + result.ToString() + _
                 " with " + modulus.ToString() + " left over")
   End Sub
```

The change here is in the line that divides the two numbers and stores the product in our result variable. I changed the divide symbol from a forward slash (/) to a backslash (\). In VB Express the forward slash divides two numbers and returns a Double—a value that may have digits (lots of them) after the decimal point. It's not a whole number. If you try to store a Double value into an Integer, Visual Basic will quite happily, and quietly, round the number to the closest integer. After mentioning earlier that I like to be explicit in my code, it might seem strange that I let Visual Basic get away with this. The alternative is to tell Visual Basic exactly what I expect it to do, like this:

```
result = CType(divisor \ dividend, Integer)
```

CType does something called a *cast*, converting what would normally be a Double answer into an Integer. In simple math like this VB will do it for me without me having to CType it, but there is of course an argument that typing in CType shows anyone reading the code explicitly what is going on behind the scenes. In fact many languages (C# and Java, for example) force you to do an explicit cast of data types. I'll leave it to you to decide which style you prefer.

The backslash here is an integer divide. It expects to divide two numbers and return a whole number result. If the result is not a whole number, the backslash truncates it. In other words, the integer divide cuts off everything after the decimal place. Try running the program now and you'll see the result in Figure 3-6.

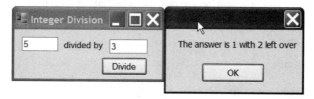

Figure 3-6. *You need to be very careful about which divide symbol you use, to prevent rounding errors.*

Other Number Types

If the only kind of number you could work with in VB was an integer, a lot of people would wander off to other development languages. Thankfully, VB has some more-complex numeric data types to play with. The most common are Decimal and Double, the rest being variations on that theme (search the online help for "built-in data types" to see the full list).

The Decimal variables can hold values with a staggering number of decimal places, but a smaller number range than Double. Conversely, Double variables have fewer decimal places than Decimal numbers, but a much greater physical number range. The golden rule when working with them is that if you are doing something that requires an incredibly high degree of precision (such as financial calculations or some scientific work), use Decimal. For anything else use Double.

Both Decimal and Double are declared exactly the same way that you would declare an Integer variable. For example:

```
Dim myDouble As Double
Dim myDecimal As Decimal
```

Boolean Values

I want to touch on a simple data type here that I'll talk about in much greater detail toward the end of this chapter: the Boolean data type.

There was a famous English chap by the name of George Boole. George is known today as the inventor of calculus law and Boolean algebra. The latter, in a nutshell, is responsible for much of the logic that goes on in computers today because it focuses on logic, trues and falses, 1s and 0s, the heartbeat of your PC.

A Boolean data type can hold just one of two values, True or False:

```
Dim trulyStunningAuthor As Boolean = False
Dim macTheDogDrools As Boolean = True
```

The True and False values are keywords in VB that you can write out longhand just as in those two examples.

There's not much more to say—you'll see a lot of these guys later in this chapter, when you start to look at conditions and loops.

Characters and Text

Aside from numbers, perhaps the most common type of data you'll work with in your programs will be *text*. There are two types of text—*characters* (which are the individual letters and symbols you see on this page), and *strings* (which are combinations of characters that form pretty much anything from a word to a novel). I'll explain characters first, since they're the more trivial.

A character is declared with the Char keyword, and you specify Char values by placing them in double quotes:

```
Dim aCharacter As Char = "s"
```

It's actually quite rare these days that you need to do much with single characters, so I'll move on.

Strings (text) are declared with the keyword String, and string data is also always held inside double quotes:

```
Dim aString as String = "Pete was here!"
```

As you can see, you can store pretty much anything you want in a string, including letters, numbers, punctuation, and a lot more besides.

The String class also has a ton of methods that you can use to manipulate the characters in the string itself. You'll soon find, when you start writing your own programs, that these will get used a lot.

If you want to find something inside a string, there are five methods that you can use: Contains(), IndexOf(), LastIndexOf()x, StartsWith(), and EndsWith(). Contains(), StartsWith(), and EndsWith() just return a True or False value. For example:

```
Sub Main()
    Dim person As String
    person = "Joseph R. Bloggs"

    If person.EndsWith("Bloggs") Then
        Console.WriteLine("Yup, we have a Bloggs here")
    End If
    If person.StartsWith("Joseph") Then
        Console.WriteLine("
This is definitely a Joseph")
    End If

    If person.Contains("R.") Then
        Console.WriteLine("The middle initial is R")
    End If

    Console.ReadLine()
End Sub
```

If you wish to go ahead and key that into a console application, feel free. When the program runs, it produces output like that in Figure 3-7.

As you can see, the Contains(), StartsWith(), and EndsWith() methods are really easy to use. You just pass them the string you want to search for, and they return True or False depending on whether they could find a match.

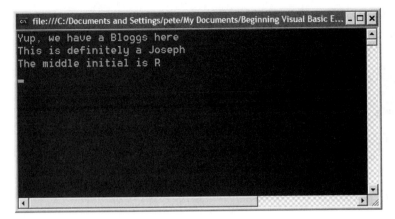

Figure 3-7. *The Contains(), StartsWith(), and EndsWith() methods let you easily see what's inside a string.*

IndexOf() and LastIndexOf()work a little differently. Both methods will tell you at which character position another string was found, or -1 if there was no match. If you have a string that might contain more than one instance of another, LastIndexOf() will return the last character position that a match was found. Here's an example:

```
Sub Main()
    Dim quote As String

    quote = "Alas, poor Yorik, I knew him well."

    Console.WriteLine(quote.IndexOf(","))
    Console.WriteLine(quote.LastIndexOf(","))
    Console.WriteLine(quote.IndexOf("Bob"))

    Console.ReadLine()
End Sub
```

If you key this into a console application project, the output will look like Figure 3-8.

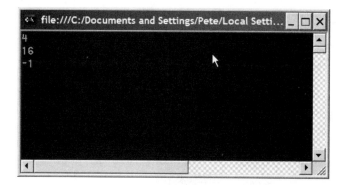

Figure 3-8. *The IndexOf() methods let you find where one string exists in another.*

As you can see, the first call to IndexOf() returns 4, telling us that there is a comma at position 4 in the string. But wait a second. If you look at the actual string, the first comma is really the fifth character. The reason IndexOf() returns 4 is that it counts the first character as character number 0. Think of IndexOf() then as telling you how many characters to ignore before it finds a match. If you look at it that way, IndexOf() is telling us that the comma appears after the fourth character in the string.

LastIndexOf()works the same way. It tells us that the last comma in the string appears after character number 16.

If you try to find a string that doesn't exist, like "Bob," both IndexOf() and LastIndexOf() return -1.

You'll most often use these methods in conjunction with another one, called Substring(). Substring() effectively slices up the string into pieces. You can use it to find everything in a string after a certain character, or you can tell it to give you a certain number of characters from the string, starting at a certain position. For example:

```
Sub Main()
    Dim numbers As String
    numbers = "One Two Three Four"

    Dim position As Integer = numbers.IndexOf("Two")

    Console.WriteLine(numbers.Substring(position))
    Console.WriteLine(numbers.Substring(position, 3))

    Console.ReadLine()
End Sub
```

If you key that in and run it, you'll see the output in Figure 3-9.

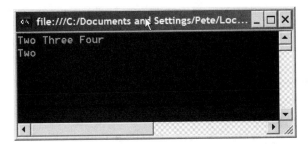

Figure 3-9. *IndexOf() and Substring() together let you slice up a string.*

This program first uses IndexOf() to find where in the string the word "Two" is. It then passes the value to Substring(). If you pass a single number into Substring(), it gives you everything from the position you specify onward. That's why the program outputs "Two Three Four."

You can also pass a second number to Substring(), which is the number of characters to extract. The second call then passes in 3 as that second number, meaning we just pull the word "Two" out of the string.

Incidentally, the more ambitious among you may be interested to know that .NET has an incredibly powerful set of objects that live in System.Text.RegularExpressions. These objects provide methods you can call to do some pretty complex stuff to strings of text. In fact, regular expressions use a language all of their own, so for now I'll leave it to you to explore the online help if you are already familiar with them and want to get a grip on how they work in .NET.

Arrays

Knowing how to work with single pieces of data is useful, but what if you want to work with a bunch of the same type? For example, you might want to hold a list of people's names in your program, or perhaps a list of stock symbols in a stock-tracking application. That's where arrays come in.

Arrays are not a special new data type, but rather a way of telling Visual Basic that you want a variable to hold more than one of a specific type of data. You declare them like this:

```
Dim stockTickers(9) As String
```

This example sets up an array to hold 10 strings (numbered 0, 1, 2, and so on up to 9). The parentheses following the variable name show VB that you want to work with an array.

You could also set up an array by specifying the values that it should hold on the same line as the declaration:

```
Dim tickers() As String = {"MSFT", "IBM", "APPL"}
```

In this case, you have an array of three strings. After the strings are in the array, they get numbered. The first is number 0 (remember how IndexOf() also treats the first element as number 0), and the last is the size of the array minus 1. So, if you have an array of four strings, the strings are numbered 0, 1, 2, and 3. This lets you get at them individually. You can also find out just how many items are in the array by using the array's Length property. This all sounds very weird and cryptic, so let's look at an example.

Try It Out: Working with Arrays

Start up a new console application. When the code window appears, declare a string array just as in the preceding example. You can see the code here:

```
Sub Main()
    Dim names() As String = {"Pete", "John", "Dave", "Gary"}
End Sub
```

Add some code now to print out the length of the array and also each string in the array:

```
Sub Main()
    Dim names() As String = {"Pete", "John", "Dave", "Gary"}

    Console.WriteLine( _
      "The array contains {0} items", names.Length)
    Console.WriteLine(names(0))
    Console.WriteLine(names(1))
    Console.WriteLine(names(2))
    Console.WriteLine(names(3))

    Console.ReadLine()
End Sub
```

If you run the application now, you'll see a console window like the one in Figure 3-10, showing the array length and each item in the array.

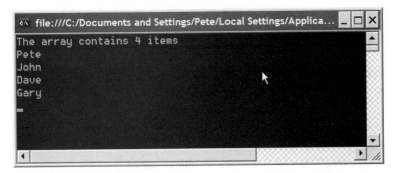

Figure 3-10. *You can access elements of the array by typing the array name, followed by the index of the element you want inside parentheses.*

Imagine, though, that you had an array with a thousand items in it. Typing `Console.WriteLine()` for each one would be tedious in the extreme. Thankfully, VB gives us the handy `For Each` command. Go ahead and change the code so that it looks like this (I've highlighted the changes for you):

```
Sub Main()
    Dim names() As String = {"Pete", "John", "Dave", "Gary"}

    Console.WriteLine( _
        "The array contains {0} items", names.Length)
    For Each name As String In names
        Console.WriteLine(name)
    Next

    Console.ReadLine()
End Sub
```

As you can see, the `For Each` command is quite easy to use. It's a *loop*, a block of code that runs over and over (more on these in a while). In the case of the `For Each` command, the block runs, walking through each element of the array, storing each element into a variable that you specify. In this case, you set up a new string variable called `name` that you'll use to grab each element "in" the `names` array.

Inside the `For Each` block, you just write out the value of that new variable. In fact, you could extend this program even further and bring in some of the handy stuff you saw that integers can do to make the output even better. Go ahead and make another couple of changes:

```
Sub Main()
    Dim names()As String = {"Pete", "John", "Dave", "Gary"}

    Console.WriteLine( _
        "The array contains {0} items", names.Length)

    Dim index As Integer = 0
    For Each name As String In names
        Console.WriteLine("Names({0}) = {1}", index, name)
        index += 1
    Next

    Console.ReadLine()
End Sub
```

This time around, you're setting up an integer variable to keep track of how many items in the array you've looked at. Inside the `For Each` loop, you use the += operator to add 1 to that variable, and also print out the current index value, along with the current array element. Run the program, and your console window should look a little more informative than it did (see Figure 3-11).

I'll cover more on loops and the different kinds of loops you can use a little later in this chapter.

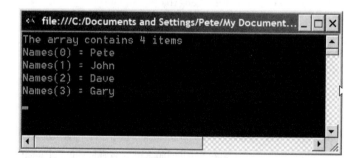

Figure 3-11. *By adding an integer counter variable, along with some neat use of Console.WriteLine(), you can make your program become more informative.*

Making Decisions

I touched on how to get VB to make decisions in the "Writing Conditional Statements" walk-through in the previous chapter. Time to look at the details.

If Statements

I don't think I've ever come across a programming language that didn't have an If statement.

The format is quite simple, as you saw in the preceding chapter:

```
If somecondition Then
End If
```

Notice that If, as with all VB keywords, is typed out with a capital first letter. If you forget to type this yourself, the VB editor will fix it for you. The If statement always evaluates what follows as a Boolean True or False value. For example:

```
If  1 = 2  Then
    // Do something
End If
```

This code will never work, because 1 does not equal 2. The = symbol means "is equal to" and is just one of a whole bunch of comparison operators that you can use in building your conditions. The full list is shown in Table 3-1.

Table 3-1. *The Conditional Operators Available to You in VB*

Symbol	Meaning
=	*Is equal to*—compares the value on the left to see whether it is equal to the value on the right
<>	*Not equal to*—compares the value on the left to ensure that it's not the same as the one on the right
<	*Less than*—checks whether the value on the left is smaller than the one on the right
>	*Greater than*—checks whether the value on the left is bigger than the one on the right
<=	*Is less than or equal to*—checks whether the value on the left is less than or equal to the value on the right
>=	*Is greater than or equal to*—checks whether the value on the left is greater than or equal to the value on the right
Not	*Not*—returns True if the entire condition is *not* true

The last item in the list (Not) is an interesting one. It negates the whole condition. For example:

```
If  Not (myAge = entryAge)) Then

End If
```

Normally, you'd expect a True value to get returned, causing the block following the If command to run if myAge and entryAge were both the same. Wrapping them in parentheses and sticking a Not at the front turns it all around. The block following the If condition will run If myAge is Not equal to entryAge.

How about this, though:

```
If  Not ( myAge <> entryAge ) Then
End If
```

Confusing, isn't it. This is equivalent to just testing myAge = entryAge, and it demonstrates something quite important: negative conditions are confusing. Try to avoid using negative conditions if you possibly can. It's hard for us humans to think in terms of negative conditions, and so using Not and <> too many times makes your code quite hard to read—and that can be a big deal when you're up against a deadline and can't find that last bug. As a general rule of thumb, use only positive conditions (Not negative ones).

Typically, newcomers to VB spend their first few months writing code that always has a condition following the If statement, but you don't have to. The If just expects to see a True or False value as the condition, so you can use single Boolean variables, or even function calls, in the condition part. This can make your code really slick and easy to follow. Let's take a look.

Try It Out: Using Functions As Conditions

You're going to revisit our password example from the previous chapter, writing a simple form to check that the user enters the same password twice, just as if they were changing it in some application. Create a Windows application in Visual Basic 2005 Express and drop some controls on the form so that it looks like Figure 3-12.

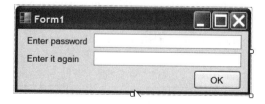

Figure 3-12. *Drop some controls onto your form and set up their text properties so that your form looks like the one shown here.*

Just to make sure your code looks the same as mine, set the Name of the first textbox to password1, and the second to password2 (see Figure 3-13).

Figure 3-13. *Set up the name properties of the controls by using the Properties window, as always.*

When you're finished setting up the properties, double-click the OK button on your form to drop into the code editor. What you could do at this point is write a simple If followed by a condition to check that the two words entered are the same. In fact, in an example this trivial that would make a lot of sense, but it wouldn't really teach you anything.

Instead, add a new function to the code underneath the button's event handler:

```
Private Function PasswordsValid( _
    ByVal firstPassword As String, ByVal secondPassword As String) _
    As Boolean

    Return (firstPassword.Equals(secondPassword))


End Function
```

Notice that this is not a Sub, as we have used in the preceding chapters. A Function is a special kind of Sub that can return a value, in this case a Boolean value. Other than the word "Function," the other difference with how this function is written are the words As Boolean at the end of the Function definition. It looks in some ways just like a variable declaration. You're just letting VB know here that the data type this function returns is a True/False, or Boolean, value. Also, as you type this in, you don't need to type in the words ByVal. VB will automatically put them in for you. I'll cover what they mean later. The final, very important, piece of information you need to know about this function is that because it returns a True or False value, you can actually call it as part of an If statement, as you'll see shortly.

Next, I'm sure you already noticed that the function contains just one line of code—a Return statement. The Return statement is returning the result of a condition. You take two strings into the function (firstPassword and secondPassword) and just do a simple comparison of the two to check that they are the same. The result of a condition is always a Boolean True or False value, so it's fair enough to just return this. You've probably also spotted that you don't compare the two strings with the = operator, but instead use the Equals() function. When you're using strings, the = operator will actually call Equals() behind the scenes. However, in terms of strings and objects, = should really just check to the see whether the two objects refer to the same space in memory, not that they contain the same value. To clarify, then, when comparing strings, use the Equals() method rather than =. It saves heartache, as you'll see when you've learned more about objects, trust me.

With your function coded up, it's dead easy to add some code to the button's click handler to use it. Type code in so that your click event handler looks like this:

```
Private Sub Button1_Click(ByVal sender As System.Object, _
    ByVal e As System.EventArgs) Handles Button1.Click

    If (PasswordsValid(password1.Text, password2.Text)) Then
        MessageBox.Show("Congratulations! They match.")
    Else
        MessageBox.Show("They don't match - try again.")
    End If
End Sub
```

Take a look at the code and see if you can figure out what it does.

Instead of using a condition, the If statement just calls PasswordsValid(), passing in as parameters whatever text the user entered into the two password boxes on the form. Because this function returns True or False, that's all you need. If the return value is True, a message box gets displayed saying that everything was okay. Otherwise, a message box is shown to indicate that there was a problem.

As you can see here, Else adds a certain something to a basic If statement, letting you set up a code block to run if the If condition is not True.

You can even go one step further if you want and use multiple If statements, like this:

```
If condition1 Then
ElseIf condition2 Then

ElseIf condition3 Then

Else

End If
```

Such things are generally frowned upon, though, if you let them get too big—there are better ways to get around having massive If...ElseIf...ElseIf statements, including object orientation and subclassing—so I'm not going to spend any more time on this right now. .

Select Statements

A bunch of If...ElseIf...Else statements quickly gets confusing, so it's frowned on for all but the simplest of checks. An alternative (as long as you don't get carried away with it as well), is the Select statement.

Unlike If, Select doesn't use conditions. You typically use an If clause to check whether one thing satisfies a condition. A Select statement lets you test a whole bunch of conditions at once. It lets you effectively code "if the value is this, do this; otherwise if it's this, do this; otherwise…" and so on. I'll just jump straight into an example to show you how it works.

Try It Out: Select Statements

Start up a new Windows project and set up your form like the one in Figure 3-14.

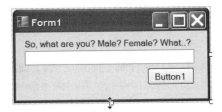

Figure 3-14. *Set up your form like this one.*

Set up the Name of the text box control to be userType.

Double-click the Button1 button to drop into the code editor. Now write some code with a Select statement to respond appropriately to the type of user keying in data:

```
Private Sub Button1_Click(ByVal sender As System.Object, _
    ByVal e As System.EventArgs) Handles Button1.Click
    Select Case userType.Text.ToUpper()
        Case "MALE"
            MessageBox.Show("So, you're a guy!")
        Case "FEMALE"
            MessageBox.Show("Hello there, m'lady!")
        Case Else
            MessageBox.Show("HELP! An Alien!")
    End Select
End Sub
```

Run the program and try keying in **Male**, **Female**, or anything else, just to check that it works as it should. You'll see a window like the one in Figure 3-15.

Figure 3-15. *You can use Select statements to easily test for a bunch of different conditions.*

Let's explore just how this works.

Obviously, you want to check what the user entered, and so the `Select` statement contains a reference to the text that the user entered into the text box inside its brackets—notice, not a condition, but a straight value. Because the user could conceivably type in data in lowercase, uppercase, or a mix of them, you also call the string's `ToUpper()` method so that no matter what they enter you can treat it as uppercase.

Inside the `Select` block, the `Case` statements list the possible values that you are interested in responding to—in this case, Male, Female, and anything else. That's really what `Case Else` does—by adding a `Case Else` statement to the block, you are telling VB's `Select` statement that if it doesn't find a match, it should do whatever follows `Case Else`.

Immediately following the `Case` statements, we just have commands to pop open message boxes. You could conceivably do anything you like here, but the general rule of thumb is that if you have more than two or three lines of code following a `Case` statement, you really should move that code into a function and call the function from the `Case` statement instead.

Just as with the `If...ElseIf` statements, there is also a risk that if you stick *huge* `Select` blocks in your code, it will become unmanageable and very hard to read and debug.

Loops

Loops use conditional statements just like our old friend the `If` statement. The difference between them of course is that whereas `If` will do something just once if a condition is met, loops will run over and over until the condition is met (`For` loops), or for as long as a condition is true (`While` loops).

While Loops

A `While` loop, as its name indicates, runs a block of code over and over *while* a condition is true. As soon as the condition fails, the loop stops. That can cause problems for newcomers until they get their heads around it, because `While` loops may never run at all; if the condition is False, the first time the While loop is met, the loop will be skipped. Alternatively, a badly coded condition could also mean the loop runs forever.

In terms of formatting, While loops look pretty similar to If statements:

```
Do While condition
Loop
```

Just like an If test, While checks the condition to make sure it's true and then runs the stuff inside the block. This can be useful, but please make sure you do something in the block so that eventually the loop stops; otherwise, your program is likely to send the computer into an endless spin cycle and stop everything else that is running as well.

As always, code helps clarify the situation, so let's take a look at a While loop in this "Try It Out."

Try It Out: While Loops

Let's make a simple Windows form that dumps the current time into a list box, for a length of time. Create a new Windows Forms application and build up a user interface like the one in Figure 3-16.

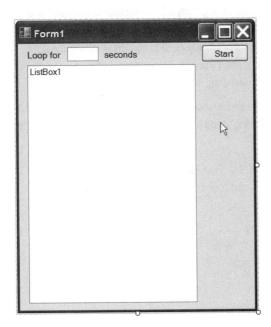

Figure 3-16. *Drop two labels, a text box, a button, and a list box onto your form to make it look like this.*

Just let VB Express assign the default names to the controls and you won't need to change anything for your code to work the same as mine.

Double-click the Start button on the form to pop open the code editor.

Each time the button is clicked, the first thing you need to do is clear out any data that may already be in the list box. Add this line to the subroutine:

```
ListBox1.Items.Clear()
```

What the code is going to do ultimately is fire items into the list box for a specific length of time. The easiest way to do that is to add the number of seconds entered in the text box by the user to the current time, to work out the time to stop. That's the next line of code to add:

```
Private Sub Button1_Click(ByVal sender As System.Object, _
    ByVal e As System.EventArgs) Handles Button1.Click

    ListBox1.Items.Clear()
    Dim endTime As Date
    endTime = DateTime.Now.AddSeconds( _
        Integer.Parse(TextBox1.Text))

End Sub
```

Let's talk through this a little just to make it clear what's happening. First a Date variable called endTime is declared. To initialize this, you take the current time (DateTime.Now) and add some seconds to it (AddSeconds()). Because the text box on the form holds strings, you need to convert whatever the user entered from a string (for example, "2") into a number (2). The Integer.Parse does that for you. By giving Integer.Parse some text containing a number, it will return the integer number on its own.

The setup is now out of the way and you can focus on the While loop itself. Key in the rest of the code. Your finished button click event handler will look like the following listing (I've highlighted the new bits you need to type in):

```
Private Sub Button1_Click(ByVal sender As System.Object, _
    ByVal e As System.EventArgs) Handles Button1.Click

    ListBox1.Items.Clear()
    Dim endTime As Date
    endTime = DateTime.Now.AddSeconds( _
     Integer.Parse(TextBox1.Text))

    Do While DateTime.Now < endTime
        ListBox1.Items.Add(DateTime.Now.TimeOfDay.ToString())
    Loop

End Sub
```

As you can see, the While loop is quite straightforward. It runs *while* the current time is less than the time you are supposed to stop at. Inside the list you just take the current time of day, convert it to a string, and add it to the list box. Run the app and key a number (**2** is a good bet) into the text box; then click the Start button to see what happens (see Figure 3-17). Bear in mind that you don't have any error checking on this application just yet, so be sure to enter a number and not anything else.

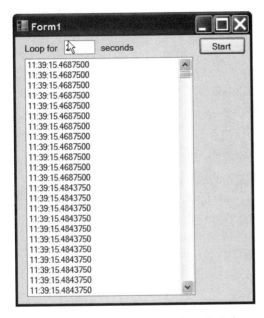

Figure 3-17. *Run the app to see the While loop working.*

If a While loop runs while some condition is true, an Until loop runs until a condition is met. It's the reverse of a While loop. I'm not going to walk you through a complete "Try It Out" on this because it's so simple to grasp once you understand While loops.

The format of an Until loop looks like this:

```
Do

Loop Until condition
```

So, if we were to change our loop in the previous example to use an Until loop, it would look like this:

```
Do
    ListBox1.Items.Add(DateTime.Now.TimeOfDay.ToString())
Loop Until DateTime.Now > endTime
```

Because the two loop types are so similar, you may be wondering which you should use. There is no simple answer to that, but there is an important subtle difference between the two. The code in an Until loop will always run at least once. It runs, and then the condition is checked. A While loop, on the other hand, checks its condition before the code runs, so there's a strong chance that sometimes the code in the loop might not even run once. That subtle difference often plays a big part in helping you choose which loop format to use (personally, I prefer While loops).

For Loops

A While loop runs for as long as a specific condition is met. A For loop, on the other hand, runs a specific number of times, until a condition is met.

The syntax is quite hard to remember at first, but you'll get it with a bit of practice:

```
For somevariable as sometype = startvalue to endvalue
```

That's hard to get your head around if you haven't seen it before, but the real code is a little easier to read. Take a look at this simple console application (feel free to start a console application and key this in if you want to experiment):

```
Sub Main()
    For index As Integer = 1 To 10
        Console.WriteLine(index)
    Next
    Console.ReadLine()
End Sub
```

The For loop here declares a new Integer variable called index, and then simply counts from 1 to 10. If you wanted to go backward, from 10 to 1, you'd add step -1 to the end of the statement, like this:

```
Sub Man()
    For index As Integer = 10 To 1 step -1
        Console.WriteLine(index)
    Next

    Console.ReadLine()
End Sub
```

It's not really so difficult, is it.

If you were to key in and run the program (the one that counts up), you'd see something like Figure 3-18.

Figure 3-18. *The loop runs ten times, counting from 1 to 10.*

There are two ways to get out of a For loop prematurely, something you'll want to do sometimes. The first is to change the index inside the loop. For example:

```
Sub Main()
    For index As Integer = 1 To 10
        Console.WriteLine(index)
        If index = 5 Then
            index = 11
        End If
    Next
    Console.ReadLine()
End Sub
```

This checks for a specific number in index, your loop's index variable, and then sets index to something that breaks the For loop condition. If you do this, bear in mind that the loop will finish what it's doing before stopping.

A much better way (and this applies to While and Until loops as well) is to use the Exit command. If you wanted to break out of a For loop, you'd type Exit For. To leave a While loop, you'd type Exit While. When you actually type in the word Exit, Visual Basic's IntelliSense will pop up, showing you the various code constructs you can break out of and letting you choose one.

It's worth also mentioning that you can use a keyword called Step with a For loop to control how much the index variable changes. For example:

```
For evenNumbers As Integer = 2 To 20 Step 2

Next
```

This causes the loop to count from 2 to 20 in steps of 2. Equally, you could use a negative step to count backward:

```
For countdown As Integer = 10 To 1 Step -1

Next
```

This counts down from 10 to 1, since the step each time is –1.

Summary

This chapter has covered pretty much the core essence of Visual Basic. You've seen how to create variables and then how to write code to work with them. That code can make decisions, it can loop, and so on. Now you've got the basics down, you can move into the real meat, starting with functions and methods (same thing) in the next chapter. Hang in there—you don't have far to go now before you can start making beautiful Windows applications with cool user interfaces. You have to learn to walk first, though.

CHAPTER 4

███

Classes and Object Orientation in Visual Basic 2005

I think Douglas Coupland first documented geeks' obsession with LEGO bricks in his novel *Microserfs* (HarperCollins, 1995). In that book, a bunch of disillusioned programmers from Microsoft leave the safety of Redmond and form their own Silicon Valley start-up to make a computerized version of LEGO kits, thus freeing geeks all over the world to build new models no matter where they are (so long as they have a laptop with them).

The obsession is simple to explain. LEGO building is object-oriented programming. Each LEGO brick has data (its color, size, shape, and so on) and functionality (it exposes a set of connectors that allow it to connect to other bricks). Encapsulation of data and functionality is a key tenet in object-oriented programming. However, LEGO is also a great demonstrator for other key goals of object orientation.

Using the basic LEGO building blocks, you can create more-complex components for later use. For example, you could take a bunch of blocks and connect them to form a house. The house is a "superset" of the basic building block in that it does everything the basic building block does, but adds to it. A house, for example, will still expose those little round bumps that allow it to connect to yet more blocks, but it also has specific functions in terms of housing the little LEGO guys, forming a LEGO community, or even being the object of a menacing monster's destructive whims (mine were). In that respect then, LEGO blocks support the basic object-oriented tenets of inheritance, absorbing the data and functionality of one object into a far more specialized object.

The previous chapters focused on the essential tools and skills that you'll need to create the basic building blocks of your application. This chapter brings all those tools together and shows you just how to use them to create classes, the building blocks of a Visual Basic 2005 application, and all the neat things that you can do as a result.

Classes and Objects

Every piece of code you write in VB lives inside a class. For example, you should be familiar by now with this:

```
Public Class Form1

End Class
```

So, if VB is an object-oriented programming language, and objects are like LEGO bricks, where do classes fit in? If I give you a LEGO brick, a nice small chunky one with two rows of four connectors on top, that's an object. However, the description "a small chunky LEGO brick with two rows of four connectors" is the definition of the object. That description is in effect a class. It tells you what kind of object you are after, along with the properties and functionality that define the object.

Look at it another way. As I said in Chapter 2, Bill Gates is a billionaire. Sentences like that, with the words "is a" in the middle, tend to define a relationship between a class and an object. Bill Gates then is an object, and Billionaire is the class, or type of object. You know that Billionaire implies certain functionality and data (has lots of money, can buy a small country, and so on), and so an *instance* of that class is a real and tangible thing that does everything the class says it can. Get used to the word "instance." When we talk about objects and classes together, we typically say that an object "is an instance of" a specific class. It's kind of like saying a cookie cutter is a class, and applying the cookie cutter to some dough produces an instance of the class.

Creating Classes

Creating a class in Visual Basic 2005 Express is trivial. With a project open in the Solution Explorer, right-click its name and then choose Add ➤ Class, as you can see in Figure 4-1.

After you choose to add a new class to the project, a dialog box appears, asking you to confirm the name of the class. You can see the dialog box in Figure 4-2.

Figure 4-1. *Right-clicking on a project in the Solution Explorer pops up a context menu that lets you add new elements into the project.*

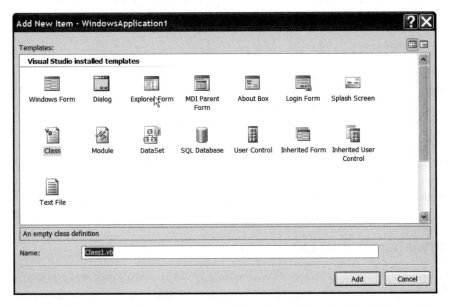

Figure 4-2. *Adding in a class pops open a dialog box asking for information about the class, specifically its name.*

After you've chosen a name for the class file and clicked Add, the class is added to the solution, ready for you to open up the code editor and start writing code. If you double-click the class, the code editor should show a nice new empty class, just like the ones that you have already seen. Here's the code for a new class I added called Class1:

```
Public Class Class1

End Class
```

You don't have to let VB Express create classes for you, though. There is nothing stopping you from just going ahead and adding hand-coded classes to any source file in the project. You've already done this, in fact, in some of the examples earlier in the book.

The format of a class is really simple. Just start off with the word Class, followed by a name for the class. The end of the class is marked in the source with the words End Class. For example:

```
Class ANewClass
End Class
```

Notice how this class differs subtly from the one that VB Express builds automatically. If VB Express had created this class, it would look like this:

```
Public Class ANewClass
End Class
```

The difference here is obvious. The class definition itself is prefixed with the keyword Public. This changes the *scope* of the class, so that it can be used from any other code within the project. You'll look at scoping in more detail a little later in this chapter, so don't worry about it too much.

Classes bring with them two special kinds of subroutines as well that let you write code that will be executed only when an object is created from a class, and then when the object is later destroyed. The former are called *constructors*, and the latter, *finalizers*.

Using Constructors and Finalizers

Constructors are special methods. They don't return any value of any kind, and just contain code that should run as soon as an object is created. A class can have more than one constructor as well, with each constructor having a different set of parameters. The exact method used to instantiate the code determines just which constructor will run. I know that's a bit confusing if you've never come across this stuff before, so let's take a hands-on look.

Try It Out: Constructors and Finalizers

Create a new console project in the usual way. When the code editor appears, add a new class called `TestClass.vb` to the project. As a reminder, you can do this by right-clicking on the name of the project in the Solution Explorer and choosing Add ➤ Class from the context menu that appears. Don't forget to set the name of the class to `TestClass.vb`.

After a very short delay, the code window will change to show the new class, just as in Figure 4-3.

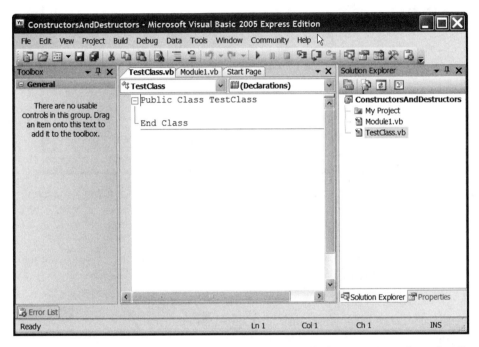

Figure 4-3. *Adding a new class to the solution automatically drops you into the code editor for that new class.*

Let's go ahead now and add a constructor. The VB Express code editor can actually help you do this. At the top of the code window are two drop-down boxes. If you look at Figure 4-3 again, you can see that these currently show TestClass in one, and (Declarations) in the other. If you were working on a source file that had more than one class in it, you could use the drop-down at the top left of the editor to quickly jump from one class to another. As you add code into a class, the drop-down at the right lets you quickly jump from subroutine to subroutine (actually, subroutines and functions inside a class are more commonly called *methods*). With a blank class like ours here, you can also use the drop-down on the right to create the class constructor. Simply click on it, and choose New from the list that appears, as in Figure 4-4.

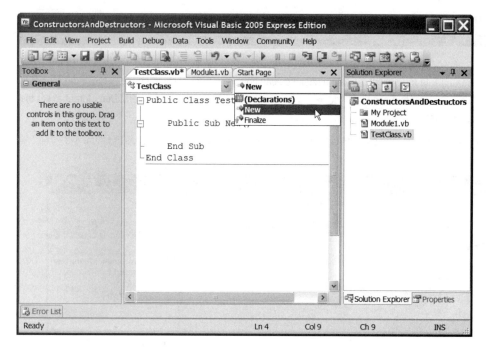

Figure 4-4. *You can use the Declarations drop-down in the code editor to help you quickly create constructors for classes.*

As soon as you click New, an empty constructor method will be inserted into the code, as you can see in Figure 4-4. Go ahead and add a line of code to this method:

```
Public Sub New()
    Console.WriteLine("TestClass just got instantiated")
End Sub
```

As soon as the class is instantiated, this code causes a message to be written out to the console. You can of course test this out by adding some code to the application to actually instantiate the class.

Double-click on Module1.vb in the Solution Explorer to jump back to the code that you first saw when you created the project. You could also switch to Module1.vb by using the tabs at the top of the editor. Notice that there are two—one for Module1.vb and another for the new class you just added into the project.

Change the `Main()` method so that it creates an instance of the new class in order for you to see the constructor at work:

```
Sub Main()
    Console.WriteLine("About to create an instance of TestClass")
    Dim newClass As New TestClass()
    Console.WriteLine("All done!")
    Console.ReadLine()
End Sub
```

All that's happening here is that you are outputting a bunch of text to let you know just what's going on in the program and creating an instance of the class.

Creating an instance of the class (creating an object, in other words) is quite easy. You just declare a variable the same way that you would declare an integer or a string, but set the type to the name of the class in question. Then, create the new class with the words `New TestClass()`. Notice the parentheses at the end of the class name—looks like you're calling a subroutine, doesn't it, and the reason is that you are. The subroutine that gets called is the constructor (if you take a look back at the code for the constructor itself, you will notice that it doesn't have anything in its parameter list either).

Run the program now and you'll see a console window like the one shown in Figure 4-5.

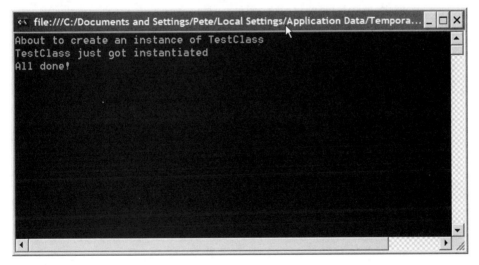

Figure 4-5. *When the class gets instantiated, the constructor runs, and the code you wrote into that constructor outputs a message.*

Constructors are really quite similar to standard subroutines, except that they don't return any value. So this means that you can define a bunch of constructors as long as they all have different "signatures." You'll look at this in a lot more detail later in the chapter, but just to give you a taste, let's go ahead and create an additional constructor and see how it's used.

Click the TestClass tab at the top of the IDE to bring the `TestClass.vb` source back into view. Right underneath the constructor you wrote a short while ago, add another one (you'll need to type this one in entirely by hand):

```
Public Class TestClass
    Public Sub New()
        Console.WriteLine("TestClass just got instantiated")
    End Sub

    Public Sub New(ByVal name As String)
        Console.WriteLine("Instantiated by {0}", name)
    End Sub
End Class
```

This constructor has a different signature in that it takes a single string parameter while the old one takes no parameters at all.

Click the Module1.vb tab to return to the main code, and then write some code to use this constructor:

```
Module Module1

    Sub Main()
        Console.WriteLine("About to create an instance of TestClass")
        Dim newClass As New TestClass()
        Dim anotherClass As New TestClass("Me")
        Console.WriteLine("All done!")
        Console.ReadLine()
    End Sub

End Module
```

You may have noticed, by the way, that this code is in a module, not a class. I'll talk about modules a little later. For now, just think of them buckets used to hold shared code. If you run the program now, you'll see that the console shows output from the new constructor (see Figure 4-6).

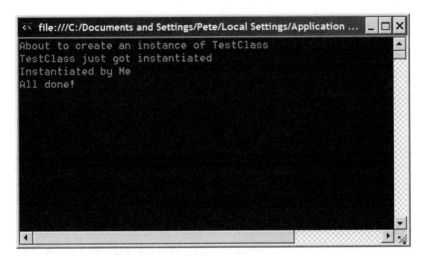

Figure 4-6. *Adding constructors allows you additional control over what happens when objects are created.*

So now you can control what happens when an object gets created from one of your classes. But what about when an object gets destroyed? For example, in the code so far, at the end of the program the object is no longer needed and so it gets destroyed. It's sometimes useful to have additional code run when that happens. For example, when you know a little more about .NET, you may have allocated memory in that class that you need to return to Windows when the object dies. Alternately, you might have some connections open to files, websites, or even databases that need closing. That's where finalizers come in.

Although a class can have many constructors (as long as they all have different signatures), a class can have only one finalizer. The finalizer is a special subroutine called `Finalize`, and you can add it to the class by selecting it from the drop-down again, just as when you created your first constructor earlier.

Let's add a finalizer to `TestClass` to make it tell us when it dies.

Back in the TestClass.vb source, select Finalize from the declarations drop-down, and then add some code to the finalizer, like this:

```
Public Class TestClass
    Public Sub New()
        Console.WriteLine("TestClass just got instantiated")
    End Sub

    Public Sub New(ByVal name As String)
        Console.WriteLine("Instantiated by {0}", name)
    End Sub

    Protected Overrides Sub Finalize()
        Console.WriteLine("TestClass object just died")
        MyBase.Finalize()
    End Sub
End Class
```

Run the program now and watch the console very closely as you hit the Enter key to stop the program. The two finalizer messages will flash onto the console for a mere fraction of a second as the program stops running.

This is actually better than the equivalent C# program. In C#, the program would crash, highlighting an important lesson about finalizers (they are called destructors in C#) and how garbage collection works in .NET.

You need to be careful about adding finalizers to your classes because you really don't have any control over just when those finalizers are run. The reason is that .NET's garbage collector (the behind-the-scenes bit of techno-wizardry that frees up memory used by objects when they are no longer needed) is nondeterministic. It runs when it can but offers you no guarantees as to when that will be, or what resources will be available to your code when it does run. In this example, the garbage collector kicks in when the program finishes, and is getting ready to clean up the two objects you created in your Main() function. However, at that point, the Console object has already been removed. Your finalizer then tries to use it and gets a nasty slap on the wrist. (This is of course a highly simplified view of how garbage collection works, but it should suffice for most of you for now.)

For this reason most people avoid using finalizers in their classes, preferring instead to add a method to the class called `CleanUp()` or `FinishUp()` or something similar that they call by hand. That way, any code you have in there to close down connections, output statuses, and so on, runs when you want it to run, giving you more control over just what facilities are still available to that code at runtime. In fact, there's an even better way in .NET. If you implement the `IDisposable` interface (we cover interfaces later in the book), you can add a `Dispose()` method to the class. You can be certain that if you implement this interface, `Dispose()` will absolutely get killed when you are done using an object.

I've touched on methods in the previous chapters. Let's take a more detailed look.

Methods

Methods are what breathe life into your classes. It's great that you can add constructors and finalizers to a class to get the class to do things when it's instantiated and destroyed, but it doesn't really move code-based objects into the same realm as objects in the world around us. We need our objects to do things!

Methods allow us to add functionality to a class. For example, if I were writing a `Car` class in a video game, I'd probably want functions in that class to start the car, put it in gear, accelerate, brake, turn, and stop.

When you add a method to a class, there are really only three things that you need to think about: what kind of data does it return, what's its name, and what's its signature. The first two are fairly obvious. *Signature* is the number and type of parameters passed to the method. For example, if you had a method that added two numbers and returned the result, the signature would be two number parameters (probably either integers or doubles).

The return type can be absolutely any type that you could define a variable from, including other classes. The example of a method that adds two numbers returns either an `Integer` or a `Double`. It could equally well return a `SumResult`, which could be a special class you defined to hold the result of mathematical sums.

FUNCTIONS AND METHODS

I have a bad habit of using the words "function" and "method" interchangeably. A *function*, strictly speaking, is a block of code with a name that can be called, and that returns a value. In VB, these are usually defined with the `Function` keyword you saw earlier. C programs, for example, consist of little more than a big bunch of functions.

When object-oriented programming came along, some way was required to differentiate between a function or subroutine outside of a class, and a function or subroutine inside of a class. The latter was called (and is now known as) a *method*. Because everything you do in Visual Basic 2005 ultimately lives inside a class, I tend to refer to everything (subroutine or function) as a method.

Let's go ahead and look at a simple example.

Try It Out: Methods

Let's make a trivial calculator just to show how to work with methods in a class. Start up a new Windows application and drop controls on the form so that it looks like mine in Figure 4-7.

Figure 4-7. *Drop some controls on the form and resize it so that it looks like this.*

If you can't guess already, the way that this is going to work is that you'll enter values in the two text boxes, choose something to do to them (add, subtract, and so on) from the combo box, and then click the Calculate button to calculate a result. In order for your code to work the same as mine, you'll need to change some properties on the controls, specifically the Name properties. Set the Name properties as shown in Table 4-1.

Table 4-1. *Name Properties of the Controls*

Control	Name Property
First text box	value1Box
Second text box	value2Box
Third text box	resultBox
Combo box	operation
Button	calculateButton

Before you drop down into the code, you need to add some values to that combo box so that the user has something to choose at runtime. Click on the combo box on the form and take a look at the Properties window (if you can't see it, press F4 to bring it into view). If you scroll down the Properties list, you'll eventually find one called Items. Click that property and you'll see a button appear with three dots (…). Click it to open the String Collection Editor. You can see this and the property in question in Figure 4-8.

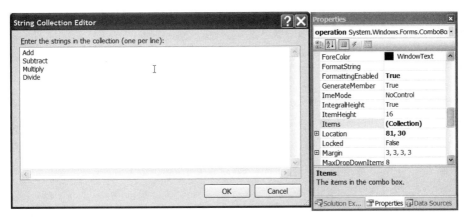

Figure 4-8. *Click the button in the Items property of the combo box to open the String Collection Editor.*

Add four items as shown (it's important to keep the text of the items exactly as I have in the screen shot—you'll see why in a minute). Also change the `DropDownStyle` property of the control to `DropDownList`.

Now you can start on some code. Add a new class to the project. Name it `Calculator.vb`—this class will hold all the methods that bring your somewhat simple calculator to life. After the class has been added to the project, you should see the GUI editor disappear to be replaced with the code editor for the class.

Just as you added items into the combo box list, you're going to need four methods: one for adding, one for subtracting, another for division, and a final one for multiplication. These are all quite simply methods that perform a calculation and return a value, so go ahead and key them in all at once. I've highlighted the code you need to add in the following listing:

```
Public Class Calculator

    Public Function Add(ByVal value1 As Double, ByVal value2 As Double) _
      As Double
        Return value1 + value2
    End Function

    Public Function Subtract(ByVal value1 As Double, ByVal value2 As Double) _
      As Double
        Return value1 - value2
    End Function
```

```
Public Function Multiply(ByVal value1 As Double, ByVal value2 As Double) _
    As Double
    Return value1 * value2
End Function

Public Function Divide(ByVal value1 As Double, ByVal value2 As Double) _
    As Double
    Return value1 / value2
End Function
```

```
End Class
```

All the methods here have different names but the same signature. Notice how each method takes two Double parameters, for example. Also, when defining the signature for a method, you'll notice that the code doesn't just list two doubles as the signature. Each parameter to the method is given a name. This name can then be used inside the method to refer to the actual value passed in, just as if you'd declared a couple of variables. So, taking a look at the Add() method, you take in two doubles, called value1 and value2, and use those to return their sum.

The keyword Return is used to pass a value back out of the method. In the case of these simple methods, you want to tell the Calculator class to do something (add, subtract, multiply, or divide) and then get the result of that calculation "returned" to you. Notice also how each method is a function that returns a Double:

```
Public Function Divide(ByVal value1 As Double, ByVal value2 As Double) _
    As Double
```

(I've used the _ symbol to split long lines of code so that they fit nicely into the book's pages.) Adding As Double after the end of the function signature tells Visual Basic that the value you are going to return here is a double, and so the compiler expects to see a Double value following the Return statement. You could have set these up as strings instead, in which case you would need code in the method to convert the result of the calculation from a double to a string.

Double-click Form1.vb in the Solution Explorer to drop back into the form editor, and then double-click the Calculate button on the form to drop into the code editor to hook up the Click event for that button.

I cover events and everything else to do with GUI programming in Chapter 8, but there's something interesting to note here. Take a look at the screen shot in Figure 4-9.

Figure 4-9. *Double-clicking a control drops you into the code editor for its default, or standard, event. This event is itself a method.*

At their simplest level, events are methods that VB knows about, but which you fill in the code for. So when the button gets clicked at runtime, its Click event fires and VB looks for one or more methods to run as a result. In Figure 4-9 you can see this. The button's Click event is a subroutine called calculateButton_Click, which is passed two objects as its signature. I won't go into detail on what those objects are or what they mean just yet, but the point is that just as every piece of code you write in VB lives in a class, every single line of functioning code you write in your classes lives in methods. That includes code to respond to things happening on Windows Forms.

Back to the code. Let's bring together everything you've done so far in the book—from creating variables to making decisions, to creating objects and actually calling methods on them—to fill in the code for this click event handler.

Because all the methods that you are going to call to make the calculations expect to be passed Double values, the first thing you need to do is extract the data from the text boxes on the form and convert it to doubles. For this you'll need a couple of variables, plus of course one for the result:

```
Private Sub calculateButton_Click(ByVal sender As System.Object, _
    ByVal e As System.EventArgs) _
    Handles calculateButton.Click

    Dim value1 As Double = Double.Parse(value1Box.Text)
    Dim value2 As Double = Double.Parse(value2Box.Text)
    Dim result As Double = 0.0

End Sub
```

So, here you've set up three variables—value1, value2, and result—and you've given them initial values. I should point out that we're assuming ideal conditions here and that the user really is going to enter something that should convert into a double. If they don't, we're in trouble. There is a VB method to get around this problem called TryParse(), but for our example it overcomplicates the code. Go ahead and look up TryParse() in the online help, and we'll also touch on it later.

You'll recall from the preceding chapter that all the number data types (Double, Integer, and so on) have a Parse() method that you can call to translate a string into a number. Because the text boxes hold text (strings), you use Double.Parse() here to convert the text the user enters into numbers that you can store in your variables.

The next thing you need to do is use your new Calculator class to create an object that you can call methods on. That's quite easy to do:

```
Dim value1 As Double = Double.Parse(value1Box.Text)
Dim value2 As Double = Double.Parse(value2Box.Text)
Dim result As Double = 0.0

Dim calc As New Calculator()
```

A variable is set up to hold the object of type Calculator. You then use New Calculator() to create an object and run the standard constructor. I didn't actually get you to write a constructor into the class, so all this will do is create a new object but not run any special code when that object comes to life.

With the object created, all that remains is to figure out just which method to call on it. You'll use a Select statement to look at the text in the combo box and decide which action to take:

```
Private Sub calculateButton_Click(ByVal sender As System.Object, _
    ByVal e As System.EventArgs) _
    Handles calculateButton.Click

    Dim value1 As Double = Double.Parse(value1Box.Text)
    Dim value2 As Double = Double.Parse(value2Box.Text)
    Dim result As Double = 0.0

    Dim calc As New Calculator()
```

```
Select Case operation.Text
    Case "Add"
        result = calc.Add(value1, value2)
    Case "Subtract"
        result = calc.Subtract(value1, value2)
    Case "Multiply"
        result = calc.Multiply(value1, value2)
    Case "Divide"
        result = calc.Divide(value1, value2)
End Select

resultBox.Text = result.ToString()

End Sub
```

The Select statement takes a look at the current text in the combo box (the currently selected item) and then decides which method to call on your new calc object. The result of the method call is stored in the result variable, which at the very end is copied back into the Result text box on the form.

Run the application now to see it in action. Just enter some values (numeric) in the first two text boxes, choose an operation from the combo, and then click the Calculate button to call the class and see the result (it should look like Figure 4-10 if all goes well).

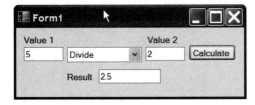

Figure 4-10. *The calculator application running*

NAMING VARIABLES AND PARAMETERS TO METHODS

You'll notice that I've named the first two variables `value1` and `value2`, which are the same names I gave to the Double parameters of the methods back in the `Calculator` class. This isn't a requirement. I could have called them Mickey and Goofy and it wouldn't have mattered. So long as I pass data types that match a method's signature to the method, I can call them whatever I want. More on this when we get to scoping later in this chapter, so not long to wait.

Visual Basic 2005, like most other programming languages that support object-oriented programming, allows you to use polymorphism. It's a strange name, I know, but it's actually quite a simple concept. *Polymorphism* allows you to have more than one method in a class with the same name. As long as the signatures on the methods differ, you are free to create as many methods with the same name as you like. It's a wonderful thing, liberating you to "phrase" your method calls just the way that feels most natural. In some instances, for example, you might need to pass only one parameter to a method, while at other times it makes sense to pass three or four. Polymorphism allows you to define a method for each situation, and it's used a heck of a lot in the .NET Framework itself.

For a brief demonstration of what it means, run up a new VB Windows Forms project (or the calculator one you just finished working on) and drop into the code editor by double-clicking the form in the form editor. Now, in the code editor just type in `MessageBox.Show(` and no more than that. You'll see an IntelliSense pop-up appear, as in Figure 4-11.

Figure 4-11. *IntelliSense is an awesome invention when you're working with polymorphic methods.*

With the IntelliSense pop-up displayed, just tap the down arrow on your keyboard. What you are seeing now are all the different variations of the `MessageBox.Show()` method that Microsoft provides. If you just wanted to display a message box with some text, and aren't too concerned about icons and such, you'll find a method signature near the top of the list that takes just a single string parameter. Polymorphism is very handy.

Time to try a quick example (just a short console application this time).

Try It Out: Polymorphic Methods

Start up a new console application in Visual Basic 2005 Express, and when the Solution Explorer appears, add a new class called `Names.vb` to the project.

What we'd like is for `Names` objects to say Hello but to use the proper level of respect based on who they are talking to. So go ahead and drop a `SayHello()` method into the class for normal everyday folks:

```
Public Class Names

    Public Sub SayHello(ByVal person As String)
        Console.WriteLine("Hi there {0}", person)
    End Sub

End Class
```

So far, so good. Now, add another `SayHello()` method in there for addressing royalty:

```
Public Class Names

    Public Sub SayHello(ByVal person As String)
        Console.WriteLine("Hi there {0}", person)
    End Sub

    Public Sub SayHello(ByVal person As String, ByVal title As String)
        Console.WriteLine("{0} {1}, we are most graced by your presence {0}", _
            title, person)
    End Sub

End Class
```

Notice that the method has exactly the same name as the previous one, but the signature (the parameters passed into the method) differ. This time two strings are passed in, instead of just one.

Let's see this in action. Drop back into `Module1.vb` (you should know how to do that by now—click the tab at the top of the editor, or double-click it in the Solution Explorer) and add a few lines to the `Main()` function:

```
Sub Main()

    Dim greeter As New Names()

    greeter.SayHello("Pete")
    greeter.SayHello("Most regal majesty", "King Fozznib")

    Console.ReadLine()

End Sub
```

Run the program and you'll see the output, as in Figure 4-12.

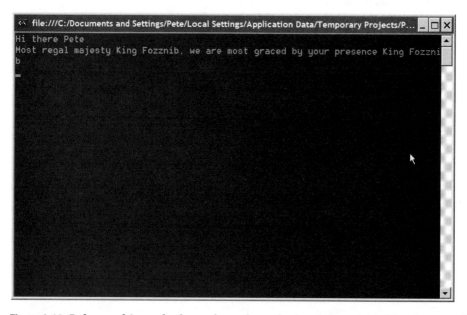

Figure 4-12. *Polymorphic methods can keep the code simple but also add quite some flexibility to your code.*

That's all there is to it.

There is one important point to bear in mind. The polymorphic aspect (having more than one method with the same name) depends on the signature of the method. The signature is just the number and types of parameters passed to the method. So, for example, if you have these two methods in your class, then it wouldn't compile:

```
Public Sub SayHello(ByVal person As String)

End Sub

Public Sub SayHello(ByVal personsName As String)

End Sub
```

In this case the signatures are the same. Even though the names of the parameters differ, the types and the number of them don't. Therefore, VB sees the preceding methods as the same method and thus they're not polymorphic. Similarly, the following will cause a compiler error:

```
Public Sub SayHello()

End Sub

Public Function SayHello() As Integer

End Function
```

In this case the return types are different (since one is a function, and the other is a subroutine that returns nothing), but return types are not part of the method signature and thus again VB sees these two as exactly the same method.

Visual Basic 2005 Express is pretty good at spotting problems like this before you even try to run the program. If you put two methods with the same name in a class without differing signatures, the code editor will give you a hint about the problem, as you can see in Figure 4-13.

```
Public Sub SayHello()
        'Public Sub SayHello()' and 'Public Function SayHello() As Integer' cannot overload each other because they differ only by return types.
End Sub

Public Function SayHello() As Integer

End Function
```

Figure 4-13. *When you make obvious mistakes in the code editor, Visual Basic 2005 Express will underline the problem and give you a hint when you move the mouse over the offending line of code.*

Properties and Members

The purest definition of an object says that it is an encapsulation of data, and the functionality to work with that data. So far you've looked at functionality only in the form of methods. Where does the data come in? Hopefully you remember all about variables from the preceding chapter. Variables in the class (actually in the class, not inside a method of the class) are how you add data to the class for the methods to work with.

Variables defined in a class, and seen and used only by the methods in that class, are called *members*. Variables that are defined in the class for all to see are called *properties*, or *fields*. You've seen how to use them already; when you drop a control onto a form and then set up its name by using the Properties window, what you are actually doing is setting a property inside a class (it's actually a property on an object, because by dropping the control—the class—on a form, you've created an object).

Let's take a look at a simple console-based example.

Try It Out: Adding Members and Properties to a Class

Start up a new console project, and then immediately add a new class called `Person.vb` to the project.

First, add some members (hidden, private data) to the class:

```
Public Class Person

    Private _forename As String
    Private _surname As String

End Class
```

There are two things to notice here.

First, the keyword `Private`. This is covered in a lot more detail in the "Scoping" section later in this chapter. For now, what it means is that this variable, or member, is private to the class. When someone creates an object from this class, they can't see the two variables you've created here. Private members provide a way to store data inside an object that only the class methods can get at and work with.

Second, notice how I've prefixed the names of the variables with an underscore symbol. This is *not* a requirement of Visual Basic, but I think it is a good habit to get into. As you write more and more of your own classes and add more and more data into them, it's quite useful to be able to look at the code and instantly tell whether something you are working with is a property of the class or a private member. Prefixing member names with an underscore helps in this respect. On the other hand, the IDE and IntelliSense are pretty good about showing you what the scope of a variable is, and some people hate the idea of using a scope prefix on their variable names. It's another area where personal preferences play a big part in how you choose to write your code.

Next, add a property to the class:

```
Public Class Person

    Private _forename As String
    Private _surname As String

    Public FullName As String

End Class
```

This time, the member is `Public`, the same as most of the things you've seen declared in classes so far. This means that anyone using the class as an object can also see and interact with this variable, reading data from it and setting data into it just like a property in a control. Before you drop back into `Module1.vb` and actually use this class, add a method to make the class do something. You'll just take in a person's surname and forename and then set up the contents of this property:

```
Public Class Person

    Private _forename As String
    Private _surname As String

    Public FullName As String

    Public Sub SetName(ByVal forename As String, ByVal surname As String)
        _forename = forename
        _surname = surname
        FullName = _forename + " " + _surname
    End Sub

End Class
```

Drop back into the `Module1.vb` code and you'll finish up this program to see it working, and more important see how to use a property in your code:

```
Module Module1

    Sub Main()

        Dim scientist As New Person()
        scientist.SetName("Albert", "Einstein")

        Console.WriteLine("Fullname = {0}", scientist.FullName)

        Console.ReadLine()

    End Sub

End Module
```

The first thing you do is create an object (called `scientist`) from the `Person` class. Next, the `SetName()` method is called, passing in a person's surname and forename. Finally, you use the `FullName` property on the class to write out the resulting full name to the console. Note that using properties of an object is different from calling methods; when you refer to a property of an object, you don't follow the name of the property with parentheses. Parentheses on the end of something mean you're calling a method. A lack of parentheses here means you are using a property instead of calling a method.

Run the application to see the result, which should be completely as expected (you can see the output from my program in Figure 4-14).

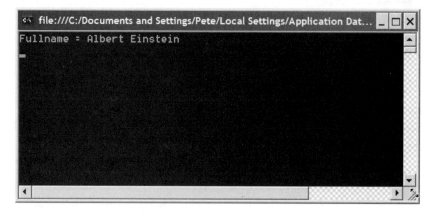

Figure 4-14. *Properties enable us to get at the "public" data inside an object.*

THE DIFFERENCE BETWEEN PROPERTIES AND FIELDS

Technically, what we have here is a field. To users of a class, properties and fields appear to work the same way. However, with a property you can also add in code that runs as soon as the property is set or read. You'll look at that shortly.

It all looks good, but this program has a problem. The interface that you've exposed on the class implies that your users should call SetName() to set up the name of the person in question, and that's the only way it should be done. However, making the FullName variable public (turning it into a field in the class) means that users could write code like this:

```
scientist.FullName = "Tom Mouse"
```

Doing that completely bypasses your SetName() method, which could be less than ideal in a real application. The solution is to turn that field into a true property by using getters and setters.

Let's take a look at turning this field into a proper property by using getters and setters.

Getters and Setters

Ideally, you just want users of your Person class in the preceding example to read the FullName, and not write it or change it. That's really easy to do.

Try It Out: Adding a Getter to a Property

Load up the preceding example and take a look at the Person.vb source.

Change the property definition by adding the word ReadOnly to it:

```
Public Class Person

    Private _forename As String
    Private _surname As String

    Public ReadOnly FullName As String
```

```
Public Sub SetName(ByVal forename As String, ByVal surname As String)
    _forename = forename
    _surname = surname
    FullName = _forename + " " + _surname
End Sub
```

```
End Class
```

That would appear to solve the problem—or does it? You can prefix members and property definitions with the word ReadOnly to stop people setting them, but it causes other problems. Try to run the program and you'll see what I mean. You'll see a message box appear as in Figure 4-15.

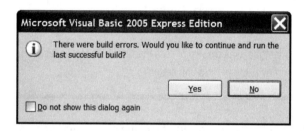

Figure 4-15. *Setting a field to read-only is not always a good idea.*

Click the No button, and the error list appears proclaiming that the "ReadOnly variable cannot be the target of an assignment." Well, duh! We knew that, that's what we wanted right? Well, no. Double-click that error in the error list, and VB Express will highlight the exact line of code that's causing the problem (see Figure 4-16).

```
Start Page  Person.vb  Module1.vb

Person                                                    SetName

Public Class Person

    Private _forename As String
    Private _surname As String

    Public ReadOnly FullName As String

    Public Sub SetName(ByVal forename As String, ByVal surname As String)
        _forename = forename
        _surname = surname
        FullName = _forename + " " + _surname
    End Sub

End Class
```

Figure 4-16. *Read-only properties can't be written by anyone including code in the same class.*

So, obviously, that's not the quick and easy solution you need. Getters and setters solve this. Before I show you the code change to make, think about this. At the moment, your `SetName()` method stores three values: `surname`, `forename`, and `FullName`. Another way to do this would be for the `SetName()` method to store only the surname and forename, and then have the `FullName` property itself calculate what it should be when someone asks for it.

First, remove the `FullName=` line from the `SetName()` method. It will look like this:

```
Public Sub SetName(ByVal forename As String, ByVal surname As String)
    _forename = forename
    _surname = surname
End Sub
```

Now, make the following changes to the `FullName` property:

```
Public Class Person

    Private _forename As String
    Private _surname As String

    Public ReadOnly Property FullName() As String
        Get
            Return _forename + " " + _surname
        End Get
    End Property

    Public Sub SetName(ByVal forename As String, ByVal surname As String)
        _forename = forename
        _surname = surname
    End Sub

End Class
```

That's a *getter*. By adding the word `Property` to the definition of `FullName`, Visual Basic instantly popped open a bunch of code to fill in, labeled `Get` and `Set`. I deleted the `Set` because we don't want to set this property's value, just get it. `Get` is a function that returns the data type of the property. So, because our `FullName` property is a string, `Get` is a function that returns a string. Now, properties that have a `Get` function but no `Set` subroutine are read-only, so I also added the word `ReadOnly` before the keyword `Property`; otherwise, the program wouldn't compile again. You'll find you can now run the program; it will compile just fine and work just as it did before. It's a much more "robust" design now, though.

Because you added only a `Get`, and not a `Set`, the property is effectively read-only. If you try to add code into `Program.cs` that sets `person.FullName`, you'll get a compile error identical to the preceding one. So this really does solve the problem.

But what if you wanted to give the user the flexibility to set the FullName property and then automatically have it set up the surname and forename values inside the class? Realistically that would be unwise—it's adding code that you don't really need into the class. You should have either a writeable property *or* that SetName() method, not both. For the sake of a full example, though, we'll go ahead and do just that. We'll stretch our coding legs a little here and use some of the methods on the string to split a larger string into two parts.

I'll walk you through this step-by-step, so drink that coffee and keep up.

First, remove the word ReadOnly, and add Set to the property:

```
Public Property FullName() As String
    Get
        Return _forename + " " + _surname
    End Get
    Set(ByVal value As String)

    End Set
End Property
```

Like Get, Set is a method. The difference of course is that Get returns a value (it's a function), and Set expects one and returns nothing (it's a subroutine). You automatically get a parameter that you can use in your property Set code called value. This is the value that the user of your class is trying to set into the property.

What you need to do is take this value and get the forename and surname from it. One way to do this is to find the first space in the words, because the surname and forename are always separated by a space. That's not going to work, though, for "John Wilkes Booth" or "Lee Harvey Oswald." A better way to do it would be to "split" the string based on spaces:

```
Set(ByVal value As String)
    Dim parts() As String = value.Split(" ")
End Set
```

It looks terribly complex, but it's really not. In the case of this Set, value will be a String, and String has a method on it called Split(). The Split() method returns an array of strings (after it has split one string into many, you need a place to store the many different words that result).

Split() expects to be passed a list of all the possible things that could be used to split the string. We're interested only in spaces. We pass just one value into Split()—a space.

So, the result of calling Split() will be that you get an array of strings, called names, that hold the various names in FullName. If you had tried to set the property to John Wilkes Booth, you would have an array of three strings, the first item being John, the second Wilkes, and the third Booth.

We're interested in only the first and last entries, so all that's required now is a couple of lines to get just those two entries:

```
Set(ByVal value As String)
    Dim parts() As String = value.Split(" ")
    _forename = parts(0)
    _surname = parts(parts.Length - 1)
End Set
```

You just set the _forename member to the first item in the array (remember, the first item in an array is always numbered 0), and set the _surname member to the last item in the array (if you have an array of 10 strings, the last item is item number 9). Even if the user just entered a single name (Jason, for example), Split() would still return a single element array.

That's all there is to it. All that remains is to change the code in Module1.vb to test it out:

```
Sub Main()

    Dim scientist As New Person()
    scientist.SetName("Albert", "Einstein")

    Console.WriteLine("Fullname = {0}", scientist.FullName)

    Dim badguy As New Person()
    badguy.FullName = "John Wilkes Booth"

    Console.WriteLine("Fullname = {0}", badguy.FullName)


    Console.ReadLine()

End Sub
```

Notice that you're intentionally setting FullName to a three-part name. When you run the program, though, you'll find that only the forename and surname are used, just as we had hoped. You can see the new output in Figure 4-17.

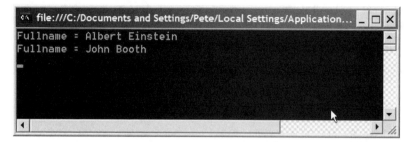

Figure 4-17. *Notice how John Wilkes Booth is now split into John Booth, and all you did was set a value into a property.*

Scoping

There are three VB keywords that I haven't spent a lot of time explaining but that you've seen quite a few times: `Public`, `Private`, and `Shared`. These are all vital keywords that provide you with even more flexibility in how you design the structure of your programs, and more specifically your classes. However, it's really hard to explain what they are and what they do if you haven't been introduced to classes, methods, variables, and properties.

This explanation is going to be a little dry, but it's essential to understanding scoping. Hang in there.

Public

Take a look at a stereo in a car. The stereo is a box embedded in a bigger system (the car itself), which exposes an interface in the form of buttons, slots, a read-out, and maybe one or two knobs. All these things are exposed by the object for you, the user, to interact with. They are known as the *public* interface. Properties, and methods within objects that are public, are part of the class's interface. A simple class for a car stereo with the public interface may look like this:

```
Public Class CarStereo

    Public CurrentTime As Date
    Public NowPlaying As String

    Public Sub SetStation(ByVal stationNumber As Integer)

    End Sub
```

```vb
    Public Sub StoreStation(ByVal stationNumber As Integer)

    End Sub

    Public Sub TuneRadio(ByVal frequency As Double)

    End Sub

    Public Sub TurnOn()

    End Sub

    Public Sub TurnOff()

    End Sub

    Public Sub ChangeVolume(ByVal level As Integer)

    End Sub

End Class
```

As you can see, this is a simple class with a bunch of public methods and properties to enable users of objects from this class to use it.

Now, because these things are public, they can all interact with each other. For example, calling SetStation() would undoubtedly do something to update the NowPlaying property.

Private

Behind the sleek user interface of any car stereo is a complex set of chips, circuits, and wires that make the stereo do its job. You, the user, don't need to see these things—the public interface of the class provides you with a simple way to control them. However, there will be stuff behind the scenes that all code in the class needs to work with. By expanding the definition of the class, you get this:

```vb
Public Class CarStereo

    Public CurrentTime As Date
    Public NowPlaying As String

    Public Sub SetStation(ByVal stationNumber As Integer)
    End Sub
```

```vb
    Public Sub StoreStation(ByVal stationNumber As Integer)
    End Sub

    Public Sub TuneRadio(ByVal frequency As Double)
    End Sub

    Public Sub TurnOn()
    End Sub

    Public Sub TurnOff()
    End Sub

    Public Sub ChangeVolume(ByVal level As Integer)
    End Sub

    Private _tuner As Tuner

End Class

Public Class Tuner
    Public Frequency As Double
    Public FM As Boolean

    Public Sub ChangeFrequency()

    End Sub
    Public Sub Play()

    End Sub

    Private Sub ConnectToSpeaker()

    End Sub
End Class
```

Just as your car's dashboard is made up of various objects, each with its own function, so too is your car stereo. It has a tuner embedded inside, for example, to tune to different radio stations. A tuner is not something anyone would normally want to use outside of the box, but it is a vital component, so in the new code notice how a new class is created, but it's private. This means that only code that lives inside the same namespace (CarStereo, if you take a look at the top of the source) can use the Tuner class. It's private to that namespace.

The tuner is a private variable within the Stereo class as well. It's used by most of the other methods, especially the public ones, within the Stereo, but it's not exposed as a public part of the interface to the stereo's user.

You'll also notice that the Tuner has a private method of its own, called ConnectToSpeaker(). The stereo box itself doesn't need to know how the Tuner makes noise; it just wants it to do so. The Tuner then has a private method just for hooking up its own output to the stereo's speaker.

Shared

Shared methods are where my stereo analogy falls down a little. Everything you've seen so far in this walk-through is collectively called *instance members*. You need to create an instance of a class (an object) in order to use instance members, and even then there may be restrictions (Public can be used by anyone, Private cannot). *Shared methods*, on the other hand, are known as *class members*. These are methods and properties/variables that can be used without actually generating an object. In addition, shared methods can be public or private. A brochure for stereos, for example, may tell you about the stereo but until you go and buy one (and turn the class into an object), you can't access the instance members. The brochure, then, could be thought of as being a shared method of the class.

Shared methods in particular are very useful when you need a block of code that you can call over and over but that doesn't really apply to an instance of a class. A good example (which you'll come across later in the book) is getting connection info to talk to a database. This is typically a string that's stored in a config file (a text file) that the application needs to read in order to be able to connect to the database. The signature of the method, at least, would look like this:

```
Public Class DatabaseStuff
    Public Shared Function GetConnectionString() As String

    End Function
End Class
```

This looks pretty much like any other method definition, doesn't it, with the obvious addition of the word Shared. What this means is that the method can be called like this:

```
    Dim dbString As String = DatabaseStuff.GetConnectionString()
```

Notice that instead of creating an object from the class first, and prefixing the name of the method with the name of the object, you can just use the class name, in this case DatabaseStuff. No instantiation required.

This is called a shared method. You'll see a lot more about shared methods throughout the rest of the book, in large part because the starting point for every .NET application is a shared method called Main() that you've seen a few times now.

DON'T USE SHARED METHODS EVERYWHERE

At my last job, a company director felt the need to get involved in coding on an internal project. He'd had a lot of experience with classic ASP and Visual Basic, but this was to be his first .NET project.

I kick-started his work and gave him a brief hands-on walk-through of things he should know. Included in that demo, I created a shared method to grab a database connection string, just as I've just shown you.

I next saw his code about a month later, and to my horror found he had about 30 classes in his project with every single method being a shared method. This is bad. Don't do it.

If you use shared methods all the time, you aren't giving .NET a chance to clean up memory from unused objects (because you are never creating objects, just calling class methods on classes). The net result is that your program bogs down and starts to get slow. More to the point, by using shared methods you are forgoing all the benefits that object-oriented programming can bring you, such as inheritance and encapsulation of data and functionality.

Using shared methods everywhere is an easy trap to fall into if you come from a classic VB background, so be aware of it and try to use them sparingly.

Summary

As usual, we've covered a lot in this chapter—more than I had originally planned, in fact. But, it's all vitally important. Visual Basic 2005 is an object-oriented programming language and so everything you do will make use of the OOP facilities the language provides.

By using these tools effectively and really working in a true OOP style, your programs can become a lot easier to maintain, extend, and work on than their non-object-oriented cousins. But, you'll notice that so far you haven't really looked at just what is a good way to use these facilities to design a great OOP app. The bad news is that I don't really have the time or scope to do that in this book. Throughout the rest of this book and especially in the next chapter (where you'll look at some of the more advanced OOP features of Visual Basic 2005), I'll try to coax you toward the good habits and away from the bad. But it's well worth picking up one or two other books after you have Visual Basic 2005 figured out to get a good grip on just what is, and what isn't, good OOP design.

CHAPTER 5

■ ■ ■

More-Advanced Object Orientation

By now you should have a good grip on the structure of the code that goes into a Visual Basic 2005 application. The preceding chapter in particular brought together the elements that make the most fundamental building blocks of all the code that you'll write: classes.

There's more to it than that, though, including the "design" point of view. In this chapter you'll take a look at key features of OOP, including inheritance and interfaces, and something very scary sounding, but quite painless, called virtual methods and abstract classes. You'll also take a peek at some of the things going on behind the scenes when you use objects, particularly when you start passing them around between methods.

After a brief interlude in the next chapter, we'll move our focus more toward building functional and useful Windows applications, so I'll try my best here to not only get you up to speed on these slightly more advanced OOP concepts, but also give you some pointers on the whys and wherefores of OOP and Visual Basic 2005. Just why do we do something one way and not another? Just why do we have all these neat, but initially confusing, features such as inheritance?

Inheritance

I drive a well-worn Jeep. My dad drives an even more loved Ford, the UK equivalent of a Ford Taurus. Both these objects have something in common; at their very core, they are cars. I can jump in my Dad's car and know that the controls all work the same as in my Jeep, and in fact the same as in any other car. Similarly, my Dad can jump in my Jeep and know that it too does everything a car should do, but with the added ability to move troops, guests, or hoards of squealing children through muddy bogs and ravines.

Both the Ford and my Jeep "inherit" functionality from a base class: the Car. Look around the room you're in and you'll see a myriad of other examples of inheritance in the real world. The notebook I'm writing this on is a computer, but with the added advantage that it's portable. My chair has the same functions as any other chair in the world, but with the added bonus of a bendy back and wheels. My dogs, Mac and Tosh, are just like any other dogs in the world, but with additional functionality geared toward yipping and drooling.

Inheritance lets you specialize objects to a specific purpose. Perhaps you want a text box that accepts only numbers, and that beeps whenever the user presses a key. That can be achieved by creating a new TextBox class that automatically inherits all the functionality of the standard text box class. That way you get the "base" class to handle all the drawing of the control and its contents, but provide your own custom code to handle beeping and numeric-only entry.

Let's start out with a simple (and a little dull—sorry) example of just how to do the inheritance thing.

Try It Out: Inheritance

To keep things simple for now, start up a new console application and add a new class to it called Car.vb. When the code editor appears, add in the constructor, just as in Figure 5-1. (You recall that you can do this by just clicking in the drop-down list at the top right of the code editor and choosing New.)

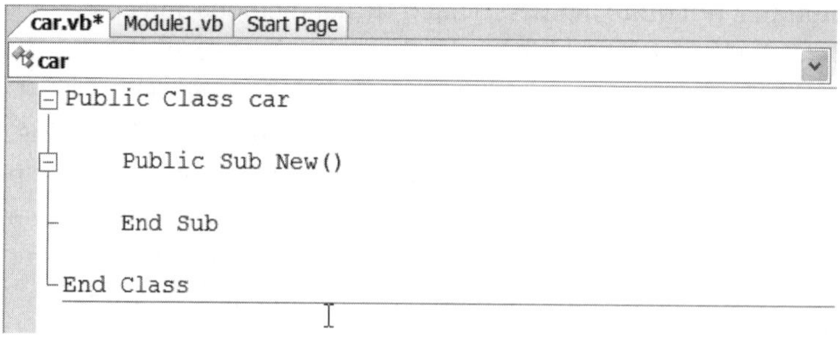

Figure 5-1. *Add a new class called Car.vb to the solution.*

Still in the code editor for the Car class, add Drive() and Brake() methods as I've highlighted in the following code:

```
Public Class Car

    Public Sub New()

    End Sub
```

```
Public Sub Drive()
    Console.WriteLine("We're now whizzing down the road")
End Sub

Public Sub Brake()
    Console.WriteLine("The car comes to a screeching stop")
End Sub


End Class
```

Now add another class to the project, this time called `OffRoader.vb`. Because an off-roader (4 x 4, SUV, call it what you will) inherits all the basic functionality of a car, you need to set up this new class to inherit from the base `Car` class. You do this simply by typing `Inherits` on the first blank line in the class. This opens an IntelliSense drop-down list for inheritance, as you can see in Figure 5-2.

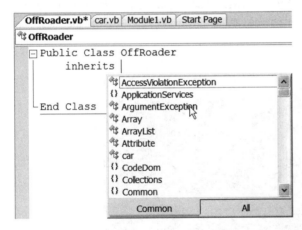

Figure 5-2. *Typing the Inherits keyword tells Visual Basic 2005 Express that you want to inherit another class. IntelliSense helps you choose the class.*

Choose Car from the list, or just type in `Car`, and your class will look like this:

```
Public Class OffRoader
    Inherits Car



End Class
```

That single tiny change sets up the OffRoader class to inherit from the Car class. So, now the OffRoader can do everything the Car can. Drop back into the Module1.vb source and add some code to the Main() function to show this in action:

```
Module Module1

    Sub Main()
        Dim myJeep As New OffRoader()
        myJeep.Drive()
        myJeep.Brake()

        Console.ReadLine()
    End Sub

End Module
```

Run the program now and you'll see that even though you haven't added any real code to the OffRoader class, it will work just as if it were a Car class (in that you can call the Drive() and Brake() methods). See Figure 5-3.

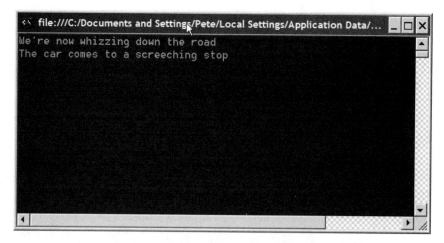

Figure 5-3. *Inheritance lets you instantly "inherit" functionality into a new class (called the subclass).*

Of course at this point it would be easy to add functionality to the OffRoader class, perhaps a DriveOffRoad() method, but that doesn't really show you much.

Something else that inheritance lets you do is treat one type of object as another. For example, even though OffRoader may have additional methods and functionality over a car, it is still a Car. Therefore, OffRoader objects can be treated as Car objects in your application.

Go ahead and make a change to the Main() function to show this:

```
Module Module1

    Sub Main()
        Dim myJeep As New OffRoader()

        Dim aCar As Car
        aCar = myJeep

        aCar.Drive()
        aCar.Brake()

        Console.ReadLine()
    End Sub

End Module
```

If you run the application again at this point, you'll find it works exactly the same as it did before; the OffRoader object is now being treated as a standard Car.

Virtual Methods

Inheritance on its own provides you with a means to make one class inherit the functionality of another. Usually, after doing that, you'll add more functionality to specialize the subclass. However, you can also override the functionality in the base class, effectively replacing the way that even that inherited functionality works. Why on earth would you want to do this? Why not just change the base class?

Well, that's certainly an option. But, if you have a bunch of code already relying on the functionality in the base class, perhaps also some other classes inheriting from it, the last thing you want to do is to take the risk that changing the base class would introduce unwanted behavior in the rest of the application. It's much safer in those specialized cases to create a subclass that overrides the functionality you need to change. Another example of why you'd want this of course is when you want to change the way a class works, but you don't have access to the source code of the original class. This is always the case when you want to change the way that a class in the .NET Framework works, unless of course you work for Microsoft.

The solution is virtual methods. Making a method *virtual* involves nothing more than putting the word Overridable in front of its name. After that's done, subclasses can override the virtual method with the Overrides keyword. Let's extend that car example to see it in action.

Try It Out: Virtual Methods

Load up the example you were working on earlier, and change the Car class's Drive() method as shown:

```
Public Class Car

    Public Sub New()

    End Sub

    Public Overridable Sub Drive()
        Console.WriteLine("We're now whizzing down the road")
    End Sub

    Public Sub Brake()
        Console.WriteLine("The car comes to a screeching stop")
    End Sub


End Class
```

By adding Overridable to the method definition in the base class, you've told Visual Basic that this method can be overridden in a subclass. The only subclass you have is the OffRoader class, so bring up its source. You'll add a Drive() method to this class that overrides the virtual method in the base class.

In the class type, beneath the constructor, type in Public Overrides and then press the spacebar. IntelliSense pops up, asking you which method you want to override, as you can see in Figure 5-4.

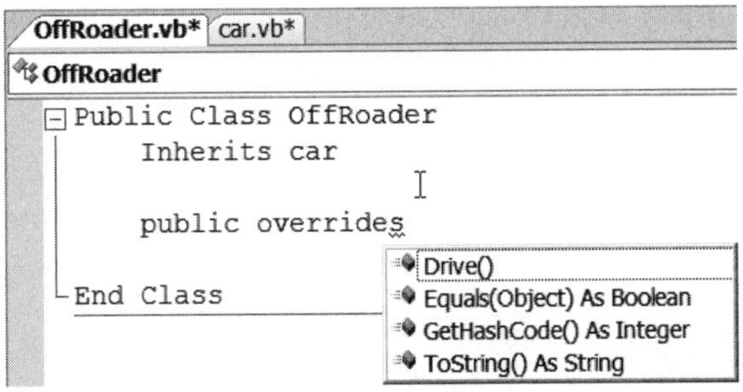

Figure 5-4. *Typing **Public Overrides** followed by a space causes IntelliSense to pop up, asking you what you want to override.*

Double-click `Drive()` from the list (or use the arrow keys and then press Enter on the selected one), and VB Express will fill in the rest of the method signature and put in some code for you:

```
Public Overrides Sub Drive()
    MyBase.Drive()
End Sub
```

The new method includes a call to `MyBase.Drive()`. This means that unless you remove that line and put in some code of your own, the `OffRoader.Drive()` method will automatically use the `Drive()` method from the base `Car` class.

Remove that line and change the method:

```
Public Overrides Sub Drive()
    Console.WriteLine("You zoom down a rocky ravine!")
End Sub
```

Finally, just to tidy up the code a little, change the `Main()` subroutine (in `Module1.vb`) to look like this:

```
Module Module1

    Sub Main()
        Dim aCar As Car = New OffRoader()
        aCar.Drive()
        aCar.Brake()

        Console.ReadLine()
    End Sub

End Module
```

Once again you have a Car object variable that's getting an OffRoader object stored in it. Run the program now and you'll find that, even though you are dealing with a variable that references Car objects, it's the OffRoader object's Drive() method that gets called at runtime (see Figure 5-5). Handy, isn't it.

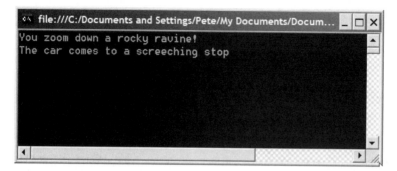

Figure 5-5. *Even though you are using a Car object variable, you call the actual object's Drive() method—OffRoader.Drive()—at runtime, thanks to virtual methods and overriding.*

Virtual methods are particularly handy when writing functions. As you've seen, by putting a specific instance of a class into an object variable that references the base class, you can treat all subclasses as a general base class. This makes it easy to write methods that take base class parameters (that is, a Car object as a parameter) and then just work, even if someone (including you) passes in an instance of a specific subclass.

Abstract Methods and Classes

Virtual methods are great when you think there is a chance that someone might want to override your code in a subclass. There are occasions, though, when you not only want someone to override your methods, but also want to prevent someone from instantiating a base class on its own. That's where abstract methods and classes come into play. To use the car analogy once again, you can't walk into a car dealership and say "I want a car" and expect instant satisfaction. Car is a generic base class that really means very little. Most people actually want a specific instance of a subclass of Car.

Abstract methods have no code in them. When you declare a method as MustOverride, you are effectively saying, "This method must be implemented by a subclass."

You declare an abstract class with the `MustInherit` keyword, and you declare an abstract method with the `MustOverride` keyword. For this reason, a lot of VB programmers call these things *MustInherit classes* and *MustOverride methods*. The rest of the world, though, calls them abstract, so if you plan on speaking to a Java, C#, or C++ programmer in your future, it's a good idea to learn the terminology they use.

When you think about it, a class with a method that can't actually do anything until it is subclassed and overwritten, is itself somewhat useless. Therefore, if you declare an abstract (`MustOverride`) method in a class, you also need to declare the class as `MustInherit`. Here's an example of what that looks like:

```
Public MustInherit Class GameGraphic

    Public MustOverride Sub Draw()

End Class
```

This tiny class could represent the very simplest foundation for a graphic in a game. Until it's subclassed into something more specific (for example, `PlayerGraphic` or `AlienInvaderGraphic`), it's useless. By using `MustInherit` and `MustOverride`, you force whoever subclasses `GameGraphic` to implement the `Draw()` method. If the subclass doesn't actually include a `Draw()` method, the compiler will throw an error. Also, just as when using virtual methods, there is nothing stopping you from putting methods with code into the base abstract class. This would let you provide a base class with functionality to do common tasks, but still require a subclass to implement a key function before the class can be used.

Take a look at an example before you move on.

NOTINHERITABLE CLASSES

Before you leave the world of special classes, there is one more kind that you should know about but that doesn't really warrant an example: `NotInheritable` classes.

Just as you can create an abstract class by placing the keyword `MustInherit` in front of the class definition, you can create a `NotInheritable` class by using the word `NotInheritable` in the same way that you would `MustOverride`.

`NotInheritable` classes are the polar opposite of abstract ones. Whereas an abstract class cannot be turned into an object and must be subclassed, `NotInheritable` classes cannot be subclassed and must be turned into objects. Use `NotInheritable` classes when you absolutely never want someone to subclass. A good example of this in the .NET Framework itself is the `System.String` class. `System.String` is marked as `NotInheritable` because the developers of the Framework did not want people overriding functionality in the `String` data type. This makes sense because `System.String` is used so much that it would be silly to override it, and potentially break the way it works and all code that relies on it.

Try It Out: Declaring and Using Abstract Classes

Start up a new console application and as before add a `Car.vb` class to the project. When the code editor appears, type in this for the `Car` class:

```
Public MustInherit Class Car

    Public MustOverride Sub Describe()

End Class
```

You won't add all the other functionality here, so consider this a car in a brochure. All cars in brochures have just one function, and that is to describe themselves.

Now, let's start to add another class, called `OffRoader`. Just type in the highlighted lines directly underneath your `Car` class (sure, you could add another class file, but for this example it's handy to keep everything in one place).

```
Public MustInherit Class Car

    Public MustOverride Sub Describe()

End Class

Public Class OffRoader
    Inherits Car
```

As soon as you hit the Enter key on the end of the `Inherits` line, VB Express automatically sees what you are trying to do and lends a helping hand, adding code to your class so that it looks like this:

```
Public Class OffRoader
    Inherits Car

    Public Overrides Sub Describe()

    End Sub
End Class
```

You are subclassing a `MustInherit` class with a `MustOverride` method, so Visual Basic intelligently shows you the work you need to do. Add the highlighted code to this new class, and then add a third class, `Sedan`, underneath, like this:

```
Public MustInherit Class Car

    Public MustOverride Sub Describe()
```

```vb
End Class

Public Class OffRoader
    Inherits Car

    Public Overrides Sub Describe()
        Console.WriteLine("Big, with big wheels and a big engine")
    End Sub
End Class

Public Class Sedan
    Inherits Car

    Public Overrides Sub Describe()
        Console.WriteLine("Just your average kid taxi")

    End Sub
End Class
```

Once again, as soon as you type in `Inherits Car` for the `Sedan` class, VB jumps in and adds a stub of the methods that you need to code.

Back in the `Module1.vb` source, add a new method and some code to `Main()` to bring the program to life:

```vb
Module Module1

    Sub Main()
        Dim jeep As New OffRoader()
        Dim ford As New Sedan()

        DescribeCar(jeep)
        DescribeCar(ford)

        Console.ReadLine()
    End Sub

    Public Sub DescribeCar(ByVal theCar As Car)
        theCar.Describe()
    End Sub

End Module
```

First, you've added a new method called `DescribeCar()`. This takes a `Car` object as a parameter and then calls its `Describe()` method.

`DescribeCar()` takes a `Car` object as a parameter, but `Car` is an abstract class and can't actually be turned into an object. So, what's happening here? Well, you can still use abstract classes as parameters. What you're saying is that the parameter passed to the method will be a subclass of `Car`, and as such can do anything `Car` can do. Because `DescribeCar()` is an abstract method, you know that any subclass of `Car` must provide a full implementation of that method, as the classes `OffRoader` and `Sedan` do.

Run the program now and you'll see output like that in Figure 5-6.

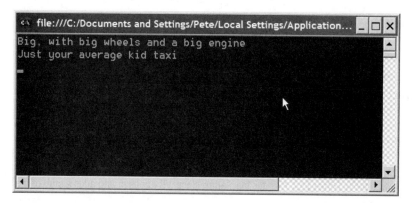

Figure 5-6. *OffRoader and Sedan can be passed to DescribeCar() because they both inherit from Car and implement all the abstract methods as required.*

Beware Shadows

There's a special keyword in Visual Basic 2005 that I'm not a big fan of: Shadows. Shadows looks, on the surface anyway, to do exactly the same thing as Overrides does, but beneath the surface it does strange and sinister things.

The idea behind Shadows is that the designers of Visual Basic 2005 wanted to give you a way to "hide" functionality. You can use Shadows to not only replace a base class's method, but also to remove it completely, and even replace instance variables within the class. For example, take a look at this code:

```
Public Class Car
    Public Sub Describe()
        Console.WriteLine("I am a generic car")
    End Sub
End Class

Public Class OffRoader
    Inherits Car

    Private Shadows Sub Describe()
        Console.WriteLine("I am an offroader")
    End Sub

End Class
```

It looks innocent enough, doesn't it. We have a base Car class, and an OffRoader class that inherits from it. Now, look at the Describe() sub in the OffRoader class. Notice anything strange?

```
    Private Shadows Sub Describe()
```

Describe() in the Car class is Public. If you have a Car object, you can call Describe() on it. Describe() in the OffRoader class, on the other hand, is Private. What this means is that if you have an OffRoader object, you can't call Describe() on it, because it's now Private. Even worse, if you treat an OffRoader object as a Car, you can call Describe() on it—like this:

```
Public myOffRoader As Car = New OffRoader()
myOffRoader.Describe()
```

Confusing, isn't it? Here we have an OffRoader object that used Shadows to hide the Describe() method, but Describe() can still be called if you treat the object as an instance of Car–in that case, it's the Car.Describe() method that gets called.

The situation gets even more confusing if you leave Describe() in the OffRoader class as public. When you do that, if you call Describe() on an OffRoader object, you get the new message printed out. However, if you treat the OffRoader as a Car object, you'll see the old message printed when Describe() is called.

I know developers who love this feature, but to me it violates the number one rule that you all should adhere to when writing code: the code should be obvious! When you have a bunch of objects subclassing each other, and some of them hiding methods, some using Shadows to temporarily override them and so on, the code gets very confusing very quickly. My advice: use Overrides, MustInherit, and NotInheritable where you can.

Let's take a look at Shadows in action.

Try It Out : Using Shadows

Start up a new console project. When the code editor appears, change the code so it looks like this:

```
Module Module1

    Sub Main()
        Dim truck As New OffRoader
        Dim car As Car = CType(truck, Car)

        truck.Describe()
        car.Describe()
        Console.ReadLine()
    End Sub

End Module
Public Class Car
    Public Sub Describe()
        Console.WriteLine("I am a generic car")
    End Sub
End Class

Public Class OffRoader
    Inherits Car

    Private Shadows Sub Describe()
        Console.WriteLine("I am an offroader")
    End Sub

End Class
```

This is pretty much the same code that you just saw. In addition, the `Main()` subroutine includes code to instantiate the class and use it. Let's take a look:

```
Sub Main()
    Dim truck As New OffRoader
    Dim car As Car = CType(truck, Car)

    truck.Describe()
    car.Describe()
    Console.ReadLine()
End Sub
```

The code here first creates an instance of the `OffRoader` class, called `truck`. A second variable, of type `Car`, is then set to point at the same single object. The `Describe()` method then gets called on both `truck` and `Car`. Run the code and you'll see the output in Figure 5-7.

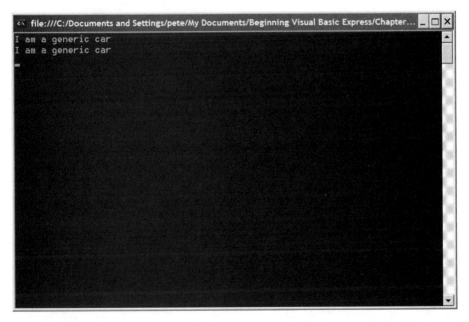

Figure 5-7. *When you run the code, the same message appears for both calls to Describe().*

Now, this may seem odd. After all, `OffRoader` creates a `Describe()` method that shadows the base `Car.Describe()` method. So, surely that means we should see two different output messages.

The reason we don't is subtle. Take a look at the definition of `Describe()` in the `OffRoader` class:

```
Private Shadows Sub Describe()
    Console.WriteLine("I am an offroader")
End Sub
```

This method is `Private`. The other `Describe()` method, the one in the `Car` object, is `Public`. So, what you did here is create a `Describe()` method that replaces the one in `Car` but that is `Public`. Confused? What happens at runtime is that because the new `Describe()` method is `Private`, the runtime tries to find `Describe()` in a subclass. In our case this means it finds `Describe()` in `Car` and calls it. The problem with this approach can be demonstrated by adding a new method to the `OffRoader` class. Go ahead and make the following highlighted change:

```
Module Module1

    Sub Main()
        Dim truck As New OffRoader
        Dim car As Car = CType(truck, Car)

        truck.ShowMe()
        car.Describe()

        Console.ReadLine()
    End Sub

End Module
Public Class Car
    Public Sub Describe()
        Console.WriteLine("I am a generic car")
    End Sub
End Class

Public Class OffRoader
    Inherits Car

    Private Shadows Sub Describe()
        Console.WriteLine("I am an offroader")
    End Sub

    Public Sub ShowMe()
        Describe()
    End Sub

End Class
```

Here, you've added a method to `OffRoader` called `ShowMe()`. This method in turn just calls `Describe()`. Run the code again and you'll see the output in Figure 5-8.

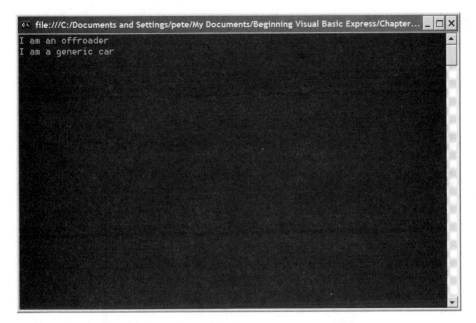

Figure 5-8. *Now when you run the application, you see two messages.*

This time you see two messages. Why? Well, ShowMe() in OffRoader calls Describe(). It is able to access the private shadowed Describe() method, so you see two messages.

So, given all these problems with Shadows, why even use it? Well, there is a valid use. You can use Shadows to protect your methods. If you are subclassing and expect that a method in a base class may change, or even that a new method may be added with the name of a method you are using, Shadows can protect you from that change, and thus protect code that uses your own class.

Interfaces

Abstract classes provide us with a way to force people using the class to implement some functionality. Another way of thinking about it is that an abstract class binds a subclass to support a specific *interface*. Visual Basic 2005 also has a specific Interface type for just this purpose. Unlike an abstract class, you can't put functionality of any kind inside an Interface. An Interface just specifies a set of method signatures that a supporting class must provide.

Let's take a look (this won't be a complete example, but it is handy to see how to create an interface type and to see the support that the Visual Basic 2005 Express IDE gives you when it comes to implementing it).

Create a new console project and add a new `Car.vb` class to the project, just as before. When the editor appears, erase all the code except for the namespace definition. Your code window will look like the one in Figure 5-9.

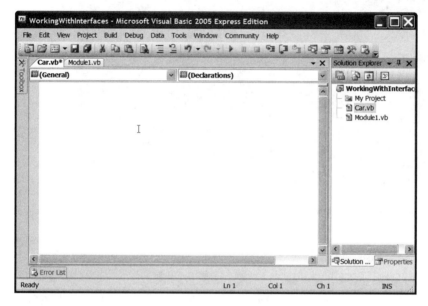

Figure 5-9. *Erase all the code in the Car.vb class so that just the namespace definition remains.*

Now go ahead and declare the interface:

```
Public Interface ICar

End Interface
```

A WORD ON NAMING

We tend to name classes and interfaces a little differently. A class name always uses a capital letter at the start of each word in its name—for example, FactoryEmployee, GameGraphic, Car, and so on.

Just like a class, interfaces use a capital letter as the first letter of each word in the interface name, but traditionally begin with a capital I—for example, IFactoryEmployee, IGameGraphic, ICar.

This difference makes it easy when you're glancing through your code to see just what is an interface and what is a class. It's also the standard used to name classes and interfaces within the .NET class library, so it makes a lot of sense for us to adopt the same standards.

Interfaces never contain any code or variables, just methods. Even then the methods are declared with no body, just as when you declared an abstract method earlier.

Add a few methods to this interface:

```
Public Interface ICar

    Sub TurnOn()
    Sub TurnOff()
    Sub Drive()

End Interface
```

You'll notice of course that there are no Public or Private modifiers on the methods in the interface. Everything in an interface is public because the very nature of a VB interface is to define a public interface supported by a class.

Let's create a class now that implements this interface, just to see the special help Visual Basic 2005 Express gives us when working with interfaces.

Underneath the interface, type in this:

```
Public Class OffRoader
    Implements ICar
```

As soon as you press the Enter key, VB Express automatically drops a bunch of code into your class, as you can see in Figure 5-10.

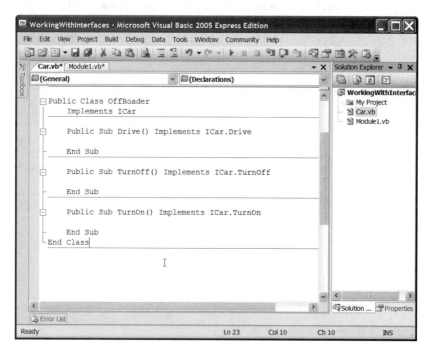

Figure 5-10. *When you implement an interface with a class, VB automatically generates the Interface stubs for you.*

The keyword `Implements` tells Visual Basic that this class implements the named interface. Every single method in the interface is now in your class. Also, notice how every single method in the class from the interface also uses the `Implements` keyword. This lets VB know that the method in question is a part of this class's implementation of the interface, not simply a generic class method.

If a class implements an interface like this, it must provide code for absolutely every method within the interface. Interfaces, then, are like a contract. By implementing an interface in a class, the person writing the class is committing to a contract that says he will make sure the class does everything the interface says that it should.

Every method within the class has the same name as the method in the interface. That's what implementing the methods *implicitly* is all about. Now, Visual Basic will let you inherit from only one base class, but a class can implement as many interfaces as you like. For example, a Jeep class could implement OffRoader and Car interfaces, showing the world that it does everything both interfaces say it should. This becomes a problem, though, when a class implements two or more interfaces that have the same method names in them. For example, an OffRoader interface may also have a Drive() method, just like the class. This is why every interface method in the class explicitly identifies the interface and method that it's implementing. Also, there's nothing stopping you from implementing more than one interface within a class. In fact, you can even implement a number of interfaces that support the same method name, because in code you explicitly identify which interface a method implementation belongs to.

```
Public Class OffRoader
    Implements ICar

    Public Sub Drive() Implements ICar.Drive

    End Sub

    Public Sub TurnOff() Implements ICar.TurnOff

    End Sub

    Public Sub TurnOn() Implements ICar.TurnOn

    End Sub
End Class
```

You have even more flexibility, in that if you wish you can implement a method from an interface and change its name too, like this:

```
Public Sub DoSomething() Implements ICar.TurnOn
```

Finally, bear in mind that at runtime an interface acts pretty much like an abstract class; although you can't create an object directly from an interface (that would be silly, because an interface has no code), you can treat objects as interfaces. For example:

```
Dim mycar As ICar = New OffRoader()
mycar.Drive()
```

Even though you're not going to get this project working, don't throw it away; you'll come back to it in a second.

Let's move on to a new feature of Visual Basic 2005, the partial class.

Partial Classes

Imagine that you had a very complex class that also implemented a very complex interface. As you add code to the class, it would soon become quite confusing as you try to figure out just which parts are the private methods of the class, which are the public methods, and which are required methods that implement the interface. It's a problem that's plagued Java and C++ programmers for years, and one of the things that helps make code written in those languages so daunting to newcomers.

However, Visual Basic 2005 has *partial classes*. Simply put, you don't need to dump all the code of a single class into a single file. You can break the code into multiple physical files on your computer—for example, one file to handle the interfaces that the class implements, another to hold private methods, and another to hold the class's own unique public methods. When you start a Windows Forms project in Visual Basic 2005 Express, the IDE automatically makes every form you create a partial class. This means that as you drop controls onto the form, the IDE can populate a hidden partial class file with information about the controls on the form, leaving the main code file that you work with free of anything other than the code you write.

Let's take a look at how this works.

Try It Out: Partial Classes

Load up the interfaces project you were just working on.

The first thing you need to do to create a partial class is to simply tell VB Express that your `OffRoader` class is partial. Change the class definition by removing all the code inside it and adding the word `Partial` to its declaration:

```
Public Interface ICar

    Sub TurnOn()
    Sub TurnOff()
    Sub Drive()

End Interface


Partial Public Class OffRoader


End Class
```

Now add another class file to the project (right-click the project in the Solution Explorer and then follow the usual steps) and call this one OffRoader_Interfaces.vb. When the code editor appears, add the Partial keyword once again and make the OffRoader class implement your interface:

```
Partial Public Class OffRoader_Interfaces
    Implements ICar
    Public Sub Drive() Implements ICar.Drive

    End Sub

    Public Sub TurnOff() Implements ICar.TurnOff

    End Sub

    Public Sub TurnOn() Implements ICar.TurnOn

    End Sub
End Class
```

The net result of course is that you now have the source code for your OffRoader class in two files. One file contains code that implements the interfaces that OffRoader supports. The other contains (or will, if you add more code to this) the code that makes OffRoader do its thing.

USED .NET BEFORE?

If you've used .NET before, you'll probably remember the nightmare code tangle that was the result of the Windows Forms editor. To enlighten the rest of the readers, when you drag and drop controls onto a form to design the user interface of a Windows application in Visual Basic 2005 Express, what's happening behind the scenes is that the VB Express IDE is actually generating code for you.

In previous versions of Visual Studio .NET, this code would get dropped into a code region within your form's source and would easily get mixed up with your own source. As you added more and more controls to your form's user interface, the source for the form would grow and grow in size and eventually become quite confusing.

In Visual Basic 2005 Express and Visual Studio 2005, partial classes are used. The IDE will generate code in a separate hidden source file, leaving your form's source file completely empty and a lot less confusing to work with. Take a look for yourself—go ahead and create a new Windows Forms project, and then double-click on the form that appears. You'll notice that the class definition for the form itself is a partial class.

Casting Types

When you start to work with inheritance, abstract classes, and interfaces, the ability to treat one object as another becomes more and more important. In fact, even if you don't use inheritance and interfaces in your projects (you should, really), you'll still need to know how to cast one type of object as another. The reason for this of course is that the .NET class library makes extensive use of inheritance, abstract classes, and interfaces.

There are a couple of rules about just what you can cast objects into. Simply put, you can only cast an object down to something it inherited from, or back to the original type of object that was created. This is probably easier to illustrate with a diagram (see Figure 5-11).

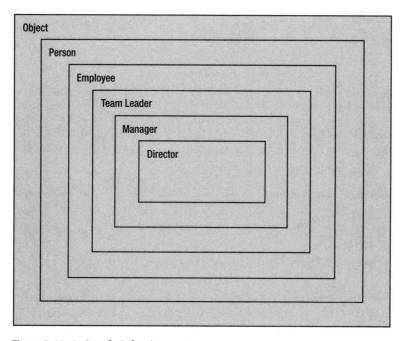

Figure 5-11. *A simple inheritance tree*

In this example, if you went ahead and created a Director object, you could cast it down into pretty much any of the objects it inherited from. In VB you can inherit from only a single object (although you can implement multiple interfaces), so it's quite painless to build nice easy-to-follow inheritance trees like this one.

So, a Director object could easily be treated just like a standard Employee one with code like this:

```
Dim myEmployee as Employee = myDirector
```

Visual Basic 2005 is pretty smart at automatically spotting that you can convert one object into its superclass (the one it inherited from). Sometimes, though, you'll need to help it out, particularly when you need to convert a base object reference into the more specific subclass type. Let's look at an example.

Try It Out: Casting and Type Evaluation

Start up a new console application and add a new class to it called Employee.vb. When the code editor for the new class appears, add some code, like this:

```
Public Class Employee            .
    Public Sub Hire()
        Console.WriteLine("I got hired")
    End Sub
End Class


Public Class Director
    Inherits Employee
    Public Sub GetHiringBonus()
        Console.WriteLine("I also got a bonus")
    End Sub
End Class
```

So, here you have an Employee class with a single method, and a Director class that inherits from it, adding the GetHiringBonus() method to the mix. Drop back into the Module1.vb code and type the bolded code in and I'll talk you through it when you're finished:

```
Module Module1

    Sub Main()

Ind:   delDim newHire As Employee = New Director()
        newHire.Hire()

        If TypeOf newHire Is Director Then
            CType(newHire, Director).GetHiringBonus()
        End If

        Console.ReadLine()
    End Sub


End Module
```

The first thing the code does is create a new object, called newHire. The object type is Employee, but you store a new Director object inside. This works, because Director subclasses Employee and can thus be treated the same in code.

The next line calls Hire(), the method you added to the Employee class. Even though this is really a Director object, the call works because on the one hand you're treating the object like an Employee object, and on the other hand Director subclasses Employee and automatically gets its own Hire() method as a result.

Now, what if you needed to get back to the original Director object? Because you are working with an object variable declared as Employee, you can't just call GetHiringBonus() on it. So, the next thing you need to do is see whether the object you are working with is really a Director. That's where the TypeOf and Is keywords come into play:

```
If TypeOf newHire Is Director Then
```

All this does is see whether the "type of" your object is a Director.

If the object is really a Director (it is), you need to "cast" it back into the Director type. That's what CType does. CType attempts to convert one object into another type:

```
CType(newHire, Director).GetHiringBonus()
```

You can either store the result of the call to CType into another variable, or just call methods on it. What it does here is attempt to convert your newHire object (an Employee) into a Director. It then calls GetHiringBonus() on the resulting Director object.

Run the program now and you'll see the output in Figure 5-12.

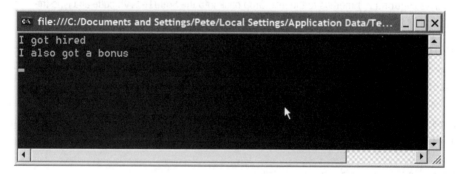

Figure 5-12. *You can use CType to convert one object to another, and TypeOf to check whether one object is another.*

You can also use CType to convert between the built-in Visual Basic types, for example converting a Double to an Integer.

Reference Types and Value Types

All that brings us nicely on to reference types. Take a look at this code:

```
Sub Main()
    Dim a As Integer = 2
    Dim b As Integer = a * 2
    b = b + 10
End Sub
```

Without keying it in, what do you think the values of a and b are at the end of this program? You'd be right if you said that a is 2 and b is 14. Integer is one of the simple data types that you looked at in Chapter 3. When you say something like a = b, the value inside b actually gets copied into a.

Now, look at this code:

```
Module Module1

    Sub Main()
        Dim myEmployee As New Employee()
        myEmployee.Name = "Pete"

        Dim newEmployee As Employee
        newEmployee = myEmployee

        newEmployee.Name = "Dominic"
    End Sub

End Module

Public Class Employee
    Public Name As String
End Class
```

What do you think the values of myEmployee.Name and newEmployee.Name are at the end of Main()? Strangely, both are set to Dominic.

Objects are known as reference types, so setting objectA = objectB doesn't copy objectB into objectA. Instead objectA is set to reference objectB. In some other languages this would be called a *pointer*. Assigning one object to another will only set both variables to reference the same object in memory.

At the end of the day, that's all object variables do anyway. When you create an object, the .NET runtime creates it in the memory of your computer and then stores a reference to it inside your variable. So what really happens when you assign one object variable to another is that the reference is copied, but the object pointed to remains the same.

It's because of this that casting works. Because object variables don't actually hold objects, it's easy to tell Visual Basic exactly what type of object a variable points to. Of course, behind the scenes Visual Basic works some magic so that you don't try to cast the impossible, but you don't need to ever worry about that unless the compiler gives you an error.

This also brings us onto the ByVal keyword that you've seen Visual Basic adding to your methods, for example:

```
Sub SayHello(ByVal name As String)


End Sub
```

ByVal indicates that the actual value of any variable passed to this method is copied into the method's name parameter. The alternative would be ByRef:

```
Sub SayHello(ByRef name As String)


End Sub
```

In this case, a pointer to the variable itself is passed into the subroutine. This means that if the subroutine changes its name in any way, then it will also be changed in the code that called the subroutine. I'm not going to dive into a full "Try It Out" here, but here's some example code that you can key in yourself:

```
Module Module1

    Sub Main()

        Dim someValue As Integer = 12

        SafeSubroutine(someValue)
        Console.WriteLine("Some value is {0}", someValue)

        UnsafeSubroutine(someValue)
        Console.WriteLine("Some value is now {0}", someValue)

        Console.ReadLine()

    End Sub
```

```
Public Sub SafeSubroutine(ByVal a As Integer)
    a = a * 10
End Sub

Public Sub UnsafeSubroutine(ByRef a As Integer)
    a = a + 50
End Sub


End Module
```

What this program does is create a variable (someValue) and then pass it to one routine ByRef, and another ByVal.

SafeSubroutine gets the value ByVal. So, it adds 10 only to its own local copy of the number.

UnSafeSubroutine, on the other hand, gets the value ByRef. So, when it adds 50 to the number, it's actually adding 50 to our original variable. If you do key this in and run it, you'll see the output in Figure 5-13.

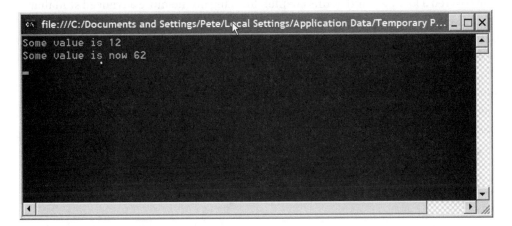

Figure 5-13. *By passing a value to a routine, ByRef actually passes a "reference" to the original variable over to the subroutine.*

Obviously, using ByRef can introduce some very nasty side effects into your programs, so why on earth would you want to use it? Well, the answer is simple. When you are working with classes and objects of your own, you'll often need to pass the object to a subroutine ByRef because there's no easy way for Visual Basic to extract the "value" of a custom class you developed.

BOXING AND UNBOXING

Since we're talking about reference and value types, and casting, now would be a great time to mention a little behind-the-scenes "gotcha." Every type in .NET derives from the base `System.Object` type, which effectively means that you can treat anything as `System.Object`. You need to be careful doing this, though, because of how .NET works with reference and value types differently.

Without going into a massive amount of detail, value types are stored on a small chunk of memory called the *stack*. Reference types, on the other hand, live on the *heap*, the larger "main" memory, if you like, in your PC. If you cast a value type to a reference type, it gets *boxed*. This means that .NET will allocate a lump of heap memory for a real object, and then move the value into that lump. If this happens a great deal in your program, you could notice performance problems because boxing takes time. *Unboxing* is the reverse. When you cast from a `System.Object` type to a value type, the wrappers get torn off the heap object, and the value is then moved to the stack, another costly maneuver if speed and performance is your primary goal.

Just something to be aware of.

Summary

We've covered a lot of ground in this chapter, focusing on the more advanced stuff that you are likely to want, or need, to do with objects. Object references, interfaces, and casting can take a little while to get used to if you are new to the world of Visual Basic 2005, but they are invaluable tools that will stand you in good stead.

The next chapter wraps up your introduction to the features of the Visual Basic 2005 language with a look at exceptions. With that out of the way, you'll be ready to start learning all about what it takes to use Visual Basic 2005 Express to write great Windows applications.

CHAPTER 6

■ ■ ■

Handling Exceptions

Occasionally programs go wrong. As users, we see these events as crashes. As programmers, we see them as exceptions, exceptional circumstances that cause the program to do something we really didn't want it to do.

In the Microsoft .NET Framework, exceptions serve two purposes. On the one hand, they are the first stages of a nasty crash (if left unchecked) that will leave your users less than amused and potentially cause them to lose data, or at least faith in your program. On the other hand, exceptions are the mechanism that all of the .NET Framework class library uses to tell your code something has gone wrong. If your code chooses to ignore the exception, you get a crash. Smart programmers, though, know how to handle them and deal with them intelligently so that the users of your program don't wander off to something more stable.

In this short chapter you'll take a look at the world of exceptions. You'll see how to make your own exceptions and learn just why that's a useful skill to have. You'll also see how to handle exceptions raised by either your code or .NET itself. I'll also try to give you a little insight into what are the right and wrong ways to work with exceptions, and why exceptions are not always a good idea.

Understanding Exceptions

Like everything in .NET, an *exception* is an object. Specifically, an exception is an object that inherits functionality from System.Exception. The actual type of the exception is a good indicator as to roughly what went wrong, while the data contained inside the exception object can pinpoint exactly what happened, where, and why.

In less-technicalspeak, an exception is your program complaining. You ask some object to do something, and it finds that it can't for whatever reason and complains loudly. It complains by creating an object based on System.Exception, filling in some fields telling you exactly why it can't do something, and then stopping altogether.

Let's take a look at a brief example.

Try It Out: What Is an Exception?

Let's write a simple Windows division application that's bound to fail in spectacular fashion. Start up a new Windows Forms application and drop some controls onto the form as shown in Figure 6-1.

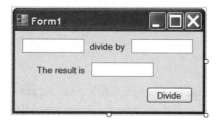

Figure 6-1. *Arrange controls on your application's form like this.*

As always with Windows GUI examples, you'll need to set up the names of the controls so that they are the same as mine so the example code works on your machine. The first text box should be named dividendBox, the second is divisorBox, and the third is resultBox. Set the name of the button control to divideButton.

Double-click the Divide button to start writing the code to respond to the button being clicked. Just go ahead and fill in the method as shown here:

```
Public Class Form1

    Private Sub divideButton_Click(ByVal sender As System.Object, _
        ByVal e As System.EventArgs) Handles divideButton.Click

        Dim dividend As Double = Double.Parse(dividendBox.Text)
        Dim divisor As Double = Double.Parse(divisorBox.Text)

        resultBox.Text = (dividend / divisor).ToString()

    End Sub
End Class
```

First, a Double variable is created to hold the dividend in the calculation. Double.Parse() is used to turn the text in the dividendBox into a Double value that you can work with. The same technique is used to get the divisor's Double value.

Finally, the `resultBox`'s text is set to the result of the dividend divided by the divisor. Notice that you've enclosed the calculation in parentheses. This enables you to treat the entire calculation just as if it were a `Double` value or variable, and call `ToString()` on it to turn the result into text.

Run the program and key in **12** in the first text box, **3** in the second, and click the Divide button. Everything runs great, and you'll see the result of 4 displayed in the result box, just as in Figure 6-2.

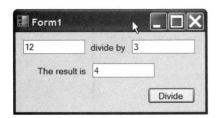

Figure 6-2. *Enter valid numbers into the first two text boxes, and the program will run just fine.*

Now type **12** in the first text box and the word **three** in the second, and click the Divide button. The result is shown in Figure 6-3.

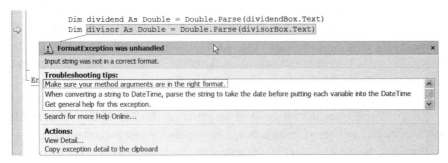

Figure 6-3. *This is what exceptions look like when you run a program from within the IDE. To your users, they look much worse.*

An exception occurs because `Double.Parse()` expects to be given a string containing numeric data, but you gave it straight text. When an exception occurs while running a program from the Visual Basic 2005 Express IDE, the program will stop and the line of code that failed will be highlighted, just as you can see. In addition, a dialog box appears, explaining what the exception was, in this case "FormatException was unhandled," along with some options for things that you can do. Click the link in that box that says View Detail. This takes you to a detailed view of the exception, shown in Figure 6-4.

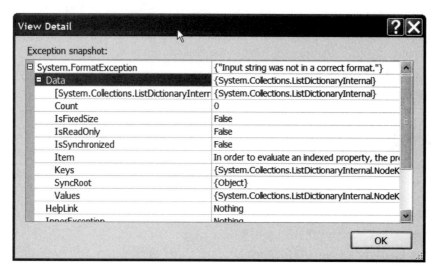

Figure 6-4. *Clicking View Detail allows you to drill down in more detail into just what went wrong with the program.*

Click the + sign beside the first item in the list to view the detail of the exception, as I have in Figure 6-4.

There are quite a few interesting insights into the exception here. What you're looking at is the type of exception (System.FormatException) and some of its properties. Of most interest is the Message property, which tells us that, as we expected, "Input string was not in a correct format." You'll also notice a property called InnerException. When an exception occurs, it could be "caught" by other code and then transformed into a new type of exception. For example, a method deep in a class may fail to parse some text into a Double, causing a FormatException to occur. This may get caught by some other code and transformed into a custom CantDoItException that you wrote yourself. In that case FormatException would become the *inner exception*. It's a little like Russian dolls, with more-generic exceptions containing more-specific ones, each exposed through the InnerException property. You'll see more of this in a little while.

For now, click the OK button to get rid of the dialog box, and then stop the program either by pressing Ctrl+Alt+Break or by clicking the VCR-like Stop Debugging button on the Visual Basic 2005 Express toolbar (see Figure 6-5).

Figure 6-5. *You can click the square icon on the Debug toolbar to stop the program.*

ON THE OTHER HAND...

It's worth pointing out that you could have used the `TryParse()` method instead of `Parse()`. The big difference between the two is that `TryParse()` returns a `True` or a `False` value to indicate whether it could do the conversion, rather than raising an exception when things go wrong. Also, `TryParse()` takes a lot of parameters specifying exactly the format that should be used on the string, the string itself, and the variable that you want the parsed value dumped into. Using this method can get a little complicated and certainly detracts from what we're trying to achieve here. Feel free to take a look at `TryParse()` in the online help.

Handling Exceptions

Visual Basic 2005 includes three keywords to give you some control over exceptions at runtime; Try, Catch, and Finally. Anything inside a Try block is code that you want to run. Code in the Catch block runs only when something goes wrong (and an exception occurs), and code in the Finally block is code that must always run no matter what.

Let's see all this in action by fixing the broken division program you started earlier.

Try It Out: Catching Exceptions

The example you worked on earlier in this chapter has a pretty significant problem. If the user enters text in the text boxes, the program will crash. You'll fix that now. Bring up the project again and go back into the code behind the button's Click event. Add a `Try...Catch` block:

```vb
Public Class Form1

    Private Sub divideButton_Click(ByVal sender As System.Object, _
        ByVal e As System.EventArgs) Handles divideButton.Click

        Try
            Dim dividend As Double = Double.Parse(dividendBox.Text)
            Dim divisor As Double = Double.Parse(divisorBox.Text)

            resultBox.Text = (dividend / divisor).ToString()

        Catch ex As Exception
            MessageBox.Show("Something went horribly wrong!")
        End Try

    End Sub
End Class
```

If you run the program after this change and enter text in one of the text boxes, you'll find the program no longer crashes and instead shows a message box when something goes wrong.

Of course, this code doesn't actually do anything with the exception. When the error occurs and is caught, there's absolutely no indication of what the error was or how it occurred. Changing the code to find out this stuff is easy. Replace the existing `Catch` block with this one:

```
Catch ex As Exception
            MessageBox.Show("Something went horribly wrong: " + _
                ex.Message)
        End Try
```

Make that change, and when the error occurs you'll see a much more informative message about just what went wrong (see Figure 6-6).

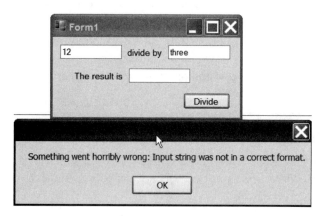

Figure 6-6. *By adding a parameter to the Catch block, you can reference the exception in code.*

This still isn't perfect, though. In fact, this is terrible, and you should never write a `Catch` block like this. When I first learned Java (which uses a similar `Try...Catch` syntax), it took me a while to realize just why this is so terrible.

Every exception inherits from `System.Exception`. When an exception occurs at runtime, Visual Basic 2005 looks for a `Catch` block that most closely matches the type of exception that occurred. If all you have is a `Catch` block that catches generic exception types, then you are effectively telling VB that all exceptions, regardless of type, are handled in that one block. This is bad because although you may think that only one thing could ever trigger the Catch block, you'll inevitably find something unexpected happening, which will get caught by the Catch block you've written. At that point something unexpected has happened to trigger the exception, and your code is assuming the wrong reason the exception was thrown. A much better way to write the code is like this:

```
Private Sub divideButton_Click(ByVal sender As System.Object, _
    ByVal e As System.EventArgs) Handles divideButton.Click

    Try
        Dim dividend As Double = Double.Parse(dividendBox.Text)
        Dim divisor As Double = Double.Parse(divisorBox.Text)

        resultBox.Text = (dividend / divisor).ToString()

    Catch formatEx As FormatException
        MessageBox.Show("Please enter numbers, not text")
    Catch ex As Exception
        MessageBox.Show("Something unexpected occurred:" _
            + ex.Message)
    End Try

End Sub
```

This is much better. Now the code will respond to FormatException exceptions by displaying a message telling the user exactly what went wrong. If any other kind of exception occurs, though, you'll get a detailed message about the unexpected exception.

There's still a problem with the code, but it's a subtle one. If you perform a valid calculation and then try one that fails, the result text box will still show the result of the previous successful one. You can use a Finally block to fix that. (You could also fix this problem by clearing out the text box before you even try to calculate anything, but then I wouldn't be able to show you how the Finally block works at all—so forgive the slightly inelegant code solution here.)

When an exception occurs, the code stops. It stops at the point where the exception occurs and then it jumps to the nearest Catch block (more on how that's calculated in a minute). So, any code beyond the line that fires the exception doesn't run. A Finally block solves this by telling VB that no matter what happens, whether the code succeeds or fails, the code in the Finally block must be run.

Let's make some changes to the code to use a `Finally` block:

```
Private Sub divideButton_Click(ByVal sender As System.Object, _
    ByVal e As System.EventArgs) Handles divideButton.Click

    Dim result As String = String.Empty

    Try
        Dim dividend As Double = Double.Parse(dividendBox.Text)
        Dim divisor As Double = Double.Parse(divisorBox.Text)

        result = (dividend / divisor).ToString()

    Catch formatEx As FormatException
        MessageBox.Show("Please enter numbers, not text")
    Catch ex As Exception
        MessageBox.Show("Something unexpected occurred:" _
            + ex.Message)
    Finally
        resultBox.Text = result
    End Try

End Sub
```

Although this example is trivial, our use of exception handling rocks! This is a much better way to do things. Now the code creates a string variable. The result of the division is stored in that variable, and the variable is dumped into the text box in the `Finally` block. So, if the division fails now, the text box with the result will be cleared. If it works, the text box shows the result.

Visual Basic's exception handling support also provides a feature no other .NET language has—*conditional catches*. With these you can specify `Catch` blocks that run only when a certain exception type occurs and some other condition is true. You write them like this:

```
Try

Catch ex As Exception When a = 10

End Try
```

In this case, the code in the `Catch` block will run only if an exception occurs when variable a is set to 10.

Bubbling Exceptions

So far the code you've seen has the Catch block right there with the code that you're expecting to throw an exception. However, exceptions can bubble up.

Let's say you're writing a method named FireEmployee(), that calls method ProduceTerminationDocuments(), that calls method PrintEmployeeLetter(), and that in turn throws an exception. Visual Basic 2005 will search for the first Catch block in PrintEmployeeLetter(), ProduceTerminationDocuments(), and FireEmployee() that matches. If you had a Catch in ProduceTerminationDocuments(), for example, that matches the exception better than a handler in PrintEmployeeLetter(), then ProduceTerminationDocuments()' exception handler will fire.

Here's a brief code demonstration:

```
Module Module1

    Sub Main()

        Try
            DoSomething()
        Catch ex As Exception
            Console.WriteLine("There was an exception: " + ex.Message)
        End Try

    End Sub

    Public Sub DoSomething()
        Dim aNumber As Double = Double.Parse("This will throw!")
    End Sub

End Module
```

If you were to key this in, the Catch block in Main() would trigger, even though the exception is actually thrown in DoSomething().

The moral of the story: you don't need to catch an exception where it happens. If it makes more sense to catch it in a calling method, then do so. However, if you're writing code that someone else is going to call, don't forget to document that your code could throw an exception, and just what type of exception it could throw.

Throwing Exceptions

There's a school of thought in Java, C#, and Visual Basic 2005 (again, I mention Java just because it has exactly the same exception-handling syntax as C#, which in turn has the same syntax as Visual Basic 2005) that says if your code encounters something wrong, throw an exception. There's another school of thought that says return a value that indicates an error. The guys in this second group tend to be old-school C and C++ guys because those languages didn't have a rich exception-handling mechanism.

For example, let's say you had a method that logged a user in. Without exceptions you could write it like this:

```
Public Function LoginUser(ByVal name As String, _
    ByVal password As String) As Boolean


    Dim loginSuccessful As Boolean

    ' Code here  to actually try to log in
    ' and set loginSuccessful to true or false

    Return loginSuccessful

  End Function
```

What you're indicating here is that there is a return value that will be set to True if the user successfully logs in, and False if the user doesn't. Perhaps you don't want the person calling your function to let their application go any further if the user fails to log in. The problem with this approach, though, is twofold.

First, you're relying on something you can't enforce. You return False if the user can't log in and you *hope* that the person calling the code checks the value you return and does something with it. You have no guarantee that the person will, though.

Second, remember in the discussion of subroutines in Chapter 2 how I spoke about programming by intent? Well, this method name doesn't do that. The method name LogInUser() implies that this method will log in a user no matter what. It doesn't indicate that something needs to be checked or could go wrong.

So, you have two choices: either you can change the name of your method to something more obvious or you can throw an exception. Personally, I prefer the latter. This method will log a user in, no matter what. *If* something horrible happens, an exception can get thrown and the person calling this code (could be you, of course) will have no choice but to either deal with it or have their application crash.

So, how do you do that? Visual Basic 2005 has a special keyword built in for throwing exceptions: the aptly named Throw keyword. All you need to do is pass this a valid Exception object and the exception is thrown. So, you could change that preceding fragment of code to this:

```
Public Sub LoginUser(ByVal name As String, _
    ByVal password As String)


    Dim loginSuccessful As Boolean

    ' Code here  to actually try to log in
    ' and set loginSuccessful to true or false

    If Not loginSuccessful Then
        Throw New Exception("The user failed to log in")
    End If

End Sub
```

Now, at the end of the method, if the user didn't manage to log in correctly, you create a new Exception object and throw it.

The constructor to the Exception object can take a single string parameter, as you can see. This sets up the Message property of the exception so that the code that catches this exception can tell the user something useful about what went wrong.

But this code is just as bad as a Catch block that catches generic exceptions. It's not really very specific, is it? It's a much better idea to create a specific type of exception, either by using one of the Exception classes from the .NET Framework, or by creating your own. Here's how you'd create your own:

```
Public Sub LoginUser(ByVal name As String, _
    ByVal password As String)


    Dim loginSuccessful As Boolean

    ' Code here  to actually try to log in
    ' and set loginSuccessful to true or false
```

```
        If Not loginSuccessful Then
            Throw New LoginException("The user failed to log in")
        End If

    End Sub
    ...
    ...
    ...
Public Class LoginException
    Inherits Exception
End Class
```

Although this will work, the code is pretty bad from a design standards point of view. When you define your own exception types, there really are a number of important rules you must follow in the new class. Let's take a look.

Custom Exceptions

Exceptions have lots of overloaded constructors, so when you create your own exception classes you really need to implement each of these three constructors. Also, all exceptions should be *serializable*. It's a confusing term this early on in your Visual Basic career, but it's a simple enough concept. When a class is serializable, Visual Basic 2005 knows how to turn that class into something that can be stored on disk, or transmitted over the network, at runtime. Thankfully, you don't need to do anything special to make a class of your own be serializable, other than let .NET know that's what you need.

Visual Basic provides a great snippet to walk you through all these requirements when you create your own exception types. In the code editor, simply right-click, choose Insert Snippet ➤ Common Code Patterns ➤ Exception Handling ➤ Define an Exception Class. The Visual Basic snippet system will then automatically dump a bunch of useful code into the editor, like this:

```
<Serializable()> _
Public Class ProblemException
    Inherits ApplicationException
```

```
    Public Sub New(ByVal message As String)
        MyBase.New(message)
    End Sub

    Public Sub New(ByVal message As String, ByVal inner As Exception)
        MyBase.New(message, inner)
    End Sub

    Public Sub New( _
        ByVal info As System.Runtime.Serialization.SerializationInfo, _
        ByVal context As System.Runtime.Serialization.StreamingContext)
        MyBase.New(info, context)
    End Sub
End Class
```

The first line of code here is an *attribute*. Attributes are beyond the scope of this book, so think of them simply as markers that the .NET runtime can use to find out information about a class. In this case, the attribute tells the .NET runtime that this class is serializable, just as every exception class should be.

Notice also that this class does not inherit from Exception. Instead it inherits from ApplicationException. According to the official Microsoft Framework Design Guidelines, this is wrong. The snippet that ships with Visual Basic 2005 Express has a bug! You should always derive your custom exceptions from the base Exception type. Deriving them from ApplicationException deepens the inheritance chain, making things a little more convoluted than perhaps they need to be. Also, by extending ApplicationException in all cases, you actually forgo the benefits that can be had from either reusing or extending the more specific exception types in the framework. In short then, when using this snippet, change the base class from ApplicationException to Exception.

The three constructors provide you with a means to add custom code when this exception is created. For example, you may want to automatically store information about this exception in a log file each time it gets created. Although you may never need to add any custom code, it is generally accepted to be good programming form to at least have these placeholders generated, as the snippet does for you. Then if you need to later add custom code, it's a fairly painless exercise.

Finally, as with all snippets, the most important thing to remember about this code is that after the snippet adds it, change the highlighted areas (in this case it will be the class name) to the specific class name you want to use.

Summary

Exceptions do happen in programs. Sometimes you'll even expect one to happen, and at other times you'll need to code for the worst, just in case something goes wrong.

VB's `Try...Catch...Finally` block lets you catch and work with the exceptions, bubbling them up to other code if necessary.

This pretty much concludes our tour of the major language features of Visual Basic 2005. There are still nuances to learn, but they are out of the scope of a beginner's book. You're sure to pick them up as you work through the rest of the book, building real Windows applications, and as you start to work on your own programs.

So without further ado, let's dive into the rest of the treats Visual Basic 2005 Express has to offer so you can start to learn how to really use the tool to write great applications.

CHAPTER 7

■ ■ ■

How Visual Basic 2005 Express Helps You Code

You've hopefully already noticed that Visual Basic 2005 Express provides quite a few tools and neat IDE tricks to help you develop your applications. Before you dive into learning all about writing Windows applications, now would be a good time for me to introduce each of these features properly. These features, if you master them, can make you incredibly productive at your development work. A chap on the team I'm currently working on, for example, has memorized every single shortcut key within Visual Studio 2005 and can crank out code at a blinding pace. Whether that's a good thing remains to be seen, but as you'll see there are plenty of features given to you in VB Express to help you be really productive.

Building a User Interface

Microsoft likes to say that Visual Studio 2005 (and that includes Visual Basic 2005 Express) provides a great "design experience." What they mean is, Visual Basic 2005 Express includes a bunch of tools to make life for the user-interface builder a heck of a lot easier than it used to be. Some of us, for example, still remember a time when it took about 50 lines of meticulously crafted code just to get a window to appear with the words "Hello, World" inside it. In VB Express this can be achieved without manually typing in any code at all.

The key to this ease is, of course, the Toolbox, shown in Figure 7-1.

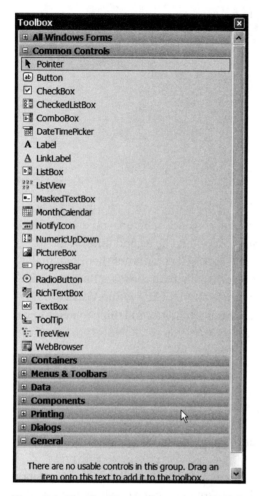

Figure 7-1. *The Toolbox is the source of all the elements of your user interfaces.*

The Toolbox contains the controls that you will want to use to build your user interfaces. You've come across it already in the few samples in previous chapters that required you to build a Windows user interface. All you need to do is click and drag a control from the Toolbox onto the windows in your project. You can also double-click anything in the Toolbox, and it will magically appear on the current project window. It's worth bearing in mind, though, that the Toolbox is context sensitive; it will show only the tools that apply to what you're currently working on. For example, when you work on source code in the code editor, the Toolbox looks like the one in Figure 7-2.

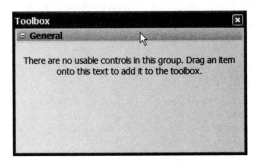

Figure 7-2. *The Toolbox changes based on the work you are currently doing within VB Express.*

So, what really happens when you drag and drop something from the Toolbox onto a window? Well, code happens. Out of sight, Visual Basic 2005 Express creates a variable in your class (remember, a form or window is really a class) of the type of control that you select, and then goes ahead and sets up property values to size and position the control, as well as to set the properties you define in the Properties window. If you want to see the code that VB Express creates, just click the Show All Files button in the Solution Explorer. You can see this button in Figure 7-3.

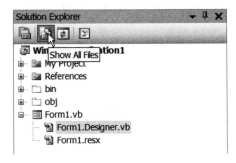

Figure 7-3. *The Show All Files button shows you all the files that VB Express creates behind the scenes. Handy for digging around.*

Let's go ahead and take a peek behind the scenes.

Try It Out: Exploring the Behind-the-Scenes Code

Fire up a new Windows project in VB Express; then drag and drop a Button control from the Toolbox to the window in your application. You'll end up with the Visual Basic 2005 Express form editor looking similar to Figure 7-4.

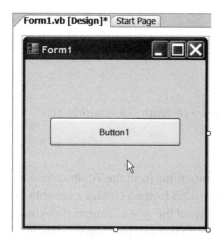

Figure 7-4. *Drag and drop a button onto a form. Behind the scenes, VB Express generates code in response.*

With that done, click the Show All Files button and you'll see your Solution Explorer change, as in Figure 7-5.

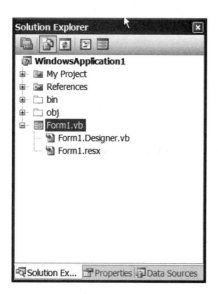

Figure 7-5. *When you click the Show All Files button, new files appear in the Solution Explorer.*

Notice that a plus sign appears next to your form name in the Solution Explorer. Click the plus sign and you'll see the source file that VB Express has been working on behind the scenes, a file called `Form1.Designer.vb`. It's a partial class just like the others you looked at back in Chapter 5. Double-click that file to view the code.

The method that will be of most interest to you is the `InitializeComponent()` method. It starts off like this:

```
Private Sub InitializeComponent()
    Me.Button1 = New System.Windows.Forms.Button
    Me.SuspendLayout()
    '
    'Button1
    '
    Me.Button1.Location = New System.Drawing.Point(39, 90)
    Me.Button1.Name = "Button1"
    Me.Button1.Size = New System.Drawing.Size(214, 45)
    Me.Button1.TabIndex = 0
    Me.Button1.Text = "Button1"
    Me.Button1.UseVisualStyleBackColor = True
```

Notice the button stuff. You dragged and dropped a button on the form, and VB Express created a member in the class called `Button1`. What you see here is a bunch of code setting up the `Location`, `Name`, `Text`, and `Size` properties of the button. In short, this code sets up the button exactly where you have positioned it on the form, at the size you set, with any other properties you set.

Obviously, the more controls you add to the form, and the more properties that you set on those controls, the bigger and more complex this code gets. But you never have to see this code or work with it. It's nicely hidden away in a partial class, letting you focus on the real code in the main class file.

Using Property Smart Tags

Talking of properties, now is a good time to introduce the property smart tags feature. Start up a new Windows project, if you don't already have one open, and drag and drop a `DataGridView` control onto the form (you can find that control in the Data section of the Toolbox). What you'll see will look like Figure 7-6.

The smart tag (the small arrow attached to the top right of the control) can be clicked to quickly access common properties and property-editing tasks associated with the control. In the case of a `DataGridView` for example, most people want to set up the grid's columns and general appearance, and also specify whether the grid should allow sorting, paging, and so on.

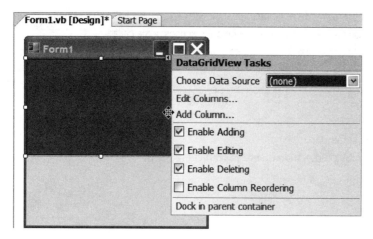

Figure 7-6. *Controls now have smart tags attached to them to provide you with quick and easy access to common properties and property-editing tasks for that control.*

Click in the center of the grid to select it and press the Del key to get rid of it. Then drop a simple text box onto the form. Notice that even a control as simple as the humble text box also has smart tags attached, although the text box's smart tag does nothing more than let you specify that the box will hold multiple lines of text.

Experiment with dropping controls onto a form at your leisure to see which do and which do not support smart tag property editing.

Aligning Controls

I used to have a hard time making my Windows user interfaces look good. How big should the controls be? How much space should I put between them and between controls and the edge of my window? These are important questions, and it took a while to figure out how to consistently produce the right results so that my Windows applications looked professional, or at least had some semblance of professionalism to them.

Microsoft realized this of course, and Visual Basic 2005 Express comes with a handy set of automatic tools to make life simple.

Try It Out: Aligning Controls

Start up a new Windows project (if you already have one open, don't worry about getting rid of it—a great feature of VB Express is in-memory projects that you don't have to save and that don't litter your hard disk with files you don't need).

When the form appears, double-click the Button control in the Toolbox three times, so that you create three different buttons on your application's form. The form will look like mine in Figure 7-7.

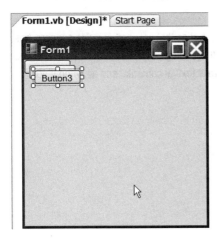

Figure 7-7. *Double-click the Button control three times to create three buttons on your application's form.*

Drag the buttons so that they are spread all over the form, nicely spaced out. Now move one toward the top-left corner of the form. As you near the corner, you'll see guidelines appear, helping you position the button at exactly the correct, recommended distance from the top and left of the form, as you can see in Figure 7-8.

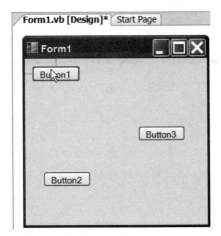

Figure 7-8. *As you move the controls around, you'll notice guidelines appear to help you position the button precisely the right distance from the edges of your form.*

When you have both the left and top guides in view, release the left mouse button to drop the Button control. Now grab another Button control and drag it underneath the one you just positioned. This time different guides appear to show you the correct distance to place the control from the one above it, as well as where to position it so that its left or right edge is aligned.

Grab that third button and move it to the right of one of the others. Notice that yet another guide appears, this time aligning the text in the buttons (see Figure 7-9). You can still use the guides to align the tops or bottoms of the Button controls, but you can also align based on the control's textual contents, and all without you having to do a thing.

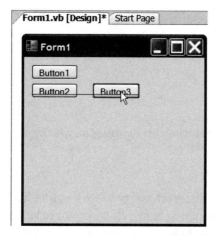

Figure 7-9. *Guides even let you align the contents of controls to each other.*

You'll come to love the guides over time.

Setting Tab Orders

Imagine that you had a form like the one in Figure 7-10.

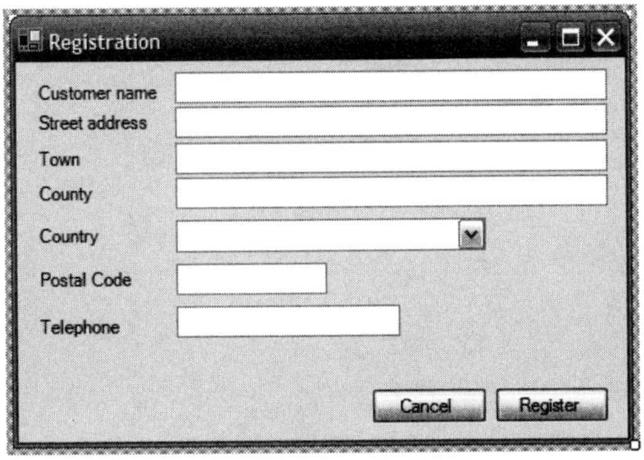

Figure 7-10. *All forms require some attention to navigation order, especially when they get a little complex like this one.*

That's a pretty complex form. Now imagine that you came across this form in an application you had installed—perhaps it's part of a registration dialog for an application you adore. Out of the box there are a few assumptions you and any other user would make about how this form works. Perhaps the biggest assumptions are that when you start editing the form, the cursor will start in the topmost text box, and that pressing Tab will take you down through all the text boxes in the form until you reach the bottom one. You would quickly lose faith in the program if pressing the Tab key moved you all over the form in a seemingly random order.

When you design your user interfaces, Visual Basic 2005 Express provides you with help in specifying the tab order of the controls on forms.

Take a look at the View menu (see Figure 7-11).

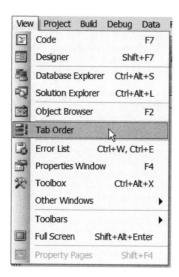

Figure 7-11. *Visual Basic 2005 Express's View menu*

If you select the Tab Order item from the View menu, the form you are working on changes to Tab Order mode, just like mine in Figure 7-12.

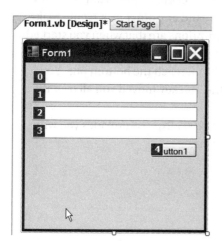

Figure 7-12. *Selecting Tab Order from the View menu shows you the current tab order of the controls on the form.*

In Tab Order mode, all you need to do to set up the tab order of the controls on the form is to simply click on them one by one. Don't forget to click on the Label controls as well, because you can set a hot key for a label by using & in the label's Text property (for example, &Next to display <u>N</u>ext); when you select a label by pressing its hot key, focus moves to the next control in sequence.

When you are finished clicking away, just press the Esc key on the keyboard to leave Tab Order mode. What could be easier?

Using IntelliSense

We've touched on IntelliSense in some of the examples in earlier chapters. It's the part of Visual Basic 2005 Express that pops up tip boxes in the code window to help you remember the syntax of methods to call and so on. You can even bring it up at any time in the code editor by pressing Ctrl+spacebar. It's a lot more than just a neat pop-up window, though.

IntelliSense can help you spot bugs and problems with your code before you run the program. It can also automatically resolve some problems for you. In fact VB Express's IntelliSense features can even be used to write code for you in some instances, thanks to a great feature called code snippets.

Automatically Fixing Namespace Problems

Methods and properties live in classes, and classes live in namespaces. The .NET Framework alone includes a huge number of namespaces, and an even larger number of classes. Remembering what lives where can quickly become a real problem. IntelliSense can help.

Fire up a new console application and I'll demonstrate.

There's a class in one of the framework namespaces called WebClient, a great class that lets you download stuff from the Internet (web pages, files, and so on). The only problem I ever have with it, and indeed with a great many other classes in .NET, is remembering where it lives; is it System.Web.WebClient or System.Net.WebClient?

Add some code to the Main() function to create a WebClient object:

```
static void Main(string[] args)
{
    WebClient myClient = new WebClient();
}
```

If you try to run this program now, you'll get an error because you haven't told VB Express where to find the WebClient class (either by fully naming it or by adding an Imports clause to the top of the source file).

Take a look at the code in the editor and you'll notice that IntelliSense has drawn a blue squiggle underneath WebClient. You should also notice a small red box at the end of the squiggle. Hover the mouse over the red box and a drop-down box will appear. Click it, and you'll see an option to fix your code, as shown in Figure 7-13.

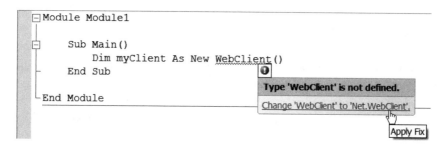

Figure 7-13. *IntelliSense can automatically spot namespace problems and offer you solutions.*

To fix the code, simply click on Change WebClient to Net.WebClient. IntelliSense will change the name to the correct fully qualified name for you.

Using Code Snippets

Just as it's easy to forget which namespaces to use for which classes, new programmers in Visual Basic 2005 (or indeed any programming language) frequently have a hard time remembering how to structure blocks in the language. For example, when I learned C years ago, I used to have real issues remembering whether the condition or the increment came first in a for loop. (It's the condition, right?) IntelliSense code snippets can help you out here.

If you don't still have the console application open, create a new one just to get into the code editor so you can try this out.

Right-click on a blank line in the Main() method and choose the Insert Snippet option from the context menu. A list of code categories will appear, as shown in Figure 7-14.

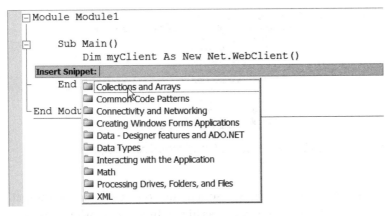

Figure 7-14. *Snippets are prewritten blocks of code that IntelliSense can add to your programs for you.*

Each item in the list is a category of code snippet. If you wanted to drop a loop into your code, you would click the Common Code Patterns category. If you needed to do something on the Internet, Connectivity and Networking would be a great place to start looking. For now, just click the Common Code Patterns category. The list will change to show you some more categories, and also display a web-style "breadcrumb" to let you quickly jump back to the list view you were just looking at. You can see this in Figure 7-15.

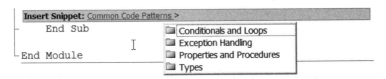

Figure 7-15. *Clicking a category shows you more categories and also displays a breadcrumb trail above the list that you can use to quickly jump back to a previous place in your snippet search.*

Click the Conditionals and Loops category and you'll see a list of actual code snippets, just like those in Figure 7-16.

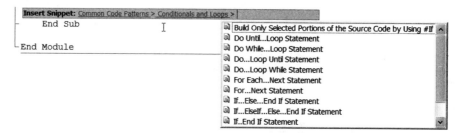

Figure 7-16. *Finally, the snippet window shows you a list of actual code snippets.*

Click the For...Next entry. The snippet will be inserted into your code, and the snippet window will vanish. Notice that the resulting code has highlighted areas inside it, as in Figure 7-17.

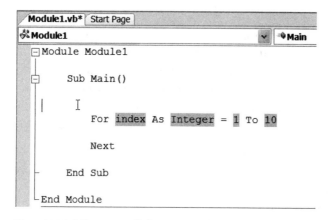

Figure 7-17. *When you click an actual snippet, it gets inserted into your code. The areas you need to customize are highlighted for you.*

The highlights show you the parts of the code snippet that you need to change. For example, in our For loop here, the name of the variable in the loop is highlighted, as is its data type. Simply type in a new variable name and hit Tab and you'll move to the next highlight. When you've changed the data type (if you need to), hit Tab again to move to the value that the For loop will start at.

As you can hopefully see, snippets can save you a lot of time when you are getting up to speed with the language and features of the .NET Framework. Feel free to spend some time exploring what other snippets are included before we move on.

Summary

Visual Studio has always been the IDE of choice for millions of developers around the globe simply because it makes programming easier. With Visual Studio 2005 and the Express tools, it just got even better.

In this chapter you took a look at some of the GUI aids for Windows user-interface design, as well IntelliSense and code snippets. I picked these items for a full explanation because they warrant it, especially if you've never used Visual Studio before. There are still a lot of other neat features to explore on the menus, so feel free to click away to your heart's content before moving on. Don't forget, online help can get you out of a bind if you find something particularly strange.

You're all set now to start learning how to write Windows applications. See you in the next chapter.

■■■

CHAPTER 8

Building Windows Applications

Now we get to the good stuff: using Visual Basic 2005 Express to create beautiful Microsoft Windows applications, complete with windows, dialog boxes, buttons, text boxes, lists—in fact, everything you see in the professionally packaged Windows applications out there. The bad news, of course, is that this isn't something that you can just pick up (or I can write about) in one chapter. There's a lot of ground to cover. It's fun ground, though.

In this chapter we'll cover the basics of building a user interface with VB Express, before diving into the details of just what a Windows application is and what it means to you. Along the way, you'll explore some of the most common elements you'll see in any Windows application user interface, namely buttons, text boxes, and labels.

That may not sound like a lot, but you have to bear in mind that you'll also be looking at the fundamental concepts behind how a Windows app works, and these are concepts that you'll need to know and be aware of no matter what elements you stick in your application's user interface.

So, without further ado…

How Windows Programs Work

It's handy to have the wonderful world of .NET application building put into context. Just how do Windows programs really work? If you think about it hard enough, Windows programs should be impossibly complex to create. A program consists of a number of windows, each containing a number of controls ranging from menus and toolbar items, to buttons, drop-down lists, text boxes, and much more. At any point, users could click on and interact with any control they can see. The golden rule with a graphical user interface is typically, "If they can see it, they can use it."

Just think about that for a second. Your programs need to be able to handle absolutely any permutation of controls being used, in any order, and for pretty much any purpose (just because you want a user to enter a number for his age in a text box rarely means he will). Thankfully, Visual Basic 2005 Express simplifies this a great deal, and in the process simplifies just how Windows programs really work (in effect, it hides a lot of the underlying complexity of Windows away from you).

Hidden away, out of sight from you, is something called the *message loop*. Whenever something happens to an application (even something as simple as the user moving the mouse), the Windows operating system catches that and fires off a message, a data structure that holds lots of information about what just happened. The message loop of a program just sits there checking and rechecking to see whether there are any new messages, and if there are, it grabs them so that no one else can, and fires them off to the appropriate window. Historically, you'd have to write the code for the message loop and add code to each and every window you create to catch the messages and respond accordingly.

In Visual Basic 2005 Express, all of this complexity is taken care of for you through *events*. Each and every control and window in your application is capable of generating a number of different events. For example, when the user presses the Tab key to move the cursor from one text box to another, the first text box generates a LostFocus event, while the second generates a GotFocus event. When a user clicks a button, the button generates a Click event.

In VB Express, your part in all this is simple: you write code to "handle" these events. For example, if you want something to happen when the user clicks a button, you write code to handle the button's Click event.

So, how do you do that? It's very easy. You already know that when you drag a control from the Toolbox onto a form, you can use the Properties window to set various properties that define how the control should look and behave. Well, the Properties window is also an event browser. If you select a control and then click the lightning bolt button at the top of the Properties window, the list changes to show you all the possible events that the selected control can generate (see Figure 8-1).

All you need to do now is find the event you are interested in, and then do one of three things to start writing code:

- Double-click the event in the list to generate a brand new method in your code for the event.

- Type in a method name next to the name of the event to have VB Express generate a method with the name you specify.

- Click the drop-down arrow in the entry area next to the event name and choose some event code that's already been written to reuse that code for this event.

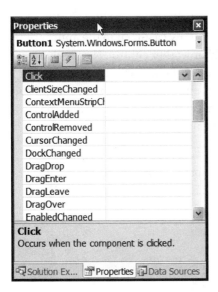

Figure 8-1. *Clicking the lightning bolt at the top of the Properties window changes it to show all the events that a control can generate.*

The last item in that list is quite important. *Event handlers* (the code you write to respond to an event) are really little more than methods with a special signature. It is totally possible and acceptable to have one event handler respond to the same event on many different controls. For example, if you have a bunch of text boxes in a window and you want them all to be validated the same way, you'd just hook up the Validating event of all the text boxes to the same event handler.

The question then arises, if you do that, how do you figure out just which control fired the event in the first place? After all, if you have 20 text boxes in a window all using the same Validating event, you'll probably want the code in that event to be able to figure out just which one of the 20 fired the event in the first place. Well, all event handlers look pretty much the same. For example, here's the Click event for a button:

```
Private Sub Button1_Click(ByVal sender As System.Object, _
    ByVal e As System.EventArgs) Handles Button1.Click
End Sub
```

The first parameter passed to any event handler is called sender and it's typed as an object. This is actually the control that fired the event. By casting it to the appropriate object type, you can interact with it just as you would any other control. Notice also how Button1_Click actually specifies at the end of the subroutine definition Handles Button1.Click. This is the connection among a control and an event and your code. If you used the event browser to link one event handler to more than one control, that Handles statement would be expanded to a list of controls, like this:

```
Private Sub Button1_Click(ByVal sender As System.Object, _
    ByVal e As System.EventArgs) Handles Button1.Click, _
        Button2.Click, Button4.Click, Button3.Click


End Sub
```

Common Properties and Events

Every single control that you drop onto a form to build your application's user interface is a subclass of System.Windows.Forms.Control. What this means to you, of course, is that every visual control you'll ever use will inherit a common set of functions, properties, and events from that base System.Windows.Forms.Control. If you take a look at the online help for System.Windows.Forms.Control, you'll see that the list is in fact huge, but the good news is that you don't need to memorize everything there.

On the properties side, the most common properties that you'll want to work with are listed in Table 8-1.

Table 8-1. *The Most Common Properties You'll Ever Work With*

Property	Description
Name	This is the name of your control. When you name a control, an instance variable is created in your form's class with the same name.
BackColor	The background color of the control. Its actual effect varies from control to control, but it's usually pretty obvious. Clicking the ellipsis (...) button in the Properties window brings up a color browser that you can use to choose a color.
ForeColor	The color of the text or foreground within the control. Like the BackColor control, clicking the ellipsis (...) button in the Properties window brings up a color browser that you can use to choose a color.

Property	Description
Text	For most controls, this property is the text that the user sees inside the control. On a button, for example, it's the text that appears within the button itself. For a TextBox control, it's the text that the user enters.
Size.Width, Size.Height	Width and height belong to the size structure embedded in every control. Usually you don't have to do anything with these properties at all, because you typically set them by dragging the resize handles in the visual designer to make the control the size you want.
Location.X, Location.Y	Just like Size.Width and Size.Height, these properties are typically set as a result of you moving the control around on the form with the mouse at design time. The X value specifies how far from the left edge of the form the control should appear, and the Y value specifies how far down from the top edge of the form it should appear.
Font	This is an object embedded inside every control. It exposes properties such as Font.Name, Font.Size, Font.Bold, and so on. Normally this is best set by clicking the ellipsis (…) button next to the Font property in the Properties window.
Anchor	This is also a complex property. It's best set by clicking the drop-down arrow next to the property value in the Properties window, where you can choose which sides of a control to *anchor*. Anchoring a control makes it respond to changes in the form's size, so if you anchor all four sides of a control, it will grow and shrink as the form itself does at runtime.
GenerateMember	This is a Boolean (True/False) value. Every time you drop a control onto a form, you get a new variable in your class with the same name as the Name property of the control. However, you won't always want this to happen. For example, you'll rarely need access to a Label control from within code. Just set this to False for those controls that you don't actually need to work with inside your program code.

Of course, there are other common properties, but these are by far the most useful and frequently used.

Similarly, there is a huge list of events that every control can generate. For example, all visual controls in .NET can fire off a Click event in response to the user clicking them with the mouse, and also Validating and Validated events to let you check the contents of the control after the user has finished messing with them. Rather than listing them all here, I'll have you look at the events as you explore each of the controls throughout the rest of this chapter and the rest of the book.

Buttons in All Their Glory

I'd like to introduce you to perhaps the simplest, and most common, of all the controls in the Toolbox—the humble Button control. The button, while sporting a wealth of properties that let you change its general appearance, is really designed to do just one thing: click. In fact, it does a little more than that. It can be depressed, and it can pop up after being depressed—if only life were as simple. If you really wanted to take the button to the very bleeding edge, you could even get it to do things when the mouse travels over it, when it's dragged, or when things are dropped on it. See, not so simple a control after all, is it.

Let's take a look.

Try It Out: Working with Buttons

Start up a new Windows project. When the form editor appears, drop a button onto the form's surface, as in Figure 8-2.

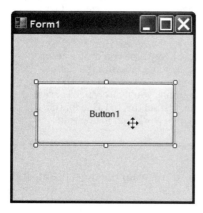

Figure 8-2. *Drop a button onto the form, like this.*

Select the button by clicking it just once, and if the Properties window is not currently visible, press F4 on the keyboard (or select Properties Window from the View menu) to bring it into view.

Notice at the top of the Properties window there is a button that looks quite like a lightning bolt. Click this, and the Properties window will change to show you a list of all the events that the button can respond to. You can see this in Figure 8-3.

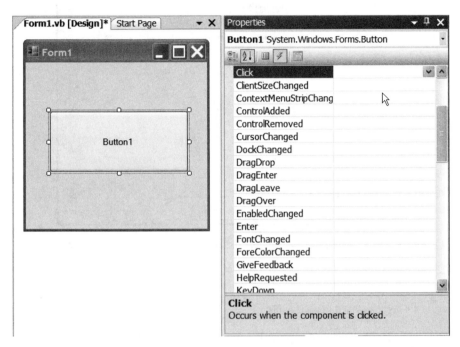

Figure 8-3. *The Properties window also shows you the list of all the events that a control supports.*

Events, as I explained earlier, are raised by controls, more often than not as a result of the user doing something. There are a few events in the list, though, that have very little to do with the user. The Paint event is a good example. This event fires whenever the button needs to redraw itself—for example, when it reappears after being covered by another window.

Let's take a look at some of the events in action. Scroll down the list of events and find the MouseEnter event.

Double-click in the entry area to the right of the event name (MouseEnter), and your code window will appear, looking like mine in Figure 8-4.

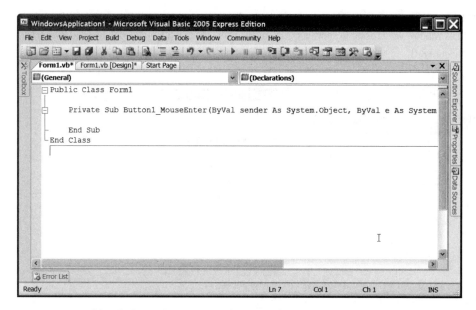

Figure 8-4. *Double-clicking the event in the event list drops you into the code editor for that event.*

Add some code to the event so that it reads like this:

```
Private Sub Button1_MouseEnter(ByVal sender As System.Object, _
    ByVal e As System.EventArgs) Handles Button1.MouseEnter
    Button1.Text = "The mouse is over me"
End Sub
```

What you're saying here is that when the mouse enters the control, you'll change the Text in the control.

Go back to the form editor by clicking its tab at the top of the code window, and reselect the button. This time find the MouseLeave event in the event list and click it once. Notice the drop-down button in the entry area next to the event name (see Figure 8-5).

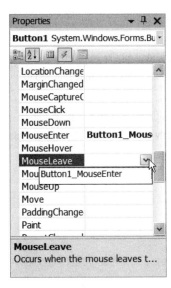

Figure 8-5. *The event drop-down lets you set up one method to work with many different events.*

Clicking the drop-down button shows you a list of event handlers you've already written that could be used for this event as well. These aren't necessarily event handlers for just the currently selected control; if you had a few buttons on the form, you could have them all use the same event handler.

For now, though, just double-click in the entry area beside the event name (MouseLeave) to go into the editor for that event. Change the code so that it looks like mine here:

```
Private Sub Button1_MouseLeave(ByVal sender As System.Object, _
    ByVal e As System.EventArgs) Handles Button1.MouseLeave
    Button1.Text = "The mouse is not over me"
End Sub
```

Run the application and wave the mouse over the button—the caption will change as the button's events fire.

Stop the program that is running by closing down the window in the usual way when you are finished exploring.

Every control has a default event that logically fits the control. With a button, for example, the default event is Click. Double-click the button on the form editor and you'll see the code window open up, ready for you to fill in the button's Click event.

I mentioned earlier that an event could be called by many controls. But the problem is that so far the code you've written pretty much assumes which control triggered it (you explicitly set Button1's Text property). This is exactly where the two parameters passed to the event come into play:

```
Private Sub Button1_Click(ByVal sender As System.Object, _
    ByVal e As System.EventArgs) Handles Button1.Click


End Sub
```

The first parameter, sender, can be used to figure out which control sent the event through. Let's add some code to the click event handler to demonstrate this:

```
Private Sub Button1_Click(ByVal sender As System.Object, _
    ByVal e As System.EventArgs) Handles Button1.Click

    Dim clickedButton As Button = TryCast(sender, Button)
    If Not clickedButton Is Nothing Then
        clickedButton.Text = "I was clicked"
    End If


End Sub
```

I'll walk through the code just in case some of it doesn't make sense. First, a new object variable is created to hold a button. On the same line of code, a new Visual Basic command called TryCast is used. Before Visual Basic 2005, if you wanted to convert an object (such as sender) into another type of object (such as Button), you'd use a command called CType. The problem is, if sender is not actually a Button, you end getting a runtime exception, meaning that you'd have to write exception handlers into the code. In addition, dealing with exceptions takes quite some time at runtime, and we want our application to remain quite "snappy." TryCast solves this problem. It attempts to convert one object into another type. If the conversion is successful, the result is the converted object. On the other hand, if the conversion can't be performed, the result is a special Visual Basic data type called Nothing.

The very next line of code checks to see whether your object is Nothing. Assuming it's not, clickedButton's Text property is set to I was clicked. In English, if the sender of the event is a button, you set its Text property. Go ahead and run the application to try this out (see Figure 8-6). Notice of course that adding a click handler doesn't in any way affect the MouseEnter and MouseLeave events you already coded.

Figure 8-6. *Clicking the button now changes its caption, even though you didn't refer to the button by name in code.*

Stop the program that is running again and add a second button to the form. Bring up its events list and use the drop-down next to the Click event to give it the same event handler as the one you just coded.

If you run the application now, you'll find that you can click each button, and in each case the appropriate button's caption gets set.

So what about that second parameter to the event, the EventArgs parameter? This is an object that provides some useful information about the event that just fired. On a command button it's actually not that much use, but you will see it used quite extensively when you get into some of the more-complex controls later in the book (the grid controls, for example). On those controls, the parameter is used to pass specific information back to your code—for example, which item in a list was clicked.

Entering Text

Although command buttons may be one of the most common types of control that you'll drop on a form, perhaps one of the most common things you'll want to let users do with your forms is enter information. Visual Basic 2005 Express provides a bunch of controls to enable this, covering everything from entering small amounts of text to making choices by using radio buttons and check boxes.

Text Boxes

You've seen text boxes already in some of the example programs that you've developed so far. They are typically used to grab a small piece of information from a user (such as the user's name, or a brief description of a product in a stock management program). Like the button, text boxes provide a great deal of functionality beneath the surface, and a mass of events they can respond to. The most interesting of these are listed in Table 8-2.

Table 8-2. *The Most Useful Events of a Text Box*

Event	Description
Enter	Occurs when the user clicks on, or tabs into, a text control and is ready to start entering information.
Leave	Occurs when the user clicks on another control or tabs out of a control, and finishes entering information.
Validated	Happens when validation of the control has finished.
Validating	Happens when the control wants to validate its contents—you write code to do the validation.
TextChanged	Occurs when the text inside the control changes, usually as a result of the user doing something.

In terms of functionality, the humble text box packs a whole lot in. You can type on the keyboard to enter text, and the control automatically supports backspacing, deleting, and navigating around the text with the keyboard cursor keys. You can cut and paste by using the Windows Clipboard without having to write any special code. You can also select part or all of the text and have the text box automatically highlight the selected text. In fact, out of the box without any effort on your part, the text box works just the way users would expect a text box in any other Windows application to work. Aren't user interface standards great!

All this functionality brings with it some interesting properties that you haven't really seen yet. Table 8-3 lists some of the most important.

Table 8-3. *Some of the More Interesting Properties Attached to a Text Box*

Property	Description
CausesValidation	A True/False property that tells the text box whether it should raise validating events.
Lines	A text box can hold multiple lines of text, and this property, a string array, provides access to the lines in the control.
PasswordChar	Setting a character in here, such as *, lets you hide the text in the control from the user—great for handling password entry.
Multiline	A True/False property that indicates whether the control can hold more than one line of text.
Wordwrap	If you have a lot of text in the control spread over multiple lines, setting this to True ensures that a word doesn't get split over two lines in the control.
Text	You know this one—the text inside the control.

Property	Description
SelectedText	The text that the user has selected inside the control.
SelectionStart	The beginning of the selection, indicated by the number of characters into the text in the text box.
SelectionLength	The number of characters inside the text box that the user selected.

Let's take a look at some of these in action.

Try It Out: Handling Selections in Text Boxes

Start up a new Windows project and drop a text box and button onto the form so that it looks like mine in Figure 8-7.

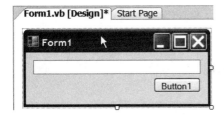

Figure 8-7. *Arrange a text box and button onto your form so that it looks like this.*

To start getting into some good habits, you'll set some names on the important controls. Set the name of the TextBox control to inputBox, and the name of the Button control to showButton.

What you're going to do in this application is pop up a message box when the button is clicked that shows you exactly what's in the text box, what's selected inside the text box, and information about the selection. First, though, you need to make sure that the user actually selected something inside the text box.

Double-click the Show button to open the code window so you can start working on the button's Click event. Change the code to read like this:

```
Private Sub showButton_Click(ByVal sender As System.Object, _
    ByVal e As System.EventArgs) Handles showButton.Click

    If inputBox.SelectionLength = 0 Then
        MessageBox.Show("Select some text in the textbox")
    End If

End Sub
```

As you can see, you can take a look at the SelectionLength property of a text box to see whether the user has selected anything inside the box. If the user hasn't, in this code you display a message box pointing out the error to the user.

Next, you need to do something with any information entered into the text box. What you are going to display is the text itself, the selected text, and information about how long the selection is and where it starts. That's a lot of data to display, so obviously you are going to have to split it over a number of lines in the message box. In addition, it makes sense to build the message string to display over a number of lines.

Although you could simply create a string variable and keep adding to it, that's not really a good habit to get into. Instead, you'll use a StringBuilder object (for a detailed explanation of just why you need to be careful of how you work with strings, see the "Never Keep Adding to a String" sidebar following this exercise). Go ahead and add an Else block to the code and kick it off by declaring a StringBuilder object:

```
Private Sub showButton_Click(ByVal sender As System.Object, _
        ByVal e As System.EventArgs) Handles showButton.Click

    If inputBox.SelectionLength = 0 Then
        MessageBox.Show("Select some text in the textbox")
    Else
        Dim builder As New System.Text.StringBuilder()
    End If

End Sub
```

With that done, you can start to add stuff into the string. Personally, I really like the way Console.WriteLine() works, where you can put parameters into the string itself with braces ({1}, {2}, and so on) and then dump a bunch of parameters at the end of the call to replace those in the string. The same thing can be achieved with the String.Format() command. Take a look:

```
    Else
        Dim builder As New System.Text.StringBuilder()
        builder.Append( _
            String.Format("The textbox contains {0}" + vbCrLf, _
            inputBox.Text))
    End If
```

Here you are adding some text onto your string that says, "The input box contains," followed by the text inside the input box, followed by a new line symbol (vbCrLf) to start a new line of text in the message.

NEVER KEEP ADDING TO A STRING

Strings are *immutable,* which is really a posh word meaning they can't be changed, ever. But hang on a minute, we've seen code that changes a string variable from one value to another, and we've seen code that extends a string by adding new text onto the end of it. If strings are immutable, how does that work?

Well, that's the problem. Whenever you try to change something in a string variable, either by reassigning text to the string, or by adding stuff to it, what actually happens is that the string that was in the variable gets thrown away. Behind the scenes, the .NET common language runtime creates a new chunk of memory to hold the new string. The new string gets dumped into the new block of memory, and the variable is updated to point to this new memory location. The net result, of course, is that this is slow, very slow. You'd hardly notice how slow if you did it now and then without thinking. If you did it inside a big loop, though, you'd soon start to notice the application slowing down.

If you want to do things to strings (add to them, change them, and so on), use a StringBuilder—as the name suggests, this is an object designed to build strings efficiently.

Add the rest of the code so that the message is built in full and displayed:

```
Else
        Dim builder As New System.Text.StringBuilder()

        builder.Append( _
            String.Format("The textbox contains {0}" + vbCrLf, _
            inputBox.Text))

        builder.Append( _
            String.Format("You selected {0} characters starting at {1}" + _
            vbCrLf, _
            inputBox.SelectionLength, inputBox.SelectionStart))

        builder.Append( _
            String.Format("The selected text is {0}", _
            inputBox.SelectedText))

        MessageBox.Show(builder.ToString())
    End If
```

This should all be straightforward enough. The second line shows the number of characters that have been selected in the string, by interrogating the `inputBox.SelectionLength` and `inputBox.SelectionStart` properties. The third line displays the actual selected text by interrogating `inputBox.SelectedText`.

Go ahead and run the program. Enter some text, select a part of it, and then click the Show button and you'll see a message box appear much like mine in Figure 8-8.

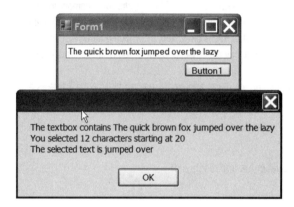

Figure 8-8. *Enter some text, select a part of it, and then click the button, and your application will look much like this screen shot.*

Just as you coded it, the message that appears tells you a bunch of stuff about the text in the text box, and what was selected inside of it.

So far, you've looked at simple text boxes with a single line of data. However, the text box is more than capable of holding a mass of text spread across multiple lines of data. Think of it as a very simple text editor. Let's take a look.

Try It Out: Working with Multiline Text Boxes

Start up a new Windows project again and drop a text box onto the form.

If you try to resize the text box so that it takes up the majority of the form, you'll find that you can't. To fix this, take a look at the text box's properties and change the `Multiline` property to `True`.

Now resize the text box so that it takes up the majority of the form.

Rename the text box `multiLineBox` and then drop a button underneath it called `showLinesButton`. Set the caption on the button to `Show Lines`. Your form should now look like the one in Figure 8-9.

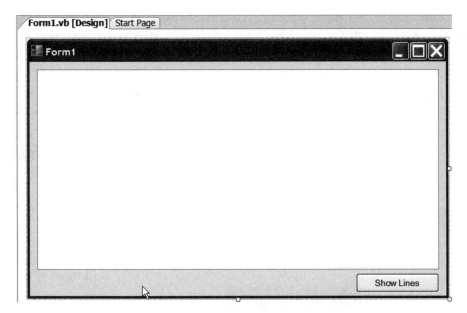

Figure 8-9. *Arrange the text box and button on the form, like this.*

You can work with a multiline text box just as you would with a standard text box. In addition, there is a Lines property that is a string array. You can use this property to get at the physical lines of text inside the text box. Let's add some code to the button's Click event to take a look.

Double-click the Show Lines button to open the editor at the button's Click event code, and add the following highlighted lines:

```
Private Sub showLinesButton_Click(ByVal sender As System.Object, _
    ByVal e As System.EventArgs) Handles showLinesButton.Click

    Dim lineInfo As New System.Text.StringBuilder()
    lineInfo.Append(String.Format("There are {0} lines..." + vbCrLf, _
        multiLineBox.Lines.Length))

    For Each line As String In multiLineBox.Lines
        lineInfo.Append(line + vbCrLf)
    Next

    MessageBox.Show(lineInfo.ToString())

End Sub
```

Just as in the earlier example, the code first creates a `StringBuilder` object, because that's the most efficient way to build a string on the fly. Text is then added to `StringBuilder` to show the number of lines in the text box. Because the `Lines` property of the text box is just an array, you can find out the number of lines in the text box with a call to `multiLineBox.Lines.Length`.

The loop simply adds each line from the `Lines` array to `StringBuilder`. The net result, of course, is that `StringBuilder` contains a long string that displays a summary of the number of lines in the text box, and then each line itself. This is displayed in a message box.

Run the application now, enter a few lines of text, and click the Show Lines button. You'll see a result like that in Figure 8-10.

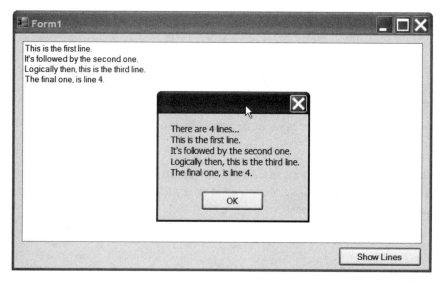

Figure 8-10. *With a multiline text box, you can work with each line of text through the text box's Lines property.*

You'll frequently need to check that the data entered by your users into a text box is valid. That's just what the Validated and Validating events of a text box are for. The Validating event fires after the user moves the focus away from the text box. So, selecting a different control on a form, or even closing the form, will cause the Validating event to fire. The Validated event occurs after the Validating event completes without being cancelled. Let's take a look.

Try It Out: Validating Text Box Contents

Start up another Windows application project in Visual Basic 2005 Express and lay out some controls on the form so that it looks like Figure 8-11.

Figure 8-11. *Lay out controls on your form so that it looks like this.*

What you want to do in this application is just check that the user enters a number (not text) between 1 and 10. In other languages, one approach to doing this would be to code up the OK button so that when it's clicked, code runs that can check what was entered into the text box. With .NET, you don't need to do that. Instead, you'll just close the form down when the button is clicked.

Set the name of the button to okButton and then double-click the button to drop into the code editor for its Click event. Just add a single line of code to close the form down, as here:

```
Private Sub okButton_Click(ByVal sender As System.Object, _
    ByVal e As System.EventArgs) Handles okButton.Click
    Me.Close()
End Sub
```

Let's set up the validation on the text box now. Set the Name property of the text box to numberBox, and then use the Properties window to find the Validating event. You can see it in Figure 8-12.

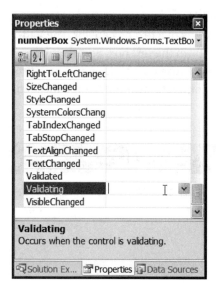

Figure 8-12. *The Validating and Validated events let us check that the data entered into a text box is as we expect it to be.*

Double-click the Validating event in the list to drop into the code editor for the event. Add the highlighted code from the following source listing:

```
Private Sub numberBox_Validating(ByVal sender As System.Object, _
    ByVal e As System.ComponentModel.CancelEventArgs) _
    Handles numberBox.Validating

    Dim numberEntered As Integer
    If Integer.TryParse(numberBox.Text, numberEntered) Then
        If numberEntered < 1 Or numberEntered > 10 Then
            e.Cancel = True
            MessageBox.Show("You have to enter a number from 1 to 10")
        End If
    Else
        e.Cancel = True
        MessageBox.Show("You must enter an integer")
    End If

End Sub
```

Walking through the code line by line, you can see that the first thing that happens is whatever is inside the text box is parsed into an integer. You could have used the Parse() method to do this, but then you'd need to write an exception handler; Integer.Parse() will throw an exception if the data you hand it is not a number. TryParse(), on the other hand, will place the number it finds into the second parameter (in this case, numberEntered). If the data it's handed is not a number, TryParse() will return False, making it ideal for use in an If statement like this.

Assuming all goes to plan, and the user entered a valid integer into the text box, the value is compared. If it's less than 1 or greater than 10, you know you have an invalid value.

Take a look back up at the event signature for a moment:

```
Private Sub numberBox_Validating(ByVal sender As System.Object, _
    ByVal e As System.ComponentModel.CancelEventArgs) _
    Handles numberBox.Validating
```

You get passed a CancelEventArgs object named e. This has a property inside it called Cancel. This is a simple Boolean (True/False) value and is set to False by default. Inside the Validating event handler, it's up to your code to set this value to True if validation fails. What you are saying here is not that you are cancelling the validation event, but instead that you want to cancel whatever event triggered the validation. For example, if the user moves the focus to another control on the form or tries to close the form down, the Validating event will fire. If there isn't any valid data inside the text box, you want to cancel the event that caused the validation to occur.

In our case, if the value entered is less than 1 or greater than 10, you set Cancel to True and display an error message to the user inside a message box. You do the same thing if the user didn't enter a number at all but instead entered text: you set Cancel to True and display a different, appropriate message (see Figure 8-13).

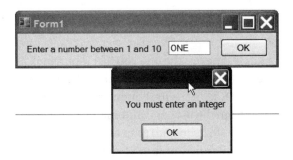

Figure 8-13. *The Validating event catches errors in your text box and displays an appropriate message.*

If the Validating event exits with e.Cancel set to False, it's safe to assume that any validation code in the event handler passed. .NET then fires the Validated event, to run code in the event of validation passing. Go back to the form editor, click on the text box again, and find the Validated event in the Properties window. Double-click it to drop into the code editor for it:

```
Private Sub numberBox_Validated(ByVal sender As System.Object, _
    ByVal e As System.EventArgs) Handles numberBox.Validated
    MessageBox.Show("Well done! Valid number entered.")
End Sub
```

All you want to do here is fire out a message letting the user know that all the validation completed successfully. If you run the program and enter a valid integer into the text box, you'll see this working (see Figure 8-14).

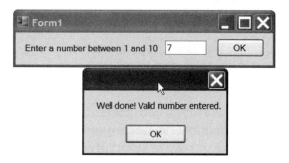

Figure 8-14. *Enter a valid value in the text box and the Validated event will fire, enabling you to display a congratulatory message.*

I should point out that this is just a trivial example. There are much better ways of handling validation, as you'll see later.

The MaskedTextBox Control

Visual Basic 2005 Express includes two types of text boxes: the one you just took a look at and the MaskedTextBox control. The MaskedTextBox control is a special kind of text box that can limit the data a user enters and also format it on the fly. For example, you could use a masked edit control to get a large number from the user and automatically format it with thousands separators. Another typical use would be to grab a zip code from the user and make sure that what the user enters is only digits and the correct length.

AN ALTERNATE VIEW OF THE MASKEDTEXTBOX

To be frank, the MaskedTextBox is a bit of a party crasher among controls. It's a control that was originally in Visual Basic, and the .NET version is functionally identical to that control and was included to ease VB developers' migration to .NET.

That's certainly a great and worthy reason to include a control, but I don't like this control at all. Since the time the control was first conceived, user interface standards have marched on, taking development tools with them. Today there are far better, less user-jarring ways to achieve the same thing. If you want to validate data in a control, use the Validating and Validated events. If on the other hand you want a specific kind of data (and by far the most common is a date), check out the date pickers that I'll cover shortly.

Just what the user can and cannot enter into the control is governed by the `Mask` property. In here you enter a series of characters that denote just what is expected from the user at that position in the text. For example, entering `00/00/00` tells the control to expect two digits, followed by a slash, then two more digits, followed by a slash, and then two more digits—just like a date, in fact. The full list of characters that can be used to set up the mask can be found in the online help under `MaskedTextBox.Mask` property, as you can see in Figure 8-15.

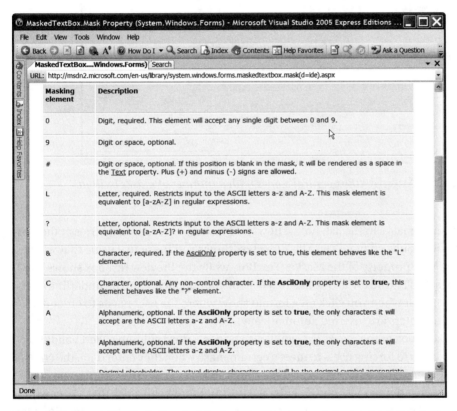

Figure 8-15. *The online help for the MaskedTextBox control shows the full list of values to enter into the Mask property to set up the control.*

Thankfully, Microsoft doesn't expect you to commit the list to memory and has supplied a number of built-in masks that you can get to from the control's smart tag when it's on a form. When you click the MaskedTextBox control's smart tag and then choose Set Mask from the menu that appears, a dialog box is displayed that lets you select from any of the built-in mask formats (see Figure 8-16).

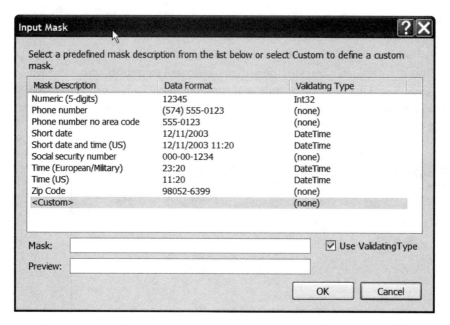

Figure 8-16. *The MaskedTextBox control comes with a number of masks built in.*

As you select masks in the list, notice how the Mask and Preview text boxes at the bottom of the dialog box change. The Mask text box shows you the actual value that will be fed into the Mask property of the MaskedTextBox, while the Preview text box shows you what the MaskedTextBox will look like to a user of your application. The underline characters that appear when you click on a format show where the user needs to enter data. Any other characters are inserted automatically.

If you take a look at the masks list, you'll also notice a third column called Validating Type. In addition to forcing users to meet a certain mask when they enter data, the control can also check that the resulting data will fit into a specific type. For example, you could select a mask that defines just how to enter a date, but there's still a risk that a user would put the day and month of the date in the wrong order. In that case, using a validating type of System.DateTime will ensure that the data entered not only is in the right format but also is a valid DateTime value. The data type shown here is entered into the ValidatingType property of the MaskedTextBox, a property that you can access only from within your code (it's not shown in the Properties window).

You don't have to use a ValidatingType, though. Just like a standard TextBox control, the MaskedTextBox control uses the Validated and Validating events to let you programmatically check that the value entered by the user not only conforms to the correct visual format but also contains a valid value.

In addition, the MaskedTextBox can automatically fire an event (the MaskInput-Rejected event) if the data entered by the user fails to match the mask. The reason this event exists is that if the user tries to enter something invalid into the box, the box will beep, but nothing more. Writing code into the MaskInputRejected event handler for a MaskedTextBox lets you provide the user with more information, usually by means of an ErrorProvider or ToolTip control.

Adding ToolTip Help

Another feature that your users might expect to find in your applications is ToolTips. Don't go overboard, though; as annoying as it can be to not have ToolTips in confusing entry dialog boxes, it can quickly get really tiresome when you can't move the mouse more than a millimeter without yet another ToolTip popping up.

Go ahead and start up a Windows application and produce a form like my registration one from Chapter 7. You don't have to copy it precisely; just put an assortment of labels and text boxes onto the form.

When you're finished editing your form, double-click the ToolTip menu control in the Control palette. Notice how even though ToolTips are visible at runtime, the ToolTip control doesn't actually sit on the form's surface (see Figure 8-17).

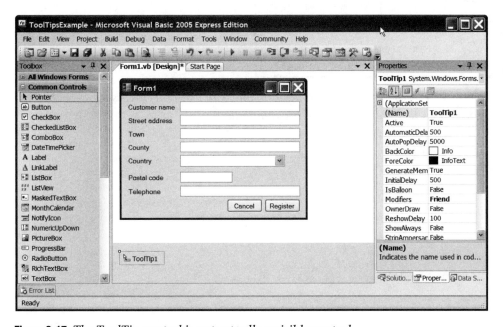

Figure 8-17. *The ToolTip control is not actually a visible control.*

Adding a ToolTip control to a form merely makes it possible to show ToolTips. It doesn't actually set up, display, or hold the tips themselves. Now that you have that control on the form, though, click on one of the text boxes and take a look at the Properties window. You'll see a new property called `ToolTip On ToolTip1`. This is the ToolTip that you want displayed when the ToolTip control is enabled and the mouse is over the control. You could have more than one ToolTip control on a form and enable them or disable them at runtime by setting their `Enabled` properties to `True` or `False`. In that way, you could display different kinds of tips based on the user (from novice to expert, for example).

Put something into this property and set up the `ToolTip On ToolTip1` properties on some of the other controls. Then run your program.

At runtime you'll find that if you move the mouse over a control that has a ToolTip set and let it hover there for a while, a ToolTip will pop up (see Figure 8-18).

Figure 8-18. *With a ToolTip control on the form and enabled, ToolTips associated with controls can be displayed at runtime. It's automatic.*

Try It Out: Adding an ErrorProvider

The validation example from earlier in the chapter puts up a message box when validation fails. This is a pretty neat visual way for an author to get your attention with some sample code in a book, but it's not very elegant from a user interface perspective; suddenly the user needs to stop what she is doing and focus her attention on a new window that's just appeared. It will also become really tedious if you have a complex form with a few dozen input areas that all need validation.

.NET provides a wonderful little control called an ErrorProvider that can help you out. The ErrorProvider exists solely to display icons and error messages for controls with problems. Load up the code you were just working on and then find the ErrorProvider control in the Toolbox. You can see what it looks like in Figure 8-19.

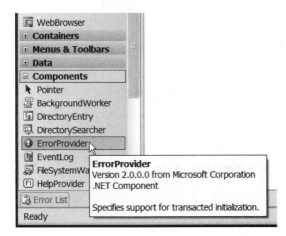

Figure 8-19. *The ErrorProvider gives you a wonderful way to draw a user's attention to problems on a page.*

Double-click the control in the Toolbox to add it to the form. Notice that this is also a nonvisual control; it doesn't actually appear on the form, but instead appears in the nonvisual controls area underneath the form editor.

What happens behind the scenes, of course, is that by double-clicking the ErrorProvider in the Toolbox, you just added a new `ErrorProvider` object into the form's class, just as if you'd written the code by hand yourself.

Drop into the code window now by pressing F7 and find the Validating event handler you wrote in the preceding "Try It Out." What you're going to do here is remove the two `MessageBox` lines and instead use the ErrorProvider to feed error messages back to the user.

Replace both `MessageBox.Show` lines with the following highlighted code:

```
Private Sub numberBox_Validating(ByVal sender As System.Object, _
    ByVal e As System.ComponentModel.CancelEventArgs) _
    Handles numberBox.Validating


    Dim numberEntered As Integer
    If Integer.TryParse(numberBox.Text, numberEntered) Then
        If numberEntered < 1 Or numberEntered > 10 Then
            e.Cancel = True
            ErrorProvider1.SetError(numberBox, _
                "You have to enter a number from 1 to 10")
        End If
    Else
        e.Cancel = True
        ErrorProvider1.SetError(numberBox, _
            "You must enter an integer")
    End If


End Sub
```

As you can see, the ErrorProvider is really quite easy to use. You just need to call `SetError()` and pass in the name of the control with the error, and the error message itself. At runtime, an error icon is displayed next to the offending control along with a pop-up ToolTip when you move the mouse over this icon. You can see this in Figure 8-20.

Figure 8-20. *The ErrorProvider displays an error icon and a ToolTip containing the error message next to a control.*

You really should bear the ErrorProvider in mind when writing your own applications. It's a much better way of providing feedback to users than the somewhat jarring standard of throwing a message box up on-screen for each and every error.

Choosing Things: Radio Buttons and Check Boxes

I'm sure you've seen option dialog boxes in Windows programs that ask you choose to turn certain things on or off, or to select one from a handful of options. Take a look at the Options dialog box from Microsoft Word in Figure 8-21 to see what I mean.

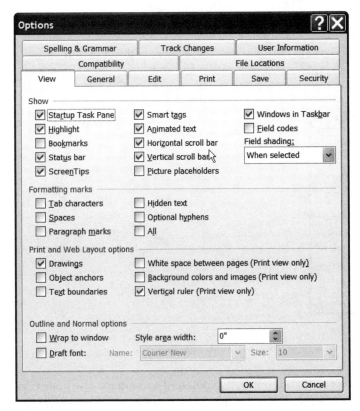

Figure 8-21. *Lots of applications use controls that limit the number of possible things the user can choose.*

Aside from lists and drop-down lists, which I'll cover later in this book, the two most common types of control you'll use for this are the RadioButton and the CheckBox. You can see these in Figure 8-22.

Figure 8-22. *The RadioButton and CheckBox controls limit the number of possible things a user can do or choose.*

Although they look similar, the two controls work in very different ways. The check box (that's the square one) simply forces the user to choose one of two things. Think of it as a switch; it could be on or off, black or white, yes or no, male or female—you get the idea.

The radio button, on the other hand, is mutually exclusive. What that means is that you can select only one radio button from a group. You would use this when you want the user to choose from a very small number of possible things. I recently came across a good example of this on a flight-booking website. Radio buttons were used to force the user to choose the class of ticket: Economy, Business, or First.

There is a catch, though, with radio buttons (isn't there always): they are mutually exclusive *within their container*. Take a look at Figure 8-23.

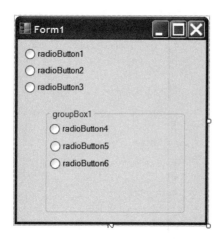

Figure 8-23. *Radio buttons are mutually exclusive within their container.*

Figure 8-23 shows two sets of radio buttons in two different containers. The first set is placed directly on the form, so selecting any of them will instantly deselect any other in that group.

The second set is contained within a group box and works the same way. This means that even though there are six radio buttons in total, they are split into two groups of three, and the user would be free to choose two at once: one from the first group, and one from the second. Go ahead and build this form in VB Express and then run the program to see what I mean.

So, radio buttons and check boxes look similar but work in different ways. At a code level, though, they work the same way, exposing the same events and properties to work with them. At an event level, there really is just one event that you'll be most interested in working with: the CheckedChanged event. It does exactly what it says, firing whenever the user clicks in a control to check or uncheck it.

In terms of properties, the controls support all the standard ones for appearance (Font, Text and so on), but also expose a Checked property. This is a Boolean (True/False) property. If the control is currently checked (selected), the property is True. If it's False, the control isn't checked.

Let's take a look at an example and focus on the RadioButton control.

Try It Out: Radio Buttons

You're going to produce a small form here for a fictitious flight-booking system. The form itself is the window the user will see when asked to confirm the class of ticket required, so you need to write code to figure what the user chose. You'll do it the hard way first.

Start up a new Windows project. Then resize the form in the project and drop some radio buttons and a command button onto it so it looks like mine in Figure 8-24.

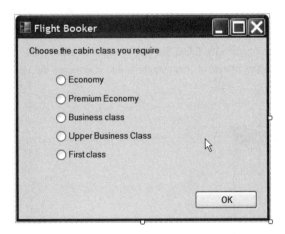

Figure 8-24. *Arrange controls on your application's form so it looks like this.*

You can tell from the screen shot just what the Text properties of all the controls should be. Set the Name of the command button to okButton, and then set the names of the radio buttons to economyRadio, premiumRadio, businessRadio, upperRadio, and firstRadio.

With that out of the way, you can start coding. What I'd like to happen is that when the OK button is clicked, a message box appears confirming the class of ticket the user just selected. As I said a little while ago, you'll do this the hard way first. That way, when I show you an alternate method shortly, you'll appreciate it all the more.

Double-click the OK button to open up the code window and key this in:

```
Private Sub okButton_Click(ByVal sender As System.Object, _
    ByVal e As System.EventArgs) Handles okButton.Click
  Dim ticketClass As String

  If economyRadio.Checked Then
      ticketClass = "Economy class"
  ElseIf premiumRadio.Checked Then
      ticketClass = "Premium economy class"
  ElseIf businessRadio.Checked Then
      ticketClass = "Business class"
  ElseIf upperRadio.Checked Then
      ticketClass = "Upper business class"
  Else
      ticketClass = "First class"
  End If

  MessageBox.Show("You have requested a seat in the " + _
      ticketClass + " section of the aircraft")

End Sub
```

Run the application after you've set up the click event handler. You'll find that you can click a radio button, then the OK button, and see a message telling you just what kind of ticket you ordered. You can see this in Figure 8-25.

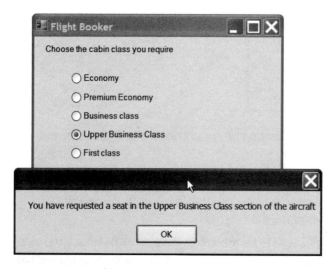

Figure 8-25. *Providing you typed in all the code correctly, this is what the result will look like.*

There's not a huge amount of code to type in there, but you'll probably agree that it doesn't look very elegant, did take you a little while to key in, and is generally just a bit hard to read. This is the way things used to be done prior to .NET's arrival.

The code itself is actually quite simple. It declares a string variable to hold the name of the ticket type the user ordered, and then takes a look at the Checked property of each and every radio control on the form in order to figure out just what should be put into the string variable.

Because .NET supports shared event handlers, the same thing could be achieved with a lot less code, and in a much more readable way. From a coding style point of view, this is a good thing, because lots of code, or hard-to-read code, inevitably leads to bugs.

In the click event handler for the button, delete all the code you just typed in, except for the call to MessageBox.Show(). Then add the string variable back in, but near the top of the class itself to make it a member variable of the class. When you are finished, the class will look like this:

```
Public Class Form1

    Dim ticketClass As String

    Private Sub okButton_Click(ByVal sender As System.Object, _
            ByVal e As System.EventArgs) Handles okButton.Click

        MessageBox.Show("You have requested a seat in the " + _
            ticketClass + " section of the aircraft")

    End Sub
End Class
```

Okay, so this change makes the button's event handler a lot more obvious. It shows a message telling the user the type of ticket he just ordered. You just need to write some code now to set up the variable with the correct type of ticket.

Go back to the form editor by selecting the designer tab at the top of the code window. Just as a memory refresher, it looks like the one in Figure 8-26.

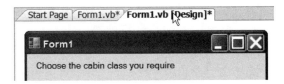

Figure 8-26. *You can switch between the code and design views for a form by using the tabs at the top of the code editor window.*

> ### FEELING LAZY?
>
> There's nothing wrong with being a lazy programmer. Lazy programmers tend to find the best, most efficient ways of doing things simply because they are too lazy to do things the laborious way.
>
> So if you're feeling lazy, try holding down the Ctrl key on your keyboard and then clicking each radio button on the form. You'll find that you can select them all at once this way. You can also then set all the radio button event handlers in one fell swoop, rather than clicking through by hand.
>
> See, it pays to be lazy sometimes.

Click the first radio button, and then using the Properties window, click the lightning bolt to see the list of events for the control. Click in the entry area next to the CheckedChanged property, just once. In other examples, you would have double-clicked this to automatically drop into the code window with an event handler created and named for you by VB 2005 Express. This time around, you're going to give the event handler your own name. Type in TicketTypeChanged.

When you press the Enter key, the code editor will open. As you've probably guessed from the name, this event fires whenever the Checked property of a radio button changes. The important thing to note is that this event fires both when a radio button is selected and when it's deselected—it's not like a Click event on a button, which would fire only when the user explicitly pointed at the control with the mouse and clicked it.

Now, don't bother writing any code into the event handler just yet. Instead, head on back to the designer view and select the next radio button. This time, in the event list click the drop-down arrow beside the CheckedChanged event and select the event handler you just created. Repeat the process for the remaining radio buttons on the form and you'll end up with them all having the same event handler for their CheckedChanged event.

When you've set the radio buttons all up, press F7 to drop into the code window once again.

Take a look at the event handler method you created:

```
Private Sub TicketTypeChanged(ByVal sender As System.Object, _
    ByVal e As System.EventArgs) _
    Handles economyRadio.CheckedChanged, upperRadio.CheckedChanged, _
    premiumRadio.CheckedChanged, firstRadio.CheckedChanged, _
    businessRadio.CheckedChanged


End Sub
```

Notice that you get two parameters passed to the event. The first one is really useful because it is the control that fired the event. You can use this to figure out just why the event fired (was the control deselected or selected). More to the point, you can pull the text out of the control's Text property and use that to set up your ticketClass member variable.

Add code that looks like this to the event handler:

```
Private Sub TicketTypeChanged(ByVal sender As System.Object, _
        ByVal e As System.EventArgs) _
        Handles economyRadio.CheckedChanged, upperRadio.CheckedChanged, _
        premiumRadio.CheckedChanged, firstRadio.CheckedChanged, _
        businessRadio.CheckedChanged

    Dim ticketTypeButton As RadioButton = CType(sender, RadioButton)
    If ticketTypeButton.Checked Then
        ticketClass = ticketTypeButton.Text
    End If

End Sub
```

The first thing this new code does is cast the sender parameter to a RadioButton; you know that it will work because this code gets called only in response to a RadioButton on the form calling it.

After that's done, you can just take a look at the Checked property to see if the event fired because the sender control got selected. If it did, the contents of its Text property are copied into your member variable.

Run the program now and you'll find that it works just as it did a short while ago. The difference, of course, is that now it's a lot smaller and much more readable.

Date Pickers

If you want to work with dates in your user interface, there are two controls that you are going to have to get to grips with: the DateTimePicker control and the MonthCalendar control. Deep down, you need to learn only the MonthCalendar control, because the DateTimePicker is really a text box with a MonthCalendar attached to it. Therefore, we'll focus on the MonthCalendar control here.

The MonthCalendar control is fantastic. You just drag it onto a form in your application and instantly you have a graphical calendar display, as you can see in Figure 8-27.

Figure 8-27. *The MonthCalendar control provides an interactive graphical calendar view.*

If you resize the MonthCalendar control, then rather than stretching the month view, you actually get to see more months, as you'll see shortly in the next "Try It Out."

In terms of formatting, the MonthCalendar control has an extensive set of properties to let you completely customize the way the control works. You can change the colors of the title bar on the control with the TitleBackColor and TitleForeColor properties, and change the colors within the calendar view itself with the standard ForeColor and BackColor properties. Aside from the cosmetics, you can also change how the calendar displays dates by using the properties shown in Table 8-4.

Table 8-4. *The Most Common Properties of the MonthCalendar Control*

Property	Description
ShowToday	Set to True, and the calendar control will display today's date right at the bottom of the calendar itself.
ShowTodayCircle	Set to True, and today's date will also be circled in red within the calendar.
FirstDayOfWeek	This is an enum and can be set to Monday, Tuesday, and so on, to set which day of the week appears as the first day of the week in the calendar view.
MaxDate, MinDate	The maximum and minimum dates that the MonthCalendar control will allow the user to move to.
SelectionRange.Start, SelectionRange.End	Sets up two dates, and the MonthCalendar control then selects all dates between and including those dates.
BoldedDates, AnnualBoldedDates	These properties both take arrays of DateTime objects and set those dates to bold. The AnnualBoldedDates array bolds the dates passed in as you scroll from year to year.

In terms of events, the MonthCalendar control raises all the usual ones (Click, LostFocus, GotFocus, and so on), but also exposes two just for working with dates: DateSelected and DateChanged.

The DateChanged event fires whenever the selected date changes, either by virtue of program code changing it, or the user clicking on a date in the calendar. The DateSelected event, on the other hand, fires only when the user clicks on a date with the mouse.

The DateTimePicker is a much simpler control. In fact, you work with it pretty much like a text box; it's just that at runtime the user gets a drop-down arrow to click on for displaying the calendar, as in Figure 8-28.

Figure 8-28. *The DateTimePicker works just like a text box, but with a down arrow to display and choose from a calendar view.*

You get at the date selected from the calendar through the control's Text property, just as with a text box. Also, you can enter data directly into the text box part of the control and it will automatically check whether the data entered is a date, and then highlight the appropriate date in the drop-down calendar. Additionally, the control does still expose the formatting properties I mentioned earlier to format the view of the drop-down calendar itself.

Anyway, let's take a look at these two controls in a "Try It Out."

Try It Out: Working with the DateTimePicker and MonthCalendar

Start up a new Windows application project and drop a Label, DateTimePicker, Button, and MonthCalendar control onto the form, as in Figure 8-29.

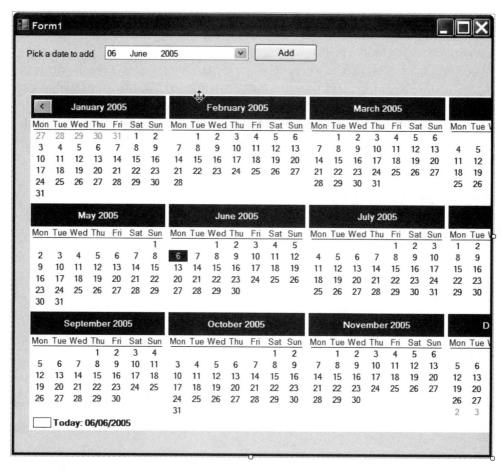

Figure 8-29. *Arrange your controls like this. The MonthCalendar control will initially show just one month, until you resize it to show more.*

What you are going to do with this application is select dates from the picker and display them in bold in the calendar view. Conversely, when the user clicks on a date in the calendar view, you'll have that date shown in the picker automatically.

As usual, to ensure that your code looks the same as mine, you'll need to set the Name properties for the controls. Set the name of the button to addButton, the DateTimePicker to specialDate, and the MonthCalendar to calendar.

Let's write the code first to move a date chosen in the MonthCalendar view into the DateTimePicker. Select the MonthCalendar and then click the lightning bolt at the top of the Properties window to show the events that the control supports. Find the DateSelected event and double-click it to drop into the code editor, ready to write the event handler.

When the user chooses a date in the MonthCalendar view, the event that's raised gets passed a
DateRangeEventArgs object called e. This contains two useful properties: Start and End. These are used
when the user selects a range of dates. We're only interested in one though, so you can just use

e.Start

in your code to get at the date chosen. The problem is that the value Start holds a DateTime value, while
you are going to need a string to set the text property of the DateTimePicker. So, you'll need to call
ToLongDateString() on the Start value to convert the selected date into a string. Confused? It's actually
simple. Go ahead and add code to the event handler so that it looks like the following code:

```
Private Sub calendar_DateSelected(ByVal sender As System.Object, _
        ByVal e As System.Windows.Forms.DateRangeEventArgs) _
        Handles calendar.DateSelected

    specialDate.Text = e.Start.ToLongDateString()

End Sub
```

As you can see, you get Start from the DateRangeEventArgs object, and call ToLongDateString() on
it to convert the selected date into text. The result is stored straight into your DateTimePicker control's Text
property.

Now to set up the other half of the story. When the user selects a date from the DateTimePicker control, you
want the date to show up in bold in the MonthCalendar control. The MonthCalendar control has a property
called BoldedDates, which is an array of DateTime objects. What you need to do is grab that array and add
a new element to it. You can do this quite easily because Visual Basic lets you change the size of an array with
a call to Redim Preserve. Double-click the Add button to drop into the code editor and then add the following code:

```
Private Sub addButton_Click(ByVal sender As System.Object, _
        ByVal e As System.EventArgs) Handles addButton.Click
    Dim boldDates() As System.DateTime
    boldDates = calendar.BoldedDates

    ReDim Preserve boldDates(calendar.BoldedDates.Length + 1)

    boldDates(calendar.BoldedDates.Length + 1) = _
        System.DateTime.Parse(specialDate.Text)

    calendar.BoldedDates = boldDates
End Sub
```

Let's walk through what this does. First, you create an array of `DateTime` objects. Because you don't know how big this array needs to be, no size is specified inside the parentheses.

Next, you copy the `BoldedDates` array from your calendar control into the new array. In order to add a new bolded date, you now need to resize the array. This is done by calling `Redim Preserve`. It actually uses the same format to resize an array as delcaring it. You specify the name of the array, its size, and its type. For the size, you just grab the length of `BoldedDates` and add 1 to it.

Next, you copy the date the user selected from the drop-down into the last element in your array. To do this, though, you need to ask the `DateTime` data type to parse the text the user selected into the right format.

Finally, you copy your new array, complete with new date, back into the `BoldedDates` property on the calendar.

Run the program now. Click a date in the MonthCalendar view to see it in the DateTimePicker. Then choose a new date in the DateTimePicker and click the Add button to see that date appear in bold in the MonthCalendar.

Summary

You covered a lot of ground in this chapter, looking at the most common properties and events of all controls, as well as drilling down into event handling. You also took a look at some of the most common controls you'll use in your apps, including buttons, text boxes, date and time controls, radio buttons, and check boxes. In fact, armed with your knowledge of Visual Basic 2005 Express, you could probably go some way now to developing a simple Windows application on your own.

The journey, though, is far from over. In the next chapter you'll take a look behind the scenes at event handling and I'll equip you for the more complex controls and chapters to come.

CHAPTER 9

■ ■ ■

Windows and Dialogs

In the preceding chapter you covered much of the basics behind building a user interface. You took a look at building a user interface by dropping controls onto a form, and also the common events and properties associated with those controls. Of course, you also took a look beneath the covers at the sort of code you'll need to write to breathe life into your glorious user interfaces.

One element, though, was conspicuous by its absence: the window itself. Nearly all applications you use on a daily basis consist of more than one window. Many will pop open dialog boxes to prompt you for information when you want to load or save a document. Others may have a user interface that consists of many windows. In fact, a great many Microsoft Windows applications even seem to have special code in them that can spot when things happen to the windows themselves, confirming whether you really want to quit, for example, when you click the Close button on a window and things like that.

So, that's the focus of this chapter. You'll learn pretty much everything you'll ever need to know to work with windows and dialogs in an application. You'll see how to open, close, and hide windows in code, how to change the visual style of a window, and even how to put a window inside another window. You'll also explore just how to use and develop dialogs for your applications, and I'll talk you through how to harness the power of Windows' built-in dialogs (the Open, Save, and Print dialogs, for example).

Windows (or Forms)

You probably have noticed by now that I tend to use the word "form" a lot when what I actually seem to mean is "window." It's a hangover from the old days of Visual Basic that just stuck around in the .NET world. The thing that you drop controls onto in the visual designer part of Visual Studio 2005 is a form. At runtime it's a window. Ultimately though, we're talking about exactly the same thing but in different environments: the designer and at runtime.

You've worked through a few examples now of adding controls to windows to build up user interfaces, and it's easy to fall into the trap of thinking that the window or form is really just some dumb container thing that you draw on at design time. There's a lot more to it than that, though. You see, understanding the form, its properties, events, and methods is key to bringing multiple windows, dialogs, and container windows into your applications. In fact, when you take a look at the "Common Dialogs" section, you'll see that Windows itself provides some pretty complex ready-made forms for you to just pick up and go.

Let's start off with the basics.

The Main Window and How to Change It

You've probably noticed by now that when you start a Windows Forms project in Visual Basic 2005 Express, you start with a project that contains a single form. When you run the program in the editor, the window appears, and when you close the window, the application stops running. How come?

In Chapter 8 I gave a quick introduction to how Windows programs work beneath the covers, particularly the event-handling system. If you write a Windows application the old-fashioned way using C or C++, the entire program is controlled by a single loop that watches for new event messages to appear. The loop grabs the message and forwards it onto the window concerned, and you then need to have some fairly nasty-looking code in place to respond to all the different kinds of event messages that you expect the window and its controls to respond to. It's a project setting that controls just which window gets loaded at runtime, and thus which window is the first to receive messages.

PEEKING INSIDE .NET

Passionate programmers, ones who really love to write code and try things out, typically destroyed all their toys as children. We like to know how things work, and invariably enjoyed pulling things apart to see, much to the chagrin of our parents.

You can do the same with .NET, but without the heartache of it ceasing to work after you do. When you hit F5 or click the Run button on the toolbar, the VB compiler comes to life, turning your lines of code into something called Microsoft Intermediate Language (MSIL). The .NET runtime then looks at this MSIL and turns it into something the computer can actually work with in order to run the program.

There is a great tool out there called Reflector, from a guy named Lutz Roeder, that can do the reverse, turning MSIL into C# or even Visual Basic 2005 code. If you want to take a look at exactly what `Application.Run()` really does behind the scenes, download Reflector (http://www.aisto.com/roeder/dotnet/), load up your program, and take a look. This is a great way to take a peek at the inner workings of .NET itself, and of course to learn programming techniques from the talented people at Microsoft.

When you first create a Windows project in Visual Basic 2005 Express, you'll notice in the Solution Explorer a strange item called simply MyProject. Double-clicking this opens up the project properties window, which you can see in Figure 9-1.

Notice the third text box down on the left: Startup Form. If you have more than one form in the project and want a different one to appear (perhaps a form designed as a splash screen welcoming users to your application), all you need to do is select the new form from the drop-down and close the properties page.

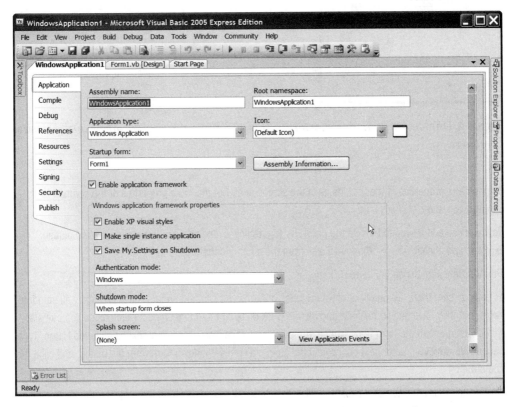

Figure 9-1. *The project properties govern which form starts when you run the program, among other things.*

Opening and Closing Windows

A Form (System.Windows.Forms.Form) is a class. All you need to do to display it is instantiate the class as an object and call the Show() method. What could be easier? Similarly, to close a window, just call the Close() method.

Try It Out: Opening and Closing Windows

Start up a new WinForms project and drop two buttons onto the form that appears, as in Figure 9-2.

Figure 9-2. *Drop two buttons onto the form. These will be used to control opening and closing windows.*

Set the `Text` properties of the buttons as in the screen shot. Set the `Name` properties of the controls to `openButton` and `closeButton`.

Now you can add a second form to the program. Right-click on the name of the project in the Solution Explorer, and choose Add ➤ Windows Form from the submenu that appears.

The Add New Item dialog in Figure 9-3 appears.

As you can see, there are plenty of different types of forms you can add. In fact these are really all standard forms, but they have had some code and design work done on them to make your life easier. You can also specify the name of the form here. Notice at the bottom of the dialog there is a text box labeled Name. Type **SecondWindow.vb** into the text box, select the plain old empty Windows form from the dialog, and click the Add button.

After a short delay, the Solution Explorer will update to show the new form in the project, and the new blank form will also appear in the form editor. Let's go ahead and add a label to this form so that it stands out as your new window. Drop a Label control onto the form as in Figure 9-4.

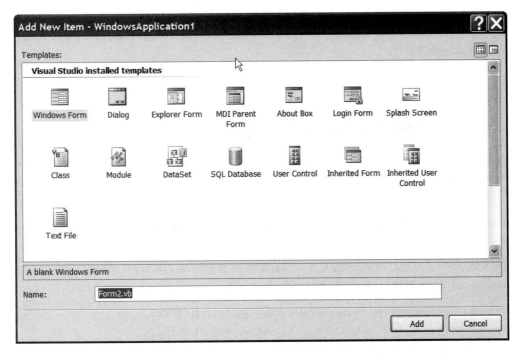

Figure 9-3. *When you choose to add a new item to the project, Visual Basic 2005 Express displays the Add New Item dialog.*

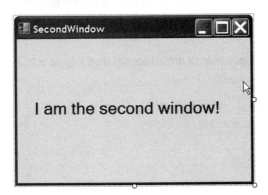

Figure 9-4. *Drop a Label control on the form, and use its Text and Font properties to make it look like this.*

Okay, so now you have two forms in your application, you need to get some code added to those buttons on the first form to work with the second. Use the tabs at the top of the form editor to return to Form1's design mode (see Figure 9-5).

Figure 9-5. *As you add new files to the project, you can move between them by using both the Solution Explorer and the tabs at the top of the designer.*

Double-click the Open Window button to drop into its Click event, and you'll add code to open up your new window.

Because a form is a class, all you need to do is instantiate an object from it. Now you know why we spent so long looking at how to do this earlier in the book.

```
Private Sub openButton_Click(ByVal sender As System.Object, _
    ByVal e As System.EventArgs) Handles openButton.Click
    Dim newWindow As New SecondWindow()
End Sub
```

Notice that the second form's class name is SecondWindow, and the filename in the Solution Explorer is also SecondWindow.vb. When you add a new form to a project and set its name, VB Express is smart enough to set the Name property of the new form to be the same as the filename, which saves you the hassle of setting it yourself.

Instantiating the second form just creates a new window in memory; it doesn't actually show it on-screen. To display it, you need to call a method on your newWindow object:

```
Private Sub openButton_Click(ByVal sender As System.Object, _
    ByVal e As System.EventArgs) Handles openButton.Click
    Dim newWindow As New SecondWindow()
    newWindow.Show()
End Sub
```

Run the program now. When the window comes into view, click the Open Window button to display the second window. There's a bit of a problem with the program currently, though. Click the Open Window button a few times—you may need to rearrange the windows on-screen in order to find it (see Figure 9-6). Each time the Open Window button is clicked, it creates a brand new instance of the second window and displays it. This may be fine for some applications, but it's not at all what we were aiming for.

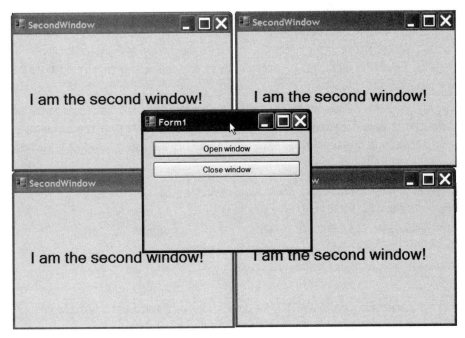

Figure 9-6. *Clicking the OpenWindow button multiple times creates multiple instances of the second window and shows them all.*

What we'd really like to happen is for the Open Window button to create just one instance of the second window. You can do that by making the local newWindow variable in the button's click handler a member of the class, instead of local to the subroutine. Stop the program that is running by closing down all the windows, or clicking the Stop button on the VB Express toolbar, and change the code for the click handler, like this:

```
Public Class Form1

    Dim newWindow As SecondWindow = Nothing


    Private Sub openButton_Click(ByVal sender As System.Object, _
        ByVal e As System.EventArgs) Handles openButton.Click

        If newWindow Is Nothing Then
            newWindow = New SecondWindow()
        End If

        newWindow.Show()
    End Sub
End Class
```

By moving the newWindow variable out of the event handler, it becomes a member variable accessible to all code in your first form. Initially, you set the value of the variable to Nothing, effectively meaning that it's empty and doesn't actually reference a live object. The code in the click handler then just has to check whether the newWindow variable is still Nothing, meaning the second window is not shown yet. If that's the case, a new window is created and shown.

In fact, moving the newWindow variable into the class makes it relatively easy for you to add code now to the Close Window button. Go back to the designer view for Form1 and double-click the Close Window button to open up the code editor for its click handler. Add some code to work with the newWindow variable, like this:

```
Private Sub closeButton_Click(ByVal sender As System.Object, _
    ByVal e As System.EventArgs) Handles closeButton.Click
    If Not newWindow Is Nothing Then
        newWindow.Close()
        newWindow = Nothing
    End If
End Sub
```

If you run the program now, you'll find that clicking the Open Window button produces only one second window. You can also now click the Close Window button to shut the second window.

There's still a problem, though. If you open a second window and then close the window down by hand, by clicking its Close icon at the top right of the window, you can't go ahead and click the Open Window button again; as far as it's concerned, the window is still open.

There are a number of ways around this. You could get the second window to call a method on the first when it closes down, but that's a little complex right now. You could change the window style to prevent the second window from showing a Close Window button at all, but that's a little forceful from a user experience perspective.

A much better solution exists using the Application class. As the name suggests, Application has a bunch of methods and properties that you can use to find out the state of the current application. It has an array property called OpenForms that you can use to get at each and every form the application has opened. You can also just look at its Count property to see how many forms are open. (An alternate way to see which windows are open, for example, is to use a For Each loop over the OpenForms collection.) Go back to the code for the Open Window and Close Window button Click events and change them, like this:

```
Public Class Form1

    Dim newWindow As SecondWindow = Nothing


    Private Sub openButton_Click(ByVal sender As System.Object, _
        ByVal e As System.EventArgs) Handles openButton.Click
```

```vb
        If Application.OpenForms.Count = 1 Then
            newWindow = New SecondWindow()
        End If

        newWindow.Show()
    End Sub

    Private Sub closeButton_Click(ByVal sender As System.Object, _
        ByVal e As System.EventArgs) Handles closeButton.Click

        If Application.OpenForms.Count = 2 Then
            newWindow.Close()
        End If
        newWindow = Nothing
    End Sub
End Class
```

After this change, the Open Window button will work only if there is only one form (the first form) open. Similarly, the Close Window button will work only if there are two windows open (the first and the second). Try the app now, and it works perfectly. You can open a window by using the Open Window button, and close it by either using the Close Window button or by manually closing the window by clicking on its own Close icon. Either way, the Open Window button will still work perfectly (see Figure 9-7).

Figure 9-7. *By checking the Application.OpenForms.Count property, you can ensure that only one second window is ever displayed.*

Of course, the OpenForms array provides a lot more information than just a Count property. You could iterate through it with a For Each command and actually grab each and every form that's opened and interrogate their properties.

Styles

I mentioned in the previous section that you can change the style of a form to remove the standard Close icon on the window. In fact, you can do much more than that. You can remove each of the Close, Maximize, and Minimize icons individually, as well as change the actual border style and title bar style of the window. By doing this, you can also prevent the window from resizing at all. There are even properties to control the maximum and minimum sizes that a user can make a window. If you want to go really nuts, you can even make the window transparent. The properties to do all this are shown in Table 9-1.

Table 9-1. *Properties That Control How the Window Looks at Runtime*

Property	Description
ControlBox	Set to False to remove the Close, Maximize, and Minimize icons from the form.
MaximizeBox	Set to False to disable the Maximize icon from the window.
MinimizeBox	Set to False to disable the Minimize icon from the window.
Opacity	Set to a value between 0 and 100 to control transparency of the window. For example, set the property to 0 and it becomes completely transparent.
MaximumSize	Set MaximumSize.Width and MaximumSize.Height to limit the maximum size a user can resize a window to.
MinimumSize	Set MinimumSize.Width and MinimumSize.Height to limit the smallest size a user can resize a window to.
FormBorderStyle	Select a style from the drop-down list in the Properties window to govern how the border and title bar look. Possible values are None, FixedSingle, Fixed3D, FixedDialog, Sizable, FixedToolWindow, and SizableToolWindow.

The great thing about writing Windows applications with VB Express is that it's such a visual development environment. All of those properties (with the exception of the Opacity property) can be changed at design time and will instantly update the form in the designer. Go ahead and play with them to see what they all do.

For the Opacity property, just start up a new WinForms project, set the Opacity property of the main form in the project to 25, and run the project to see what happens (see Figure 9-8).

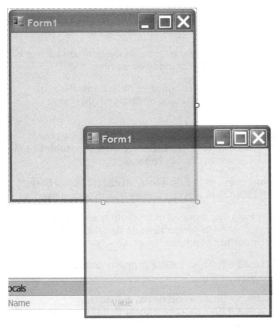

Figure 9-8. *The Opacity property can be used to make forms transparent. This is good for informational dialogs, which I'll cover later in this chapter.*

The Life and Times of a Form

Forms also support a lot of events that you can code up to respond to changes in the form's state. In fact, forms have so many events that it can be hard at times to know just which one you should add code to.

When a form loads up at runtime, the following events fire, in the order shown in Table 9-2.

Table 9-2. *Events That Fire on a Form When It Is First Shown*

Event	Description
Move	This event fires when a form is moved. At start-up, the location of the form is set before anything else happens; hence the event fires.
LocationChanged	As soon as a move is complete and the form has determined where on the screen it lives, the LocationChanged event fires.
StyleChanged	Whenever a form's FormBorderStyle changes, or its control box or Maximize or Minimize icons are enabled or disabled, this event fires.
BindingContextChanged	This is used for data binding, something I cover much later in the book. The event fires whenever the data sources (database tables and so on) that it is supposed to display change.
Load	This used to be the first event to fire on a form in classic Visual Basic. In .NET, though, this event fires directly before a form is displayed.
Layout	After the form is displayed, it may need to reposition any controls it contains (if they are anchored in position, or docked). This event fires before that repositioning happens.
VisibleChanged	This event fires whenever a form's Visible property changes from True to False, or vice versa.
Activated	After the form has been positioned and displayed and has rearranged itself, this event fires to let you know that it is now the current active form.
Shown	This event fires after everything else to let you know that the form is now visible and ready for use.
Paint	This event fires whenever the form, or a control, needs to redraw itself. You would typically put code here to do any custom drawing you need, something I cover later in the book.

When the form closes down, the events in Table 9-3 fire.

Table 9-3. *Events That Fire on a Form When It Closes Down*

Event	Description
MouseCaptureChanged	This means the form is no longer responding to mouse events, and is the first event to fire when it closes. It stops the user from queuing up lots of events to a form that is about to go away.
FormClosing	This event fires just before the form closes down. It can be cancelled, to stop the form closing, by setting e.Cancel to True (e is the name of the second parameter to the event handler).
FormClosed	This event fires after the form successfully closes down.
Deactivate	When the form no longer has focus (the user clicks on a different form, switches application, or closes the form down), this event fires.

That's a lot of events for something so simple as opening and closing a window, I think you'll agree. Incidentally, this sequence isn't documented in the online help and so to confirm it I simply started a new WinForms project and coded up every single event handler. Feel free to do the same if you want to explore the events in more detail; it's a great way to become familiar with all the events that a form offers. Also bear in mind that there are still a great many events not included here that fire on a form, just as they would on a normal control, such as Click and DoubleClick.

The most commonly used of all these events are probably the Load, Paint, FormClosing, and FormClosed events. I'll cover Paint later in the book when we look at drawing and graphics in .NET.

The Load event is used a lot to set up any data that might be needed by the form. In fact, if you eventually decide to move into the world of ASP.NET web development, you'll find that WebForms also have a Load event that gets used for the same thing. A typical example might be loading up data from a database and storing it into member variables in the form class that the controls on the form use, or running some code to do something special with the form's controls that perhaps .NET doesn't support out of the box.

FormClosing and FormClosed, on the other hand, are used to control shutting down of a form. You get a FormClosing event when the user, or program code, tries to shut down a form. This event gives you the opportunity to cancel the form closing, typically by displaying a message box that asks the user whether he is really sure he wants to close the form down, perhaps because there's data on the form that still needs to be saved.

The FormClosed event, on the other hand, is the point of no return for a form. If that event fires, you know for certain that the form is about to shut down. Therefore, most people use that event to contain code that must be run as the last thing the form does before it goes away completely.

Try It Out: Stopping a Form from Closing

Start up a new WinForms project and drop a CheckBox control on the form. Set the Text property of the control as shown in Figure 9-9.

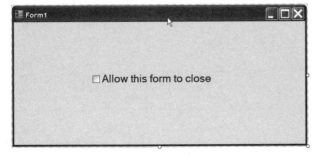

Figure 9-9. *Drop a CheckBox control onto your form and set its Text property as shown.*

Set the Name property of the CheckBox control to letFormCloseButton.

Click on the form itself, and then find the FormClosing event in the Properties window and event browser. You can see the event in Figure 9-10.

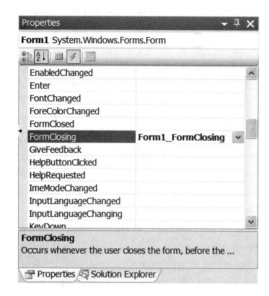

Figure 9-10. *Just as you can with a control, you can browse the full list of events for a form in the Properties window.*

Double-click the entry area next to the event to drop into the code editor. What I want you to do here is check to see whether the check box has been clicked before you allow the form to close down.

Take a look at the event handler code you currently have:

```
Private Sub Form1_FormClosing(ByVal sender As System.Object, _
    ByVal e As System.Windows.Forms.FormClosingEventArgs) _
    Handles MyBase.FormClosing

End Sub
```

The second parameter passed into the handler, e, is of type FormClosingEventArgs. This object has a Boolean property called Cancel. Usually Cancel is set to False, meaning, "Don't cancel this event." However, your code can decide to set it to True. If this happens, the form will stop unloading instantly, effectively cancelling the user's request to close the form down.

Go ahead and add some code to do just that:

```
Private Sub Form1_FormClosing(ByVal sender As System.Object, _
    ByVal e As System.Windows.Forms.FormClosingEventArgs) _
    Handles MyBase.FormClosing

    If Not letFormCloseButton.Checked Then
        e.Cancel = True
    End If

End Sub
```

Run the program now. If you try to close the form by clicking its Close icon, it will steadfastly refuse. Click the check box and try to close the form, and it goes away nicely.

When you take a look at message boxes shortly, you'll see how to actually question users about their decisions graphically.

MDI (Multiple Document Interface)

User interfaces tend to have fashions and phases much like anything else in life. In the mid-90s Multiple Document Interface (MDI) was extremely popular, but today the trend seems to be more toward Outlook-style user interfaces with a single window showing everything but subdivided into moving frames.

Despite that, MDI is still a useful user interface technique. An MDI application has a single parent form that "contains" inner forms. These inner forms typically each hold a document, or some specific piece of information, hence the name Multiple Document Interface. SQL Server's Query Analyzer, for example, still uses MDI for its user interface (see Figure 9-11).

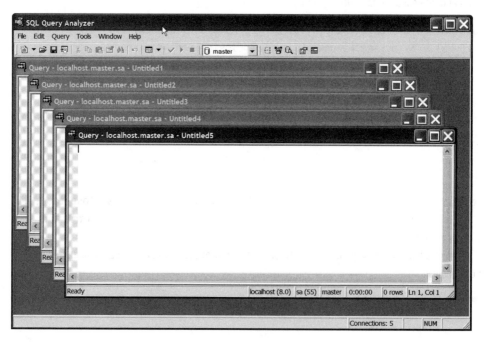

Figure 9-11. *SQL Server is one of the few Microsoft products that still uses MDI for its user interface paradigm.*

The great thing is, if you need to produce this kind of user interface, it's very easy to do with .NET.

Start up a new WinForms project in Visual Basic 2005 Express. When the main form appears, click on it once and look in the Properties window for a property called IsMdiContainer (see Figure 9-12).

Figure 9-12. *Setting a form's IsMdiContainer property to True lets it contain other child forms.*

Set this property to True. You'll notice the form change style—its color will darken and the border will change slightly. This is to show you in the editor that this is now an MDI container form.

Prior to .NET you were limited in which controls you could drop onto an MDI container form. Typically you'd just want a menu bar, toolbar, and status control on the form. However, because we haven't covered those controls just yet, and .NET does let you put other controls onto an MDI container, drop a button on the form, near the top. Call it newWindowButton (see Figure 9-13).

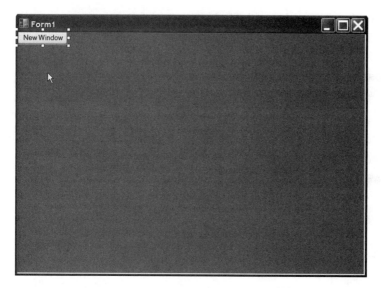

Figure 9-13. *.NET lets you drop controls onto container forms, something that you couldn't do very easily before.*

Now, let's add a child form to the project. Just as you did in the earlier example with more than one form, right-click on the project in the Solution Explorer and use the pop-up menu to add a new form to the project. Call it ChildForm.vb.

When that's done, go back to the MDI form and double-click the button to drop into the code editor for its Click event. What you're going to do is open a form just as you did before, but this time you'll make it an MDI child form. You do that simply by setting a form's MdiParent property to the form that is the parent. Confused? Go ahead and type this code in:

```
Private Sub newWindowButton_Click(ByVal sender As System.Object, _
     ByVal e As System.EventArgs) _
     Handles newWindowButton.Click
    Dim newChild As New ChildForm()
    newChild.MdiParent = Me
    newChild.Show()
End Sub
```

Notice the second line of code there. Because your code is inside the MDI container form, you can just set the `MdiParent` property of the new form to `Me`. Because your code lives inside a form, the keyword `Me` is used to refer to that form.

Run the application now, and click the button in the MDI form a few times (see Figure 9-14).

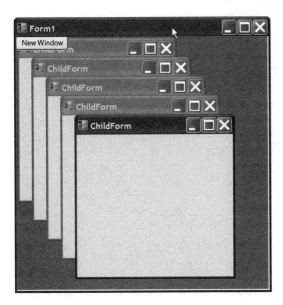

Figure 9-14. *MDI containers "contain" child forms.*

Every new form that opens up is "contained" within the parent. You can't drag the windows outside of the parent form at all. If you keep clicking the button, you'll quickly find that the MDI container becomes a bit of a mess with new windows all over the place. Thankfully, it's very easy to rearrange them through code.

Forms have a method called `LayoutMdi()` that does something useful only when the form in question is an MDI container. The method takes one property, an enum from `MdiLayout` that can be any of `MdiLayout.ArrangeIcons`, `MdiLayout.Cascade`, `MdiLayout.TileHorizontal`, or `MdiLayout.TileVertical`. Let's add a couple more buttons to your MDI container to see `LayoutMdi()` at work.

Drop two more buttons onto the MDI container, and name them `cascadeButton` and `tileButton` (see Figure 9-15).

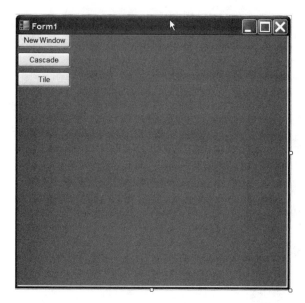

Figure 9-15. *Drop two more buttons onto the MDI container form.*

Double-click the Cascade button and add a line of code to call LayoutMdi():

```
Private Sub cascadeButton_Click(ByVal sender As System.Object, _
      ByVal e As System.EventArgs) _
      Handles cascadeButton.Click
    Me.LayoutMdi(MdiLayout.Cascade)
End Sub
```

Now go back to the editor and double-click the Tile button to drop into its click event handler and add a similar line of code:

```
Private Sub tileButton_Click(ByVal sender As System.Object, _
      ByVal e As System.EventArgs) _
      Handles tileButton.Click
    Me.LayoutMdi(MdiLayout.TileHorizontal)
End Sub
```

In both cases, all you need to do is call LayoutMdi() and pass in the appropriate value. Run the application now, create a few child windows, and try out the two new layout buttons (see Figure 9-16).

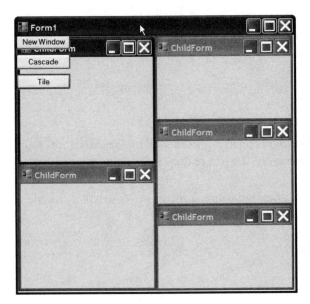

Figure 9-16. *Arranging MDI child windows is as easy as calling this.LayoutMdi().*

Dialogs

There is another kind of window that you haven't explored yet, but you have used it in a number of examples: the dialog box. A *dialog* is a special window that pops up to provide information to, or get information from, the user. It's special in that it's *modal*: when a dialog is on-screen, you can't interact with any other window in the application until the dialog has gone away. You've used a few of them in the examples, courtesy of the MessageBox class.

Using a Simple Message Box

A MessageBox control is perhaps the simplest of all possible dialogs in a Windows application, and it's provided for you through the .NET MessageBox class. As you've already seen a few times, all you need to do is type

```
MessageBox.Show("Your message goes here")
```

and a message box dialog will appear on-screen at runtime with whatever text you specify. There are actually quite a few overloads of the MessageBox.Show() method call that allow you to specify not just the message to display, but also the caption of the dialog, what buttons to display inside it, and what icon to display next to the text. MessageBox.Show() will even return a value to you that you can check to see exactly which button the user clicked to make the dialog go away.

Probably the most common overload of the MessageBox.Show() method looks like this:

```
MessageBox.Show(<message>,<dialog caption>, <buttons>, <icon>)
```

The first two parameters are both strings. The first is the actual message that you want to show in the message box, and the second is the text to display in the title bar of the dialog.

The buttons parameter is another enumerated value, from MessageBoxButtons. It can be one of the following values:

- MessageBoxButtons.AbortRetryIgnore

- MessageBoxButtons.Ok

- MessageBoxButtons.OkCancel

- MessageBoxButtons.RetryCancel

- MessageBoxButtons.YesNo

- MessageBoxButtons.YesNoCancel

Obviously, these all refer to the number of buttons to display and the text within them. Similarly, the icon is specified as an enumerated value from MessageBoxIcon, and can be one of MessageBoxIcon.Asterisk, MessageBoxIcon.Error, MessageBoxIcon.Exclamation, MessageBoxIcon.Hand, MessageBoxIcon.Information, MessageBoxIcon.None, MessageBoxIcon._Question, MessageBoxIcon.Stop, or MessageBoxIcon.Warning.

As if all those enumerated values aren't enough to make your head spin, the Show() method will also return an enumerated value from DialogResult. The values here correspond to the name of the button that was pressed—for example, DialogResult.OK, DialogResult.Retry, DialogResult.Cancel, and so on.

Try It Out: Using a Message Box Properly

Earlier in the chapter, I mentioned using a message box to cancel a form closing down. That's exactly what you are going to do now.

Create a new WinForms project and drop into the code editor for the form's FormClosing event handler. What I'd like you to do is put up a message box that asks the user whether she really wants to quit, and that displays Yes and No buttons. This is quite easy to do. Go ahead and add some code:

```
Private Sub Form1_FormClosing(ByVal sender As System.Object, _
      ByVal e As System.Windows.Forms.FormClosingEventArgs) _
      Handles MyBase.FormClosing

    MessageBox.Show("Are you sure you want to close the form down?", _
        "Really quit?", MessageBoxButtons.YesNo, _
        MessageBoxIcon.Question)

End Sub
```

The call here just displays the question, sets the title of the message box to "Really quit?" and specifies that you want Yes and No buttons, and a Question icon in the message box.

The next thing you need to do, though, is figure out what the user actually pressed. `MessageBox.Show()` returns a value of type `DialogResult`, so you'll need a variable here of the same type to catch the return value:

```
Private Sub Form1_FormClosing(ByVal sender As System.Object,_
      ByVal e As System.Windows.Forms.FormClosingEventArgs)_
      Handles MyBase.FormClosing

    Dim result As DialogResult
    result = MessageBox.Show(_
     "Are you sure you want to close the form down?",_
       "Really quit?", MessageBoxButtons.Yesno,_

    End Sub
```

All that remains is to check the result value, and if the user pressed the No button, meaning "No, I don't want to close the form down," you can set e.Cancel to True to cancel the closing:

```
Private Sub Form1_FormClosing(ByVal sender As System.Object, _
        ByVal e As System.Windows.Forms.FormClosingEventArgs) _
        Handles MyBase.FormClosing

    Dim result As DialogResult
    result = MessageBox.Show("Are you sure you want to close the form
down?", _
            "Really quit?", MessageBoxButtons.YesNo, _
            MessageBoxIcon.Question)

    If result = Windows.Forms.DialogResult.No Then
        e.Cancel = True
    End If

End Sub
```

That's all there is to it. Run the application now and try to close the form and you'll see the message box exactly as you specified it (see Figure 9-17). If you click Yes, the form closes; if you click No, it doesn't.

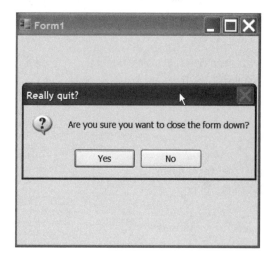

Figure 9-17. *Message boxes like this are typically used to get important information quickly from the user.*

Feel free to play with the various Messagebox.Show() options, and we'll catch up in the next section.

Creating Your Own Dialog Box

Message boxes are undeniably handy, unless you need to display a custom dialog of exactly your own design. Think back to the Microsoft Word Options dialog from the previous chapter for a minute (see Figure 9-18).

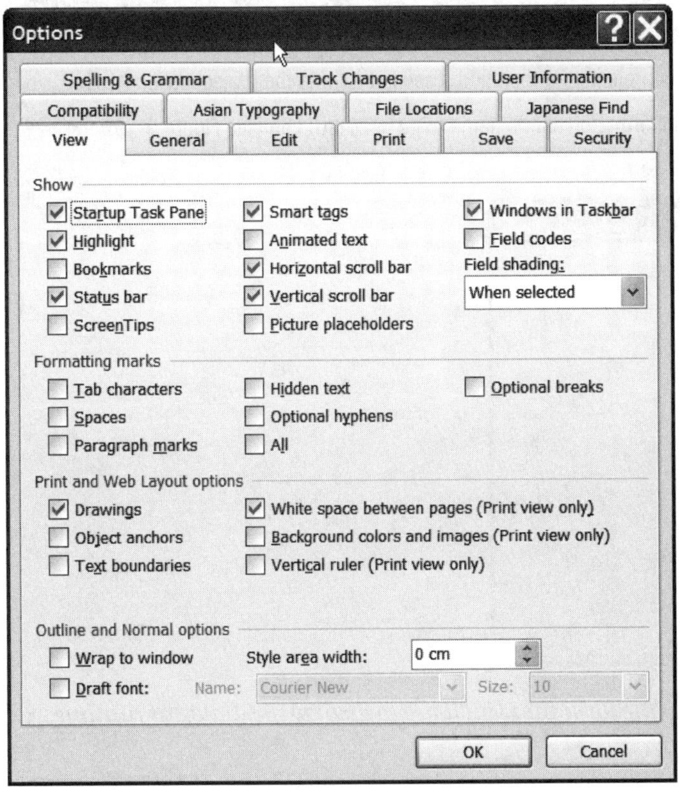

Figure 9-18. *The Word Options dialog*

There's no way you are going to be able to achieve all that with a standard message box. You can, however, turn a standard form into a dialog by using almost no code.

First of all, every form has a ShowDialog() method that shows the form modally (remember, a modal form is one that must be closed before any other in the application can be interacted with). In addition, all forms have a DialogResult property that you can set with a DialogResult value. ShowDialog() will return this to you so you can see what the user did with the dialog. In addition though, buttons also have a DialogResult property, which you can set at design time. If the button is clicked at runtime, the form is hidden (not deleted), and its DialogResult value is set into the form's DialogResult value.

Best of all, don't forget that when you display a form you are effectively working with an object, an object that can expose properties like any other object. What this means is that you can query those properties after the call to ShowDialog() to get key values from the form. This is all best shown with a "Try it Out."

Try It Out: Implementing Your Own Custom Dialog

Once again, create a new WinForms project, and then add a second form to the project called Dialog.vb. Drop a button onto Form1 (the main form) and set its name to getNameButton (see Figure 9-19).

Figure 9-19. *Drop a button onto the form that you'll use to display the dialog at runtime.*

Now go back to the designer for the new dialog form. Drop some buttons, a text box, and a label onto the form. Set the captions as in Figure 9-20 and name the text box nameBox (you don't need to worry about setting up the Name properties for the buttons because you won't need any code in them).

Figure 9-20. *Design your dialog like this. Don't worry about giving the OK and Cancel buttons decent names, because they won't need any code.*

Next, press F7 to drop into the code for the form, and add a single property to the form, like this:

```
Public Class Dialog
    ReadOnly Property UserName() As String
        Get
            Return nameBox.Text
        End Get
    End Property
End Class
```

It's a simple enough property that just grabs the value out of the text box at runtime and returns it.

Go back into the designer view for the dialog now and you'll set up the buttons to work as dialog buttons are supposed to.

First, click on the form and find the `AcceptButton` property. This property tells the form which button acts as an OK button and is automatically triggered when the user presses the Enter key on the keyboard. Set it to the OK button. Now find the `CancelButton` property. This tells the form which button to press when the user presses Esc on the keyboard, just as the user would to quickly get rid of a dialog. Set the `CancelButton` property to the Cancel button on the form.

Click the OK button now and take a look at its properties. You'll find a property called `DialogResult`. If you click on the drop-down in the property entry area, you'll see all the dialog result values, as in Figure 9-21.

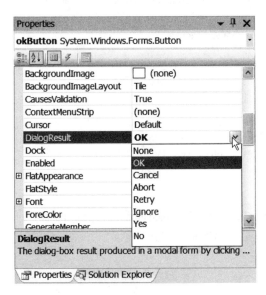

Figure 9-21. *You can set the DialogResult property of a button to any of theDialogResult-enumerated values.*

Set it to OK. Next, select the Cancel button and set its DialogResult property to Cancel in the same way.

That's all there is to it; your dialog is now complete with the only code you had to write being a short bit to expose a property. Time now to code up the main form to run the dialog and do something with it.

Go back to the main form's designer and double-click the button you dropped on it earlier to go into the code editor for its Click event.

All you want to do here is display your dialog and then have it do something only if the user clicks OK in it. That's easy to do:

```
Public Class Form1


    Private Sub getNameButton_Click(ByVal sender As System.Object, _
        ByVal e As System.EventArgs) Handles getNameButton.Click
        Dim nameDialog As New Dialog()


        If nameDialog.ShowDialog = Windows.Forms.DialogResult.OK Then


        End If
    End Sub
End Class
```

As always, the first thing you need to do is create an instance of the form. With that done, you can call ShowDialog() to see whether the result is DialogResult.OK. Let's add one more line of code now to grab the text the user entered into the dialog from the property that you exposed:

```
    Private Sub getNameButton_Click(ByVal sender As System.Object, _
        ByVal e As System.EventArgs) Handles getNameButton.Click
        Dim nameDialog As New Dialog()


        If nameDialog.ShowDialog = Windows.Forms.DialogResult.OK Then
            MessageBox.Show("This .NET stuff could really catch on!")
        End If
    End Sub
```

Run the program now. When the main form appears, click the button. The dialog form will appear, modally. Try clicking back on the main form while the dialog is on display to confirm that you can't.

Enter some text now into the text box on the dialog and hit the Enter key, or click the OK button when you are finished. Notice how even though you didn't write any code to close or hide the dialog, it automatically goes away when you do this. That's because the OK button has a `DialogResult` value, and .NET automatically knows that it needs to respond to this button being clicked by closing the form.

The result of the code is that you are returned to the main form and message box, telling you the text that you entered into the dialog (see Figure 9-22).

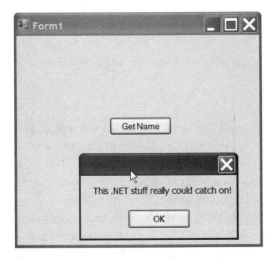

Figure 9-22. *This is what you should see if everything went right.*

Common Dialogs

You may have noticed that nearly all Windows applications use the same dialogs. For example, when you go to open a file, you see a file Open dialog that always look the same. Similarly, if you are using a program that lets you choose colors or fonts, the dialogs to let you make the choices are identical from program to program. Before I learned how to develop Windows applications, I naively assumed that developers had to go to great lengths to make their dialogs always look and behave the same way. Instead, those dialogs are part of Windows itself and are available to you within VB Express as handy controls. You can find them all in the Dialogs section of the Toolbox (see Figure 9-23).

Figure 9-23. *The common Windows dialogs are all grouped together in the Dialogs section of the Toolbox.*

As you might expect by now, they all work exactly the same way as any other dialog (custom or message box). You call ShowDialog() to open up the dialogs at runtime, and then check the result to see whether the user clicked the OK or Cancel buttons. The only differences between the common dialogs from a code point of view are the properties that they expose. The OpenFileDialog and SaveFileDialog controls, for example, expose a property called FileName that is the name of the file the user chose. Both those controls also expose a Filter property that you can use to limit the files that the user sees in the dialogs. For example, if I wanted my user to be able to see .txt files and everything else, I'd set the filter to Text Files|*.txt|All Files|*.*. This means display text files to the user, but filter what the user sees to files ending in .txt. The file dialog displays a File Type drop-down that will also show All Files, which will show all files in the dialog.

The Color dialog, on the other hand, exposes a Color property that can be used to set any other color property you may want. Similarly, the Font dialog contains a Font property.

Let's take a look with the last "Try It Out" of this chapter.

Try It Out: Working with the Common Dialogs

Start up a new Windows application and drop a label and three buttons on the form, as in Figure 9-24.

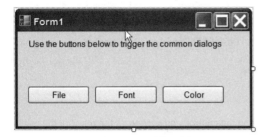

Figure 9-24. *Arrange your controls like this.*

Next, drop OpenFileDialog, FontDialog, and ColorDialog controls onto the form. Notice that instead of appearing on the form, they appear underneath it (see Figure 9-25). These aren't actually visible controls; you need to call code on them to show the dialogs at runtime.

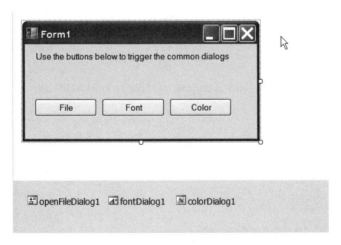

Figure 9-25. *When you drop a common dialog control onto a form, it appears in the area underneath the form.*

Double-click the File button you put on the form, and add some code to show the dialog and display the name of the file the user selected:

```
Private Sub Button1_Click(ByVal sender As System.Object, _
        ByVal e As System.EventArgs) Handles Button1.Click

    If OpenFileDialog1.ShowDialog() = Windows.Forms.DialogResult.OK Then
        MessageBox.Show("You chose " + OpenFileDialog1.FileName)
    End If

End Sub
```

Straightforward enough, isn't it. You call ShowDialog() on the control, and so long as the result of the call is that the OK button was pressed, you display the name of the file selected in a message box.

Code up the Font button now (go back to the designer and then double-click the Font button):

```
Private Sub Button2_Click(ByVal sender As System.Object, _
        ByVal e As System.EventArgs) Handles Button2.Click

    If FontDialog1.ShowDialog() = Windows.Forms.DialogResult.OK Then
        Label1.Font = FontDialog1.Font
    End If

End Sub
```

The code is almost identical, except this time if the OK button is pressed, you take the font that the user selected and set the label's font to the same thing.

Finally, code up the click handler for the Color button:

```
Private Sub Button3_Click(ByVal sender As System.Object, _
    ByVal e As System.EventArgs) Handles Button3.Click

    If ColorDialog1.ShowDialog() = Windows.Forms.DialogResult.OK Then
        Me.BackColor = ColorDialog1.Color
    End If

End Sub
```

That's it. Run the program now to see the dialogs in action (see Figure 9-26).

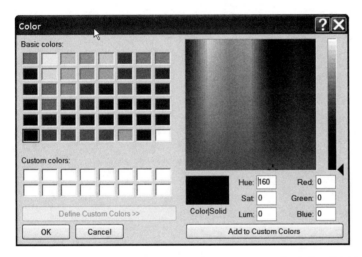

Figure 9-26. *The common Color dialog in action—look familiar?*

Summary

Well, we certainly covered a lot of ground in this chapter. It's so easy when you start out with Windows programming to take the humble window for granted, but as you've seen here there's a whole lot more to it than meets the eye. In fact, there's a lot more to it than I could cover here (the idea is to get you up to speed coding, after all, and not to publish the world's first 10,000-page .NET encyclopedia). Take a look at the online help for the form to see the full list of all its properties, methods, and events, and of course have fun experimenting with the samples in this chapter to further explore the wonderful world of forms and dialogs.

CHAPTER 10

■ ■ ■

Lists

So far you've looked at the most common (and simplest) controls that you're likely to use in your programs. You've also explored the capabilities of the form and dialog boxes. Now it's time to move on to some more-complex controls, namely the list controls.

The *list controls* (there are five in total, not including the grid, which you'll look at in Chapter 16) give you a means to display large amounts of data to the user, and give the user a way to select items of data for your code to work with. All of the controls we'll cover here (the ListBox, ComboBox, CheckedListBox, and TreeView) do pretty much the same thing. They let you display a single item of data in a list—for example, the names of all the files in a certain directory, DVDs in your DVD collection, employees in your company, and so on. As you work through the controls, though, you'll also notice that each adds capabilities to the basic ListBox control.

A CheckedListBox, for example, displays a list of items but with check boxes beside them to provide an easy way for users to select multiple items. A TreeView, on the other hand, takes the basic concept of a list and then makes it hierarchical, so that list items can contain other list items, much like a table of contents in a book, where each chapter contains sections, and the sections may in turn contain subsections.

By the end of this chapter, you'll be even further down the road to being able to develop some fairly complex WinForms user interfaces without any help.

So, let's go.

The ListBox Control

As the name suggests, the *ListBox control* displays a simple list of items within a box. It's used a lot in many Windows applications, so I'm sure you've come across it before. To jog your memory, take a look at Figure 10-1.

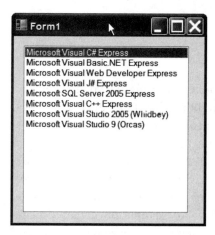

Figure 10-1. *A simple ListBox control*

As the number of items in the list grows, a scroll bar appears down the right side of the control to let the user easily move through the items in the list. The size and position of the actual bar within the scroll bar also gives a good indication of just how big the list is. If it's a very small bar, the list is likely to be quite large. If on the other hand the bar is quite large, the list is going to be quite small. (You can see this in Figure 10-2.)

The ListBox control exposes a property called Items that you can use to add items to the list. You can use this property either through code, or even in the Properties window. In the form editor, just drop a ListBox on a form, and then find the Items property and click on the ellipsis button (…) in the property's input area to open the String Collection Editor dialog in Figure 10-3.

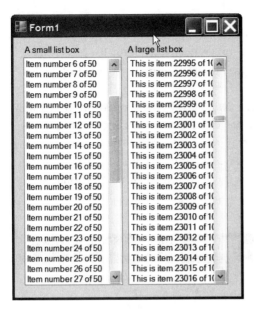

Figure 10-2. *The size of the drag bar in the scroll bar gives a good indication of the number of items in the list, as well as where you are in moving through it.*

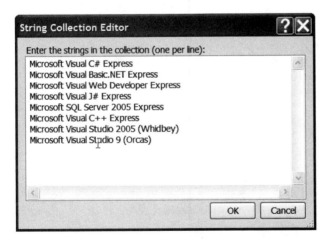

Figure 10-3. *Clicking the ellipsis button next to the Items property in the Properties window opens up this editor to add items to the list at design time.*

You can also get at this editor by using the smart tag attached to the list box. Just click on the tag and then click Edit Items from the menu that appears.

The String Collection Editor dialog is great if you know just what the list box contains ahead of time, but more often than not you'll want to programmatically control the list contents at runtime.

The Items property is actually a Collection, a .NET class that goes beyond what a standard Visual Basic array can do. With a Collection you can easily add and remove items, something that's tricky to do with a standard array, and even provide methods for sorting and searching within the collection. You'll look at collections in some detail later in the book, but for now let's cover the basics as they apply to working with the various list controls.

Try It Out: Adding Items to the ListBox.Items Collection

Start up a new WinForms project and add a list box, label, text box, and button to the form as shown in Figure 10-4.

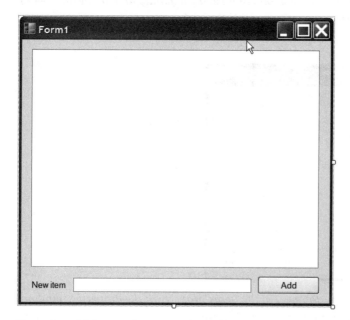

Figure 10-4. *Add controls to your form, like this.*

Try resizing the list box vertically, and you'll find that you are somewhat limited. By default, the list box will accept only a horizontal size that allows it to show complete items. For example, there's a possibility you would set a size that at runtime would mean the bottom item on the list is cut in half. You can get around this limitation by setting the IntegralHeight property of the ListBox to False. This allows you to set any height you want.

Set the Name property of the TextBox to newItemBox, of the Button to addButton, and of the List to demoListBox. I'm sure you can guess what you are going to do here. The user will enter text into the text box, and then click the button to add the text to the list box.

Double-click the button to drop into the code editor, and change the method to look like this (I'll talk you through it when you're finished):

```
Public Class Form1

    Private Sub addButton_Click(ByVal sender As System.Object, _
        ByVal e As System.EventArgs) Handles addButton.Click

        demoListBox.Items.Add(newItemBox.Text)
        newItemBox.Text = ""

    End Sub
End Class
```

As I mentioned earlier, the Items property on the ListBox is something called a Collection. Collections have an Add() method on them to add new items into the collection. In the case of ListBox.Items, this translates to adding an item into the list box. So, the code just takes the string of text entered into the text box and adds it into the Items collection. When that's done, the text box is cleared out, ready for the next piece of text to be entered.

Go ahead and run the program now to see how it works (see Figure 10-5).

Figure 10-5. *Click the Add button to add the text from the text box into the Items collection of the ListBox.*

Easy, isn't it?

Okay, so now you can add items to a list box. What about deleting items, though, or working with the items themselves in code to find out what's in the list box?

Working with the items in the list box is very much like working with items in an array. A container exposes elements inside the container in the same way that an array does. So, for example, if you needed to get at the third item in the list box in code, you might write the following:

```
Dim thirdItem As String = myListBox.Items(2)
```

Notice that just like an array, the elements are zero based, meaning the first element is number 0, the second is number 1, and so on.

You can find out just how many items are in a list box by looking at the Items.Count property. For example:

```
Dim itemsInList As Integer = myListBox.Items.Count
```

Also, just as with an array, you can use a For Each statement to iterate through all the items in the list box. For example:

```
For Each currentItem As String In myListBox.Items
    Console.WriteLine(currentItem)
Next
```

There are two methods available to you if you want to remove items from the list. The first is `Items.RemoveAt()`. This requires that you know the position of the item you want to delete, something you can find out through the selection properties of the list box (more on those in a minute as well). You simply use

```
myListbox.Items.RemoveAt(4)
```

for example, to remove the fifth item (remember, the list is zero based). The second method is `Items.Remove()`. This requires you to have an object the same as the one you want to delete. For example, if your list contained only strings and you knew that one of them was the word `listbox`, you could use the following:

```
myListbox.Items.Remove("listbox")
```

It gets a little more complicated if you have objects in the list other than simple strings, but more often than not you'll remove by index with the `RemoveAt()` method. Let's see how that works, and also take a look at selecting items in a list box and putting more than just strings into it.

Let's round out the discussion on the ListBox control with a nice meaty example that also builds on the dialog stuff you did in the preceding chapter. What you'll do is use a dialog to gather simple employee information, and then populate a list box with the employees the user enters. In addition, you'll display that employee information when the user clicks on an item in the list box, and also handle deleting of employees.

This will be an unusually big "Try It Out," the reason being that most of the other list controls work in a similar fashion. In effect then, we're killing a lot of birds with one stone (apologies to the ornithologists out there).

Try It Out: Adding Other Objects to a List, Selecting, and Deleting

Start up a new WinForms project and then add a new class to the project called `Employee.vb`. The first thing you'll do is create a simple `Employee` class to hold information about the employees in the company. Double-click the class to open up the code editor and then add three fields and a `ToString()` method to the class:

```
Public Class Employee
    Public FirstName As String
    Public LastName As String
    Public JobTitle As String

    Public Overrides Function ToString() As String
        Return LastName + ", " + FirstName
    End Function
End Class
```

Remember back when we were looking at objects and Visual Basic, I mentioned that all classes are actually subclasses of System.Object? Well, System.Object implements a ToString() method, so that in turn means that every single class you'll ever use also has a ToString() method. In this code you are overriding the base implementation of ToString() with your own one specific to the Employee class so that at runtime if anyone calls ToString() on an Employee object, they'll get something meaningful returned.

Normally I wouldn't bother implementing ToString() on my own classes. But, the ListBox control uses it. You see, you can add any kind of object you like to the ListBox.Items collection. At runtime, when the list needs to be displayed, the code inside the ListBox control calls ToString() on every object in the Items collection and displays the results. Usually when we just add strings to the collection, ToString() just returns the value of the string, and so it appears that ListBoxes just hold text. As you'll see, though, the ability to add any object to a ListBox makes it a very versatile beast indeed.

Next, you'll need to create a dialog in order to add or edit employees. You'll use one dialog for both functions, which is a lot less complicated than it might sound if you are an ex-VBer.

Add a new form to the project called EditDialog.vb. When the form appears in the designer, drop a few controls on it, just as in Figure 10-6.

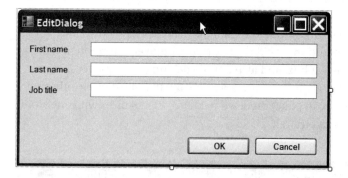

Figure 10-6. *Drop some controls onto the form to make a generic add and edit employee dialog.*

You'll need to set up quite a few properties on these controls so that the dialog works as a dialog, and so that your code matches mine. Set up the properties as shown in Table 10-1.

Table 10-1. *Properties of the Controls on the Dialog*

Control	Property	Value
First Name label	Text	First name
Last Name label	Text	Last name
Job Title label	Text	Job title
First Name text box	Name	firstName
Last Name text box	Name	lastName

Control	Property	Value
Job Title text box	Name	jobTitle
OK button	Name	okButton
	Text	OK
	DialogResult	OK
Cancel button	Name	quitButton
	Text	Cancel
	DialogResult	Cancel
Form	AcceptButton	okButton
	CancelButton	quitButton

From a user interface (UI) point of view, that's all you need. The buttons have their DialogResult properties set so that the form can work and behave just as a dialog should, and you have entry areas for the three main properties of the Employee class. The next step is to write some code behind this form.

Here's the strange bit. Because this is a dialog and will be used just for data entry, you don't need to code up any events at all to get this form working properly at runtime. What you do need, though, is a way to get an Employee object into and out of the form at runtime, in order to set up the form for an edit and retrieve the data the user entered. Hit F7 to drop into the code view, but outside of any event handler.

The first thing you are going to need is a private member to hold the employee object that the dialog is working on:

```
Public Class EditDialog
    Private _employee As Employee = Nothing
End Class
```

The next thing you are going to need is a public Employee property so that other code using the dialog can get at the employee data:

```
Public Class EditDialog
    Private _employee As Employee = Nothing
    Public Property StaffMember() As Employee
        Get

        End Get
        Set(ByVal value As Employee)

        End Set
    End Property
End Class
```

So far, so good. Let's code up the Set part of the property first, because that's the easiest. Other code using this dialog will set the StaffMember property only if the dialog is to be used to edit that data. Think about that for a second. If you were adding a new staff member, you wouldn't want to pass in any employee information because the whole purpose of using the dialog would be to get that new employee information from the user. If, on the other hand, you wanted to use the dialog to update an employee's information, it makes sense that you'd pass the employee in question into the dialog, by setting the StaffMember property to a valid Employee object:

```
Public Class EditDialog
    Private _employee As Employee = Nothing
    Public Property StaffMember() As Employee
        Get

        End Get
        Set(ByVal value As Employee)
            _employee = value
            firstName.Text = _employee.FirstName
            lastName.Text = _employee.LastName
            jobTitle.Text = _employee.JobTitle
        End Set
    End Property
End Class
```

So, when an Employee object is passed into the dialog, you'll store it in your member variable, and also set the values from the object into the three text boxes on the dialog, ready for the user to edit.

The Get code for the property is a little more complex, but not much. Because the form can be used to get new employee information as well as to edit an existing employee, the Get code needs to check first whether the dialog is aware of an Employee object already:

```
Public Class EditDialog
    Private _employee As Employee = Nothing
    Public Property StaffMember() As Employee
        Get
            If _employee Is Nothing Then
                _employee = New Employee()
            End If
        End Get
        Set(ByVal value As Employee)
            _employee = value
            firstName.Text = _employee.FirstName
            lastName.Text = _employee.LastName
            jobTitle.Text = _employee.JobTitle
        End Set
    End Property
End Class
```

So, if the _employee member variable in the dialog is Nothing, meaning you are adding a new employee, you'll go ahead and create a brand new Employee object. All that remains then, in both add and edit cases, is to copy the values from the dialog's text boxes into the fields of the Employee object and return it:

```
Public Class EditDialog
    Private _employee As Employee = Nothing
    Public Property StaffMember() As Employee
        Get
            If _employee Is Nothing Then
                _employee = New Employee()
            End If

            _employee.FirstName = firstName.Text
            _employee.LastName = lastName.Text
            _employee.JobTitle = jobTitle.Text

            Return _employee

        End Get
        Set(ByVal value As Employee)
            _employee = value
            firstName.Text = _employee.FirstName
            lastName.Text = _employee.LastName
            jobTitle.Text = _employee.JobTitle
        End Set
    End Property
End Class
```

That's all the work you need to do on the dialog. I know that we have spent quite a bit of time here working on a dialog that on the surface has nothing to do with a list box, but you'll find that you'll develop a lot of very similar dialogs if you have lists in your applications that you want your users to be able to edit and add to. The key point here is that the dialog itself contains no real code. All it has is a property to hold the data that the dialog is working with. The rest of the work is handled by simply setting the control's properties on the form.

Before you move on to developing the list box form that will drive the entire application, just take stock of where you are. You have an Employee class that holds basic information about an employee but that also includes a ToString() method, which of course means you can actually add Employee objects to a list box directly. Also, you have a dialog to work with that data, to handle getting information about a new employee as well as to update existing employee information. All you need to do is work with the StaffMember property on the dialog.

Double-click Form1.vb in the Solution Explorer to bring up the main form in the designer window. Drop some controls onto the form so that it looks like Figure 10-7.

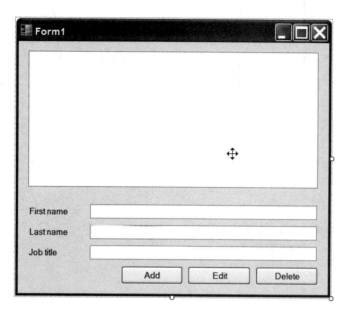

Figure 10-7. *Drop controls onto the main form to hold the list, display information about an employee, and handle adding, editing, and deleting employees.*

Once again you'll need to set up some properties on these controls. Pay special attention to the text boxes as well. You are going to use these to display information about any employee selected in the list box, but not to enter data. For that reason you need to disable the text boxes to prevent the user from entering information into them. Set up the properties as shown in Table 10-2.

Table 10-2. *Properties of the Controls on the Main Form*

Control	Property	Value
List box	Name	employeeList
First Name text box	Name Enabled	firstName False
Last Name text box	Name Enabled	lastName False
Job Title text box	Name Enabled	jobTitle False
Add button	Name Text	addButton Add
Edit button	Name Text	editButton Edit
Delete button	Name Text	deleteButton Delete

You'll write code here in such a way that you can keep running the application to test it out after you add each method. I'm not going to explicitly tell you to run the application, though, so use your own judgment as to when would be a good time, and when wouldn't.

First, let's write the code to add a new item to the list box. Double-click the Add button to drop into its click event handler. All you need to do here is show the dialog and then add the new employee object it creates into the list box:

```
Public Class Form1

    Private Sub addButton_Click(ByVal sender As System.Object, _
        ByVal e As System.EventArgs) Handles addButton.Click

        Dim newEmployeeDialog As New EditDialog()
        If newEmployeeDialog.ShowDialog() = Windows.Forms.DialogResult.OK Then
            employeeList.Items.Add(newEmployeeDialog.StaffMember)
        End If

    End Sub
End Class
```

Quite simple, isn't it. First you create a new instance of the dialog, and then you call ShowDialog() on it to display the employee dialog modally (that is, you must finish work on the dialog before you can continue to use the controls on the main form). If the user clicks OK in the dialog, you assume that the user is happy with the data entered and so you add the dialog's StaffMember property value (a new Employee object) into the list box. The result, of course, is that the new employee appears in the list.

Let's look at deleting an item from the list now. To delete an item from the list, you need to find out which item is selected. There are two properties on the ListBox control that you can use to do this: SelectedItem and SelectedIndex. SelectedIndex will give you the index number of the item selected. So, if the user has clicked the first item in the list box, the SelectedIndex property will return a value of 0. If on the other hand the employee hasn't selected anything, the SelectedIndex property will return -1.

Go back to the form editor view and double-click the Delete button to drop into its click handler. The first thing you need to do is make sure that the user has actually selected something. If the user hasn't, you need not go any further:

```
    Private Sub deleteButton_Click(ByVal sender As System.Object, _
        ByVal e As System.EventArgs) Handles deleteButton.Click

        If employeeList.SelectedIndex = -1 Then Return

    End Sub
```

If the code moves beyond this point, you know that the user has selected something. The next step then is to make sure that the user really does want to delete that item, and then do so:

```
Private Sub deleteButton_Click(ByVal sender As System.Object, _
        ByVal e As System.EventArgs) Handles deleteButton.Click

    If employeeList.SelectedIndex = -1 Then Return

    Dim result As DialogResult = _
        MessageBox.Show("Really delete this employee?", _
        "Delete", MessageBoxButtons.YesNo, _
        MessageBoxIcon.Question)

    If result = Windows.Forms.DialogResult.Yes Then
        employeeList.Items.Remove(employeeList.SelectedItem)
    End If

End Sub
```

First, a message box is shown with two buttons (Yes and No) and a question mark icon, asking whether the user is sure about removing the item. If the user answers yes (the result of the MessageBox.Show() call will of course be DialogResult.Yes), you call Remove() on the ListBox's Items property, passing in the actual item that the user currently has selected.

Armed with your newfound knowledge of how to figure out just what the user has selected, you can easily code up the Edit button now. Go back to the design view of the form and double-click the Edit button.

Once again, the first thing you need to do is make sure the user really has selected something:

```
Private Sub editButton_Click(ByVal sender As System.Object, _
        ByVal e As System.EventArgs) Handles editButton.Click

    If employeeList.SelectedIndex = -1 Then Return

End Sub
```

Now things get a little more tricky, but it's the user's fault (you'll find it always is). You see, users (and to be honest, that includes you, even though you wrote the code) expect things to happen a certain way. They expect in this application to be able to click on an item in the list, click Edit, edit the details, and then see them change in the list. For example, if a staff member gets married, she may change her surname. So, a user will expect to see the surname in the list change after completing editing.

The problem with this is purely technical (another thing you'll find is that users don't care about your technical excuses for why it's hard to make a program do something—they just want you to get it done). When you pull the SelectedItem out of the list to edit it and pass it to your dialog, you are actually passing a copy of the original object, not the object itself. This means that in code terms there will be two employees exactly the same: the one that's displayed in the list, and the one you're editing in the edit box.

There are a number of solutions to this problem. You could grab the actual object from the list itself, and not use SelectedItem. You could also declare a method on the dialog and pass the object to it by reference. I don't like that. I'd much rather work with the properties that Microsoft gave me, instead of working around them. Besides, I also like my program code to tell me exactly what's going on, rather than having things seemingly work by magic. It's also good experience for you to do things "the hard way."

My solution, then, is this: First you store the index of the item the user has selected. Then you pass SelectedItem to the dialog. When the user has finished editing, you delete the original item from the list and insert (not add) the edited version back in at the same location. The user won't see any of this stuff going on behind the scenes, but will just be happy (subconsciously—Pete's Third Rule of Users is that they subconsciously love what you do right, and verbally chastise you for what you do wrong) that the program works the way it should. Let's take a look.

First, let's store SelectedIndex, instantiate our dialog, and pass SelectedItem to it:

```
Private Sub editButton_Click(ByVal sender As System.Object, _
        ByVal e As System.EventArgs) Handles editButton.Click

    If employeeList.SelectedIndex = -1 Then Return

    Dim employeeNum As Integer = employeeList.SelectedIndex
    Dim editEmployeeDialog As New EditDialog()
    editEmployeeDialog.StaffMember = employeeList.SelectedItem


End Sub
```

Great. Now you can call ShowDialog() in the usual way and do something only if the user closes the dialog by clicking the OK button:

```
Private Sub editButton_Click(ByVal sender As System.Object, _
        ByVal e As System.EventArgs) Handles editButton.Click

    If employeeList.SelectedIndex = -1 Then Return

    Dim employeeNum As Integer = employeeList.SelectedIndex
    Dim editEmployeeDialog As New EditDialog()
    editEmployeeDialog.StaffMember = employeeList.SelectedItem

    If editEmployeeDialog.ShowDialog() = Windows.Forms.DialogResult.OK Then

    End If

End Sub
```

I'll talk you through the next bit line by line. Assuming the user clicked the OK button, you now need to remove the original selected item from the list:

```
    If editEmployeeDialog.ShowDialog() = Windows.Forms.DialogResult.OK Then
        employeeList.Items.RemoveAt(employeeNum)
    End If
```

Next, you need to put the Employee object that your dialog has back into the list at the same position as the original selected one. For this, you can use Items.Insert() instead of Items.Add(). It takes two parameters: the first is the position in the list you want to insert the item into, and the second is the item itself:

```
    If editEmployeeDialog.ShowDialog() = Windows.Forms.DialogResult.OK Then
        employeeList.Items.RemoveAt(employeeNum)
        employeeList.Items.Insert(employeeNum, _
            editEmployeeDialog.StaffMember)
    End If
```

Finally, you just need to select the newly inserted item. Remember Pete's Third Rule of Users; if they see the item they just edited get deselected, they won't be very happy, and as a consequence, neither will you.

```
    If editEmployeeDialog.ShowDialog() = Windows.Forms.DialogResult.OK Then
        employeeList.Items.RemoveAt(employeeNum)
        employeeList.Items.Insert(employeeNum, _
            editEmployeeDialog.StaffMember)
        employeeList.SelectedIndex = employeeNum
    End If
```

Ta-da! All done. All that remains now is the final piece of code to update the text boxes on the form to show information about the currently selected user. As the user clicks on people in the list, you want their details displayed on the main form.

To achieve this, you just need to hook into the ListBox's SelectedIndexChanged event. As its name suggests, this event fires whenever the `SelectedIndex` property changes. There are some side effects to be aware of. First, the event will fire even if the code in your program puts a value into `SelectedIndex`. In our case, when a user edits an item, that's great. The event will fire after the user successfully edits an item, and you can use the code inside the event to update the text boxes accordingly. Second, the event will also fire when the user deselects something—for example, when the user deletes an employee. It is important in the event handler to check whether an employee is selected. If it's not, you can clear out the text boxes, and if it is, you just need to copy the `Employee` properties into the text boxes. Here's the code:

```
Private Sub employeeList_SelectedIndexChanged( _
        ByVal sender As System.Object, _
        ByVal e As System.EventArgs) _
        Handles employeeList.SelectedIndexChanged

    If employeeList.SelectedIndex <> -1 Then
        Dim currentEmployee As Employee = employeeList.SelectedItem
        firstName.Text = currentEmployee.FirstName
        lastName.Text = currentEmployee.LastName
        jobTitle.Text = currentEmployee.JobTitle
    Else
        firstName.Text = String.Empty
        lastName.Text = String.Empty
        jobTitle.Text = String.Empty
    End If


End Sub
```

So, if the `SelectedIndex` is not -1 (meaning the user has chosen something), you grab the `SelectedItem` (casting it to an `Employee` object of course) and then copy the properties of the employee into the text boxes. Alternatively, if nothing is selected, you set all the text boxes to the same value, which is an empty, blank string.

If you haven't already done so, run the program now. Notice that as you add entries, they appear in the list. Notice also that as you select entries in the list, the details of the employee appear at the bottom of the form. Finally, notice that when you edit an entry, even if you change all the details of the employee, the list updates to reflect the changes, and the employee remains selected and in the same place within the list (see Figure 10-8).

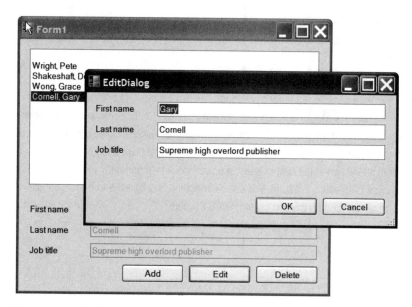

Figure 10-8. *The finished list box editing application*

Here's a thought on changes you could do yourself. A ListBox can automatically sort the contents it's displaying. To make it do this, just set the Sorted property of the ListBox to True. If you do this, though, that's really going to cause problems for your current edit code. So it will need to change to grab the actual selected item from the Items collection and pass it directly to the editing dialog.

Also, a list box can be used to select more than one entry (the user holds down Shift and clicks two items, or holds down Ctrl and clicks a bunch of them). To enable this functionality, you just need to set the SelectionMode property of the ListBox to either MultiSimple (Shift-selecting items), or MultiExtended (Shift- and Ctrl-selecting items).

If multiple select is enabled, you'll no longer be able to rely on the SelectedIndex and SelectedItem properties. Instead, you'll have to use SelectedIndices and SelectedItems. Both of these are collections, just like the Items property we've already covered. This means you can iterate over them with For Each, and find out just how many items are selected with either SelectedIndexes.Count or SelectedItems.Count.

The CheckedListBox Control

The *CheckedListBox control* works almost identically to a standard list box. The difference is that each item in the list has a check box displayed in front of it (see Figure 10-9).

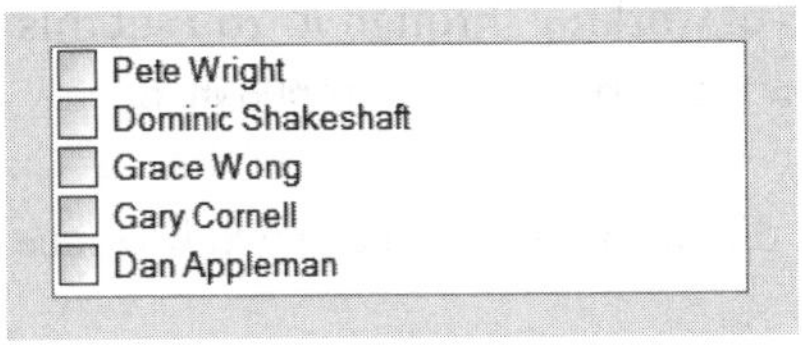

☐ Pete Wright
☐ Dominic Shakeshaft
☐ Grace Wong
☐ Gary Cornell
☐ Dan Appleman

Figure 10-9. *The CheckedListBox control*

To find out what got checked (selected) and what didn't, just take a look at the
`CheckedIndices` and `CheckedItems` properties of the control.

These work in exactly the same way as the `SelectedItems` and `SelectedIndices` on a
standard list box, but return the indexes and the items that have been checked. For example, if I wanted to print to the console every single checked item in a CheckedListBox, I'd
write code like this:

```
For Each checkedEmployee As Employee In CheckedListBox1.CheckedItems
    Console.WriteLine(checkEmployee.ToString())
Next
```

By default, the user has to select an item and then click it again to toggle the check box
on and off. You can change this by setting the `CheckOnClick` property of the control to
`True`. This means that when a user selects an item in the list, the check box will toggle.

The ComboBox Control

List boxes, whether of the checked variety or not, take up a lot of space on the form. A better alternative in many cases is a *ComboBox control* (see Figure 10-10).

Job title

Programmer
Analyst
Designer
Manager
Team Leader
Architect

Figure 10-10. *The ComboBox control offers all the functionality of a list box, but on demand.*

A combo box is really a text box with a list attached. I'm sure you've come across them
yourselves in various Windows apps. You click the button to the right of the text box to
drop down the list part of the control, or start typing and the control automatically fills in
the rest for you.

A combo box can have one of three styles and ways of working through it. You set this up by using the control's DropDownStyle property, which can be Simple, DropDown, or DropDownList.

With the Simple style set, the list is permanently on display along with the text box (see Figure 10-11).

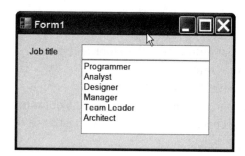

Figure 10-11. *With the Simple style set, the combo box permanently displays its list.*

The user is free to key anything into the text box or to select an item from the list. Selecting something in the list puts it up into the text box.

With the DropDownList style set, the combo box takes on a more traditional look and feel, as you can see in Figure 10-12.

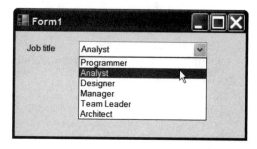

Figure 10-12. *The DropDownList style forces the user to choose an entry from the list.*

In this style, users are not free to type whatever they want into the text box. Instead, they have to click the button and choose something from the list, or type in something that already exists in the list. Doing this causes the item to be selected and once again displayed in the text box part of the control.

The final style, DropDown, looks the same as DropDownList (see Figure 10-13).

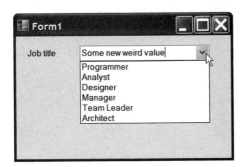

Figure 10-13. *The DropDown style of the combo looks the same as a drop-down list but allows the user to enter free text.*

With the DropDown style, users are able to enter whatever they want into the text box, or to click the button and choose something from the list.

With all three styles, one thing remains common. Whatever the user selects or manually enters, it gets displayed in the text box portion of the control. So, to find out what the user did, examine ComboBox.Text, just as if you were working with a standard text box. Of course, you can still use SelectedItem and SelectedIndex to figure out whether anything was selected from the list part of the control and to determine exactly what it was that was selected.

The TreeView Control

The *TreeView control* is a unique list control, in that it displays a hierarchical view of data. If you've used the Folders feature in Outlook, or look at the list of folders on your hard disk in Windows Explorer, you'll know exactly what I mean. Figure 10-14 shows a TreeView control.

Figure 10-14. *The TreeView control is used to display hierarchical lists of information.*

The TreeView holds a Nodes collection, each item in which is a TreeNode object. This TreeNode object also has a Nodes collection, which is again a collection of TreeNode objects. Think of it as a Russian doll, where inside each doll is a smaller one that contains even smaller ones.

Despite the potential for a horrendous amount of complexity, working with nodes is very simple. You just call Nodes.Add() and pass in the new object you wish to store in the node. Nodes.Add() then returns to you a TreeNode object so that you can, if you so desire, add child nodes to the one you just created.

Try It Out: Adding Nodes to a Tree View

Let's write a simple program to store odd and even numbers in a tree view.

Start up a new WinForms project, and drop a TreeView and a Button control onto the form as in Figure 10-15.

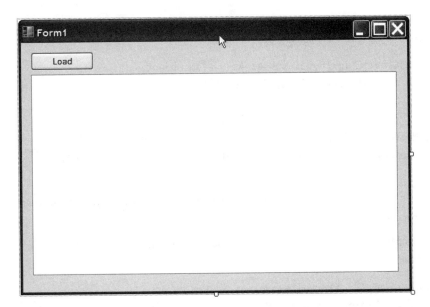

Figure 10-15. *Drop a Button and a TreeView control onto your application's main form.*

Set up the Text property of the button as shown in the screen shot, but don't worry about setting the names of the controls; you have only one of each, so your button is called Button1, and the tree view is called TreeView1.

When the user clicks the Load button, you're going to count from 1 to 500 and store even numbers in an Even Numbers node, and odd numbers in an Odd Numbers node. So double-click the button to drop into the code editor.

The first thing you need to do is clear out the TreeView. This prevents a problem of the user continuing to click the Load button and in doing so adding a bunch of duplicate nodes into the control:

```
Private Sub Button1_Click(ByVal sender As System.Object, _
        ByVal e As System.EventArgs) Handles Button1.Click
    TreeView1.Nodes.Clear()
End Sub
```

Next, you need to create nodes to hold the odd and even numbers:

```
Private Sub Button1_Click(ByVal sender As System.Object, _
        ByVal e As System.EventArgs) Handles Button1.Click
    TreeView1.Nodes.Clear()

    Dim oddNumbers As TreeNode = TreeView1.Nodes.Add("Odd numbers")
    Dim evenNumbers As TreeNode = TreeView1.Nodes.Add("Even numbers")
End Sub
```

Notice that the Nodes.Add() method returns a TreeNode object that you need to store in order to add child nodes to the two parent nodes.

All that remains is to loop through the numbers from 1 to 500 and add them into the appropriate TreeNode.Nodes collection:

```
Private Sub Button1_Click(ByVal sender As System.Object, _
        ByVal e As System.EventArgs) Handles Button1.Click
    TreeView1.Nodes.Clear()

    Dim oddNumbers As TreeNode = TreeView1.Nodes.Add("Odd numbers")
    Dim evenNumbers As TreeNode = TreeView1.Nodes.Add("Even numbers")

    For i As Integer = 1 To 500
        If i Mod 2 = 0 Then
            evenNumbers.Nodes.Add(i.ToString())
        Else
            oddNumbers.Nodes.Add(i.ToString())
        End If
    Next

End Sub
```

Here you're just using the Visual Basic Mod operator to work out the remainder of each number divided by 2. If the remainder is 0, you have an even number; otherwise, it's odd.

Run the program now and you'll see the tree view populate whenever the Load button is pressed (see Figure 10-16).

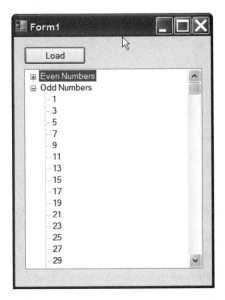

Figure 10-16. *Clicking the Load button runs your code to populate the control with nodes.*

Changing the Visual Appearance of the Tree

The TreeView control provides a lot of properties to let you completely change how it looks. At the simplest level, the three properties—ShowLines, ShowPlusMinus, and ShowRootLines—control the actual view of the list itself. They are all Boolean properties, and setting them all to False results in a tree view that looks like Figure 10-17.

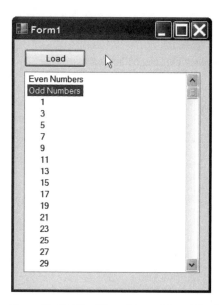

Figure 10-17. *The ShowLines, ShowPlusMinus, and ShowRootLines properties all govern the display of the tree itself.*

More usefully, though, you can change the actual view of the nodes by associating graphics with them. There is another control in the Toolbox called the ImageList. It's a container for graphics. You simply add graphics to it and then link controls on the form, such as the TreeView, to it. From that point on, controls that support the image list can grab images from it. Let's take a look.

Try It Out: Adding Images to the Tree View

Load up the tree view project you were working with earlier, and double-click the ImageList control in the Toolbox to drop it onto the form. The ImageList control is a nonvisual control, so it appears underneath the form (see Figure 10-18).

Figure 10-18. *Drop an ImageList control onto the form. Because it's a nonvisual control, it appears underneath the form in the designer.*

Click on the smart tag attached to the control and a menu appears, where you can specify the number of colors the images are to use and the size of the images (Figure 10-19).

Figure 10-19. *The smart tag on the ImageList control lets you specify the size and color depth of the images.*

Select 16, 16 and Depth32Bit and then click Choose Images. The Images Collection Editor dialog will appear, as in Figure 10-20.

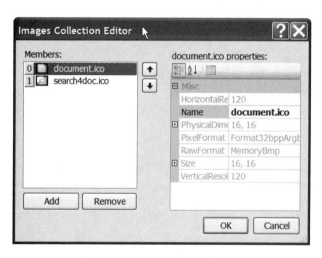

Figure 10-20. *The Images Collection Editor lets you add images to the ImageList control.*

Click the Add button and find an image on your hard disk to add to the list. Visual Basic 2005 Express ships with something called an Image Library. You can find it in the location where you installed Visual Basic 2005 Express, typically C:\Program Files_Microsoft Visual Studio 8\Common7\ VS2005ImageLibrary. Go ahead and add two images to the control, and then close the dialog.

Now that you have some images in the ImageList control, the next thing to do is associate the tree view with the image list. Click on the tree view in the designer and then find the ImageList property in the Properties window. Click in the edit area for the property and you'll see a drop-down list appear, listing all the image lists on the form (one in this case). Go ahead and select it.

The final step is to change the code that adds nodes into the tree view so that it references images to use for the nodes.

Double-click the Load button to drop back into its click event handler.

Previously, when you added a node to the Nodes collections, you just specified some text to display. The Add() method actually has a number of different overloads, a couple of which let you specify an image from the ImageList to use for the node.

Change the code, like this:

```
Private Sub Button1_Click(ByVal sender As System.Object, _
        ByVal e As System.EventArgs) Handles Button1.Click
    TreeView1.Nodes.Clear()

    Dim oddNumbers As TreeNode = _
        TreeView1.Nodes.Add("Odd", "Odd numbers", 0, 1)
    Dim evenNumbers As TreeNode = _
        TreeView1.Nodes.Add("Even", "Even numbers", 0, 1)

    For i As Integer = 1 To 500
        If i Mod 2 = 0 Then
            evenNumbers.Nodes.Add(i.ToString())
        Else
            oddNumbers.Nodes.Add(i.ToString())
        End If
    Next

End Sub
```

Instead of just passing in one string, which is the text to display in the tree view, you're now passing in five parameters. The first is called Key. It provides a way for us to search node collections by using the Find() method, like this:

```
Dim matchingNodes() As TreeNode = _
    TreeView1.Nodes.Find("Even", True)
```

This would give you an array of all the nodes called Even. If you want to specify an image to add to a node, you have to specify a key, even if you don't intend to use it.

The second parameter is the same text that you had before, and specifies the string to display in the tree view itself. The remaining two parameters are indexes into the image list. What you are saying here is that normally this node should display the first image in the image list (number 0). If the node gets selected, though, use the second image (number 1).

After you've made the code changes, run the program to see the difference (see Figure 10-21).

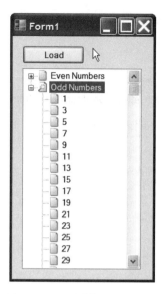

Figure 10-21. *Adding images to the TreeView gives the list a nice new look that can also be used to provide vital feedback to the user.*

Click on the Even Numbers node now and you'll see the graphic change as the list expands.

But wait—there's more!

Aside from assigning graphics to a node, you can also specify individual colors for each node in the TreeView, and even ToolTips. This is really handy, for example, if you were writing some kind of check-balancing application and wanted to show certain accounts or categories of spending in red.

Each TreeNode, just like any control in .NET, has BackColor, ForeColor, and ToolTip properties. By setting these up, you can change the look and feel of the control even more. Add a couple more lines of code to the Load event to do just that:

```
Private Sub Button1_Click(ByVal sender As System.Object, _
    ByVal e As System.EventArgs) Handles Button1.Click
    TreeView1.Nodes.Clear()

    Dim oddNumbers As TreeNode = _
        TreeView1.Nodes.Add("Odd", "Odd numbers", 0, 1)
    oddNumbers.BackColor = Color.Yellow
    oddNumbers.ForeColor = Color.Blue
    oddNumbers.ToolTipText = "The odd numbers"
```

```
Dim evenNumbers As TreeNode = _
    TreeView1.Nodes.Add("Even", "Even numbers", 0, 1)
evenNumbers.BackColor = Color.Blue
evenNumbers.ForeColor = Color.Yellow
evenNumbers.ToolTipText = "The even numbers"

For i As Integer = 1 To 500
    If i Mod 2 = 0 Then
        evenNumbers.Nodes.Add(i.ToString())
    Else
        oddNumbers.Nodes.Add(i.ToString())
    End If
Next


End Sub
```

Run the application now, and the form looks very different, as you can see in Figure 10-22. Also, notice that to get the ToolTips working, you had to add a line of code to turn the ShowNodeToolTips property to True. You can also do this at design time with the Properties window.

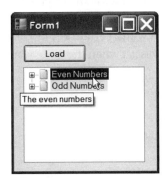

Figure 10-22. *Each node is like a tiny control; you have complete control over how it looks and even ToolTips to show.*

Responding to Selections and Finding Nodes

You haven't looked at selecting nodes yet. The tree view has an event called NodeMouse-Click. This event fires whenever the user clicks on a node. You can find out just which node the user clicked on from the event arguments object passed in. Take a look (don't key this in unless you really want to):

```
Private Sub TreeView1_NodeMouseClick(ByVal sender As System.Object, _
      ByVal e As System.Windows.Forms.TreeNodeMouseClickEventArgs) _
      Handles TreeView1.NodeMouseClick

    Dim selectedNode As TreeNode = e.Node
    Consolc.WriteLine(selectedNode.Text)

End Sub
```

To find the selected node, you just call e.Node.

After you find a node in this way, there's a bunch of stuff you can do with it. You can find out if it has children of its own by examining the Nodes.NodeCount property. This will return an integer telling you exactly how many child nodes it has. In addition, you can call Nodes.Parent to get the TreeNode that the selected node is a child of. If it's a top-level node with no parents, the return value is Nothing.

You can also quickly find out if the node contains children set with a certain key by calling Nodes.ContainsKey(). You pass in a string for the key that was set when the node was added, and you get back a True or False value. For example:

```
    Dim selectedNode As TreeNode = e.Node
    If selectedNode.Nodes.ContainsKey("PrimeNumber") Then
        Console.WriteLine("This node contains prime numbers")
    End If
```

Finally, as I mentioned earlier, you can call the Find() method on the Nodes collection of a node to find all nodes matching a certain key. The result is an array of TreeNodes.

Summary

As you can see, .NET gives a great deal of flexibility when it comes to displaying lists of data. In fact, the TreeView control when you really explore it offers a phenomenal amount of power.

When we move on to databases a little later, you'll see a grid control that does even more than all these lists. You'll also take a look at how to connect these list controls to a database to automatically show the database contents.

CHAPTER 11

■■■

Menus and Toolbars

All but the very smallest of quick hack applications have a *menu*. Even Microsoft's humble Notepad application includes an extensive menu, allowing you to access the program's property page, load and save files, reformat text, and a whole lot more besides.

On the subject of Notepad, though, its menus are somewhat "old-school." They are plain textual menus with the odd shortcut key here and there (Ctrl+S for example, to activate the File ➤ Save item) and little more. In recent years, though, Microsoft has shown the world that menus can be a lot more than just lists of text. The leader in terms of user interface standards for Microsoft Windows has always been the Office suite, and the menus in the latest version of Office are light years ahead of Notepad. Take a look at Figure 11-1.

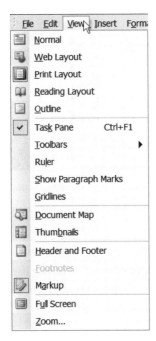

Figure 11-1. *The menus in Microsoft Office are known as "rich" menus.*

Menu items in Office include graphics in many cases. Menu items that can be toggled on and off highlight the graphic to show when certain options are enabled, and when others are not. These menus are "rich" in the level of graphic feedback they provide to users.

Visual Basic 2005 Express makes it easy to create such rich menus in your own applications. In fact, when you compare the menu creation tools to those in the very first version of Visual Studio .NET, it's really quite breathtaking to see just how far the development tools have come in just a few short years.

Typically, wherever you have a menu in a Windows application, you also have toolbars. *Toolbars* appear beneath the menu bar and provide rapid one-click access to common menu items (such as Load and Save, Undo, Cut, Copy and Paste, and so on). In addition, wherever you have a menu and toolbar, you'll typically also see a *status bar*, a special form of toolbar that always appears at the bottom of the window to provide vital feedback on what the application is doing. Once again, take a look at Microsoft Word from the Office suite (see Figure 11-2).

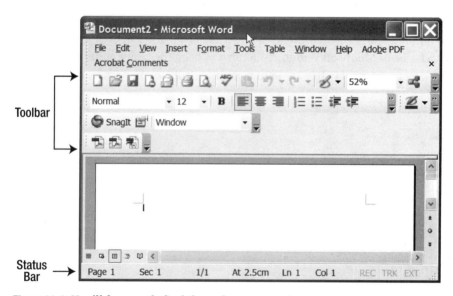

Figure 11-2. *You'll frequently find that wherever you have menus, you also have toolbars and status bars.*

The first time you look at developing a serious Windows program with all these things, the amount of graphical splendor they convey seems impossibly out of reach to all but the most accomplished developers. Just as with menus, though, the tools to let you build toolbars and status bars in VB Express are very sophisticated and very easy to use.

The Menu Controls

Visual Basic 2005 Express provides two menu controls. One, the *MenuStrip control*, lets you build the menu that lives on the top edge of a window. The other, the *ContextMenuStrip control*, lets you add context-sensitive menus, menus that appear whenever you right-click something that has a context menu attached. You've seen context menus in the VB IDE itself, for example, when you right-click an item in the Solution Explorer.

You typically use menu strips to allow access to functionality common to the entire application. Context menus, though, as you've seen, tend to be focused on one specific area and one specific piece of data. Take a look at Figure 11-3, for example.

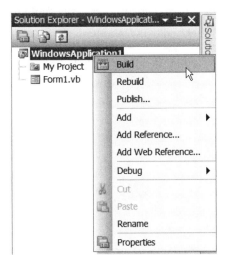

Figure 11-3. *Context menus provide functionality specific to an area of the application and the "context" the user is working in.*

I made this menu appear by right-clicking on a project in the Solution Explorer. The "context" I was in was the Solution Explorer and project management. The context menu then appears to show me things specific to projects, such as adding new items to the project and so on. Because context menus usually appear only when the user right-clicks something, they are not the most intuitive user interface element in the Toolbox. Unless users know that they can right-click something, the chances are that they might well miss your ornately designed context menu. Therefore, use context menus sparingly, or at the very least add ToolTips to controls to let users know that they can right-click something to bring up such a menu.

Let's start off with the basics and take a look at how to add a standard menu to a simple window.

Building a Menu

The menu controls (and the toolbar and status bar controls, for that matter) can be found in the Menus & Toolbars section of the Toolbox (Figure 11-4).

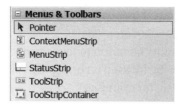

Figure 11-4. *The controls to build menus and toolbars are all grouped together in the Toolbox.*

To add a menu to a form, just double-click the MenuStrip control, and a blank, empty menu will appear on the form (see Figure 11-5).

Figure 11-5. *Double-click the MenuStrip control to add a menu onto a form.*

When you add a MenuStrip to a form, the Properties window instantly changes to show properties for the control, as you would expect. However, if you click in the menu, specifically in an area marked Type Here, the Properties window will change to show information relating to a ToolStripMenuItem.

Menus consist of ToolStripMenuItems. Each heading you see on a menu, and each item that appears underneath a menu heading is a ToolStripMenuItem. By clicking on an item and using the Properties window, you can change pretty much any aspect of the item—its colors and font, its name, the image to display alongside it, background color, and more besides. To be frank, though, most people never even touch the Properties window when building menus; for most tasks, simply clicking in a blank area of the menu and typing is enough to set up the menu just the way they like.

Before we move on to setting up images and shortcuts for menu items, let's take a quick look at how to build a simple menu and add event handlers to the items.

Try It Out: Creating a Simple Menu

Start up a WinForms project and then drop a MenuStrip control onto the window.

Click in the area of the menu that says Type Here, and type in **&File**. The leading & symbol tells Windows that you want the first letter of the menu item underlined to make it easy for users to select it by pressing Alt+F. Your menu should now look like mine in Figure 11-6.

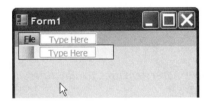

Figure 11-6. *You can create menu items by simply clicking on an area of the menu and typing.*

Notice in the screen shot that as soon as you start typing into a top-level menu item, the menu editor adds two more Type Here items: one to the right of the new menu item, and one underneath. You can use these to add new items to the menu easily. Go ahead and add in a few more options to the File menu so that it looks like Figure 11-7.

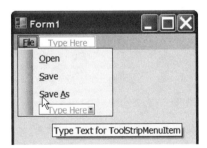

Figure 11-7. *Add more menu items to the File menu—don't forget to place an & symbol before the letter in the item that you want to be underlined.*

Each time you click to add a new menu item, you'll see that two more Type Here items appear, even as you move down the menu. This allows you to build up *submenus*, menus that expand with even more menu items when they are clicked.

You may have also noticed that as you move the mouse over an area for a new menu item, a drop-down icon appears to the right of the blank item. This allows you to add more than just text items to a menu. Move the mouse over the menu item underneath Save As and click the drop-down, and you'll see a submenu appear as in Figure 11-8.

Figure 11-8. *You can use the drop-down to the right of a new menu item area to add different types of menu items.*

As you can see, menus can also hold *separators* (which are just lines to space out the items in the menu), combo boxes, and even text boxes. The latter work just the same way that a standard combo box or text box would, but embedded inside a menu.

Choose Separator to add a separator into the list, and then add one more entry to the list, as shown in Figure 11-9.

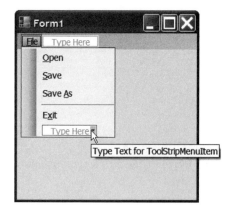

Figure 11-9. *The finished File menu*

Let's add some code now to the Exit item's event handler. To do this, double-click the menu item, just as you would double-click any other control to drop into the code editor.

Notice that the default event is a Click event for a menu item. No surprises there, then. There are a lot of other events that you can code up, but just as with menu properties, you'll rarely find yourself using them.

Type in some code to close the form when the menu item is clicked, like this:

```
Private Sub ExitToolStripMenuItem_Click(ByVal sender As System.Object, _
    ByVal e As System.EventArgs) Handles ExitToolStripMenuItem.Click
    Me.Close()
End Sub
```

That's all there is to it. As you can see, creating a menu and setting its events behind the scenes really is as simple as working with any other kind of control. Run the program now to make sure everything works, and feel free to play a bit with the menu builder. We'll catch up in the next section, where we look at graphics and shortcuts.

Adding Images and Shortcuts to a Menu

As you've just seen, building a menu is really a no-brainer. If you come from a Visual Basic background, you'll probably have your jaw on the floor at this point because the menu editor is so much easier than it was in classic VB.

All we did in the previous example was just build up a trivial text-based menu. I mentioned in the introduction that it is now possible to add graphics and other visual wonders to a menu to make your menus look just like they were pulled out of a Microsoft Office application.

The properties that handle images are the Image, ImageAlign, ImageScaling, and ImageTransparentColor properties shown in Figure 11-10.

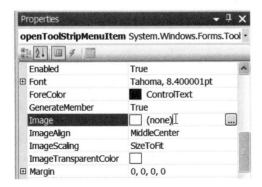

Figure 11-10. *The image properties let you transform the way a menu item looks.*

If you click in the Image property, you'll see the usual ellipsis button appear that lets you choose the image to set against the control. When you click the button, the Select Resource dialog appears, shown in Figure 11-11.

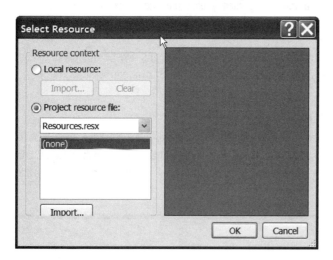

Figure 11-11. *The Select Resource dialog*

Images used inside menus must be included in the final compiled program; they can't be external files that live anywhere on the hard disk. So when you click to choose an image to set, the resource dialog appears, showing you images that are going to be embedded into your final compiled program. You can use this dialog to choose other images from the hard disk, and in doing so you'll add those images to a special folder in the Solution Explorer called Resources.

You can probably guess what the ImageAlign property does. It controls where in the menu item the image appears. Well, almost. It sets up where the image appears in the image part of the menu. Click on a menu in the designer, for example, and you'll see a shaded area to the left of the text. This is where any images get displayed, and the ImageAlign property controls where in that area the image appears. Most people leave it at MiddleCenter.

The ImageTransparentColor property is a strange one at first. When you load in an image—any image—it is likely to have a background color. Menu items also have a background color. As a result, images added to the menu could stand out horribly if the background color of the image and background color of the menu clash. The ImageTransparentColor property lets you specify a color in the image to ignore. When the menu is drawn, the color specified is never drawn, and as a result the background color and shading of the menu item itself shows through. The best way to determine the value to place into this property is to load the image in question into a drawing program such as

Microsoft Paint. Within Microsoft Paint, you can click the pipette icon and then click on the background color to select it. You can then select the Colors menu and choose Edit Colors to see the color value. You can see an example of this in Figure 11-12.

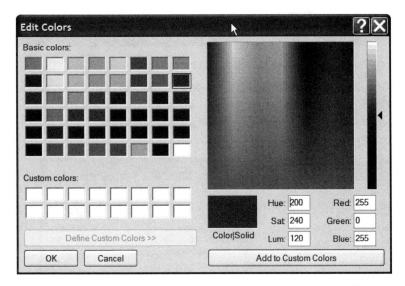

Figure 11-12. *You can use a program such as Microsoft Paint to determine the background color value. In this case the color is 255,0,255.*

After you have found out the background color (in this case 255,0,255), just key that into the ImageTransparentColor property. Instantly the background of the image in the menu will vanish.

Finally, the ImageScaling property of a menu item works hand in hand with the MenuStrip control's own ImageScalingSize properties. If you click on a MenuStrip control and look at its properties, you'll notice that by default the ImageScalingSize property is set to 16, 16. This means that images are a standard 16 dots (pixels) wide and 16 dots high. Setting ImageScaling of a menu item to SizeToFit makes the menu item resize any image you select so that it fits this size.

BACKGROUND COLORS AND THE MICROSOFT IMAGE LIBRARY

Visual Basic 2005 Express ships with a set of graphics known as the Image Library. You can find it in your VB Express directory, which is typically C:\Program Files\Microsoft Visual Studio 8\Common7\VS2005ImageLibrary.

All the images Microsoft includes have a background color value of 255,0,255, which makes using them and setting them up inside your own applications nice and easy.

Let's take a look at all this with a "Try It Out," and also see how to set menu *shortcuts*, key combinations that when pressed instantly click a menu item without the user having to mouse around to do it the hard way.

Try It Out: Adding Images and Shortcuts to a Menu

Let's go back to the menu you built earlier in the chapter. You'll add some graphics and shortcuts to it.

In the designer, select the Open item under the File menu so that its properties are displayed in the Properties window. Click the ellipsis button next to the `Image` property to open up the resources dialog you saw earlier, and then click the Import button. A typical file Open dialog will appear, as in Figure 11-13.

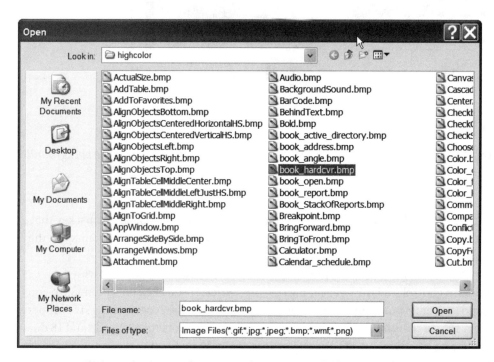

Figure 11-13. *Clicking the Import button on the resources dialog opens up a standard file dialog.*

Use the dialog to find an image on your hard disk. If you have the Visual Studio Image Library installed, go to its location and choose an image; I used the `OpenFolder.bmp` file.

After you have chosen an image, you'll be returned to the resource dialog. Click the image you just chose and then close the dialog. The menu item will redraw with the selected image, just as in Figure 11-14.

Figure 11-14. *As soon as you choose an image by using the resource dialog, the image gets drawn into the menu.*

It probably looks pretty horrible at the moment, because you haven't set the `ImageTransparentColor` property. Use your favorite paint package to find out the what the color value is, and then key the value into the `ImageTransparentColor` property. If you are using images from the Image Library that comes with VB Express, the value will either be 255,0,255 (if the icon appears with a bright pink background) or 0 (if you see it on a black background). Key this into the `ImageTransparentColor` property, and the menu will once again redraw to remove the background color.

Repeat the process a couple of times to get used to working with images, and set up the images for the Save and Exit menu items. My menu looks like Figure 11-15.

Figure 11-15. *It's best not to go crazy and put images on every single menu item. That just gets confusing. A few images, though, can make key menu items really stand out.*

Next, let's add some shortcuts. Shortcuts are really nothing to do with images, but like images in a menu, they do make menu items stand out, telling the user what key combinations can be used to invoke certain key operations within the program. After you set a shortcut key into a menu, that key combination will automatically invoke the menu item without you having to write any extra code to manage it.

Select the Open menu item once again, and then click its ShortcutKeys property in the Properties window. The rather neat mini dialog in Figure 11-16 appears.

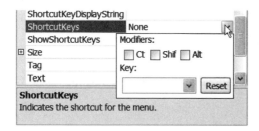

Figure 11-16. *Clicking in the ShortcutKeys property displays a handy dialog to let you easily set up the menu item's shortcut key.*

The shortcut for Open in most applications is Ctrl+O. So click the Ctrl check box in the dialog, and then choose O (for Orange) from the drop-down. When you're finished, the menu will redraw to look like Figure 11-17.

Figure 11-17. *As soon as you set a shortcut key for a menu item, the item redraws to show you what the user will see at runtime.*

Go ahead now and set the shortcuts for the other menu items: Save should be Ctrl+S, Save As should be Ctrl+Shift+S, and Exit should be Ctrl+X. The finished menu will look like mine in Figure 11-18.

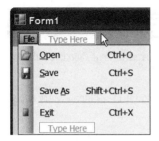

Figure 11-18. *The finished menu, with all the shortcut keys set*

Just as with images, it's not a good idea to go overboard and set up shortcut keys for every single menu item; it looks horrible and it confuses users. Choose the most important and commonly used menu items in the program and just set the shortcuts for them. In addition, pay attention to the shortcuts used by other Windows programs. The more familiar your program appears to be, the quicker users will take to it and love it.

Menus in an MDI Application

Hopefully you're quite happy with how to build menus by now, even pretty graphical ones with handy shortcut keys attached. The problem with menus really comes into play when you start implementing fairly complex MDI-type applications. Or at least, it used to.

You see, with an MDI application, the menu is hosted in the parent window. So when the user clicks on a menu item such as Save, you need to figure out in code just which window is currently open, and which document the user wants to save. In addition, though, you might not want certain menu items to be activated for all of the windows. It doesn't make any sense, for example, to have the Save menu item working when the user doesn't have any child windows open. Finally, you may want certain windows to add new menu items to the main menu bar, depending on the kind of data that those windows hold.

This sort of thing used to be a nightmare that would invariably result in loads of potentially buggy code (because the more code you write, the more chances you'll make mistakes). Not so anymore, thank goodness.

Rather than just talk you through all the potential solutions to these issues, let's just dive straight into a "Try It Out," where we'll put your newfound menu-building skills to good use.

Try It Out: Menus and MDI Applications

Start up a new WinForms project and set the IsMDIContainer property of Form1 to True. You'll recall from the preceding chapter that this turns a form into an MDI parent form.

Drop a MenuStrip control onto the form and build a file menu like the one in Figure 11-19 (don't worry about setting the images if you don't want to—it won't affect the program at all).

Figure 11-19. *Build a file menu on the MDI form, like this.*

Next, add a new window to the application and call it ChildForm.vb. Add a menu strip to this form and set it up like the one in Figure 11-20. (Again, don't worry too much about putting images into the menu items if you don't want to.)

Figure 11-20. *Set up the menu on the new child form, like this.*

Set the names of the new menu items to setToRed, setToBlue, and setToGreen, appropriately, and you're ready to code. First, let's code up the child form. When the user clicks on any of the menu items, you want to change the color of the form. Double-click each menu item to drop into the code editor, and write some code to change the BackColor property of the form. When you're finished, you'll have three event handlers that should look like this (I've highlighted the lines you need to add, as usual):

```
Public Class ChildForm

    Private Sub setToRed_Click(ByVal sender As System.Object, _
        ByVal e As System.EventArgs) Handles setToRed.Click

        Me.BackColor = Color.Red

    End Sub

    Private Sub setToBlue_Click(ByVal sender As System.Object, _
        ByVal e As System.EventArgs) Handles setToBlue.Click

        Me.BackColor = Color.Blue

    End Sub


    Private Sub setToGreen_Click(ByVal sender As System.Object, _
        ByVal e As System.EventArgs) Handles setToGreen.Click

        Me.BackColor = Color.Green

    End Sub

End Class
```

Now, if this were a real application, you'd also want the child form to have a way to save its data. In the code editor add another method, a public one called Save():

```
Public Sub Save()
    MessageBox.Show("I have saved my data!")
End Sub
```

What's going to happen is that when the Save menu item on the parent form is clicked, you are going to get the parent form to find out which child window is currently active and then call the child window's Save() method. Later in the book you'll see how to actually read and write files and databases, but for now you'll stick with a simple message box to show that something happened.

Go back to the designer for the MDI parent form now and double-click the New menu item. When this is clicked, you want to create a new MDI child window, something that you'll remember from the preceding chapter is really nice and easy to do. The code for the event handler looks like this:

```
Public Class Form1

    Private Sub NewToolStripMenuItem_Click(ByVal sender As System.Object, _
        ByVal e As System.EventArgs) Handles NewToolStripMenuItem.Click

        Dim child As New ChildForm()
        child.MdiParent = Me
        child.Show()

    End Sub

End Class
```

How about the Save item now? Go back to the designer and double-click the Save menu item and code it up like this:

```
    Private Sub SaveToolStripMenuItem_Click(ByVal sender As System.Object, _
        ByVal e As System.EventArgs) Handles SaveToolStripMenuItem.Click

        Dim formToSave As ChildForm
        formToSave = CType(Me.ActiveMdiChild, ChildForm)
        formToSave.Save()

    End Sub
```

You can look at the ActiveMdiChild property of a form to get the child form that's currently active. All you need to do when the user clicks Save, then, is cast this value to a ChildForm object (ActiveMdiChild just gives you a basic form object, so you use CType to cast this to a specific type of form), and then call the Save() method you wrote a short while ago.

You're nearly finished, but there's a problem. If you run the program now, you'll find that the Save item is always shown and clickable. In fact, if you run the program right now and click the Save item, the program will crash. Why? Well, there isn't an active child window open, so you're trying to call Save() on an object that doesn't really exist. What you need is a way to change the menu structure slightly based on what state the program is currently in.

Go back to the designer view of the MDI form and click the File menu item itself (not any of its children). Take a look at the list of events that a menu can respond to in the Properties window (Figure 11-21).

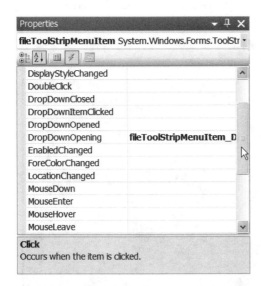

Figure 11-21. *The events that a menu item can respond to*

Two events in particular stand out: DropDownOpened and DropDownOpening. The DropDownOpened event occurs after the user clicks on a menu and its child menu items have been displayed. DropDownOpening, on the other hand, occurs when the user clicks on a menu item, immediately before the child menu items are displayed. You can use this event to change the state of the Save menu based on what the program is currently up to.

Double-click the DropDownOpening event for the File menu to drop into the code editor.

There is an array attached to an MdiParent form like this one, called MdiChildren. If this array is empty, its length property will be zero. You can use this to enable or disable the Save menu item. Type some code in:

```
    Private Sub FileToolStripMenuItem_DropDownOpening(ByVal sender As System.Ob-
ject, _
        ByVal e As System.EventArgs) Handles
FileToolStripMenuItem.DropDownOpening


        If Me.MdiChildren.Length = 0 Then
            SaveToolStripMenuItem.Enabled = False
        Else
            SaveToolStripMenuItem.Enabled = True
        End If


    End Sub
```

So if there are no child windows open, you'll disable the Save menu item. If there are child windows open, though, you'll enable the Save menu item. Perfect.

Run the program now and you'll see it works just as we thought, but with a twist. Take a look at Figure 11-22.

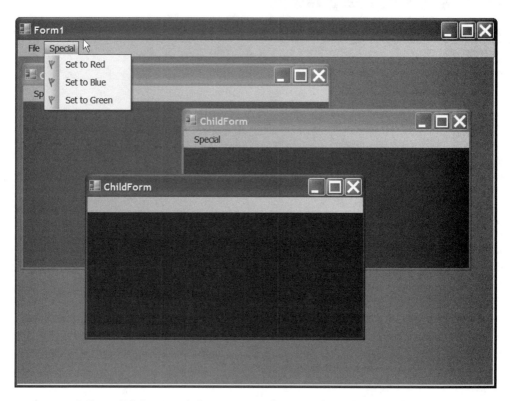

Figure 11-22. *Where did that Special menu come from on the MdiParent form?*

Notice the Special menu item on the main form? That's the menu item that you created on the child form. At runtime, the active child form will "merge" its menu with that of the parent. So, when a child form is open, the parent automatically shows new menu items that apply to the child. If you click any of the Special menu items to change the child form's color, you'll notice that they work with just the active child window, not any of the others.

Also, you'll notice that the Save item on the File menu now enables and disables based on whether there are any child windows open, and calls the Save() method on the active child window when it's clicked.

The Context Menu Control

The ContextMenuStrip control works identically to a standard MenuStrip control but has some visual differences in the designer.

When you drop a ContextMenuStrip control onto a form, the form goes into menu edit mode just as with a standard menu. However, you can't add top-level menu items (see Figure 11-23).

Figure 11-23. *The context menu strip lets you add only a single list of items.*

In addition, because figuring out which context menu you are editing items for can be quite confusing if you have more than one context menu on a form, the menu item comes with a smart tag for building the menu. Just click the tag and click Edit Items to be presented with the menu items editor shown in Figure 11-24.

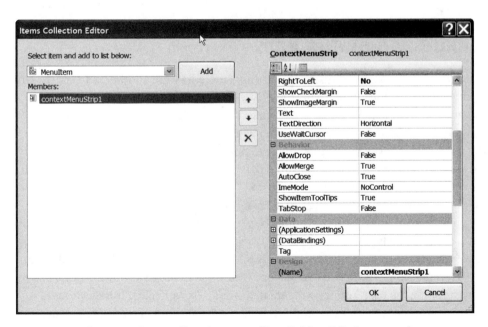

Figure 11-24. *The menu items editor is accessed by clicking Edit Items on the context menu's smart tag.*

In the dialog you just choose the type of item you want to add to the menu, by using the drop-down at the top, and then click the Add button to add it into the menu. You set up the actual text of each menu item you add, as well any other properties you want to alter, by using the properties list on the right side of the dialog.

When you're finished editing, clicking OK takes you out of the editor.

To get a context menu to display itself, just click on the control that you want the menu to attach to, and set its ContextMenuStrip property to the name of the context strip you just created. With that done, when the user right-clicks on the control at runtime, the context menu appears, as in Figure 11-25.

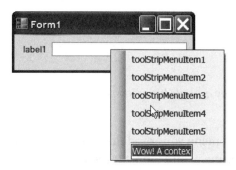

Figure 11-25. *All you need to do to enable a context menu is set the ContextMenuStrip property of a control to the name of the context strip itself.*

Toolbars and Status Bars

In earlier versions of .NET, menus were one thing, toolbars were another, and status bars were some odd little bolt-on piece of similarly incompatible technology. Thankfully, times have changed. In .NET 2.0, and of course Visual Basic 2005 Express, they are all compatible. If you know how to develop and work with a menu, you also know how to produce a toolbar, and also how to manage a status bar. This makes your life a lot easier in that you have a much shallower learning curve to climb, and it makes my job easier in that I don't have to type so much.

A toolbar provides buttons at the top of a window to allow quick one-click access to menu items and program options. A status bar, on the other hand, usually lives at the bottom of a window and typically provides feedback on just what a program is currently up to. I say "usually" and "typically" because it's really up to you, the developer, to decide where you want these controls to live on your windows (although at runtime, there's nothing stopping the user from moving them around). As with all UI things, though, it really does make sense to stick to standards unless you have a good reason not to, in order to make life easier on users getting familiar with your program.

After you add a toolbar and status bar to a form, adding elements to them works in a similar fashion to building up a menu (see Figure 11-26).

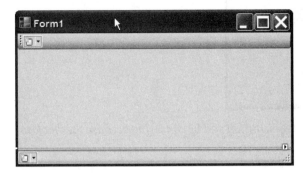

Figure 11-26. *Adding a status strip and tool strip to a form transforms its look quite considerably.*

Clicking on either control in design mode brings up a dummy drop-down button that you can click to add elements to the strip, as you can see in Figure 11-27.

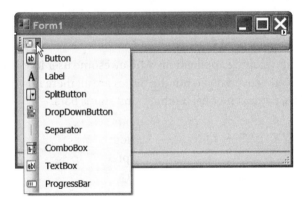

Figure 11-27. *Click the dummy button on each control to get a menu of things to add to the strips.*

On the whole, the items in the list are self-explanatory. However, on the tool strip two items often cause confusion: the DropDownButton and the SplitButton. If you add both to a tool strip and use the Image property to set up graphics for them, you'll find that they both look identical (see Figure 11-28).

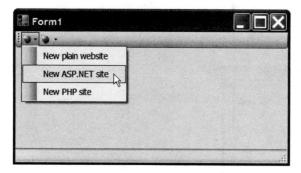

Figure 11-28. *The DropDownButton and SplitButton can be confusing because they look so similar.*

Both controls provide a drop-down menu for the user to choose from at runtime. The only difference is that a SplitButton also provides a clickable button. If the user wants to see the menu attached to a split button, the user needs to click the down arrow next to the button. Clicking the button itself triggers a Click event, as usual. Conversely, a drop-down button when clicked always shows the drop-down list of items.

Summary

You're now pretty much all set to start developing applications with awesome user interfaces. Sure, there are things that we haven't covered yet, but the basics are all there now that you know how to work with menus, context menus, toolbars, and status bars.

CHAPTER 12

■■■

Events

Now that you've had a taste of developing applications with graphical user interfaces, you may have noticed something quite important: events are everywhere. Unless you want to develop an application with a pretty user interface that does absolutely nothing, you have to work with events. You need to write code to respond to those button clicks, more code to respond to users selecting things in lists, more code to hook into text boxes and even window events. There is just no escaping events if you want to write applications for a modern operating system such as Windows.

So far, writing code for event handlers has been really simple. You either double-click a control on a form to drop into its default event handler, or you select the control in question and then use the Properties window to find the specific event that you are after. When you do that, though, Visual Basic 2005 Express writes code for you, out of sight and out of mind, that connects your event methods to the correct parts of the selected controls. The beauty of this is that although you may not have had an urge to look behind the scenes at just what's going on, after you do, a whole universe of possibilities for your code opens up.

You see, events behind the scenes are actually very easy to work with. It's a relative no-brainer to manually write code that connects your own methods to events, and it's only a tiny step beyond no-brainer to write code that raises events.

Think about that for a second. You can write code that raises events. You may have a complex object, for example, that's displayed simultaneously in a few windows in your application. Wouldn't it be great if the object itself could raise an event, just as a control does, that the windows in your application can respond to in order to redraw themselves?

That's exactly what you're going to look at in this short chapter.

Hooking Events by Hand

Let's take a glimpse behind the scenes within a simple Windows application. This isn't going to be a "Try It Out" in the traditional sense, but feel free to follow along with me to get your feet wet.

Let's say you have a simple WinForms project as in Figure 12-1.

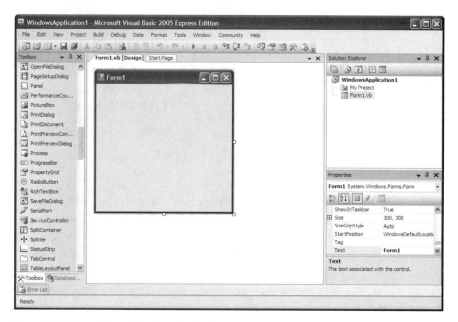

Figure 12-1. *Just about the simplest WinForms project you could possibly have*

As you already saw a while ago, there's a source file hidden out of sight that forms part of the `Partial` class for `Form1`. You can see it by clicking the Show All Files button on the toolbar at the top of the Solution Explorer, in which case the Solution Explorer changes to look like Figure 12-2.

Figure 12-2. *Clicking the Show All Files button shows the partial class source file behind Form1.*

When you add controls to a form, VB Express puts code into this file that sets up those controls based on their size and location, as well as any other property values you set. For example, dropping a button onto Form1 generates this:

```
<Global.Microsoft.VisualBasic.CompilerServices.DesignerGenerated()> _
Partial Class Form1
    Inherits System.Windows.Forms.Form

    'Form overrides dispose to clean up the component list.
    <System.Diagnostics.DebuggerNonUserCode()> _
    Protected Overrides Sub Dispose(ByVal disposing As Boolean)
        If disposing AndAlso components IsNot Nothing Then
            components.Dispose()
        End If
        MyBase.Dispose(disposing)
    End Sub

    'Required by the Windows Form Designer
    Private components As System.ComponentModel.IContainer

    'NOTE: The following procedure is required by the Windows Form Designer
    'It can be modified using the Windows Form Designer.
    'Do not modify it using the code editor.
    <System.Diagnostics.DebuggerStepThrough()> _
    Private Sub InitializeComponent()
        Me.Button1 = New System.Windows.Forms.Button
        Me.SuspendLayout()
        '
        'Button1
        '
        Me.Button1.Location = New System.Drawing.Point(104, 116)
        Me.Button1.Name = "Button1"
        Me.Button1.Size = New System.Drawing.Size(75, 23)
        Me.Button1.TabIndex = 0
        Me.Button1.Text = "Button1"
        Me.Button1.UseVisualStyleBackColor = True
        '
        'Form1
        '
```

```
        Me.AutoScaleDimensions = New System.Drawing.SizeF(6.0!, 13.0!)
        Me.AutoScaleMode = System.Windows.Forms.AutoScaleMode.Font
        Me.ClientSize = New System.Drawing.Size(292, 266)
        Me.Controls.Add(Me.Button1)
        Me.Name = "Form1"
        Me.Text = "Form1"
        Me.ResumeLayout(False)

    End Sub
    Friend WithEvents Button1 As System.Windows.Forms.Button

End Class
```

Notice the commented section labeled 'Button1. Following that comment is the code that sets up the button's size, location, name, and text properties. Notice also the very last line of code:

```
    Friend WithEvents Button1 As System.Windows.Forms.Button
```

The key here is the WithEvents keyword. When you declare an object WithEvents, you are effectively telling Visual Basic that you are aware that this object raises events, and you intend to handle some or all of them.

If you were to double-click the button on the form, the event handler that appears in your form's code looks like this:

```
    Private Sub Button1_Click(ByVal sender As System.Object, _
        ByVal e As System.EventArgs) Handles Button1.Click


    End Sub
```

You've seen this before. Look closely and you'll see that this relatively innocent-looking subroutine is suffixed with Handles Button1.Click. Because our Button control was created in the Partial class with the WithEvents keyword, you can use the Handles keyword to automatically set up which methods in your code "handle" events from the button. The name of the subroutine could be anything you want it to be, because it's the Handles statement that actually hooks the subroutine into a specific event of a specific control. By default, VB Express names event handlers as Controlname_Eventname. So, it follows then that if you wanted to manually set up an event handler, all you'd have to do is add the word Handles to the end of a method name. Realistically though, this is a pain. The subroutines you create must have the exact same signature as the event needs, so if you want to hook up events in code before runtime, it really is best to do so by using the Properties window as we've done in every example in this book.

But what if you wanted to dynamically set up event handlers at runtime? What about creating your own events from scratch? Let's dig a little deeper.

Creating Custom Events

Time to refer to the online help. First, take a look at the online help for the Button's Click event (see Figure 12-3).

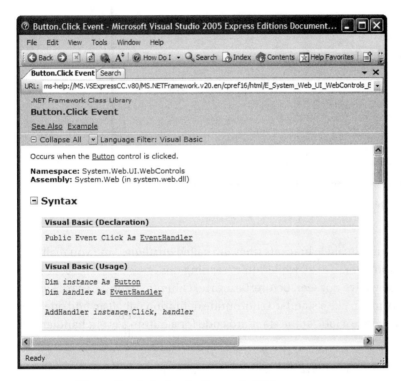

Figure 12-3. *The online help for the Button's Click event*

There are two very interesting items here. First, there's a new VB keyword that we'll come back to in a moment: Event. Second, notice that the help says this event thing is of type EventHandler. If you click on that to follow the help down to EventHandler, you get Figure 12-4.

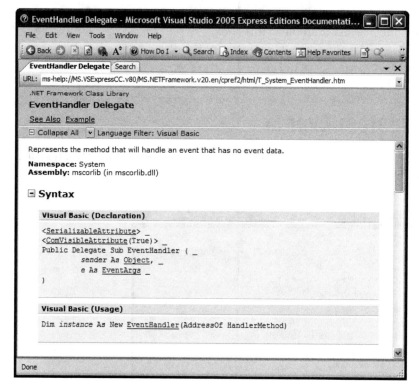

Figure 12-4. *The online help for EventHandler*

Ignoring the weird stuff in angle brackets (they are called *attributes,* and you really don't need to worry about them at all while you're reading this book), EventHandler is declared as a new type you've not seen before: Delegate. Other than the Delegate keyword, this looks pretty much like a standard subroutine definition (albeit an odd one with no code inside). In fact, take a look at the standard code for a button's event handler in a form again:

```
Private Sub Button1_Click(ByVal sender As System.Object, _
    ByVal e As System.EventArgs) Handles Button1.Click

    End Sub
```

Look familiar? It should, because the event handler in your code has exactly the same format as this Delegate thing called EventHandler. Time to reveal all.

If you were a C or C++ programmer, I'd tell you that a delegate is like an ultrasmart pointer to a function. You would wonder what's so ultrasmart about it, but the "pointer to a function" bit you'd understand and smile knowingly. Because the majority of the world's population is human, and you're reading this book because you have a life and thus don't want to learn C++, let me explain it another way.

A Delegate is a special kind of class that simply holds a list of functions to call. When you declare a delegate, you are defining a class that exists for no other purpose than to hold lists of functions. So far, so good. You declare a delegate, even though it's a special kind of class, just as you would declare a method. For example, say I had a method in my code called SayHello that looked like this:

```
Private Sub SayHello(ByVal personsName As String)

End Sub
```

Then I could declare a delegate that could keep track of functions such as SayHello, like this:

```
Public Delegate Sub HelloFunctionDelegate(ByVal SomeValue As String)
```

The key thing here is that the signature of the delegate is identical to the signature of my method. Both the delegate and my method are subroutines, and both the delegate and my method take a single string parameter. You'll recall from when you looked at method signatures a while back that the names of the parameters are not important—what is important is their type and number. As long as the delegate has the same number of parameters as the functions it's supposed to keep track of, and the same types, we're in good shape.

Now, because a delegate is really a class, simply declaring a delegate does nothing useful. We need to actually create a member variable to hold the delegate (class). It's just like saying Dim myEmployee as New Employee in code. myEmployee becomes an object variable that refers to an Employee object. With delegates, though, we use the Event keyword to do the same thing:

```
Public Event HelloFunc As HelloFunctionDelegate
```

So, HelloFunc is an event that holds a Delegate of type HelloFunctionDelegate. Hold that brain together just a little while longer; all is about to become clear.

The obvious question is, "Why would we want to store a delegate, if all a delegate can do is store lists of functions to call?" Glad you asked. The reason we'd do this is that we can actually call a delegate. Let's really let that statement sink in with a "Try It Out."

Try It Out: Delegates and Events

Create a new console project (we'll keep it simple and not let graphical controls and so on get in the way). After it's created and the code is in the editor, go ahead and add a new `Employee` class to it:

```
Module Module1

    Sub Main()

    End Sub

End Module

Public Class Employee
    Private _employeeName As String

    Public Sub HireEmployee(ByVal name As String)

    End Sub

    Public Sub FireEmployee()

    End Sub
End Class
```

Now, what we'd like to happen here is for events to fire when an employee is hired and when an employee is fired. You could declare an `HrActionDelegate` for this. Go ahead:

```
Public Class Employee

    Public Delegate Sub HrActionDelegate(ByVal name As String)

    Private _employeeName As String

    Public Sub HireEmployee(ByVal name As String)

    End Sub

    Public Sub FireEmployee()

    End Sub
End Class
```

Now that the delegate is declared, you need to let the Employee class know that it can use it as an event. Actually, you need two events: one for hiring someone, and one for firing someone. Go ahead and add the two lines:

```
Public Class Employee

    Public Delegate Sub HrActionDelegate(ByVal name As String)
    Public Event Hire As HrActionDelegate
    Public Event Fire As HrActionDelegate

    Private _employeeName As String

    Public Sub HireEmployee(ByVal name As String)

    End Sub

    Public Sub FireEmployee()

    End Sub

End Class
```

Here you're saying that the Employee class can raise two events: Hire and Fire. In addition, these events are of type HrActionDelegate. What that means, of course, is that any event handlers someone declares to respond to those events (it's just as if you had written a button here and said it could be "clicked") must have the same signature as the delegate. So, that's a subroutine that expects a single string as a parameter.

Now, you have the delegate declared and you have two events in your Employee class using it. The next step is to actually raise an event when someone gets hired or fired. Let's code up the HireEmployee() method first:

```
Public Class Employee

    Public Delegate Sub HrActionDelegate(ByVal name As String)
    Public Event Hire As HrActionDelegate
    Public Event Fire As HrActionDelegate

    Private _employeeName As String

    Public Sub HireEmployee(ByVal name As String)
        _employeeName = name
        RaiseEvent Hire(_employeeName)
    End Sub
```

```
    Public Sub FireEmployee()

    End Sub

End Class
```

The first bit is straightforward enough. When the `HireEmployee()` method is called, you store the employee name in a member variable in the class.

The next line uses the `RaiseEvent` keyword to actually raise the event. What happens is .NET then calls any handlers that have been added to the event. If there are no event handlers registered with our object, then that line does nothing.

Let's code up the `FireEmployee()` method now. Then you can get on with some code to see all this stuff in action:

```
Public Class Employee

    Public Delegate Sub HrActionDelegate(ByVal name As String)
    Public Event Hire As HrActionDelegate
    Public Event Fire As HrActionDelegate

    Private _employeeName As String

    Public Sub HireEmployee(ByVal name As String)
        _employeeName = name
        RaiseEvent Hire(_employeeName)
    End Sub

    Public Sub FireEmployee()
        RaiseEvent Fire(_employeeName)
    End Sub

End Class
```

This is pretty much the same thing. When `FireEmployee()` is called, `RaiseEvent` is used to "raise" the Fire event, passing across the name of the person that got fired.

Let's drop back into the main `Module1` code now and put all this to use. First, you need two event handlers, just as if you were creating handlers for Button clicks:

```
Module Module1

    Sub Main()
```

```
    End Sub

    Private Sub NewEmployee(ByVal name As String)
        Console.WriteLine("We just hired {0}", name)
    End Sub
    Private Sub RetireEmployee(ByVal name As String)
        Console.WriteLine("{0} just took early retirement", name)
    End Sub

End Module
```

Notice that both the handlers have exactly the same syntax as your delegate; they are subroutines and take a single string as a parameter.

All that remains then is to create a couple of Employee objects and connect the handlers:

```
Module Module1

    Sub Main()

        Dim pete As New Employee()
        Dim fred As New Employee()

        AddHandler pete.Hire, AddressOf NewEmployee
        AddHandler pete.Fire, AddressOf RetireEmployee
        AddHandler fred.Hire, AddressOf NewEmployee
        AddHandler fred.Fire, AddressOf RetireEmployee

    End Sub

    Private Sub NewEmployee(ByVal name As String)
        Console.WriteLine("We just hired {0}", name)
    End Sub
    Private Sub RetireEmployee(ByVal name As String)
        Console.WriteLine("{0} just took early retirement", name)
    End Sub

End Module
```

First, two Employee objects, pete and fred, are created. Next you connect the handlers. To do this you simply use AddHandler, which takes two parameters, as you can see. The first is the object and event you are hooking up (IntelliSense helps you here, showing you a list of events on the object that you can hook into).

The second is the AddressOf routine you want to use as your event handler. Again, the subroutine you specify here must have exactly the same signature as the delegate. It's worth also noting that you are not limited to adding just one event handler to an event. AddHandler can be used to add as many subroutines to handle the event as you like. When the event is raised, all routines you pass through AddHandler get called. You are effectively adding your event handlers to a list of functions that Employee needs to call when employees get hired or fired.

So the final step is to hire and fire some people:

```
Module Module1

    Sub Main()

        Dim pete As New Employee()
        Dim fred As New Employee()

        AddHandler pete.Hire, AddressOf NewEmployee
        AddHandler pete.Fire, AddressOf RetireEmployee
        AddHandler fred.Hire, AddressOf NewEmployee
        AddHandler fred.Fire, AddressOf RetireEmployee

        Console.WriteLine("Let the hiring and firing commence...")
        pete.HireEmployee("Pete")
        fred.HireEmployee("Fred")
        pete.FireEmployee()
        fred.FireEmployee()

        Console.ReadLine()

    End Sub

    Private Sub NewEmployee(ByVal name As String)
        Console.WriteLine("We just hired {0}", name)
    End Sub
    Private Sub RetireEmployee(ByVal name As String)
        Console.WriteLine("{0} just took early retirement", name)
    End Sub

End Module
```

Notice that all you are doing here is calling methods on the Employee objects. Those methods, because of the code you wrote earlier, fire events. The events are wired up to call the NewEmployee() and RetireEmployee() methods in your program. So, if you run the program now, you'll see Figure 12-5.

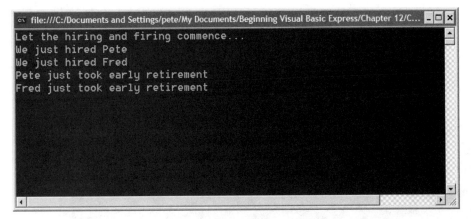

```
file:///C:/Documents and Settings/pete/My Documents/Beginning Visual Basic Express/Chapter 12/C...
Let the hiring and firing commence...
We just hired Pete
We just hired Fred
Pete just took early retirement
Fred just took early retirement
```

Figure 12-5. *When the program is run, the events fire and your event handlers catch them and output the results.*

Just to demonstrate the point I made about adding multiple handlers to an event, go ahead and double up pete's handlers, like this:

```vbnet
Sub Main()

    Dim pete As New Employee()
    Dim fred As New Employee()

    AddHandler pete.Hire, AddressOf NewEmployee
    AddHandler pete.Fire, AddressOf RetireEmployee
    AddHandler pete.Hire, AddressOf NewEmployee
    AddHandler pete.Fire, AddressOf RetireEmployee

    AddHandler fred.Hire, AddressOf NewEmployee
    AddHandler fred.Fire, AddressOf RetireEmployee

    Console.WriteLine("Let the hiring and firing commence...")
    pete.HireEmployee("Pete")
    fred.HireEmployee("Fred")
    pete.FireEmployee()
    fred.FireEmployee()

    Console.ReadLine()

End Sub
```

Because we've added our handlers twice here, if you run the program again you'll see the output in Figure 12-6.

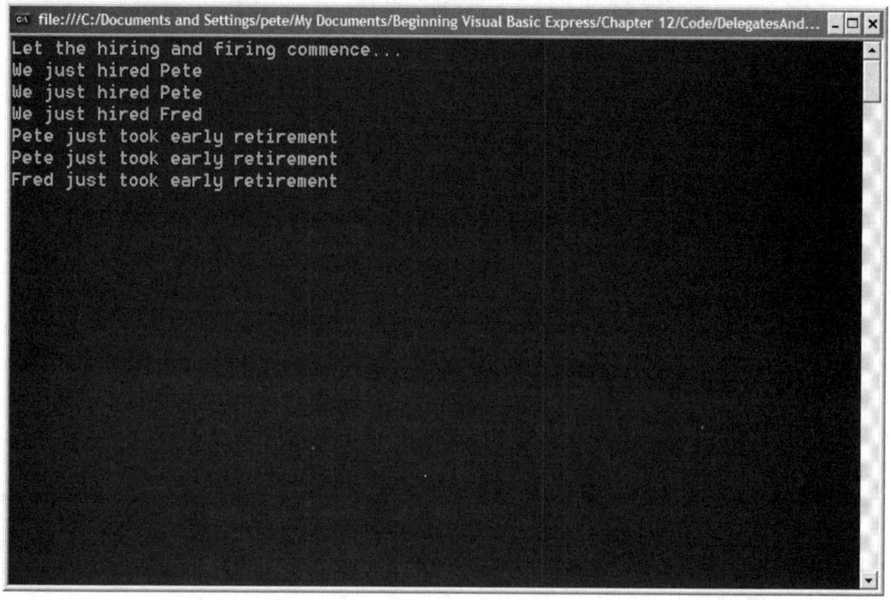

Figure 12-6. *Events can be set up to call more than one delegate method!*

Summary

The first time I came across delegates and events, my mind melted. For that reason, I've tried really hard here to lighten the subject a little. Even so, if you are confused, it may help you to reread the chapter and also just mess around with the code.

In short, a *delegate* is a list of functions to call, and an *event* is a container for delegates. At runtime you simply create instances of delegates and add them into events. You can then call the event just as if it were a standard method, and it in turn will call every single delegate method that has been added to it.

This will open up a lot of possibilities for you when you start to design really complex systems of your own later.

CHAPTER 13

■■■

Lists and Generics

You've looked at lists of data quite a lot already. Back in the early chapters, for example, I touched on arrays, the absolute simplest form of list out there, and very handy they are too from time to time. After you started to explore the world of Windows user interface programming, you came across controls that are meant to do nothing more than work with lists and present them to users (list boxes, combo boxes, and so on). What I didn't mention, though, are the subtle differences and potential problems.

Take a look at how to declare an array, for example:

```
Dim names(100) As String
```

Obviously, in your own code you'd go ahead and replace string with whatever data type you want to store in a list, even your own custom classes. There's a problem with arrays, though. How would you add items into an array? What about removing items from the array? How do you sort it?

The only answer to all these questions is code, and lots of it. Invariably the code would look pretty ugly as well, because you would have to undertake an unpleasant ReDim of the array in question. For example, let's say that we had an array of strings and wanted to add a new one into it. The code might end up looking like this:

```
Sub AddStringToArray(ByRef names() As String, ByVal newName As String)
    Dim size As Integer = names.Length

    ReDim Preserve names(size + 1)
    names(size) = newName
End Sub
```

It's not a particularly complex snippet of code, but it sure is ugly for a task as seemingly trivial as adding an item onto the end of a list. In addition, if you wanted to do something such as sort the array, the code would grow even more, and that's still not including the nasty, ugly line of code that needs to call the function in the first place:

```
AddStringToArray( myArray, "The new string");
```

All of this is really quite inefficient as well. Do that little lot enough times in a loop and you'll find the performance of your code go down through a hole. So, there's no getting away from it: arrays certainly have their uses, but they are definitely not the flexible way of working with data in the world of Visual Basic.

On the other hand, take a look at a list box. With the ListBox.Items collection (that's the key word here—collection), you can add items into the list, remove items, and even sort items. That's what collections do, but unfortunately they have limitations as well. Take a look at this line of code to add a custom object to a collection and then get it out again:

```
myListBox.Items.Add("My New String")
newString =CType(myListBox.Items(myListBox.Items.Count-1), String)
```

The big no-no here is the cast that has to take place. You see, collections store *objects,* as in System.Object. They don't store any specific type. What this means is that you have to put up with the performance cost of casting from a System.Object to the specific type you are interested in, at runtime. More problematic, though, is that with untyped collections you don't get compile-time checking. For example, if I had a string array called myArray and tried to do this

```
myArray(0) = 123
```

my program wouldn't even run. Instead, I'd get a nice compile-time error telling me that myArray is a string array and so I shouldn't add numbers to it. Now, imagine I had a collection of strings and tried to do this with it:

```
Dim myInt As Integer = CType(myListBox.Items(0), Integer)
```

That would compile just fine, because you can treat an integer as an object (you can, but you shouldn't for reasons covered earlier), but at runtime the program would crash. It's much nicer to get compile-time errors than it is to have your pride and joy crash unceremoniously in front of your users, isn't it. The crash, of course, would occur because the collection holds strings, so when I try to cast a string to an integer I get an error. It's also very, very slow. Doing this in a loop over 10,000 items would take a long time because behind the scenes .NET needs to check every access into the collection to make sure that I'm not screwing up the data types I'm working with.

So, although arrays are a little inflexible, they are nowhere near as dangerous as collections. Well, that's how it used to be, anyway.

In the .NET Framework 2.0 we get a new feature called generics, and a brand new set of collections in the new System.Collections.Generic namespace that provide all the power of arrays (including compile-time type checking), but with all the flexibility of collections. Let's take a look at how that works.

Introducing Generics

Microsoft calls *generics* "parameterized types," which even I find confusing. I prefer to think of them as classes *Of something*. For example, instead of the old-fashioned .NET 1.0 collections of objects, generics let you have collections *of* strings, or collections *of* integers, or collections *of* employees, and so on. The obvious use for them is in dealing with nice big lists of stuff, and so Microsoft very kindly provides a bunch of generics lists in the System.Collections.Generic namespace. They are listed in Table 13-1.

Table 13-1. *Types of Collections in the System.Collections.Generic Namespace*

System.Collections.Generic	Description
List	A nice simple list, which can be sorted.
SortedList	A special list that holds two "things" for every item: a key and a value. Think of it as a social security number and a person's name. The number is the key and is always unique. A sorted list will sort based on that key.
Dictionary	Another key-value type of list that enables you to instantly access any item based on its key.
SortedDictionary	Has all the benefits of a SortedList (in that it sorts items), coupled with the wonderful instant item access of a Dictionary.
LinkedList	A special list that enables each item to point forward to the next, or backward to the previous, a bit like an iron chain.
Queue	As with a real-world queue, you can get at only the first item in the queue. The first one to enter the queue is the first one out as well.
Stack	Think of a stack of plates in a restaurant. You can easily get at only the last plate added to the stack, so Stack works in a last in, first out way.

Declaring any of these for use in code requires you to use the special generic's way of working. For example, if you wanted to declare a list of aliens in space game, you would do this:

```
Dim aliens As New List(Of Alien)
```

The *type* the list is going to hold is specified using the Of keyword inside parentheses. In this case then, you have created a list that will hold objects of type Alien.

Once you have the list created, you'll find that it works like a very natural, and powerful, array. Rather than give the whole game away right now, let's dive in and take a look at each type with some examples.

Lists and SortedLists

As I gave away in the preceding section, creating an instance of a generic list is quite easy, but it can take a little getting used to. The easiest way to become familiar with the syntax is this. First, you'll need to add an Imports line to the top of the source file you are working with, to let Visual Basic know that you are going to work with classes from the System.Collections.Generic namespace.

```
Imports System.Collections.Generic
Module Module1



        :
        :


End Module
```

Next, declare a list like any other kind of object. For example:

```
Dim aliens As New List
```

As you type this in, IntelliSense will kick in and encourage you to finish off the declaration by specifying the type to use in the generic list:

```
Dim aliens As New List(Of Alien)
```

With the list created, items can be added into the list by calling the Add() method on it:

```
aliens.Add( reallyBadAlien )
```

Similarly, items can be removed from the list by calling Remove():

```
aliens.Remove( reallyBadAlien )
```

Notice, though, that with a call to Remove() you really need to pass in the actual object to remove. This isn't always convenient, though, so the generic List lets you also remove based on an index:

```
aliens.RemoveAt( 12 )
```

The preceding code line would of course remove the 13th item from the list; list items, like array items, are numbered starting at 0. Should you need to completely empty a list, a quick call to the aptly named Clear() will do just that:

```
aliens.Clear()
```

There is also a RemoveAll() method, but strangely it doesn't actually remove all items from a list. It uses something called a *predicate* to locate matching items in the list and removes just those items. We'll look at how this works in a moment.

The Add() and Remove() methods then add most of the functionality that people soon start to wish arrays had. However, lists can do so much more than arrays, particularly when it comes to finding things.

Finding Items in a List

There are seven methods that you can use to find items in a list: Contains(), Exists(), Find(), FindAll(), FindIndex(), FindLast(), and FindLastIndex().

Contains() is perhaps the simplest of them all. If you pass in an object to Find(), it will return True or False if the list contains an identical item (in terms of the values in the public properties of the object). You have to be careful with this, though. Let's take a look at why.

Try It Out: The Problem with Contains()

We'll stick with console-based applications for now to focus on the semantics of working with the generic collections rather than building complex user interfaces, so go ahead and create a new console application in Visual Basic 2005 Express.

First, add a class into Module1.vb for the wonderful canonical Employee class:

```vb
Module Module1

    Sub Main()

    End Sub

End Module

Public Class Employee
    Public Name As String
    Public Number As String
    Private m_id As Integer



    Public Sub New(ByVal name As String, ByVal number As String)
        Me.Name = name
        Me.Number = number
        m_id = New Random().Next(10000)
    End Sub
```

```
    Public Overrides Function ToString() As String
        Return String.Format("Employee Num: {0} Name: {1} id({2})", _
            Me.Number, Me.Name, m_id)
    End Function

End Class
```

It's a pretty simple class, as you can see. There are a couple of public fields in there to expose the user's name and social security number (no, I wouldn't recommend you work with social security numbers this blithely in a real application), and a private member that holds a unique internal ID. The class has a single constructor that is used to set up these three variables and a simple `ToString()` implementation to print out the employee information as text. So far, so good.

Now add some code into the `Main()` function to actually use this `Employee` class in a generic `List` (don't forget to add an `Imports` statement to the very top of the source as well):

Imports System.Collections.Generic

```
Module Module1

    Sub Main()
        Dim staff As New List(Of Employee)
        Dim newHire As New Employee("John Smith", "1101")
        staff.Add(newHire)

        If staff.Contains(newHire) Then
            Console.WriteLine( _
              "Yes the list contains the item we just added" _
                + vbCrLf + "        {0}", _
                newHire.ToString())

        End If


        newHire = New Employee("John Smith", "1101")
        If staff.Contains(newHire) Then
            Console.WriteLine("The list also contains John")
        Else
            Console.WriteLine("Nope, can't find John Smith")
        End If
```

```
        Console.ReadLine()

    End Sub

End Module
```

Before you run this, let me explain what's going on. First a generic List is created to hold Employee objects. Notice that the code includes "Of Employee" to "type" the generic list to Employee objects only.

Next, a new Employee is created and added to the list. As I mentioned in the intro, you can add items into a list just by calling the Add() method.

Next, you call the Contains() method. Naturally, because you just added the object into the list, Contains() returns True to indicate that the item is in the list. So far this should all make sense. Now we come to the problem with Contains().

The next block of code creates a new Employee object and fills in the employee name through the constructor. You're going to use this new Employee object to effectively search the List for an item. The problem is, Contains() will fail.

Go ahead and run the code and you'll see the output in Figure 13-1.

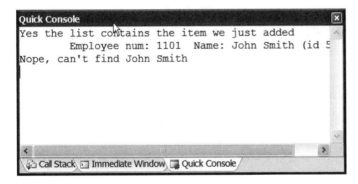

Figure 13-1. *Contains() fails to find the second object.*

The reason that Contains() fails is that it is looking for an exact object match; it's not checking properties and data within an object, but is instead searching through a list to see whether the exact same object you pass to Contains() is already in the list. Sometimes this way of working is useful. For example, you might be building a list to hold staff members who have been selected to play on the softball team. Before trying to add a staff member to the list, you could call Contains() to see whether that person is already on the team, and then add that person if not.

For the vast majority of code, though, Contains() really isn't that useful. Instead, what you'll need is a more flexible method of finding *any* object based on certain criteria. For example, find all the aliens in a video game that are still alive and need updating, or find all staff members in a certain department, or simply find that guy called Peter Wright on the payroll. That's exactly where the Find() methods come into play.

The Find() Methods

I mentioned before that there are seven Find () methods available to you when you work with a generic collection: Find(), FindAll(), FindLast(), FindIndex(), FindLastIndex(), Exists(), and Contains(). You work with all these methods in exactly the same way.

First, you create a search method, like this:

```
Function FindEmployeeByName(ByVal employeeToCheck As Employee) As Boolean
    Return employeeToCheck.EmployeeName.Equals( _
        employeeToFind.EmployeeName)
End Function
```

This method obviously works only with Employee objects, but the basic format would look the same if you were searching for integers:

```
Function FindSomeNumber(ByVal numberToCheck As Integer) As Boolean
    Return (numberToCheck = numberToFind)
End Function
```

Both methods simply compare the value passed in as a parameter to some other value, usually an instance variable in the class containing the method.

With the search method created, all that remains is to pass the address of the method to the List.Find() method.

```
Dim matchedEmployee As Employee = staff.Find(AddressOf FindEmployeeByName);
```

This calls the Find() method on a generic list and tells the Find() method to use the predicate you set up.

The Find() method itself just iterates through all the items in the list and for each item calls your predicate. In this case that means that for every item in the list, your FindEmployeeByNamePredicate() (searcher) will get called. Find() will pass your function the current item in the list, and it's up to your code in the function to return a True or False value based on whether the item passed in is the one that you were looking for.

The net result, with Find() anyway, is that when a match is made, the matching item from the list is returned. If no match is made, null is returned.

So, let's put all that in English. The Find() methods don't actually do very much. Their job is simply to move through each item in a list and call a function that you create (the predicate) to do the searching. Your job in searching a list is to create the function and return True or False to show Find() whether the item it passed was the one you were looking for.

Let's take a look at a couple of these Find() methods with some real code.

Try It Out: Using the Find() Methods

Create a new console application. In this you'll create a generic Employee list and then search for an employee by name, and also find all the employees who work in a specific department.

The first thing to do is to add an Employee class to the project. Add in Employee.vb to the solution in the usual way and key in the following code to create the Employee class itself:

```vb
Public Class Employee
    Private _employeeNumber As Integer
    Public EmployeeName As String
    Public Department As String

    Public ReadOnly Property EmployeeNumber() As Integer
        Get
            Return _employeeNumber
        End Get
    End Property

    Public Sub New(ByVal name As String, ByVal department As String)
        Me.EmployeeName = name
        Me.Department = department
        _employeeNumber = New Random().Next()
    End Sub

    Public Sub New()
        ' A do-nothing constructor
    End Sub
End Class
```

The class is straightforward. It has a constructor that takes in parameters to initialize the properties of the class as soon as an instance is created. It also has a constructor that does nothing—you'll see that in use shortly.

The class also has three members: EmployeeName and Department are standard public fields, and _employeeNumber is a private variable you just set up with a random number to make each instance of the class different from another internally. This isn't necessary; it's just to make sure that you are unlikely to end up with two instances of a class with the same public properties that are completely identical (the random number will normally be different).

Drop back into the Module1.vb code now. You need to initialize a generic Employee list with a bunch of items, and then you'll call out to two of your own methods to find first one specific employee and then a bunch of employees in a specific department. As before, don't forget to add the Imports line to the top of the source code so that you are able to work with generic lists.

```vb
Imports System.Collections.Generic

Module Module1

    Sub Main()
        Dim staff As New List(Of Employee)
        staff.Add(New Employee("Peter Wright", "IT"))
        staff.Add(New Employee("Heather Wright", "Usability"))
        staff.Add(New Employee("Dominic Shakeshaft", "Editorial"))
        staff.Add(New Employee("Grace Wong", "Management"))
        staff.Add(new Employee("Gary Cornell", "Management))

        FindAnEmployee(staff, "Peter Wright")
        FindStaffInDepartment(staff, "Management")

        Console.ReadLine()
    End Sub

End Module
```

Because you added a constructor that can take parameters to the Employee class, it's quite easy to initialize the Employee list simply passing in a bunch of new Employee objects.

With the list created, you just hand off control to two functions that you have yet to write: the FindAnEmployee() function looks for a specific employee in the list, while the FindStaffInDepartment() method lists all employees who work in a specific part of the business. Let's go ahead and code these up, in the Module1.vb source file:

```vb
Module Module1

    Private _employeeToFind As Employee

    Sub Main()
        Dim staff As New List(Of Employee)
        staff.Add(New Employee("Peter Wright", "IT"))
        staff.Add(New Employee("Heather Wright", "Usability"))
        staff.Add(New Employee("Dominic Shakeshaft", "Editorial"))
        staff.Add(New Employee("Grace Wong", "Management"))
        staff.Add(New Employee("Gary Cornell", "Management"))

        FindAnEmployee(staff, "Peter Wright")
        FindStaffInDepartment(staff, "Management")

        Console.ReadLine()
    End Sub

    Sub FindAnEmployee(ByVal staff As List(Of Employee), ByVal name As String)
        _employeeToFind = New Employee()
        _employeeToFind.EmployeeName = name

        If staff.Exists(AddressOf FindEmployeeByName) Then
            Dim matchedEmployee As Employee = _
                staff.Find(AddressOf FindEmployeeByName)
            Console.WriteLine("    {0} works in {1}", _
                matchedEmployee.EmployeeName, matchedEmployee.Department)
        End If
    End Sub

    Function FindEmployeeByName(ByVal employeeToCheck As Employee) As Boolean
        Return (employeeToCheck.EmployeeName.Equals( _
            _employeeToFind.EmployeeName))
    End Function

End Module
```

Notice that the first thing you do here is declare a new private variable. This variable is used by the actual predicate; you need some way to set up the data that you want to search for and that the predicate can access to check whether the required item has been found in the list.

The FindAnEmployee() method creates an instance of the Employee class and stores it in your private variable. The code then sets up the Name property of this new Employee instance to the value passed into your function. So, in your code you want to search for an employee called Pete Wright, so you set the name of the employee to Pete Wright.

All that remains is to call the actual Find() methods of the list:

```
If staff.Exists(AddressOf FindEmployeeByName) Then
    Dim matchedEmployee As Employee = _
        staff.Find(AddressOf FindEmployeeByName)
    Console.WriteLine("    {0} works in {1}", _
        matchedEmployee.EmployeeName, matchedEmployee.Department)
End If
```

The first one is Exists(). This just searches through the list, using the address of your predicate function, and will return True if the predicate function eventually finds a match, and False if it never does. Assuming it does, though, you drop into a code block to actually grab the matching employee and print some details.

You grab the matching employee with a call to staff.Find(). This will return the first matching object that is found. This can be a problem if there is more than one match in the list, obviously, but you'll look at a solution for that in a moment. For now take a look at the predicate function itself:

```
Function FindEmployeeByName(ByVal employeeToCheck As Employee) As Boolean
    Return (employeeToCheck.EmployeeName.Equals( _
        _employeeToFind.EmployeeName))
End Function
```

All this method does is compare the Name properties of two Employee objects: the one passed in from the list's Find() method, and the private variable you created earlier. It returns True if the employee names match, and False if they don't.

Before you go any further, you'll add some candy to the code to smarten up the output a little, and stub the second method that you haven't written yet. Go ahead and add the highlighted lines of code to your Module1.vb code:

```vb
Sub FindAnEmployee(ByVal staff As List(Of Employee), ByVal name As String)

    Console.WriteLine("Trying to find employee {0}", name)

    _employeeToFind = New Employee()
    _employeeToFind.EmployeeName = name

    If staff.Exists(AddressOf FindEmployeeByName) Then

        Console.WriteLine("    Found the employee")

        Dim matchedEmployee As Employee = staff.Find(AddressOf _
            FindEmployeeByName)
        Console.WriteLine("    {0} works in {1}", _
            matchedEmployee.EmployeeName, matchedEmployee.Department)

    Else

        Console.WriteLine("    No, I'm afraid I couldn't find the employee")

    End If
End Sub

Function FindEmployeeByName(ByVal employeeToCheck As Employee) As Boolean
    Return (employeeToCheck.EmployeeName.Equals( _
        _employeeToFind.EmployeeName))
End Function

Sub FindStaffInDepartment(ByVal staff As List(Of Employee), _
    ByVal department As String)
    '
End Sub
```

Run the program now and you'll see the output in Figure 13-2.

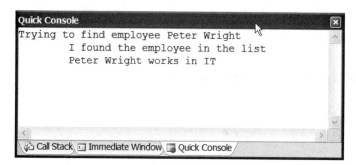

Figure 13-2. *At last, you can find items in the List.*

The Exists() and Find() methods both look for the first match and return a result.

On the other hand, the FindAll() method returns another generic List containing all matches.

Code up the FindStaffInDepartment() method and the predicate you're going to use to search for matching departments:

```vb
Sub FindStaffInDepartment(ByVal staff As List(Of Employee), _

    ByVal department As String)
    Console.WriteLine("Trying to find all staff that work in {0}", _
        department)

    _employeeToFind = New Employee()
    _employeeToFind.Department = department

    Dim matchedEmployees As List(Of Employee) = _
        staff.FindAll(AddressOf FindEmployeesInDepartment)

    For Each foundEmployee As Employee In matchedEmployees
        Console.WriteLine("    {0} works in {1}", _
            foundEmployee.EmployeeName, foundEmployee.Department)
    Next

End Sub


Function FindEmployeesInDepartment(ByVal employeeToCheck As Employee) As
Boolean
    Return (_employeeToFind.Department.Equals( _
        employeeToCheck.Department))
End Function
```

The code is really very similar to the previous example. You set up the private object with the name of the department you want to search for (it's passed into your method), and then call a Find() method (in this case FindAll()) passing in the address of the predicate you want to use to do the actual matching.

The result of FindAll(), as I mentioned earlier, is a generic List of the same type as the one you are searching. All you need to do with the result, then, is iterate over the list with a For Each command and then print out the matching object details. After you've keyed in the new code, run the app and take a look at the results. It should look like Figure 13-3.

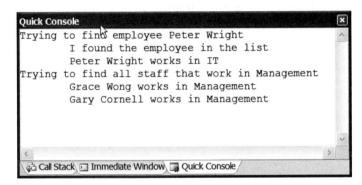

Figure 13-3. *Searching for many matches is just as easy as searching for one.*

The other functions all follow exactly the same pattern: create a matcher method, instantiate a predicate with it, and pass the predicate into the Find() method.

Sorting Lists

Sorting lists works pretty much the same as finding items in a list. Again, you create a function and then pass its address to the list's Sort() method. The function in this case, though, is called a *comparison* instead of a predicate.

A typical comparison function signature looks like this:

```
Function Compare(ByVal firstEmployee As Employee, _
    ByVal secondEmployee As Employee) As Integer
```

It takes two parameters of the same types and returns an integer. If the integer is less than 0, the first object is less than the second. If the integer is 0, the two objects are the same. It figures then, that if the integer is positive, the first object is greater than the second. It's up to the code in the comparison function to figure out how to compare two objects such as Employees, which don't have a typical numeric type value.

Let's extend the previous sample with a comparer to sort the list.

Try It Out: Sorting the List

Load up the code you worked on earlier, and add stubs for a sorting routine, and a comparison function to the Module1.vb file:

```
Sub Main()
    Dim staff As New List(Of Employee)
    staff.Add(New Employee("Peter Wright", "IT"))
    staff.Add(New Employee("Heather Wright", "Usability"))
    staff.Add(New Employee("Dominic Shakeshaft", "Editorial"))
    staff.Add(New Employee("Grace Wong", "Management"))
    staff.Add(New Employee("Gary Cornell", "Management"))

    FindAnEmployee(staff, "Peter Wright")
    FindStaffInDepartment(staff, "Management")

    SortTheList(staff)

    Console.ReadLine()
End Sub

Sub SortTheList(ByVal staff As List(Of Employee))

End Sub
Function CompareEmployees(ByVal firstEmployee As Employee, _
    ByVal secondEmployee As Employee) As Integer

End Function
```

Let's work on the comparison function CompareEmployees() first. You'll strip out the surnames of the two employees passed into the function and compare them with the string's built-in CompareTo() function:

```
Function CompareEmployees(ByVal firstEmployee As Employee, _
    ByVal secondEmployee As Employee) As Integer

    Dim firstSurname As String = _
        firstEmployee.EmployeeName.Substring( _
            firstEmployee.EmployeeName.IndexOf(" ") + 1)

    Dim secondSurname As String = _
        secondEmployee.EmployeeName.Substring( _
            secondEmployee.EmployeeName.IndexOf(" ") + 1)

    Return firstSurname.CompareTo(secondSurname)

End Function
```

I know it looks nasty, but it really isn't. The code just finds the index of the first space in the employee name (because in this example a space separates the first name and surname). Armed with this, you can call substring to strip out the second half of the employee name into two variables: firstSurname and secondSurname. With those two strings, you can return the result of string.CompareTo() to do your work for you.

With the function complete, all you need to do now is complete your SortTheList() method:

```
Sub SortTheList(ByVal staff As List(Of Employee))

    Console.WriteLine("The full list of sorted employees follows...")
    staff.Sort(AddressOf CompareEmployees)

    For Each emp As Employee In staff
        Console.WriteLine("    {0}", emp.EmployeeName)
    Next

End Sub
```

Easy, isn't it. The address of CompareEmployees is simply passed to Sort(). Just as with the Find() routines, the Sort() method just iterates through the list calling the comparison function. When Sort() is done, we iterate through the list and print out all the items in it.

Run the code and you'll notice the output of the program has changed to now show the sorted list, as in Figure 13-4.

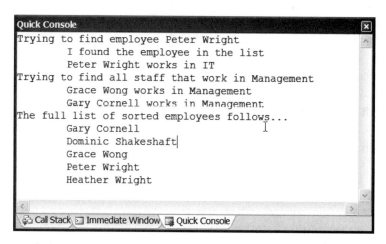

Figure 13-4. *Sorting the list is as easy as searching for items.*

Dictionaries

A straight list is great if you just want to store a bunch of information in an array-like structure, and perhaps sort it, as you saw. If you need to search for something, you've got a great deal of flexibility courtesy of the Find() methods. The search methods, though, are a little inefficient, because behind the scenes the search code in the List iterates through every single item in the list and then calls out to a predicate function that you define. Sometimes you need speed over flexibility, and that's where the generic Dictionary collection comes into play.

The Dictionary lets you store a mass of information as a combination of *keys* and *values,* just like a real dictionary, in fact. If you grab your nearest handy copy of *The Oxford English Dictionary,* you'll find that to find the meaning of a word, you look up the word. The word then, is the key. When you find the key, you find the *value* of the key, which is its textual definition.

Something quite subtle happens when you try to find something in a real dictionary as well. You know that the dictionary is ordered alphabetically. Although the dictionary holds hundreds of thousands of words, it's quite easy to zero in on a specific word definition very quickly by hand. .NET's version of a dictionary uses something called hashes. If you studied computer science in college, you probably know all about hashes. Well done. If (like me) you didn't study computer science in college, you'll have little idea of what a hash is, and the good news is that you don't need to. A *hash* is really just a unique number that gets produced after you throw a bunch of stuff (such as characters in a string) into a hashing algorithm. Armed with the hash, .NET is able to easily and quickly find a key in a dictionary, and from the key find the value. Thankfully, the base object type in .NET knows how to hash itself, and so do all the simple types (strings, and so on), so this isn't something you ever really need to worry about.

Working with a Dictionary

Because a `Dictionary` needs to store two things for every item it contains (a unique key and the matching value), you need to declare two types when you instantiate a `Dictionary`, like this:

```
Dim productList As New Dictionary( Of TKey, TValue)
```

In this snippet, we're setting up a `Dictionary` to hold products. Each product has a unique `ProductKey` object associated with it.

If you were producing an electronic version of a real-world lexical dictionary, you might instantiate the `Dictionary` like this:

```
Dim realDictionary As New Dictionary(Of String, String)
```

Here both the key and value are strings, just as in a real dictionary. Adding items to the `Dictionary` works pretty much the same as adding items to a standard list, except that you need to pass in two items to the `Add()` method:

```
dictionary.Add( key, value )
```

Getting items out of the `Dictionary` looks just like you are working with a standard array, but instead of specifying an array index, you specify the key of the item that you want to find:

```
Dim wordDefinition As String = dictionary( wordToLookup )
```

Because it's so easy to find individual items in the Dictionary based on their keys, dictionaries don't have a set of Find() methods like a list does; you don't need them:

```
dictionary.Add( "computer", "One that computes" )
Dim definition As String = dictionary("computer")
```

You can, however, check to see whether something already exists in a Dictionary, with the ContainsKey() and ContainsValue() methods. Both accept a single object as a parameter and return True or False to show whether a Dictionary contains the object passed in. You could use either of these, for example, to check whether something already exists in the Dictionary before you try to add it, and thus prevent duplicates.

Be careful though; although it's easy to find out whether a specific value is already in the list, there's no quick and simple way to grab a value from a Dictionary unless you happen to know the key. So, the ContainsValue() method really exists only to make absolutely certain that you aren't adding duplicates to the list. For example:

```
Dim authors As New Dictionary(Of Integer, String)

If Not authors.ContainsValue("Pete Wright") Then
    authors.Add(1, "Pete Wright")
End If
```

There is a way around this limitation, still using generics, that I'll show you at the end of the chapter when you take a look at creating your own generic types.

Anyway, let's pull this all this together with a nice little app to show just how to use dictionaries properly.

Try It Out: Dictionaries

In this example you're going to put together a little console app that will build a list of products, perhaps the beginnings of a product catalog application. So, first of all you need to add a new file to the project to hold the classes that define the product. Like all product catalogs, yours uses some obscure product identification code that you'll actually represent in its own product number class.

First, go ahead and add a new class file to the project—call it Products.vb. When the code editor opens, remove the class definition and replace it with two more, like this:

Public Class Product

End Class

Public Class ProductNumber

End Class

The Product class will hold the actual product details, including a name, description, and the product's unique number (you'll need that for the key in the Dictionary, because Dictionary keys have to be unique). In addition, the product number is defined in its own class because it's a little complex.

Let's start work on the ProductNumber class first. Go ahead and fill it out to look like the following code:

```vb
Public Class ProductNumber

    Public ManufacturerCode As String
    Public CategoryCode As String
    Public Number As Integer

    Public Sub New(ByVal code As String)
        Dim codeParts() As String = code.Split(New Char() {"-"})
        ManufacturerCode = codeParts(0)
        CategoryCode = codeParts(1)
        Number = Integer.Parse(codeParts(2))
    End Sub

    Public Overrides Function ToString() As String
        Return String.Format("{0}-{1}-{2}", _
            ManufacturerCode, CategoryCode, Number)
    End Function

End Class
```

The class holds three public properties that define the product number: a manufacturer code, a category code, and an actual product number. It's pretty much like some real-world product numbers I've seen. To simplify using it, the constructor takes in a string, where each part of the number is separated by a minus sign (for example, MSFT-SFTW-101). The constructor uses the string.split() method to get at each part of the product number (for example, MSFT, SFTW, and 101) in their respective properties. Finally, you override the base Object.ToString() method to get at a simple representation of the entire code as one entity again.

Next, you define the Product class itself. This one is real simple:

```
Public Class Product

    Private _productID As ProductNumber
    Public ReadOnly Property ProductID()
        Get
            Return _productID
        End Get
    End Property

    Public ProductName As String
    Public Description As String

    Public Sub New(ByVal productCode As String, ByVal name As String, _
      ByVal description As String)

        _productID = New ProductNumber(productCode)
        ProductName = name
        description = description

    End Sub

End Class
```

The Product constructor takes three parameters to allow users to create a product instance and set up the member variables in one go. Notice it takes a string as the product code, which it hands off to a new instance of the ProductNumber class for decoding.

Okay, so now you have the background out of the way, you're ready to look at the Dictionary side of things.

As I mentioned earlier, a Dictionary requires two things for every item it contains: a value and a unique key. In this Dictionary you'll use a ProductNumber object for the key, and a Product object for the value. Hop back over to the Module1.vb class file and start typing into the Main() subroutine:

```
Imports System.Collections.Generic

Module Module1

    Sub Main()
        Dim catalog As New Dictionary(Of ProductNumber, Product)

        SetupTheCatalog(catalog)

        Console.ReadLine()
    End Sub

    Sub SetupTheCatalog(ByVal dict As Dictionary(Of ProductNumber, Product))

        Dim testproduct As New Product( _
            "WBS-SFTW-101", "CoolSoftware", "A neat piece of software")

        dict.Add(testproduct.ProductID, testproduct)

        testproduct = New Product( _
            "WBS-SFTW-202", "NetSoftware", "A cool piece of Internet software")
        dict.Add(testproduct.ProductID, testproduct)

    End Sub

End Module
```

First things first—you create the Dictionary itself. Because the Dictionary requires two things for each item (the key and the value), you specify two types in the angle brackets to set this up, instead of just one when working with a simple List. Just as I said it would, the Dictionary uses ProductNumber objects as keys, and Product objects as the values.

Next, the code calls your new SetupTheCatalog() function included in the preceding code. This just creates two Products and then calls dict.add() to add them to the Dictionary. Notice again that you need to pass two objects into the Dictionary for each item: the product's unique ProductID (which is a ProductNumber object) and the new Product itself.

So far, so good. If you run the program, it will indeed create a new `Dictionary` and stick a couple of items in it, but you don't really get to see what it's doing or how. So the next step is to look at getting stuff out to check that the `Dictionary` is working properly. Let's go back and add some more code into the `Main()` function:

```
Sub Main()
    Dim catalog As New Dictionary(Of ProductNumber, Product)

    SetupTheCatalog(catalog)

    Try
        Dim numToFind As New ProductNumber("WBS-SFTW-202")
        If catalog.ContainsKey(numToFind) Then
            Console.WriteLine("Apparently, the product does exist")
        Else
            Console.WriteLine("ContainsKey fails")
        End If

        Dim foundProduct As Product = catalog(numToFind)
        If Not foundProduct Is Nothing Then
            Console.WriteLine("{0}: {1}" + vbCrLf + "    {2}", _
                foundProduct.ProductID, foundProduct.ProductName, _
                foundProduct.Description)

        End If
    Catch ex As KeyNotFoundException
        Console.WriteLine( _
            "Couldn't find the product you asked for, sorry")
    End Try

    Console.ReadLine()
End Sub
```

The first big difference between dictionary-based code and normal list-based code you'll notice straight away: you start the new code in a Try...Catch block. The reason for this is that you don't use Find() methods with a Dictionary. You don't need to, because you can directly get at items inside a Dictionary by specifying the key just as if it were an index. Take a look at the first few lines of code inside the Try block to see this:

```
Try
    Dim numToFind As New ProductNumber("WBS-SFTW-202")
    If catalog.ContainsKey(numToFind) Then
        Console.WriteLine("Apparently, the product does exist")
    Else
        Console.WriteLine("ContainsKey fails")
    End If

    Dim foundProduct As Product = catalog(numToFind)
```

The code creates a new ProductNumber object, which you use first to see whether the Dictionary contains that value as a key. This is done with a call to catalog.ContainsKey(). If this returns True, then yes, the Dictionary does contain the key you are searching for and so you go ahead and use this ProductNumber to index into the Dictionary and grab the value you want:

```
    Dim foundProduct As Product = catalog(numToFind)
```

It looks just like it would if you were grabbing something out of an array. Instead of using a number to specify an item by its array index number, you instead hand over a Dictionary key. Now, this is why the code is in a Try...Catch block.

If you try to grab an item from the Dictionary with a key that doesn't exist in the Dictionary, you get an exception. A KeyNotFoundException exception, in fact. So even if you are almost completely certain that everything is going to be fine and the key will be found, you really should wrap your code in a nice Try...Catch block just in case; the last thing you really want is for your program to blow up in front of a user just because you didn't want to type in a few extra lines of code to be supersafe. The eagle eyed among you may have noticed that if I'd restructured this code a little, then you wouldn't need a Try...Catch block at all. I could only try to grab a product if ContainsKey returns true. Obviously, if I'd done that though, you wouldn't have been able to see what happens when things go wrong and how to cope with them.

So now you're all done. You have your Product and ProductNumber classes in place, and some code to build up a Dictionary with them and then grab items. So run the code and see what happens (Figure 13-5).

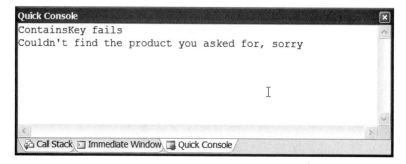

Figure 13-5. *The code fails if you don't take some special steps when working with custom classes for keys.*

It fails. Take a look at the code, though, and it's not really obvious just why it fails. After all, when you do the searching, you specify the key correctly. Looking through the function you wrote that builds up the Dictionary items, you can see that the item you're looking for really is there. So what's going on?

You may have guessed that it's the same problem you met earlier with the List. The Contains() method, and the Dictionary itself when you try to index it with a key, compares to see whether two object references (the one you say you want, and the key itself in the list) refer to exactly the same object in memory. In this case, they don't. There is a solution, though (and this applies to lists as well).

Think way back to when we talked through objects and how they work. Every single class you create in code derives from System.Object. Now, System.Object has a few handy methods in it, one of which you've already met: ToString(). There are two others: Equals() and GetHashCode(). The Equals() method is used when comparing objects. Normally when you compare two objects, the .NET default comparer kicks in that, to be frank, is pretty much useless. You can, of course, override this and provide a much more meaningful implementation. This is particularly useful when working with generic collections like the Dictionary. Now, GetHashCode() is useful in a Dictionary because you need some way of assigning a big, unique number to every object instance that you create; it's how .NET finds a specific object in a Dictionary in lightning-fast speed. Normally, this is a tricky thing to do, but in this case (ProductNumbers) it's dead easy. Because you can represent the entire product number as a unique string, you can just call the string's

GetHashCode() method. Go ahead and add these two methods to the ProductNumber class, and that should also fix your Dictionary search problem:

```
Public Class ProductNumber

    Public ManufacturerCode As String
    Public CategoryCode As String
    Public Number As Integer

    Public Sub New(ByVal code As String)
        Dim codeParts() As String = code.Split(New Char() {"-"})
        ManufacturerCode = codeParts(0)
        CategoryCode = codeParts(1)
        Number = Integer.Parse(codeParts(2))
    End Sub

    Public Overrides Function ToString() As String
        Return String.Format("{0}-{1}-{2}", _
            ManufacturerCode, CategoryCode, Number)
    End Function

    Public Overrides Function Equals(ByVal obj As Object) As Boolean
        If Not TypeOf obj Is ProductNumber Then
            Throw New InvalidCastException( _
                "Can only compare a ProductNumber to another ProductNumber")
        End If
        Return Me.ToString().Equals(obj.ToString())
    End Function

    Public Overrides Function GetHashCode() As Integer
        Return Me.ToString().GetHashCode()
    End Function

End Class
```

The Dictionary's ContainsKey() method uses Equals() to see whether a key in the Dictionary matches the one you're searching for. Your implementation of GetHashCode() just uses your ToString() override to call GetHashCode() on the string representation of the ProductNumber, and the Dictionary uses that to work out the hash code for each item.

Run the program now and you'll find it works like a charm, as you can see in Figure 13-6.

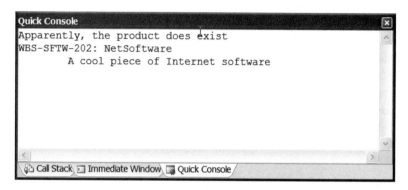

Figure 13-6. *After you've implemented the GetHashCode() and Equals() methods on your ProductNumber, everything slots into place with the Dictionary.*

Stacks and Queues

We've spent a while now looking at lists and dictionaries and how they work. The rest of the generic collections (Stack, Queue) work pretty much the same way, so we're not going to spend a great deal more time going over them in detail. However, it's certainly worth pointing out what each of these collections do and how you can use them.

Stack

It's a programming cliché, but I'm going to explain what a Stack is the same way it has been explained to generation after generation of newborn coder. Think of a Stack like a stack of plates—in fact, a stack of very, very hot plates. As you add plates to the stack, you drop them on top of the stack. However, as the stack grows, there's only one way to get a single plate out, and that's straight off the top. A stack, then, is sometimes known as a last-in-first-out data structure; the last item added is always the first item you can retrieve. The other thing with a stack, of course, is that at any time you can take a look at the item on top of the stack without actually pulling the item off.

Putting an item onto the stack is known as *pushing* it. Pulling an item off the stack is known as *popping* it. Taking a look at the top item is known as *peeking* at it. These are the same names of the methods that the Stack collection uses to work with items: Push(), Pop(), Peek(). So, you add items with Stack.Push(), remove them with Stack.Pop(), and take a look at the top item with Stack.Peek().

Queue

So if a Stack is a last-in-first-out data structure, a Queue is a first-in-first-out data structure. Think of it just as a real-life queue of people. The first person into the queue is the first person to get out of it (unless it's a huge queue and people just decide to walk away—we'll ignore that facet of the real-life structure).

Adding an item to the Queue is called *enqueuing*. Removing an item (the first item in the Queue, of course) is called *dequeuing*. As with a Stack, you can also take a Peek() at the first item in the queue. Just as with the Stack, these are the actual names of methods. Add an item with Queue.Enqueue(), remove the first item with Queue.Dequeue(), and take a look at the first item with a call to Queue.Peek().

Creating Your Own Generics

Occasionally you'll want to create your own generic type. You already know how to "use" a generic type, such as List(Of T), Stack(Of T), and so on. All you need to know now is how to create a generic type. Let's imagine you wanted to produce a class that prints out the value it contains. Okay, sure, it's a little contrived, but it gets the basic syntax out of the way:

```
Public Class PrintSomethingClass(Of T)

    Dim _value As T

    Public Sub New(ByVal valueToStore As T)
        _value = valueToStore
    End Sub

    Public Sub PrintTheValue()
        Console.WriteLine("{0}", _value)
    End Sub

End Class
```

Let's walk through this. First, the class definition:

```
Public Class PrintSomethingClass(Of T)
```

What we're doing here is creating a class called `PrintSomethingClass` and setting it up as a generic. The "type" the class will work with is T.

```
Next, take a look at the private member inside the class:     Dim _value As T
```

This is just declaring a private member variable, and the type is the type used when you instantiate the class. For example, say you instantiated the class with this:

```
Dim myObject As PrintSomethingClass(Of Integer);
```

Then at compile time, wherever you see T in the class definition, it gets replaced with Integer. Think of a generic as a way of doing a search and replace, but automatically at compile time.

So, armed with that knowledge, the method definition should be easy to follow:

```
Public Sub New(ByVal valueToStore As T)
    _value = valueToStore
End Sub
```

Again, T would get replaced with the type used to instantiate the class, Integer in our previous example.

Summary

To the uninitiated, generics can be a somewhat intimidating feature of Visual Basic. After all, Java only just got generics, and now Visual Basic has caught up, so obviously it's some big and scary new high-end language feature, right? Well, no. Generics add a great deal of flexibility to Visual Basic and allow you to create type-safe collections and classes easily.

The generic collections in fact also give you a lot of flexibility in how you manage your data within your programs in an organized fashion. As you move now toward writing your own programs, you'll find more and more use for flexible data structures such as those in the `System.Collections.Generic` namespace.

CHAPTER 14

■■■

Files and Streams

At work I write code that almost exclusively talks to huge databases. At home, though, most of the code I write deals exclusively with files and streams (I'll tell you what streams are in a moment). I have a bunch of small programs called *spiders* that hit the Internet on my behalf at set times and download data into files for me; I may download video from a favorite video news site, or have another program build me a totally unique web page with snippets of news and information from around the world. I even have programs that handle automatically backing up data for me. All these things work with files and streams.

I'm sure you've already come across files. It's hard to avoid them. When you save your family newsletter from Microsoft Word, you save it to a file. When you load up Quicken to balance your checking account, Quicken stores your checking account information along with all your transactions in sets of files. Microsoft Windows itself is nothing more than a collection of files that contain specific data and functionality to manage your computer and the programs you run.

Streams, on the other hand, you may not have heard of in a technical sense. A *stream* is nothing more than a flow of digital information. Think about your web browser for a moment. You key in a URL (such as `www.apress.com`, for example), and a web page magically appears in the browser. What actually happens behind the scenes is that the browser connects to a remote server and then opens a stream of data. That stream just happens to contain HTML information necessary to render a web page. Another way to think about it is as a stream of digital water. When you key in a URL to your web browser, you effectively tell it to stick its head in the water and take a huge gulp of all the digital water the stream contains.

So, the obvious next question is, why do we have streams and files in the same chapter? It all boils down to the great way that the .NET Framework is designed. In .NET a stream could be a source of information from a remote server, from a string variable in your own code, from a block of memory you've set aside, or more importantly from a file. If you want to read data from a file, you open its stream and grab everything you find in it. Similarly, if you want to create a new file, you open a stream and throw information into it. The great thing about .NET is that because streams apply to so many different things, you can easily write a program to handle one data source (a file, for example) and then switch it later to work with variables, or even servers on the Internet. It's a great model.

In this chapter you'll explore a couple of very handy classes that the .NET Framework provides for working with files on your computer. You'll then move into looking at streams and how to read and write files, and even how to read and write data by using streams and computers on the Internet.

I can almost guarantee that you'll use the information in this chapter pretty soon after you embark on writing programs of your own, so it's a key chapter.

Working with Files

The System.IO namespace in the .NET Framework holds everything you need to work with files and directories on your computer, as well as streams. We'll get on to streams in the next section, but first let's spend some time exploring the classes for working with files and directories.

The FileSystemWatcher Class

One of the most fun classes in this namespace is FileSystemWatcher. As the name indicates, this class can be used to watch for changes in the file system (your hard disk). You can set it up to tell you when files in a certain place, or with a certain name or type, are created, deleted, renamed, or changed. This is great for live backup programs because you can tell FileSystemWatcher to automatically fire when anything changes in one directory and then automatically update another. Another great use is in a networked environment. Let's say you need to know when someone on the network changes a specific file (perhaps the file contains a list of requirements that you and your team are to develop). The FileSystemWatcher class can be used to alert you when new requirements arrive in much the same way that Microsoft Outlook can alert you when new email arrives.

There are two ways to create and work with a FileSystemWatcher object. The easiest is to simply drag and drop the FileSystemWatcher control onto the form in a Windows Forms project. This gives you easy point-and-click access to all the properties and events of the control. The second way is to simply create the object in code. For example:

```
Dim watcher As New System.IO.FileSystemWatcher()
```

Of course, if you add an Imports System.IO; statement to the top of your class, you don't need to fully specify the namespace along with the class in code:

```
Dim watcher As New FileSystemWatcher()
```

We'll stick with the simpler method of just using the control; after all, Visual Basic 2005 Express provides features that make development easy for a reason.

Obviously, `FileSystemWatcher` is not a visual control, so when you add it to a form it appears in the area underneath the form in the form editor. You can see the properties it exposes in Figure 14-1.

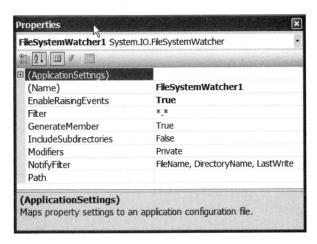

Figure 14-1. *Using the FileSystemWatcher control, you can access the properties through the Properties window.*

As you can see, there aren't a great number of properties to worry about. `EnableRaisingEvents` is a Boolean property that basically turns the control on or off. When you set this property to `True`, the `FileSystemWatcher` will start watching for changes and raise events as they occur. You specify just what you are interested in learning about through the `Filter` and `NotifyFilter` properties.

`Filter` takes a standard Windows filename wildcard to specify which files to report on. For example, setting the filter to `*.*` tells the watcher to report on changes to all files. Similarly, setting it to `*.txt` tells the watcher to report back only on changes made to text files (files whose filenames end in `.txt`).

While the `Filter` specifies the files to watch, `NotifyFilter` tells the control just which events you are interested in hearing about. `NotifyFilter` uses the `System.IO.NotifyFilters` enumeration to specify just what it is you want to see. The enumeration values and what they mean are listed in Table 14-1.

Table 14-1. *The NotifyFilters Enumerations That Control How the FileSystemWatcher Object Works*

NotifyFilter Enumeration	Description
NotifyFilters.Attributes	Watches for changes to things such as read access, write access, and so on.
NotifyFilters.CreationTime	Watches for changes in creation times of files. This will also pick up new files.
NotifyFilters.DirectoryName	Watches for directory name changes, including new directories.
NotifyFilters.FileName	Watches for filename changes, including new files.
NotifyFilters.LastAccess	Watches for when a file is accessed and reports on it.
NotifyFilters.LastWrite	Watches for when a file has new data written into it.
NotifyFilters.Security	Fires notifications when security settings on a file change.
NotifyFilters.Size	Fires notifications when a file size changes.

All of these enumeration values can be combined by using the + sign. So, if you wanted to watch for changes in file size, last access time, and last write time, you'd set up the NotifyFilter property like this:

```
myWatcher.NotifyFilter = NotifyFilters.Size + _
                NotifyFilters.LastAccess + _
                NotifyFilters.LastWrite
```

After you've set up the control, the next thing you'll want to do is actually catch the notifications themselves. This is handled through the event model. Take a look at the list of events in the Properties window within the VB Express IDE in Figure 14-2.

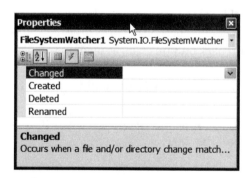

Figure 14-2. *The FileSystemWatcher is very easy to hook into with just four events.*

As you can see, the event model on FileSystemWatcher is very simple; it has just four self-explanatory events. The tricky thing is that these events relate to the filters. So, the Changed event will fire when a file change causes a filter to match. Similarly, Created will fire only when a file is created and that causes a filter to match.

Let's put all this into action with a short "Try It Out."

Try It Out: Using the FileSystemWatcher Class

The FileSystemWatcher is phenomenally powerful—and staggeringly simple. In fact, I'll warn you now that we'll probably spend more time working on our user interface in this example than we will writing FileSystemWatcher-specific code. It's a neat demo, though.

Start up a new Windows Forms application. Then drop FolderBrowserDialog, FileSystemWatcher, label, list box, and button controls onto the form so that it looks like the one in Figure 14-3.

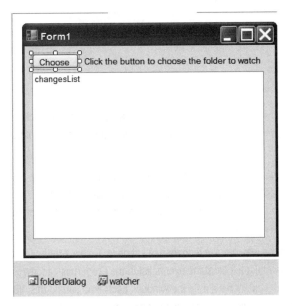

Figure 14-3. *Arrange controls on your form like this. Note that FolderBrowserDialog and File-SystemWatcher are nonvisible controls and appear underneath the form in the editor.*

Set up the name properties of the controls; the button is called chooseButton, the label is folderLabel, the list box is changesList, the folder browser is folderDialog, and the FileSystemWatcher is simply watcher.

Select the `FileSystemWatcher` and set the `EnableRaisingEvents` property to `False`; this will prevent the object from firing off events before we're ready.

The way this form is going to work is quite simple. The user will click the Choose button and then choose a folder to watch from the dialog that appears. From that point on, you'll catch events from the watcher and display information on them in the list box. It may sound like a lot of work, but it really isn't.

First, let's go ahead and code up the folder-chooser button. Double-click it to open the code editor at the button's click event handler, and then key in the following highlighted code:

```
Private Sub chooseButton_Click(ByVal sender As System.Object, _
    ByVal e As System.EventArgs) Handles chooseButton.Click

        If folderDialog.ShowDialog() = Windows.Forms.DialogResult.OK Then
            folderLabel.Text = folderDialog.SelectedPath
            watcher.Path = folderDialog.SelectedPath
            watcher.IncludeSubdirectories = True
            watcher.Filter = "*.*"
            watcher.EnableRaisingEvents = True
        End If

    End Sub
```

The first thing this code does is open the dialog. Providing the user clicks OK in the dialog, the main code block runs. This copies the selected path into the label on the form (user feedback is all important of course), before diving into setting up the watcher.

Most of the code used here to set up the watcher could have been done by using the Properties window, but I wanted to have it in code so it's explicitly documented for your future reference. The code copies the selected path into the watcher, and sets up to monitor changes in subdirectories off the changed one and to watch all files with the wildcard of *.*. Finally, we turn the control on.

The next step is to code up the event handlers on the watcher. We'll do them all at once. Go back to the form designer view and select the watcher control. Then take a look at the events list in the Properties window (which you saw back in Figure 14-2). Now double-click each event in the window. Each time you do this, VB Express will create the event handler stub and drop you down into the code editor. You'll need to keep switching back to the design view to click through all the events. Ultimately you'll end up with a block of event handler stubs that look like this:

```
Private Sub watcher_Changed(ByVal sender As System.Object, _
    ByVal e As System.IO.FileSystemEventArgs) Handles watcher.Changed

    End Sub
```

```
Private Sub watcher_Created(ByVal sender As System.Object, _
  ByVal e As System.IO.FileSystemEventArgs) Handles watcher.Created

End Sub

Private Sub watcher_Deleted(ByVal sender As System.Object, _
  ByVal e As System.IO.FileSystemEventArgs) Handles watcher.Deleted

End Sub

Private Sub watcher_Renamed(ByVal sender As System.Object, _
  ByVal e As System.IO.RenamedEventArgs) Handles watcher.Renamed

End Sub
```

All that remains now is to add some code to these handlers. The second parameter to each of these handlers lets you find out information about just why the event fired. In particular, they all have a Name property that refers to the name of the file that triggered the event. You can use this to feed data into the list box about the file that triggered the event. Go ahead and add code to the event handlers to do just that:

```
Private Sub watcher_Changed(ByVal sender As System.Object, _
  ByVal e As System.IO.FileSystemEventArgs) Handles watcher.Changed
    changesList.Items.Add(e.Name + " changed.")
End Sub

Private Sub watcher_Created(ByVal sender As System.Object, _
  ByVal e As System.IO.FileSystemEventArgs) Handles watcher.Created
    changesList.Items.Add(e.Name + " was created.")
End Sub

Private Sub watcher_Deleted(ByVal sender As System.Object, _
  ByVal e As System.IO.FileSystemEventArgs) Handles watcher.Deleted
    changesList.Items.Add(e.Name + " was deleted.")
End Sub

Private Sub watcher_Renamed(ByVal sender As System.Object, _
  ByVal e As System.IO.RenamedEventArgs) Handles watcher.Renamed
    changesList.Items.Add(e.Name + " was renamed.")
End Sub
```

And that's all there is to it. Each event just dumps out the name of the file that triggered the event along with some text to relay which event fired, and all into the list box. Run the application now. To make sure you see something, point the app at your C : \ folder and then start an application such as Notepad in Windows; you'll notice that Windows generates a lot of changes to files when you do anything, especially when you run programs. You can see the output in Figure 14-4.

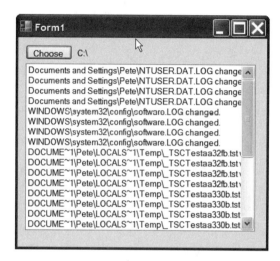

Figure 14-4. *Point the program at your C:\ folder and you'll see a lot of file changes.*

So, for a surprisingly small amount of work you now have a great tool for exploring a myriad of things Windows does behind the scenes.

The File and Directory Classes

The System.IO namespace also includes classes for dealing with files and directories on your computer: File and Directory. Actually there are four classes: File, FileInfo, Directory, and DirectoryInfo. Let me explain.

The File and Directory classes contain shared methods—you can't create instances of these classes. Obviously what that means is that you don't have to create instances of those classes to get at methods to do things such as rename, delete, and so on. FileInfo and DirectoryInfo are instance-based classes. You need to create instances of them to use the methods they contain. Which should you use? The short answer is both.

Let's say you want to find a listing of all the files in a specific directory. The Directory class's GetFiles() and GetDirectories() methods will do just that. Both these methods will give you an array of strings that you can iterate through with a simple For Each loop. Within that loop you would typically go ahead and create FileInfo or DirectoryInfo objects to let you work with that specific file or directory. The following listing shows an example:

```
Imports System.IO
Module Module1

    Sub Main()
        Dim files() As String = Directory.GetFiles("c:\")
        For Each filename As String In files
            Dim file As New FileInfo(filename)
            Console.WriteLine( _
                "{0} created on {1}, and is a {2} file", _
                file.Name, file.CreationTime, _
                file.Extension)
        Next
        Console.ReadLine()
    End Sub

End Module
```

Feel free to key this into a console-type project if you want to see it for yourself. (Don't forget to add the Imports System.IO statement to the top of the source file.) All the code does is grab a list of files by using the shared Directory.GetFiles() method and then iterate through the string array it returns. Inside the loop we create a FileInfo object to get information about each file.

I'm not going to spend a lot of time walking through every method and property on all four classes; most are self-explanatory, and a quick look at the online help or even IntelliSense in the code window will tell you all you need to know to use them. There are a few interesting ones that I will point out, though.

First, both the File and Directory classes contain shared methods to do pretty much anything you could do in Windows Explorer or inside a command prompt. For example, you can create directories by using the CreateDirectory() method, or check whether a file or directory exists by using the Exists() method. If you wanted to move or rename something, both classes expose Move() methods. In fact, the File class also gives you a Copy() method for if you need to copy something.

If you're feeling really adventurous, the File class even has Encrypt() and Decrypt() methods that will hide important information from prying eyes. These methods use your login account to build the key used to do both the encryption and decryption, so they're not terribly secure but useful in a pinch at least.

Best of all, though, the File class has ReadAllLines() and WriteAllLines() methods. ReadAllLines() will give you a string array, with each element in the string holding a single line from the file. WriteAllLines() does the reverse, taking a string array you give it and writing them out to a file. Let's take a look at these in action with a brief console-based "Try It Out."

Try It Out: Reading and Writing Files with the File Class

Fire up a new console project and add the following line to the top of the Module1.vb file:

```
Imports System.IO
```

The first thing you'll do is create a string array that you want to write out to a file:

```
Imports System.IO
Module Module1

    Sub Main()
        Dim lines(9) As String
        For i As Integer = 0 To 9
            lines(i) = String.Format( _
                "This is line number {0}", i)
        Next
    End Sub

End Module
```

So far, so good. The next step is to see whether the file you are about to write to already exists. If it does, you'll get rid of it:

```
    Sub Main()
        Dim lines(9) As String
        For i As Integer = 0 To 9
            lines(i) = String.Format( _
                "This is line number {0}", i)
        Next

        If File.Exists("c:\test.txt") Then
            File.Delete("c:\test.txt")
        End If
    End Sub
```

Now you can write out the new file contents. This is trivial to do with the File class's WriteAllLines() method:

```
Sub Main()
    Dim lines(9) As String
    For i As Integer = 0 To 9
        lines(i) = String.Format( _
            "This is line number {0}", i)
    Next

    If File.Exists("c:\test.txt") Then
        File.Delete("c:\test.txt")
    End If

    File.WriteAllLines("c:\test.txt", lines)

End Sub
```

Last but not least, you'll wrap up the program by reading back all the lines from the file and writing them out to the console. Because the File.ReadAllLines() method gives you back an array of strings, you can For Each over them:

```
Sub Main()
    Dim lines(9) As String
    For i As Integer = 0 To 9
        lines(i) = String.Format( _
            "This is line number {0}", i)
    Next

    If File.Exists("c:\test.txt") Then
        File.Delete("c:\test.txt")
    End If

    File.WriteAllLines("c:\test.txt", lines)

    For Each line As String In File.ReadAllLines("c:\test.txt")
        Console.WriteLine(line)
    Next

    Console.ReadLine()

End Sub
```

Run the program now and you'll see the output shown in Figure 14-5.

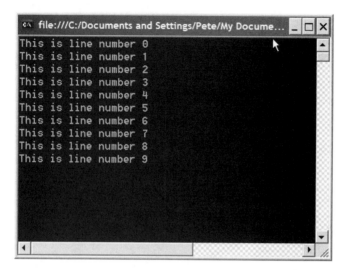

Figure 14-5. *The program successfully reads and writes data to a file.*

You'll also find a brand new file on your hard disk called `C:\test.txt`. You can open this in Notepad to see the contents.

Working with Streams

I mentioned streams back at the start of this chapter. You can think of all the data inside a file as a stream that you can both read from and write to. But we just covered how to read and write with files when we covered the `File` object. In fact, using `System.IO.File.ReadAllLines()` and `System.IO.File.WriteAllLines()` is so simple and painless to use, you may well be wondering why on earth you should even care about streams at all.

The `ReadAll...()` methods (`ReadAllLines`, `ReadAllBytes`, `ReadAllText`) are indeed simple to use, but they are "all or nothing" solutions. They don't provide you a great deal of granularity in terms of working with the data in a file; you can either read everything, or nothing at all. If you drop down to working with streams, though, you have a lot more control. Better yet, you aren't consigned to just working with files. Streams can represent data from almost any source. You can use streams to read data from a remote server on the Internet, from a string variable, from a block of memory, and of course from a file. In fact, as you dive deeper into the .NET Framework in your own projects, you'll come across plenty of times when knowing how to work with a data stream is valuable.

Just like the File and Directory classes, streams live in the System.IO namespace. This of course means that you need to add a Using System.IO statement to the top of any class file you write that needs to work with them. If you search within the online help for *stream hierarchy*, you'll see the complete list of all the stream types in the .NET Framework, some even covering weird and wonderful data sources such as DirectX graphics streams (one for the games programmers out there), Oracle database streams, and CryptoStreams for working with encrypted data. We're going to focus here on the two most common types of stream you'll use: FileStream and NetworkStream.

The Core Concepts

All streams derive from a base abstract class called System.IO.Stream. This of course means that after you know how to use one type of stream, you know how to use them all. An abstract class does, after all, just force derived classes to implement the same interface.

Similarly, the concepts for actually working with a stream apply to all streams. Although you can use methods in the Stream class for reading and writing data, the best way to work with them is to use a Reader or Writer class.

If a stream is the actual data that you want, a reader provides you with a nice easy-to-use interface to get at that data. Think of a stream as a fire hose, and a reader as a handy, controllable nozzle that you can use to get at the information without drowning in a sea of data. Conversely (and this is where the analogy falls down somewhat), a writer lets you put data back in easily.

The work flow for using a stream is simple:

1. Identify a resource containing data (that is, the file you want to work with).

2. Connect a stream to it.

3. Drop a reader or writer on top of the stream.

4. Work with the data.

Let's start putting this into real terms.

Working with File Streams

Let's say you have a file containing data that you want to read. The code for getting at that data looks like this:

```
Sub Main()

    Dim stream As New FileStream("c:\test.txt", FileMode.Open)
    Dim reader As New StreamReader(stream)

    Dim line As String = reader.ReadLine()
    Do

        Console.WriteLine(line)
        line = reader.ReadLine()
    Loop While Not line Is Nothing
    reader.Close()
    Console.ReadLine()

End Sub
```

Of course you'll also need to add `Imports System.IO` to the top of the source code, and this code does also assume that the file in question exists.

The first line of code opens the stream. Notice that when you use a file stream, you can specify not only the name, but also how you want to work with the file. In this case I'm opening the file for reading, by passing in the `FileMode.Open` value. There are a number of different values in the `FileMode` enumeration, and they are listed in Table 14-2.

Table 14-2. *The FileMode Enumeration Values*

FileMode Value	Description
FileMode.Append	Opens an existing file for writing. If the file doesn't exist, a new one is created. The stream is expecting to have data added to the end of the file in either case.
FileMode.Create	Creates a new file, again for writing. If the file exists, this will wipe out any data it contains, so use with caution.
FileMode.CreateNew	This tells the stream that we want to create a new file and we don't expect the file to already exist. If it does and we open its stream with this `FileMode`, an exception is thrown.
FileMode.Open	Simply opens an existing file, for either reading or writing. If the file does not exist, an exception is thrown.

FileMode Value	Description
FileMode.OpenOrCreate	Opens an existing file just like Open does. If the file doesn't exist, it gets created. Unlike FileMode.Append, though, FileMode.OpenOrCreate can be used to open a file for both reading and writing.
FileMode.Truncate	This is a strange one. It expects the file to already exist, and if it doesn't, an exception is thrown. If the file does exist, all the data it contains is removed, ready for us to start writing to the file as if it were a brand new one.

Moving on—once the stream has been opened, a StreamReader is created. The stream gets passed into the StreamReader's constructor in order to attach the Reader to the stream.

Finally, a loop is created to read from the file. StreamReader has a number of methods to read data from a file, ReadLine() being one of them. ReadLine() will read a line of text from a file and return it as a string. If there is no more data to be read in the file, it will return Nothing, hence the check that we have at the end of our While loop. When we are done reading, the reader is closed with a call to reader.Close(). This frees up the resources inside the computer that the stream was taking up and—more important—severs the connection to the stream itself. You should always do this.

If you like, key this code into a console project (don't forget to include the Imports System.IO line at the top of the source file) and run it. Providing you point it at an existing file, you'll see the file contents written out to the console.

So, what's the big advantage with this method over simply typing File.ReadAllLines()? The biggest advantage is that loop. Let's say that you wanted to read a file that consisted of a few gigabytes of data in order to find something specific. With File.ReadAllLines(), you'd have to sit and wait while the method slowly chugged through the entire file, filling a huge string array in your program in the process. Only when the read was complete would you be able to search the array to see whether the piece of data you were interested in was actually in the file.

With the Stream and StreamReader approach, that doesn't happen. First, in our example code here you'll always be working with only a single line of data so you don't run the risk of your computer's memory filling up. Second, it would be easy to provide visual feedback to the user (perhaps with a progress bar or animated icon) to set the user's mind at ease that the program hasn't crashed. Third, because you read the file a line at a time, you can at any point stop the read. Perhaps the data you are looking for occurs early on in the file, or perhaps the user hits a Cancel button. In either case you are free to stop the read and let the program, and its user, get on with other more pressing tasks.

You may also be thinking that that's an awful lot of code for something that the File class will let you do in just one line of code. You're right. It is. As always with Visual Basic and the .NET Framework, though, we can simplify it quite a lot. Both the StreamReader and StreamWriter classes have constructors that can take a filename as a parameter. When used in this way, the StreamReader and StreamWriter objects will handle all the mundane work of actually opening the underlying file for you. So, the preceding example could be simplified by removing the Stream variable altogether and opening the file with a simple call like this:

```
Dim reader As New StreamReader("C:\myfile.txt")
```

Admittedly, this doesn't slim down the code very much, but it does reduce some of the complexity.

The final, and perhaps most important reason to use streams, readers, and writers is for dealing with nontext. What if the file you wanted to read didn't contain nicely formatted text with a handy carriage return character to segment the lines in the file? StreamReader provides three methods for just that situation: Read(), ReadBlock(), and ReadToEnd().

StreamReader.Read() reads just a single byte from the file and returns it as an Integer value. It's important to note that this Integer is the value of the byte. If you had a file of numbers (perhaps your lottery syndicate's numbers), calling Read() would not return each in turn. What you'll get instead are the numbers that represent each and every digit of the lottery numbers. When the end of the stream is reached, StreamReader.Read() returns -1.

The Read() method can even read a number of bytes from a file in one go. Take a look at this:

```
Dim dataBlock(9) As Char
reader.Read(dataBlock, 0, 5)
```

This creates a 10-character array and then has the reader pull 5 bytes from a stream and put them into dataBlock[0] through dataBlock[4]. The second parameter to the call tells the reader which element of the array to overwrite, and the third parameter tells the reader just how many bytes to get.

This overload actually works exactly the same way as ReadBlock() works. For example:

```
Dim dataBlock(9) As New Char
reader.ReadBlock(dataBlock, 0, 5)
```

Both Read() and ReadBlock() return a number telling you just how many characters were read from the file. If it's less than the number you asked for, your code can assume that the end of the file has been reached.

Writing data to a file with a StreamWriter is almost as simple as reading. There are two methods on the StreamWriter class (Write() and WriteLine()) that you can use to send data to a stream. Write() is an overloaded method that you can send literally any kind of data to (String, Char, Byte, Integer, and so on) one data item at a time. WriteLine() is the same, but it puts a line break at the end of each item.

One thing you do need to bear in mind, though, is how you finish writing. There is a risk that data you have asked to write has not been written to the file yet. Instead it could be sitting in a file buffer within Windows. So, when you are finished writing data, you must call a method named Flush() on the writer to empty that buffer, and then close the file with a call to Close().

Let's take a look at a brief "Try It Out" to demonstrate how to work with a StreamWriter.

Try It Out: Using Write and WriteLine

Start up a new console project in Visual Basic 2005 Express. When the code editor appears, add the Imports System.IO statement to the top of the source file. Your code will look like mine in Figure 14-6.

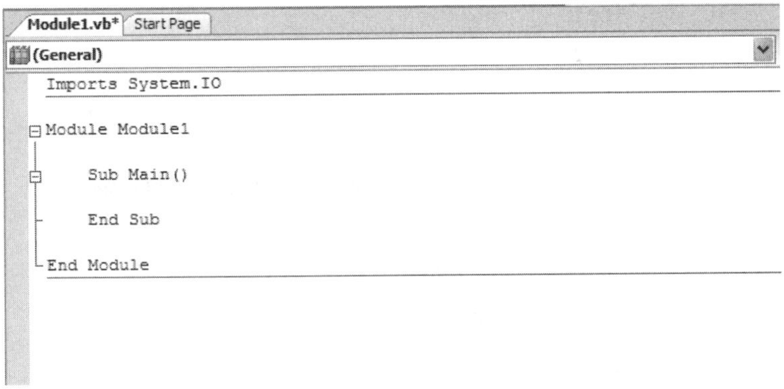

```
Module1.vb*  Start Page
(General)
    Imports System.IO

  Module Module1

      Sub Main()

      End Sub

  End Module
```

Figure 14-6. *Adding System.IO to the list of namespaces to use*

The first thing you're going to do in this program is write a new file to the hard disk. Add the highlighted code to the Main() method:

```
Sub Main()
    Dim writer As New StreamWriter("c:\myfile.txt")
    For i As Integer = 1 To 10
        writer.WriteLine(i.ToString())
    Next
    writer.Flush()
    writer.Close()
End Sub
```

The first thing you do here is create a writer and use its constructor to connect it to a stream for writing a new file. With that out of the way, the code jumps into a simple loop to count from 1 to 10.

Within the loop you just turn the loop index (i) into a string and pass it across to the writer's WriteLine() method.

Finally, when the loop is finished, the code flushes the writer and closes it down. The net result of all this of course is that you have a new file on the hard disk called C:\myfile.txt that holds numbers from 1 to 10. Let's prove that by adding in some more code to quickly read the file and write it out to the console:

```
Sub Main()
    Dim writer As New StreamWriter("c:\myfile.txt")
    For i As Integer = 1 To 10
        writer.WriteLine(i.ToString())
    Next
    writer.Flush()
    writer.Close()

    For Each line As String In File.ReadAllLines("c:\myfile.txt")
        Console.WriteLine(line)
    Next
    Console.ReadLine()
End Sub
```

Here you just use the File.ReadAllLines() method to quickly grab an array of strings from the file in order to iterate over them and write them out to the console.

Run the program now and you'll see a console like mine in Figure 14-7.

Figure 14-7. *The program writes a file and then reads it back to dump it out to the console, like this.*

When the program has finished, you'll need to tap your Enter key to close down the console thanks to our Console.ReadLine() method call at the end of the program.

So far the program did everything you'd expect it to. Let's change the WriteLine() call to Write() and see what happens. Edit the code as highlighted here:

```
Sub Main()
    Dim writer As New StreamWriter("c:\myfile.txt")
    For i As Integer = 1 To 10
        writer.Write(i.ToString())
    Next
    writer.Flush()
    writer.Close()

    For Each line As String In File.ReadAllLines("c:\myfile.txt")
        Console.WriteLine(line)
    Next
    Console.ReadLine()
End Sub
```

If you run the program now, you'll see the output is quite different. You can see mine in Figure 14-8.

Figure 14-8. *Changing the program to just call Write() instead of WriteLine() dramatically changes the format of our file.*

WriteLine() puts a line break after every piece of data you send to the file, effectively creating multiple lines of text in the file. Write(), on the other hand, just dumps everything straight to the file, warts and all.

Working with Network Streams

Now you know how to work with streams, stream readers, and stream writers, you are well equipped to work with practically any kind of stream. Let's put that theory to the test and take a look at network streams.

The basic network stream class is not found in the System.IO namespace. NetworkStream lives in System.Net.Sockets, a scary namespace full of low-level networking classes with strange names like Socket! We'll stay well away from there, because we can get at a network stream very easily via the System.Net.WebRequest class. Just as with the low-level file stuff I mentioned just now, if you really want to use sockets to directly connect to some obscure protocol on a remote server, the chances are you know what you want to do and how to do it, so I won't get in the way. The vast majority of us, though, feel warm and safe with the handy WebRequest class.

WebRequest has two parts to it—a request and a response. When you point the web browser of your choice at a remote website, the web browser first sends data to the server to tell it exactly what you want to see in the browser. The server processes the request and then gives you a response. We can get a stream from this response object. Let's dive straight into a "Try it Out" to see this in action.

WORKING DIRECTLY WITH STREAMS

You don't have to have a reader to work with a stream of data—you can sip straight from the fire hose. System.IO.Stream provides a method for reading into an array of bytes (Read()), which works the same as the reader's Read() method. You can also use ReadByte() to grab a single byte from the file. In addition to all that, you can jump forward and backward in a file by using the Seek() method. You simply pass in the number of bytes to move forward or backward, and specify where you want to move from (usually SeekMode.Current).

Although this is a powerful feature, the fact of the matter is that only a handful of you reading this will ever want to do that. It's great if you're writing code to deal with streams from strange hardware devices or binary files that you have documentation for, telling you exactly which bytes in a file do what. For that reason I'm not going to cover it here. If this is something that you need to do, take a look at the online help for Stream.Read and Stream.Seek for more information.

Try It Out: Working with Network Streams

Create a new console project and add two `Imports` statements to the top of the `Module1.vb` file so that you can work with both streams and `WebRequests`:

```
Imports System.Net
Imports System.IO

Module Module1

    Sub Main()

    End Sub

End Module
```

Now, let's work through the `WebRequest` way of doing things step by step.

The first thing that you'll need to do is create a `WebRequest` object. This is done not by just instantiating a new `WebRequest` object, but instead by calling a shared method named `Create()`:

```
Sub Main()
    Dim request As WebRequest
    request = WebRequest.Create("http://www.apress.com")
End Sub
```

This creates the object and makes the request for a web page from a remote web server. The next step is to grab the response from the server. To do this, you need a `WebResponse` object:

```
Sub Main()
    Dim request As WebRequest
    request = WebRequest.Create("http://www.apress.com")

    Dim response As WebResponse = request.GetResponse()

End Sub
```

The next step, and the most important from our point of view, is to grab the stream underneath the response and then attach a reader to it. This is handled with a call to GetResponseStream():

```
Sub Main()
    Dim request As WebRequest
    request = WebRequest.Create("http://www.apress.com")

    Dim response As WebResponse = request.GetResponse()
    Dim responseStream As Stream = response.GetResponseStream()
    Dim reader As New StreamReader(responseStream)
End Sub
```

If you're comfortable with nesting method calls inside method calls, you can simplify this code a lot:

```
Sub Main()

    Dim reader As New StreamReader( _
        WebRequest.Create("http://www.apress.com" _
        ).GetResponse().GetResponseStream() _
        )

End Sub
```

Now that you have a stream, you can get data from it just as if it were a file. Let's dump the entire web page to the console:

```
Sub Main()

    Dim reader As New StreamReader( _
        WebRequest.Create("http://www.apress.com" _
        ).GetResponse().GetResponseStream() _
        )

    Dim line As String = reader.ReadLine()
    Do
        Console.WriteLine(line)
        line = reader.ReadLine()
    Loop While Not line Is Nothing

    Console.ReadLine()

End Sub
```

Run the program now and you'll see HTML gibberish splattered all over your console window, just as in Figure 14-9.

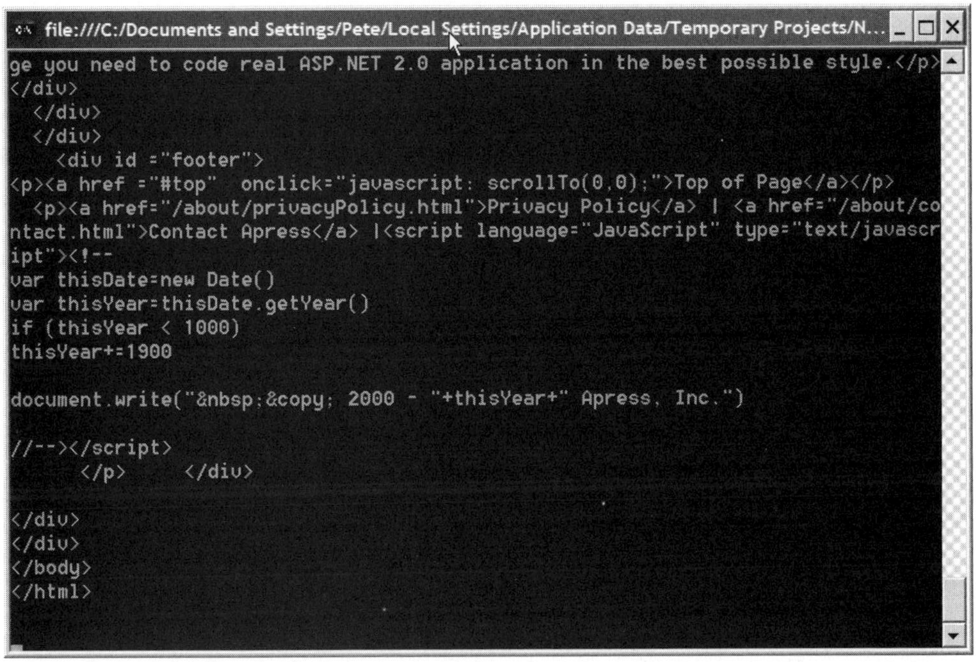

Figure 14-9. *After you have a stream, regardless of where it came from, you can work with it just as any other.*

If on the other hand you wanted to send specific data to the server, you could do so by asking the WebRequest object for its RequestStream. For example (don't type this in):

```
request.GetRequestStream()
```

From that point, you're free to attach a writer in the usual way and send data to the server.

Summary

As you've seen here, working with streams, readers, and writers is easy. When you know how to use one type of stream (a file stream, for example) you really are well equipped to work with any other. Feel free to explore the various streams, readers, and writers in the online help and experiment with the code here to find out more.

CHAPTER 15

Working with XML

In recent years eXtensible Markup Language (XML) has taken the world of computers by storm. It's the format used to store information about word processing documents, price lists on websites, and details of blog posts on people's web logs. In .NET XML can be used to send huge snippets of database data across the Internet. If you talk to a web service with your Visual Basic program (something we cover in the next chapter), the data exchanged between the web service and your program behind the scenes is XML. In short, there's no escaping XML these days.

XML is simply a way of adding structure to data. If I wanted to store a list of products in a file, I could create an XML file that looks like this:

```
<ProductList>
    <Product Reference="1234" Price="12.99">
       My super dooper widget
    </Product>
    <Product Reference="8832" Price="59.75">
       Whizz-Bang Jiggle Doobry
    </Product>
</ProductList>
```

It looks a bit like a web page, doesn't it, with all those angle brackets everywhere. The reason is that HyperText Markup Language (HTML), the *language* used to produce a web page, is itself derived from something called Standard Generalized Markup Language (SGML). SGML is the language used to define XML.

If that sounds unnecessarily complex, that's because it is. The beauty of XML is actually its simplicity. The things inside the angle brackets are called *elements* (*tags* in HTML) and they can be anything you want them to be. The only rule is that you need to both open and close all elements. For example, in the preceding snippet I have an element called <ProductList> that starts the document, and another at the end called </ProductList>. </ProductList> *closes* <ProductList>. Similarly, for every <Product> element you'll find a matching </Product> one.

Elements can also have things attached called *attributes*. In the preceding example, each product element has two attributes: Reference and Price. As you can see, you define an attribute simply by placing it after the element name and putting the attribute's value within quotation marks.

In this chapter you're going to explore the XML features of the Visual Basic 2005 Express IDE as well as the .NET Framework's support for XML. If you've never come across XML before, I would strongly urge you to take a look at `http://www.xml.com`, the spiritual home of XML on the Internet. There you'll find plenty of overview articles and tutorials on just what XML is and why it's so cool.

I should also point out that even though XML is everywhere these days, and a valuable thing to learn how to work with, you could go your whole programming life and never need to deal with it. It would be kind of like driving from one end of the country to the other on dirt roads—an interesting and colorful adventure, but perhaps not the best way to get things done.

The fact is that XML can make so many data management tasks simple, it's worth adding to your Visual Basic programming arsenal.

System.Xml

The classes that let you work with XML documents live in the `System.Xml` namespace. XML documents are like a tree. The document itself contains elements, and elements contain values, attributes, or other elements, and so on. The classes in `System.Xml` work the same way.

When you create an XML document in code, you call methods on an `XMLDocument` object. `XMLDocument` objects have a `ChildNodes` collection. Every item in an XML document, from elements to attributes and even directives (the funny elements that begin with `<?`—again see `http://www.xml.org` for more information), are represented in the framework as classes that subclass `XmlNode`. So, using the `ChildNodes` collection, which contains a bunch of `XmlNode` objects, you can get at everything inside the document.

This method of working—hitting an XML document directly—provides by far the most power and flexibility of all the ways of handling XML in the .NET Framework. However, it also requires the most work. In addition, if you're something of an XML guru, this is definitely the way you'll want to go. With that in mind, let's do a short "Try It Out" to see the `XMLDocument` object in action, before we settle down into the simpler ways of working with XML.

Try It Out: Working with XMLDocument

Most blogs these days use an XML format known as RSS to expose their content. With RSS and an RSS reader you can simply "subscribe" to a blog and have it automatically download new content to your computer and alert you when it arrives. We're not going to develop an RSS reader here, but RSS is a complex enough XML format that it's fun to explore. Let's write an application that will download an RSS feed and then show us what's inside it, in .NET terms.

First, start up a new Windows project in Visual Basic 2005 Express. When the form appears in the designer, drop a button and a list box onto it, so the form looks like Figure 15-1.

Figure 15-1. *Drop a list box and a button onto the form of your project.*

Set the Name property of the button to getXML and the Name property of the list box to xmlList. When you're finished, double-click the button to drop into the code editor for its Click event handler.

Each time the button is clicked, you'll grab the RSS feed for the Apress blogs (ablog.apress.com) and then populate the list box with a breakdown of the document's contents. So, the first thing you need to do is empty the list box and grab your XML document (and of course add an Imports statement so that you can work with the WebClient) class:

```
Imports System.Net
Public Class Form1

    Private Sub getXML_Click(ByVal sender As System.Object, _
      ByVal e As System.EventArgs) Handles getXML.Click
        xmlList.Items.Clear()
        Dim xml As String = New WebClient().DownloadString( _
            "http://blogs.apress.com/wp-rss2.php")
    End Sub
End Class
```

Don't panic if this looks a little foreign. After clearing the list box contents, the next line uses the WebClient class to download your RSS feed into a string.

Now that you have your RSS feed nicely downloaded into a string variable, the next task is to load the contents of that string variable into an XMLDocument object. First, add yet another Imports statement, this time to reference the System.Xml namespace:

```
Imports System.Net
Imports System.Xml

Public Class Form1

    Private Sub getXML_Click(ByVal sender As System.Object, _
      ByVal e As System.EventArgs) Handles getXML.Click
        xmlList.Items.Clear()
        Dim xml As String = New WebClient().DownloadString( _
            "http://blogs.apress.com/wp-rss2.php")
    End Sub

End Class
```

With that done, you can start writing code to use the XmlDocument class. XmlDocument has a handy method called LoadXml(), which is designed to load XML from a string variable into the XmlDocument object. So, all it takes to turn your downloaded RSS feed into an XML document that you can work with is just two lines of code. Add them to the Click handler:

```
Imports System.Net
Imports System.Xml

Public Class Form1

    Private Sub getXML_Click(ByVal sender As System.Object, _
      ByVal e As System.EventArgs) Handles getXML.Click

        xmlList.Items.Clear()
        Dim xml As String = New WebClient().DownloadString( _
            "http://blogs.apress.com/wp-rss2.php")

        Dim doc As New XmlDocument()
        doc.LoadXml(xml)

    End Sub

End Class
```

Now, as I mentioned earlier, XmlDocument has a ChildNodes property of type XmlNodeList. This is really just a collection of XmlNodes. In addition, each XmlNode also has a ChildNodes collection. So, you need to write a function that can progressively deal with each node and its children. It's a programming technique called *recursion*, whereby a function repeatedly calls itself, and can be very handy (if a little mind-bending). Go ahead and add this function:

```
Private Sub ProcessNodes(ByVal nodes As XmlNodeList)

    For Each node As XmlNode In nodes
        xmlList.Items.Add(String.Format( _
            "{0} - {1} - {2}", _
            node.GetType().Name, node.Name, _
            node.Value))
        If node.HasChildNodes Then
            ProcessNodes(node.ChildNodes)
        End If
    Next

End Sub
```

The function takes an XmlNodeList as a parameter and then does a simple foreach over the nodes in that collection. For each node, you print out the type of the node, its name in the document, and its value. Finally, if the node has child nodes of its own (something you can check through the HasChildNodes property), you call this function again by passing in the new ChildNodes collection. Simple, really. All you need to do now is add a call to this new function back up in the button's Click event handler:

```
Private Sub getXML_Click(ByVal sender As System.Object, _
    ByVal e As System.EventArgs) Handles getXML.Click

    xmlList.Items.Clear()
    Dim xml As String = New WebClient().DownloadString( _
        "http://blogs.apress.com/wp-rss2.php")

    Dim doc As New XmlDocument()
    doc.LoadXml(xml)

    ProcessNodes(doc.ChildNodes)

End Sub
```

Run the application now. Click the Get the XML button on the form to see the list box populated, just as in Figure 15-2.

Figure 15-2. *When you run the application, it shows you detailed information about the XML document it just downloaded.*

When the program runs, it displays three things for every item in the XML document: the .NET type of the item found, its name, and its value. As you can see, there are a bunch of .NET types that you'll need to work with if you choose to do all your XML work directly with XMLDocument. We're not going to spend too long on this because as I mentioned there are much easier ways to deal with XML. It is worth spending a little time, though, putting all those things into some perspective.

You can see the actual XML document from the Apress blogs site by pointing your web browser at http://blogs.apress.com/wp-rss2.php. It looks like Figure 15-3.

If you run the browser view of the document alongside our application, it's easy to match what the lister is showing you against what's actually in the document. The document begins with a <? tag that shows up in the lister as an XmlDeclaration object. Following that there's a comment tag (<!--), which logically maps to an XmlComment node in our document. The meat of the document follows next. Take a look at the document in IE and you'll see an RSS tag with attributes that contains a channel tag, which in turn contains title, link, description, pubDate, and a few other tags.

Looking at the lister, you can see that the RSS tag is an XmlElement, as are channel and title. The text inside the title tag is shown as an XmlText node and so on.

Because all the different types of nodes within an XmlDocument all descend from the same XmlNode class, they all have common properties such as Name and Value; our lister application exploits that.

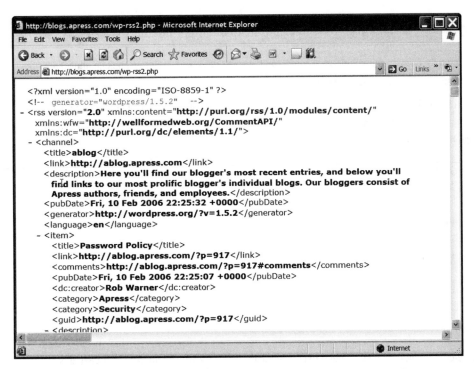

Figure 15-3. *This is what the RSS feed looks like if you load it into Microsoft Internet Explorer.*

Spend time exploring the feed in Internet Explorer and in the application to get a feel for everything in an XmlDocument. When you're finished, you can move into learning about searching an XmlDocument object.

Searching XML Documents

The standard way to search for something in an XmlDocument object is called *XPath*. It's basically a simple language, much like regex is a simple language, that lets you specify a string of characters to uniquely identify something in a document. It basically works like Windows file paths in many ways. For example, to find an element called B that is a child of element A, the XPath would be A/B. You can see the full XPath reference online at http://www.w3.org/TR/xpath, and it's worth spending the time to read it if you intend to write a lot of XML manipulation code.

Let's apply some XPath to our RSS feed document to find and list all the article titles easily.

Try It Out: Using XPath with an XmlDocument

For this example, I'll keep things uncomplicated and have you work with a simple console application. Go ahead and start up a new console-based project now.

When the code editor appears, add in some `Imports` statements. Obviously you'll need to reference `System.Xml` again to work with `XmlDocuments`. You'll also need `System.Net` once again to let you download the RSS feed you'll work with:

```
Imports System.Xml
Imports System.Net

Module Module1

    Sub Main()

    End Sub

End Module
```

Just as before, the first thing you'll need to do is actually grab the XML document (in our case this is the Apress blogs RSS feed) from a website. Add a couple of lines of code to `Main()` to do just that:

```
Sub Main()

    Dim client As New WebClient()
    Dim rssFeed As String = client.DownloadString( _
        "http://blogs.apress.com/wp-rss2.php")

End Sub
```

Next, let's load the downloaded feed into an XML document, just as before:

```
Sub Main()

    Dim client As New WebClient()
    Dim rssFeed As String = client.DownloadString( _
        "http://blogs.apress.com/wp-rss2.php")

    Dim doc As New XmlDocument()
    doc.LoadXml(rssFeed)

End Sub
```

Okay, no great surprises so far. The next thing you want to do is grab all the titles of articles from this feed. Now, looking at the actual XML in a browser, you can see that articles are called <item> in an RSS feed. The <item> tags live inside <channel> tags, and <channel> tags live inside the main <rss> tag. So, the XPath query is simply "rss/channel/item".

The XmlDocument class provides a handy method called SelectNodes() that takes an XPath query as a parameter and returns an XMLNodeList. So, let's add some code now to grab matching nodes:

```vb
Sub Main()

    Dim client As New WebClient()
    Dim rssFeed As String = client.DownloadString( _
        "http://blogs.apress.com/wp-rss2.php")

    Dim doc As New XmlDocument()
    doc.LoadXml(rssFeed)

    Dim nodes As XmlNodeList = _
        doc.SelectNodes("rss/channel/item/title")

End Sub
```

That's it. That's all there is to it. All that remains is the grunt work of actually iterating through the nodes now and printing out some information:

```vb
Sub Main()

    Dim client As New WebClient()
    Dim rssFeed As String = client.DownloadString( _
        "http://blogs.apress.com/wp-rss2.php")

    Dim doc As New XmlDocument()
    doc.LoadXml(rssFeed)

    Dim nodes As XmlNodeList = _
        doc.SelectNodes("rss/channel/item/title")

    For Each node As XmlNode In nodes
        Console.WriteLine(node.InnerText)
    Next
    Console.WriteLine()
    Console.ReadLine()

End Sub
```

Notice how inside the loop we print out the node's InnerText property, not its Value property. This threw me for a loop when I first started working with XML. Surely if I have a title node I want to get at its value to find out the title of the article in question, right? Wrong. The text inside a node, like this

```
<title>My First Blog Post</title>
```

is itself a node. You can see this if you explore the RSS feed with our lister application from earlier. The text inside an element is a special text node, and yes, it has a value you can work with. If, however, you have iterated through a list of element nodes (like title), you can get at the text inside the element only by looking at the element's InnerText.

Run the application now and you'll see the output in Figure 15-4.

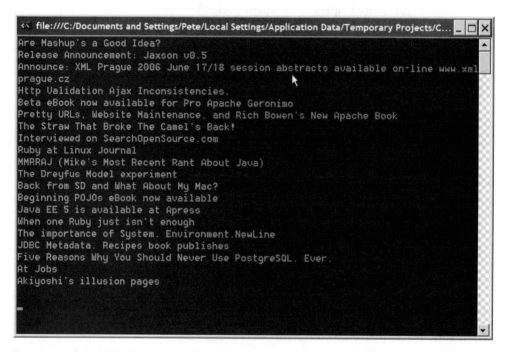

Figure 15-4. *Using XPath to iterate through a bunch of specific nodes is easy.*

Try It Out: Using XPathNavigator

Again, to focus on the code, we'll stick with a console application. Start a new console application project in Visual Basic 2005 Express. Because we're still working with XML, don't forget to add an Imports System.Xml statement to the top of Module1.vb when the code editor appears.

The first thing you are going to need is an XML document. Because the XmlDocument class can load XML data from a string, you'll build a document right inside a string. Go ahead and add this code to the top of the Main() function in Module1.vb:

```
Sub Main()

    Dim xml As String = _
            "<Order>" + _
                "<Item>" + _
                    "<Description>Some widget part</Description>" + _
                    "<Price>12.99</Price>" + _
                "</Item>" + _
                "<Item>" + _
                    "<Description>Another widget</Description>" + _
                    "<Price>50.12</Price>" + _
                "</Item>" + _
            "</Order>"

End Sub
```

So, this XML document represents the canonical Order-Items example. It contains a single order that is composed of a couple of items, each with a price and a description. What we'd like to do is sum the prices with an XPath query to get a total order price. The first step of course is going to be creating an XmlDocument object and loading the XML into it:

```
Sub Main()

    Dim xml As String = _
            "<Order>" + _
                "<Item>" + _
                    "<Description>Some widget part</Description>" + _
                    "<Price>12.99</Price>" + _
                "</Item>" + _
                "<Item>" + _
                    "<Description>Another widget</Description>" + _
                    "<Price>50.12</Price>" + _
                "</Item>" + _
            "</Order>"

    Dim doc As New XmlDocument()
    doc.LoadXml(xml)

End Sub
```

Now, to run complex XPath statements (that is, statements that do more than just grab a node by name), you'll need an XPathNavigator document. XPathNavigator is a special class that does nothing more than allow you to move around the results of an XPath query, and also evaluate numeric queries. It's created from an XmlNode object. For example, if you wanted to run a query on a specific part of a document, you could select the node to start from and then create a navigator on it to run the query on that node and its children. It's okay to just get a navigator from the document itself. XPathNavigator, though, is part of the System.Xml.XPath namespace, so you'll also need to add an Imports statement for that to the head of the Module1.vb file:

```vb
Imports System.Xml
Imports System.Xml.XPath
Module Module1

    Sub Main()

        Dim xml As String = _
                "<Order>" + _
                    "<Item>" + _
                        "<Description>Some widget part</Description>" + _
                        "<Price>12.99</Price>" + _
                    "</Item>" + _
                    "<Item>" + _
                        "<Description>Another widget</Description>" + _
                        "<Price>50.12</Price>" + _
                    "</Item>" + _
                "</Order>"

        Dim doc As New XmlDocument()
        doc.LoadXml(xml)

        Dim nav As XPathNavigator = doc.CreateNavigator()

    End Sub

End Module
```

All that you need now is to evaluate an XPath query. What you want to do is sum the values in the `Order/Item/Price` nodes. That's easy. You can simply use the XPath statement `sum(Order/Item/Price)` to do just that. The `XPathNavigator` class has a special method called `Evaluate()` that you can call to evaluate queries like this. Let's go ahead and call it, outputting the result to the console:

```
Sub Main()

    Dim xml As String = _
            "<Order>" + _
                "<Item>" + _
                    "<Description>Some widget part</Description>" + _
                    "<Price>12.99</Price>" + _
                "</Item>" + _
                "<Item>" + _
                    "<Description>Another widget</Description>" + _
                    "<Price>50.12</Price>" + _
                "</Item>" + _
            "</Order>"

    Dim doc As New XmlDocument()
    doc.LoadXml(xml)

    Dim nav As XPathNavigator = doc.CreateNavigator()
    Console.WriteLine("Total price for this order is ${0}", _
        nav.Evaluate("sum(Order/Item/Price)"))

    Console.ReadLine()

End Sub
```

Run the program now and you'll see the output shown in Figure 15-5.

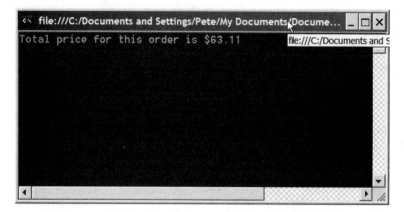

Figure 15-5. *XPath queries let us easily perform aggregations on data inside an XML document.*

The XPathNavigator object can do more than just evaluate aggregate XPath expressions. We can also pass fairly complex conditions to the navigator to grab nodes. For example, let's modify the code to print out the list of all items in the order with a value greater than 10.00.

Change the code after the creation of the XPathNavigator to look like the following highlighted code:

```
Sub Main()

    Dim xml As String = _
        "<Order>" + _
            "<Item>" + _
                "<Description>Some widget part</Description>" + _
                "<Price>12.99</Price>" + _
            "</Item>" + _
            "<Item>" + _
                "<Description>Another widget</Description>" + _
                "<Price>50.12</Price>" + _
            "</Item>" + _
        "</Order>"

    Dim doc As New XmlDocument()
    doc.LoadXml(xml)
```

```
    Dim nav As XPathNavigator = doc.CreateNavigator()
    Dim nodes As XPathNodeIterator = _
        nav.Select("/Order/Item[Price>10]/Price")

    While nodes.MoveNext()
        Console.WriteLine("Price is {0}", _
            nodes.Current.Value)
    End While

    Console.ReadLine()

End Sub
```

When you run the program this time, it will print out any price greater than 10 in value (which in this example is actually both of them—feel free to change the number 10 on the second line of code to prove that the code really does work). You can see the output in Figure 15-6.

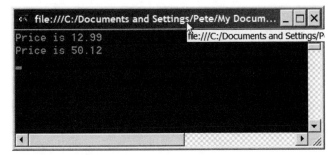

Figure 15-6. *We can use complex XPath statements to grab only a subset of all the nodes in the document.*

I'll talk you through the code. Just like XmlDocument, XPathNavigator has a Select() method that you can call to get at a bunch of nodes. It returns a type called XPathNodeIterator that lets you move through the resulting nodes one by one. It has two things we are interested in: a MoveNext() method to move from result node to result node, and a Current property to get at the current node.

After grabbing an iterator then, the next thing the code does is set up a while loop to repeatedly call MoveNext() to move through the nodes.

Within the loop you just grab the XPathNodeIterator's Current.Value property to get at the prices you want.

The XPath query itself is interesting. As I mentioned, there's a lot to XPath, and it's worth consulting the online reference for it, but the kind of query being done here is very common so I'll explain what it does. The query string itself is /Order/Item[Price>10]/Price. Working from right to left, this says that we want the Price element of every Item that has a child element called Price with a value greater than 10, of every Order.

Let's change it. Grabbing the prices is great, but really we are going to be more inclined to want to know the description of the item itself. All you need to do is change the query to return the Description element instead of the price, like this:

```
Sub Main()

    Dim xml As String = _
            "<Order>" + _
                "<Item>" + _
                    "<Description>Some widget part</Description>" + _
                    "<Price>12.99</Price>" + _
                "</Item>" + _
                "<Item>" + _
                    "<Description>Another widget</Description>" + _
                    "<Price>50.12</Price>" + _
                "</Item>" + _
            "</Order>"

    Dim doc As New XmlDocument()
    doc.LoadXml(xml)

    Dim nav As XPathNavigator = doc.CreateNavigator()
    Dim nodes As XPathNodeIterator = _
        nav.Select("/Order/Item[Price>10]/Description")

    While nodes.MoveNext()
        Console.WriteLine("Item {0} has a price greater than 10", _
            nodes.Current.Value)
    End While

    Console.ReadLine()

End Sub
```

Now when you run the application, you'll see the output changes to list the description of all items with a price greater than 10 (or whatever you've subsequently changed the code to report). You can see this in Figure 15-7.

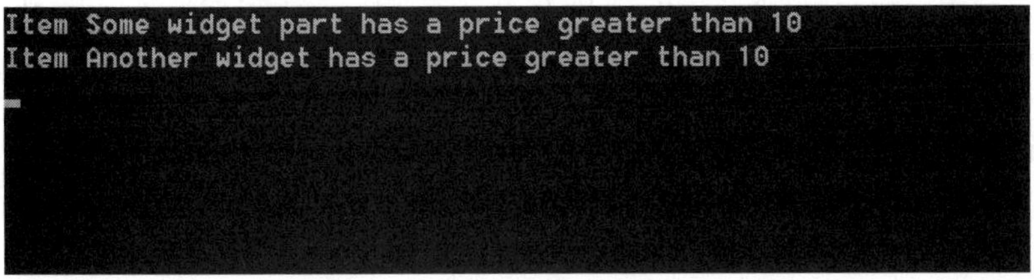

```
Item Some widget part has a price greater than 10
Item Another widget has a price greater than 10
```

Figure 15-7. *It's easy to select specific nodes based on conditions against other ones.*

Aside from selecting nodes and evaluation expressions, XPathNavigator also lets you move around a document (hence its name) with a handy set of Move methods, such as MoveNext(), MoveToFirstChild(), MovePrevious(), and so on. In fact, you can even use the Insert methods on the navigator to add nodes to a document. In all fairness, though, very few of you will ever do this— for a couple of reasons. First, XmlReader and XmlWriter (which we'll look at in a moment) are generally easier to work with, although they do add some code overhead. Second, most people don't need to do that much complex stuff with XML beyond reading and understanding a document in its entirety, or writing a new document based on an object in code. We'll cover all those things in the sections that follow.

If, however, you are a hard-core XML head, I strongly encourage you to read up on the methods in XPathNavigator and of course the XML and XPath references online. .NET's support for XML is really complete enough to fill an entire book all its own.

Reading XML Files

If you wanted to read an RSS feed and extract information from it, perhaps a listing of all the titles of articles in the feed, you could iterate through all the nodes in the XML document itself searching for one called item. When you found that node, you could then iterate through all its child nodes searching for one called title and then write even more code to extract the value of that element and print it out. You could craft an XPath expression and extract the nodes that way, as you just saw.

The XMLReader class provides an alternate, and more ".NET" way, of doing things. With the XML reader, you get intuitively named methods for navigating around a document, the ability to extract a document's contents as native .NET data types (string, int, bool, and so on), and you get a very lightweight tool for accessing huge amounts of data.

When you use the XmlDocument/_XPathNavigator combination, for example, you need to load the entire document into memory, which can be a bit of a chore if you are downloading it over a slow link and the document is huge. XmlReader lets you walk through a document node by node, without loading the whole document, processing just as much of the document as you need, and no more.

XMLReader lets you move progressively through an XML document, examining each node, attribute, or element. If you've done database programming before, it may help you to think of XmlReader as being *cursor based*. What that means is that XmlReader maintains a pointer, if you like, into the part of the document about to be read. For example, if we had this XML document

```
<SomeDocument>
        <SomeElement>
                SomeValue
        </SomeElement>
</SomeDocument>
```

we could call the XmlReader method ReadToFollowing("SomeElement") to effectively position the reader just before the opening tag of the SomeElement element. To move past the tag, we could call ReadStartElement() to position the reader immediately after the <SomeElement> tag.

XmlReader has a bunch of methods for moving around documents like this, and they are shown in Table 15-1.

Table 15-1. *The Methods of the XmlReader Class*

Method	Description
Read()	Reads the next node, and returns False if there are no more nodes to read.
ReadContentAs...()	A group of methods that read the content at the reader's current position as the specified type. For example, to grab a string you'd call ReadContentAsString(); for a float, you'd call ReadContentAsFloat(), and so on.
ReadElementContentAs()	This is the same as ReadContent() but will move the reader to the content of the named element if it's not already there. Just as with the ReadContentAs...() methods, you call the method matching the data type you are most interested in (that is, ReadElementContentAsString(), ReadElementContentAsInt(), and so on).
ReadElementString()	Because reading string elements is by far the most common operation people need to do, XmlReader includes a handy ReadElementString() method that takes the name of an element and returns its contents from the document.
ReadStartElement()	Positions the reader immediately before the next element node. You can also pass in the name of an element and the reader will jump to immediately before that element.

Method	Description
ReadEndElement()	This moves the reader to immediately after the close tag for the current node.
ReadSubTree()	Call this method when the reader is positioned on a node with children to get a new XmlReader returned just for processing the child nodes.
ReadToDescendent()	This is the method to call when you want to move the reader to a specific child node. Just pass in the name of the element you want, and the reader will jump to it if it exists, or return False if it is unable.
ReadToFollowing()	Moves the reader to the next node matching the name passed in, regardless of whether or not that node is a child node or sibling. As with the other Read methods, this returns True if the move is successful, False if not.
ReadToNextSibling()	This method is used to move the reader to the next element at the same level as the current one, with the name specified. It returns False if the read fails.
Skip()	If the reader is currently positioned on an element with children, calling Skip() skips them and moves the reader to the next node at the same level.
MoveToAttribute()	Passes in the name of the attribute of the current element to position the reader at that element.
MoveToContent()	Moves the reader to the next content node, skipping white space, processing instructions, and comments.

XmlReader is an abstract class, which of course means that you can't create one in the usual way. Instead, to create an XmlReader, you call a static method called Create() and pass in a stream or a string. Create() will return an appropriate subclass of XmlReader for you to use. In programming circles Create() is known as a *factory method*, a method that will basically create an object suited to your needs without you having to worry about working with a bunch of different types of XmlReader.

Let's see all this in action and write a simple console application to list out all the article types in the Ablog RSS feed.

Try It Out: Using XmlReader

Let's focus on the code (not the UI) with a console application. Start up a new console project in Visual Basic 2005 Express.

As before, the first thing you need to do is grab the XML document (the Apress blog RSS feed). Unlike before, the XmlReader doesn't work with the entire document but prefers streams, just reading in as much data as necessary to do the job. So, you'll need to open a stream to read the data. You can do this with the WebClient class in the System.Net namespace. Because we want to work with streams, you'll also need to use the System.IO namespace. Finally, because we're working with XML, you'll of course need to bring in the `System.Xml` namespace. So, the first order of business is of course to add three `using` statements to the top of `Module1.vb`:

```
Imports System.IO
Imports System.Net
Imports System.Xml

Module Module1

    Sub Main()

    End Sub

End Module
```

With the `using` statements sorted out, you can start work on the code. Let's open a stream to grab the RSS feed first of all. Go ahead and add a couple of lines of code to the `Main()` function:

```
Sub Main()

    Dim client As New WebClient()
    Dim rssFeedStream As Stream = _
        client.OpenRead("http://blogs.apress.com/wp-rss2.php")

End Sub
```

The code here creates a new `WebClient` and then asks it to give us a stream that we can work with to access the RSS feed. After you have a stream (whether it's from a website, a file, a memory block—it doesn't matter) you can attach an `XmlReader` to it:

```
Sub Main()

    Dim client As New WebClient()
    Dim rssFeedStream As Stream = _
        client.OpenRead("http://blogs.apress.com/wp-rss2.php")

    Dim reader As XmlReader = XmlReader.Create(rssFeedStream)

End Sub
```

As you can see, creating a reader from a stream is pretty trivial. You just have to pass the stream into the reader's constructor and you're good to go.

You'll remember when you looked at the XML format of the RSS feed earlier that the document begins with a bunch of stuff we're not particularly interested in. There are various XML directives at the top of the document, for example, to tell us that this is indeed an XML document, to reference the schema it uses, and so on. We can tell the reader to skip all this extraneous information with a call to MoveToContent():

```
Sub Main()

    Dim client As New WebClient()
    Dim rssFeedStream As Stream = _
        client.OpenRead("http://blogs.apress.com/wp-rss2.php")

    Dim reader As XmlReader = XmlReader.Create(rssFeedStream)
    reader.MoveToContent()

End Sub
```

What this actually does is make the reader suck data down from the stream until it gets to a content node. It skips any white space in the document, skips the directives, and positions the reader just before the first real XML element. This is perfect. What we're most interested in, though, are the item elements in the document. This contains information about the various blog posts that we want.

There's a method on the XmlReader listed in Table 15-1 called ReadToFollowing(). You can pass the name of an element into this method and it will make the reader advance through the document until it finds an element with a matching name. If the move is successful, the method returns True. If not, you get False. This makes it ideal for use in a loop. We can create a loop that repeatedly calls MoveToFollowing("item") to jump through each and every item in the document. Go ahead and add that loop now:

```
Sub Main()

    Dim client As New WebClient()
    Dim rssFeedStream As Stream = _
        client.OpenRead("http://blogs.apress.com/wp-rss2.php")

    Dim reader As XmlReader = XmlReader.Create(rssFeedStream)
    reader.MoveToContent()
    While reader.ReadToFollowing("item")

    End While

End Sub
```

Now the really neat part. A feature that I absolutely love about the XmlReader class is that it can generate new readers. Why would you want to do that? Well, as I've indicated, the XmlReader maintains information about where it is in a document. In this case you're looping through the items, but when you find an item, you need to jump in and process the elements it contains. You don't really want to affect what your reader is pointing at though; the while loop here is slick and simple to understand, so why complicate matters?

Instead, inside the loop you can actually generate a new reader just to process this tag and any child tags it contains, leaving your main reader unaffected. So, what you'll do here is call out to a new function, passing that function a brand new reader just for processing items in the feed. The way that you do this is by calling ReadSubtree(). That gives you a reader just for the child items within the current element:

```
Sub Main()

    Dim client As New WebClient()
    Dim rssFeedStream As Stream = _
        client.OpenRead("http://blogs.apress.com/wp-rss2.php")

    Dim reader As XmlReader = XmlReader.Create(rssFeedStream)
    reader.MoveToContent()
    While reader.ReadToFollowing("item")
        ProcessItem(reader.ReadSubtree())
    End While

End Sub


Private Sub ProcessItem(ByVal reader As XmlReader)

End Sub
```

So you created a new method stub called ProcessItem() that takes a reader as a parameter, and inside the while loop you generate a new reader for the child elements of the item tag in our RSS feed. Perfect. All you need to do now is write code into the ProcessItem() method to extract data about the feed and print it out to the console.

How can you extract data with an XmlReader()? Well, you can use ReadToFollowing() again to move the new reader to the specific item that you are most interested in. Then, you can use one of the ReadElementContentAs...() methods. These methods are some of the other strengths of the reader; you can access data from the XML document as native .NET types. If you want to grab a string, for example, you can call ReadElementContentAsString(). If you need an integer, call

ReadElementContentAsInt(), and so on. We're most interested in strings, so let's add the code to find the item, link, and title elements, extract their contents, and print them to the console:

```
Private Sub ProcessItem(ByVal reader As XmlReader)
    reader.ReadToFollowing("title")
    Dim title As String = _
        reader.ReadElementContentAsString("title", _
        reader.NamespaceURI)

    reader.ReadToFollowing("link")
    Dim link As String = _
        reader.ReadElementContentAsString("link", _
        reader.NamespaceURI)

    Console.WriteLine("{0}" + vbCrLf + "    {1}", title, link)

End Sub
```

Notice how the call to ReadElementContentAsString() requires two parameters: the name of the item that you want to read and the namespace of it. This is the XML namespace. XML documents can reference lots of different schemas and namespaces to define the elements the document can hold. Again, if this is new to you, check out http://www.xml.org to read all about it. In this case, you just pass in the main namespace of the document itself as the second parameter.

Finally, let's add a couple of console calls back up in Main() to finish the application:

```
Sub Main()

    Dim client As New WebClient()
    Dim rssFeedStream As Stream = _
        client.OpenRead("http://blogs.apress.com/wp-rss2.php")

    Dim reader As XmlReader = XmlReader.Create(rssFeedStream)
    reader.MoveToContent()
    While reader.ReadToFollowing("item")
        ProcessItem(reader.ReadSubtree())
    End While

    Console.WriteLine("All done!")
    Console.ReadLine()

End Sub
```

Run the program now and you'll see it print out the item titles and links as shown in Figure 15-8.

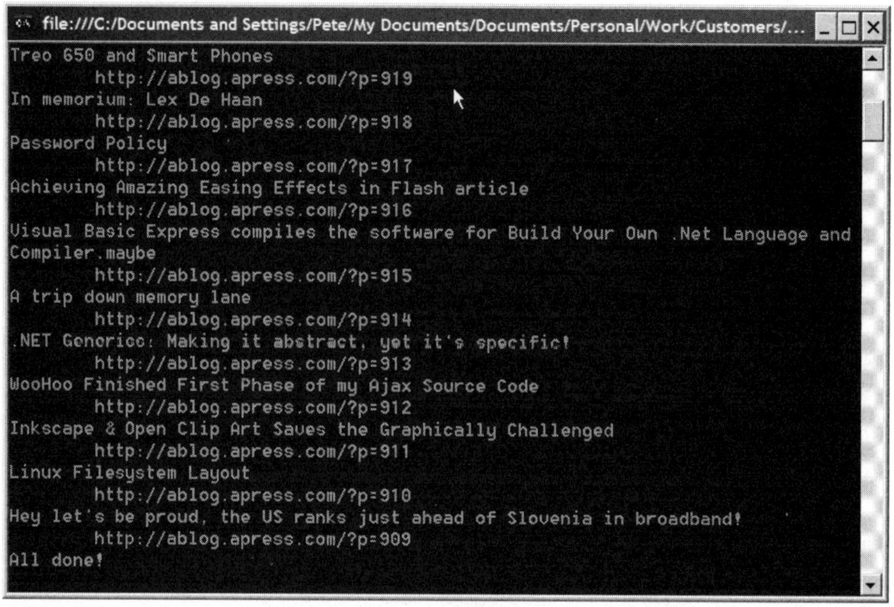

```
⚙ file:///C:/Documents and Settings/Pete/My Documents/Documents/Personal/Work/Customers/...  _ □ ✕
Treo 650 and Smart Phones
        http://ablog.apress.com/?p=919
In memorium: Lex De Haan
        http://ablog.apress.com/?p=918
Password Policy
        http://ablog.apress.com/?p=917
Achieving Amazing Easing Effects in Flash article
        http://ablog.apress.com/?p=916
Visual Basic Express compiles the software for Build Your Own .Net Language and
Compiler.maybe
        http://ablog.apress.com/?p=915
A trip down memory lane
        http://ablog.apress.com/?p=914
.NET Generics: Making it abstract, yet it's specific!
        http://ablog.apress.com/?p=913
WooHoo Finished First Phase of my Ajax Source Code
        http://ablog.apress.com/?p=912
Inkscape & Open Clip Art Saves the Graphically Challenged
        http://ablog.apress.com/?p=911
Linux Filesystem Layout
        http://ablog.apress.com/?p=910
Hey let's be proud, the US ranks just ahead of Slovenia in broadband!
        http://ablog.apress.com/?p=909
All done!
```

Figure 15-8. *Run the program to see the links and titles of articles printed out.*

Looking back through the code, using XmlReader certainly requires a lot more typing than hitting the document object model directly with XmlDocument and XPathNavigator. But look at the advantages. I think the code we just wrote is better structured and easier to follow. We're grabbing data from an XML document as native .NET data types. Better yet, RSS feeds are XML documents that can at times get *huge*. Do we really want to load a whole chunk of data into memory to process it? XmlReader lets us process a moving stream, without loading up memory, processing just as much as we need.

The counterpart to the XmlReader, with the same benefits, is of course the XmlWriter.

Writing XML

Here's the big thing with the XmlWriter. Typically, if you want to produce an XML document from code, you face two issues. The first is formatting. Although XML is a machine-readable data format, it's not unusual for people to want to be able to read (poke around is probably a better way to put it) the XML source. Second, you always produce XML documents from data you already manage. Perhaps you're writing out a set of variables you are managing to build a configuration file for your application. Perhaps you're using XML to store the contents of entire object trees. Maybe you're actually producing an RSS feed. The point is that the XML document you produce is a bloated copy of data you already have.

If you produce a document by using the XmlDocument object by hand, calling its Insert...() methods, you are actually putting into memory an even bigger copy of data you already have in memory. XmlWriter, just like the reader, is stream based. You write with it and it gets fired into the stream, without dramatically increasing memory footprint. It's also fast because you don't need to first construct a data model in memory, then open a stream, then convert the in-memory structure to a textual structure to go out on the stream. In general, XmlWriter is just a better way of working.

Let's take a look.

Try It Out: Using XmlWriter

You know, the easiest way of producing an XML document is probably to just build a bunch of strings and write them to a file. That's not really very "pure" though. Using XmlWriter also gives you the option to validate your XML document, making sure all the elements are closed properly, that attributes are declared properly, and so on. You could do it all the string way, but with a complex XML document you'd probably be damning yourself to a few very long hours of debugging. You'd also have to format the string document by hand, something XmlWriter can do for you automatically.

Start a new console application project and add an `Imports System.Xml` namespace to the top of `Module1.vb`:

Imports System.Xml

```
Module Module1

    Sub Main()

    End Sub

End Module
```

Creating an `XmlWriter` works the same way as it does on an `XmlReader`; you call a static method called `Create()`. The difference is the parameters you can pass to the method. `XmlWriter.Create()` can take a filename, a `StringBuilder` to write into a string, a stream, or even a writer already set up to talk to a file. We'll just write straight out to a file. Create the `XmlWriter` in the `Main()` function:

```
    Sub Main()

        Dim writer As XmlWriter = _
            XmlWriter.Create("c:\test.xml")

    End Sub
```

Here you're just going to write out to a file in the C drive's root directory, called `Test.xml`.

Every XML file should start with an XML directive identifying it as an XML file, and the XML standard that the file conforms to. `XmlWriter` can do all that for us with a call to `WriteStartDocument()`:

```
    Sub Main()

        Dim writer As XmlWriter = _
            XmlWriter.Create("c:\test.xml")

        writer.WriteStartDocument()

    End Sub
```

Now you can get onto producing the meat of the document. You'll produce a Customers document that contains details of a customer—it could easily be expanded to include a whole bunch of customers, but I'm trying to keep the code short.

To write an element that will contain other elements, you need to make two calls. The first is
WriteStartElement(). You pass into this the name of the element you want to create, and the
writer will write out that name surrounded by tag symbols (<>). When you're finished adding content
to the new element, a call to WriteEndElement() writes out the close tag. It's a good idea to always
write the two calls together so that you don't accidentally leave one out.

Our document will have a root element called Customers, which will contain Customer tags. Change the
code as follows to write out the start and end tags:

```
Sub Main()

    Dim writer As XmlWriter = _
        XmlWriter.Create("c:\test.xml")

    writer.WriteStartDocument()

    writer.WriteStartElement("Customers")

    writer.WriteEndElement()

End Sub
```

You can use the same pattern to build up your first customer in the document:

```
Sub Main()

    Dim writer As XmlWriter = _
        XmlWriter.Create("c:\test.xml")

    writer.WriteStartDocument()

    writer.WriteStartElement("Customers")

    writer.WriteStartElement("Customer")

    writer.WriteEndElement()

    writer.WriteEndElement()

End Sub
```

So, you have your root element, and you have a customer element in there. Now you can add some content to the new Customer element. Let's start by adding in an attribute with the customer's ID:

You write attributes by calling WriteAttributeString(), and pass in first the attribute name and then its value:

```
Sub Main()

    Dim writer As XmlWriter = _
        XmlWriter.Create("c:\test.xml")

    writer.WriteStartDocument()

    writer.WriteStartElement("Customers")

    writer.WriteStartElement("Customer")

    writer.WriteAttributeString("ID", "1234")

    writer.WriteEndElement()

    writer.WriteEndElement()

End Sub
```

That effectively makes the customer tag in the document look like this:

```
<Customer ID="1234">
```

Let's finish up by adding a child element with a value. You can do this with a call to WriteElementString() passing in the name of the new element and its value. This may seem a little limiting, being forced to just write strings, but it really isn't. XML documents are text, strings by default. In addition, all .NET types have a ToPrint() method so you can pretty much convert anything you have into a string. Reading is a different matter—it makes a lot of sense to be able to read in native .NET data types.

Add the new call into the code:

```
Sub Main()

    Dim writer As XmlWriter = _
        XmlWriter.Create("c:\test.xml")

    writer.WriteStartDocument()

    writer.WriteStartElement("Customers")
```

```
    writer.WriteStartElement("Customer")

    writer.WriteAttributeString("ID", "1234")
    writer.WriteElementString("Address", _
        "12 Somewhere Street, Sometown, 12354")

    writer.WriteEndElement()

    writer.WriteEndElement()

End Sub
```

All that you need to do now is close the document. It's a good idea to get in the habit of calling `WriteEndDocument()` on the writer as the last thing you do. This makes sure that any open tags you haven't closed are automatically closed for you. Also, you should call `Flush()` and `Close()` to make sure there's nothing hanging around in the writer that really should be written out, and that the underlying data stream is closed. Go ahead and make those changes:

```
Sub Main()

    Dim writer As XmlWriter = _
        XmlWriter.Create("c:\test.xml")

    writer.WriteStartDocument()

    writer.WriteStartElement("Customers")

    writer.WriteStartElement("Customer")

    writer.WriteAttributeString("ID", "1234")
    writer.WriteElementString("Address", _
        "12 Somewhere Street, Sometown, 12354")

    writer.WriteEndElement()

    writer.WriteEndElement()

    writer.Flush()
    writer.Close()

End Sub
```

Run the program now. If everything goes to plan, you won't see anything other than the flash of the console window coming into view and then vanishing. When the program's finished, start Notepad and load up the C:\Test.xml file you just created. You'll see the view in Figure 15-9.

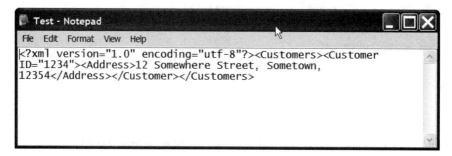

Figure 15-9. *The XmlWriter produced a well-formed but ugly XML document.*

Pretty ugly, isn't it. We can fix that easily, thanks to the XmlWriterSettings class. This class lets us build up a bunch of properties to apply to the writer to control how the resulting document is formatted.

Of particular interest to us is the XmlWriterSettings.Indent property. Setting this to True causes the resulting document to be nicely indented and formatted more as people would expect to see it. Using the XmlWriterSettings class is very easy. Make the changes shown in the following code, and then I'll talk you through them:

```
Sub Main()

    Dim settings As New XmlWriterSettings
    settings.Indent = True

    Dim writer As XmlWriter = _
        XmlWriter.Create("c:\test.xml", settings)

    writer.WriteStartDocument()

    writer.WriteStartElement("Customers")

    writer.WriteStartElement("Customer")
```

```
writer.WriteAttributeString("ID", "1234")
writer.WriteElementString("Address", _
    "12 Somewhere Street, Sometown, 12354")

writer.WriteEndElement()

writer.WriteEndElement()

writer.Flush()
writer.Close()

End Sub
```

All you need to do is create the object, set the property you want, and then pass the settings object to the `XmlWriter.Create()` call.

If you run the code and then open the `C:\test.xml` file in Notepad, the view will be very different, as you can see in Figure 15-10.

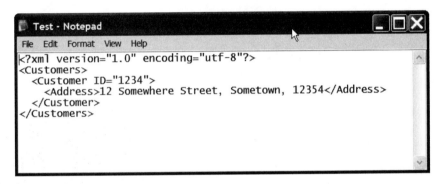

Figure 15-10. *Using XmlWriterSettings lets us format the document and control the operation of the writer.*

Feel free to wander through IntelliSense or the online help to see the other properties of the `XmlWriterSettings` object; you'll find how they are all used quite obvious.

Summary

I have to confess that we've only scratched the surface of XML support in .NET. The goal was to introduce you to the features and get you coding. There's actually enough content and features to System.Xml to fill an entire book all its own. If you are an XML fiend, I'm sure you'll have a ball browsing through the property and method lists of XmlDocument, XPathNavigator, XmlReader, XmlWriter, XmlReaderSettings, and XmlWriterSettings.

In the next chapter we'll move away from XML files as data stores and move to using fully featured SQL Server databases and the built-in database features in Visual Basic 2005 Express.

CHAPTER 16

■■■

Database Programming

It used to be the case that if you wanted to use a database in your application, you had just two choices: cheap or eye-wateringly expensive. It also used to be the case that in the world of databases you get what you pay for. At the cheap end of the scale, Microsoft's desktop database Access certainly got the job done, but it had severe limits on the amount of data it could store. Performance reading and writing large quantities of information to it from a Visual Basic application could be pretty abysmal.

The alternative, in the Microsoft world at least, was the eponymous SQL Server. Microsoft bills this as an enterprise-grade database server. It's supposed to service huge businesses with vast quantities of information at incredible speeds. As you might guess then, deploying it with your application would cost an appropriately large amount of cash.

Visual Basic 2005 Express comes with SQL Server Express, a new product from Microsoft designed to bridge the gap between Access and SQL Server, providing many of the benefits of both products. For example, a database in SQL Server Express is nothing more than a file, just as an Access database is nothing more than a file. If you intend on distributing your application to other users, this is a great thing; you can install the database along with your application just like any other file. In addition, SQL Server Express supports many of the features of SQL Server, including the database engine. Obviously there are some limitations (a limit on the maximum file size, a limit on the number of users who can simultaneously connect to the database, and so on), but by and large SQL Server Express is just like SQL Server. The big difference, of course, is that it's free.

A large part of the .NET Framework is devoted to working with databases. Also, Visual Basic 2005 Express provides many tools right inside the IDE that let you work with databases effortlessly, in many cases without ever having to have to write code. That being said, there's a lot of depth to ADO.NET (the database programming classes in the framework) that you'll never really need until you move up to the full Visual Studio 2005 package.

In this chapter I'm going to introduce you to database programming with Visual Basic 2005 Express. This won't be an extensive investigation of how to work with SQL Server databases—for that you should consult the online help. Similarly, this won't be an exhaustive examination of every feature of ADO.NET—for that, check out my other book, *ADO.NET: From Novice to Pro* (Apress, 2002). What I will cover, though, are all the most common things you are likely to want to do with a database and VB. I'll cover how to create a database, for example, how to build tables and stored procedures, and how to get information both into and out of a database by using controls on your Windows forms. By the end of this chapter you should be quite happy with writing your own data-enabled applications. For those of you wanting to go further, I'll close with some pointers to more information on the areas we didn't cover.

A Quick Walk-Through of the Tools

Before we go any further, you are going to need to download some samples from Microsoft. Simply point your browser at `http://msdn.microsoft.com/sql/downloads/` `samples` and follow the link to SQL Server 2005 Express Edition Samples and Sample Database. This will take you to a download page where you need to download the `AdventureWorksDB.msi` file. After you've downloaded it, run it to install the sample database we'll be working with in this chapter onto your computer. Please note, there have been some problems with people running this installer on machines that have the full version of Visual Studio 2005 or SQL Server 2005 installed. If that applies to you, then that's something to be aware of.

After you've downloaded the samples and installed them, you're ready to start on the walk-through.

Try It Out: Introducing the Database Tools

Start up a new Windows application project in Visual Basic 2005 Express. You're going to pull some data from the Adventure Works sample database and display it on the form—this is something that would historically have required quite a bit of code, but as you'll see here VB Express's built-in database tools make it trivial.

After the project is created, you'll need to add a reference to the database you're going to use. If this were a full enterprise-grade SQL Server database, you'd just enter a connection string to point your application at the live database. In this case, though, using SQL Express you're actually going to pull the entire database into your app, just to show how that works.

Click the Data menu and select Add New Data Source. You'll see the first page of the Data Source Configuration Wizard appear, asking you what kind of data source you want to work with. As you can see in Figure 16-1, VB Express lets you choose to use a web service, actual database, or even objects as data sources. You want a database, so click Database and then click the Next button.

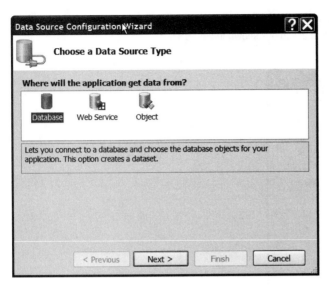

Figure 16-1. *The first page of the Data Source Configuration Wizard lets you choose the type of object you want to get data from.*

The next page of the wizard, shown in Figure 16-2, lets you set up the connection to the database. If you've used VB Express to connect to databases before, you'll be able to quickly access those database connections from the drop-down list.

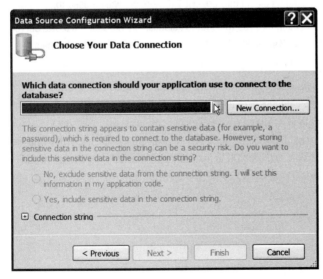

Figure 16-2. *The second page lets you reuse connections you've established before or create a new one.*

You need to set up a brand new connection to the Adventure Works database, so click the New Connection button. This brings up the Add Connection dialog box shown in Figure 16-3.

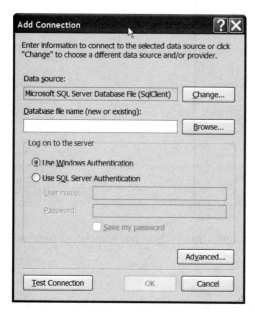

Figure 16-3. *Clicking New Connection brings up the Add Connection dialog.*

This is similar to the old ODBC connection settings dialog that pre-.NET developers will be used to.

The top of the dialog shows the type of connection that you're about to establish. In this case it's a SQL Server database file, or SQL Server Express database. You could click Change to bring up a dialog to choose a different type of database to connect to, but for our purposes this is fine.

So the next step is simply to choose the database file that you want to connect to. Click the Browse button to bring up a file dialog and then navigate to where the Adventure Works database was installed (by default this is the somewhat arcane path of C:\Program Files\Microsoft SQL Server\ MSSQL.1\MSSQL\Data_AdventureWorks_Data.mdf). After you've selected the file, click OK in the file browser to return to the Add Connection dialog, and click OK to finalize the connection. You'll return to the Data Source Configuration page. Click Next.

Straight away the dialog in Figure 16-4 appears.

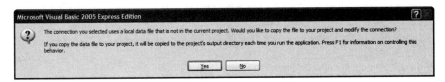

Figure 16-4. *Selecting a database file causes this dialog to appear.*

Because you are working with a SQL Server Express database, VB Express gives you the option to copy the file into your project. As the dialog indicates, doing this provides the benefit that you can easily deploy the database along with your application. You don't have to copy it, though; the connection string will work just fine with the database staying in its original location. For our purposes, copying is fine. Click the Yes button to copy the database into the project completely.

After the database is copied (you'll see it appear in the Solution Explorer), the next page of the wizard appears, as shown in Figure 16-5.

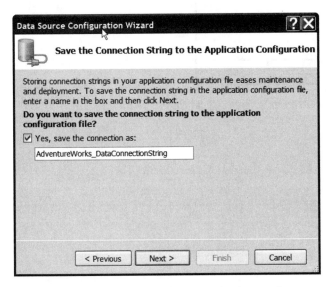

Figure 16-5. *The next page of the wizard asks you for a name to save the connection string.*

In order to tell ADO.NET where the database is, what it's called, and so on, you need a connection string. By this point the wizard has created the connection string and is advising you that the connection string will be stored in the application's configuration file. This is a file in the project called `app.config`. The database classes in the .NET Framework are able to retrieve the connection string from this file at runtime. Click the Next button.

The final stage of the wizard appears now, as shown in Figure 16-6.

Figure 16-6. *The final stage of the wizard lets you specify what will be included in your DataSet.*

A *DataSet* is a container that can mirror the structure of an entire database if necessary. At this stage of the wizard you simply need to choose which objects you want to work with. For example, if you wanted to call a stored procedure in the database and display the results in the application, you would find the stored procedure in this stage of the wizard and select it. The wizard then builds what's known as a *typed DataSet*, a class derived from the standard ADO.NET classes that provides you with easy type-safe access to tables and columns in the data, as well as methods to select that data to repopulate the DataSet on demand.

Expand the tables part of the tree and select the Contact, EmployeeAddress, and Employee tables from the list. Then click Finish.

After a brief delay, you'll find yourself returned to the designer. Take a look at the Solution Explorer in Figure 16-7.

Figure 16-7. *The Solution Explorer now has a new DataSet and the database you referenced.*

Notice that you now have a DataSet, the database, and the `app.config` file that holds the connection string included in the solution.

Double-click on the DataSet to open up the DataSet designer shown in Figure 16-8.

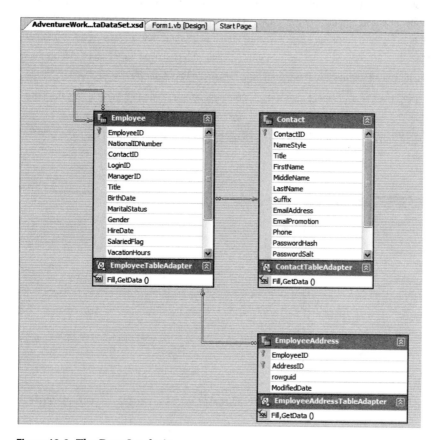

Figure 16-8. *The DataSet designer*

This shows you a graphical view of the tables, stored procedures, and views that you've selected to be in the DataSet. Notice how the relationships between the tables are drawn for you.

Each box represents both a `DataTable` object and a `DataAdapter` object. The `DataAdapter` objects are what you will use in code to grab information from the database, hence the `Fill()` and `GetData()` methods shown at the bottom of each.

Let's go ahead now and actually use the DataSet and the data adapters to grab information and display it on a form. Double-click on `Form1` in the Solution Explorer to bring up the form in the designer. Take a look at the Toolbox and find the `DataGridView` control. Double-click it to drop it onto the form, just as in Figure 16-9.

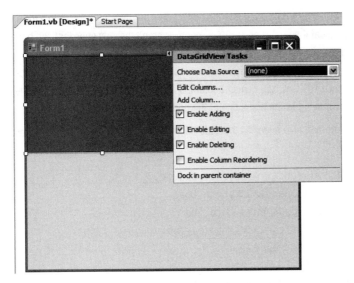

Figure 16-9. *Drop a DataGridView control onto the form.*

As soon as you drop the grid onto a form, the smart tag pops up, enabling you to configure it. All you need to do for now is point the grid at the right data source. Use the Choose Data Source drop-down list and expand the Other Data Sources Tree, then Project Data Sources, then Adventureworks, and choose the Contact table.

Still using the smart tip, select Dock in Parent Container to resize and lock the grid to the form's position. Then run the application. The form appears with the data inside it, as shown in Figure 16-10.

ContactID	NameStyle	Title	FirstName	MiddleName	LastName	Suffix
1	☐	Mr.	Gustavo		Achong	
2	☐	Ms.	Catherine	R.	Abel	
3	☐	Ms.	Kim		Abercrombie	
4	☐	Sr.	Humberto		Acevedo	
5	☐	Sra.	Pilar		Ackerman	
6	☐	Ms.	Frances	B.	Adams	
7	☐	Ms.	Margaret	J.	Smith	
8	☐	Ms.	Carla	J.	Adams	
9	☐	Mr.	Jay		Adams	
10	☐	Mr.	Ronald	L.	Adina	
11	☐	Mr.	Samuel	N.	Agcaoili	
12	☐	Mr.	James	T.	Aguilar	Jr.
13	☐	Mr.	Robert	E.	Ahlering	

Figure 16-10. *Run the program, and it will grab the data from the database and show it in the grid.*

So, with just a few mouse clicks you've added a data source to the application, dropped a control onto a form, and then got the control to "bind" to the database. `DataGridView` controls aren't the only ones that can bind to data. You can pretty much bind any control you want to a database. It's just that for the purposes of this example you get more bang for your buck with `DataGridView`. You'll also notice that you get a lot of functionality right out of the box with `DataGridView`. You can sort columns by clicking on the headings, change items you see, even add new ones by moving to the blank line at the bottom of the grid.

Stop the application that is running and then take a look at the code behind the form. The only code that was added lives in the form's Load event:

```
Private Sub Form1_Load(ByVal sender As System.Object, _
    ByVal e As System.EventArgs) Handles MyBase.Load
      'TODO: This line of code loads data into the
      'AdventureWorks_DataDataSet.Contact' table. You
      'can move, or remove it, as needed.
      Me.ContactTableAdapter.Fill( _
          Me.AdventureWorks_DataDataSet.Contact)
End Sub
```

When the form loads, the `Fill()` method is called on `employeeTableAdapter`, passing in the Employee table as the `DataTable` to load information into. These types were created on the form when you bound the grid. That's really all there is to it. Because you bound the grid view in design time, it already knows where it's expecting to retrieve data, so the only code necessary is the preceding line to make sure that data is loaded.

Let's move on now and look at all the tools available in the IDE for actually creating and working with your own databases.

Exploring the Database Creation Tools

You saw in the preceding "Try It Out" that there's a great deal of support built right into the Visual Basic 2005 Express IDE for working with an existing database. However, there are also tools in there to let you create and build your own databases from scratch.

You can add a blank database to any project in the same way that you would add any other item, such as a class or a form. Just right-click on the project in the Solution Explorer and choose Add New Item. When the Add New Item dialog box appears, select Database, give it a name, and then click Add. Doing this will also automatically generate a typed DataSet in your project and pop open the last page of the Data Source Configuration

Wizard again for you to choose which items you want to add. Obviously, with a new database you can't choose specific tables to add, so most people just click Finish when the wizard appears and leave the DataSet blank until they have their database fleshed out a bit more.

After you have a database in your project, whether it's a new one or a reference to an existing one, double-click it to open the Database Explorer on the left side of the IDE, as in Figure 16-11.

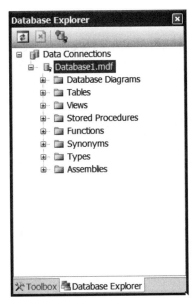

Figure 16-11. *Double-clicking the database in a project opens up the Database Explorer window.*

As the name suggests, this window lets you explore the items within your database and of course add new ones. The Database Explorer shows you a tree view of the selected database with tables, views, stored procedures, and so on. To create a new item, just right-click on the category of item you want to add into the database and select New from the pop-up menu that appears. Let's take a look.

Try It Out: Creating a Table

Create a new Windows application project and then add a new blank database to that project as outlined previously. After the database appears in the Solution Explorer, double click-it to open the Database Explorer window.

In the Database Explorer, right-click the `Tables` folder and select Add New Table. The main area of the IDE changes after a brief pause to show you the table designer in Figure 16-12.

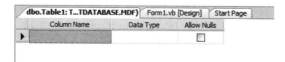

Figure 16-12. *The table designer*

You're going to create a simple blog table. The first thing you need is a unique ID for each blog entry. In the Column Name part of the grid, type **id** and then hit Tab. The view changes to show you more properties for the column as the cursor moves into the Data Type column (see Figure 16-13).

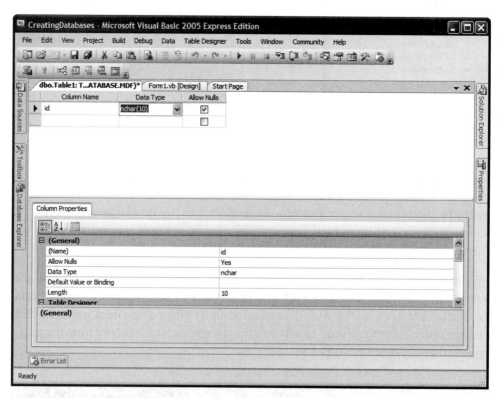

Figure 16-13. *After you enter a name for a field, additional properties for the field come into view.*

Let's make this ID field be an auto-incrementing number, so that as new blog entries are added to the table, they each get their own ID number, unique within this table. Select `bigint` as the data type and then in the Column Properties area of the designer find the Identity Specification section. Change the Is Identity property underneath Identity Specification to Yes, just as in Figure 16-14.

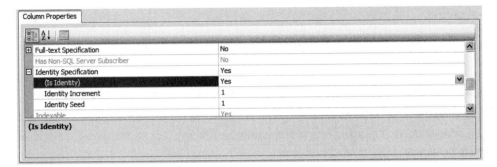

Figure 16-14. *You can set a field to be an auto-incrementing field in the properties area.*

The two properties beneath (Identity Increment and Identity Seed) will enable you to set their values. The default values here, though, are fine.

Let's add two more columns—one for the title of a blog entry and another for the blog entry's main content.

Set the name of the next column to **title** and go ahead and set the type to `varchar(100)`. That makes it a variable-length text field up to 100 characters long. Click the Allow Nulls check box to deselect it.

Now add in the final column, **postContent** with a type of `text`, and again turn off the Allow Nulls check box for the column. When you're finished, the table will look like Figure 16-15.

Column Name	Data Type	Allow Nulls
id	bigint	☐
title	varchar(100)	☐
postContent	text	☐
		☐

Figure 16-15. *Your final table design should look like this.*

Now you need to set the primary key on this table to the ID field. Just click in the ID field and then click the Set Primary Key icon on the toolbar, as in Figure 16-16.

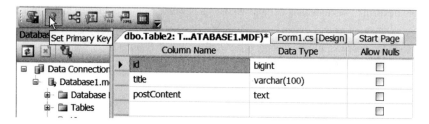

Figure 16-16. *The last stage of creating the table is to set its primary key.*

This puts a small key symbol next to the ID field. If you wanted to use more than one field to make up the primary key, you'd just Shift+click beside each field and then click the key icon.

Close the designer and you'll be asked if you wish to save the table design. Click the Yes button and then enter **BlogPosts** for the name of the table.

Your new table is now designed and ready to use. Let's put some data in it.

Find the BlogPosts table in the Database Explorer, right-click it, and select Show Table Data from the pop-up menu that appears. The table's data, which of course is empty at the moment, appears in the designer, as in Figure 16-17.

BlogPosts: Que...DATABASE1.MDF)	Start Page	
id	title	postContent
▶* NULL	NULL	NULL

Figure 16-17. *You can view and edit data in a table right within the VB Express IDE.*

Enter a couple of rows of data. You don't need to enter anything in the ID column because this is an autonumbering column and will generate its own value as you enter each row of data.

We're now in good shape to add this table to our DataSet, ready to write code with it.

Double-click on the DataSet in the Solution Explorer to open the DataSet designer, and then simply drag the table from the Database Explorer into the DataSet designer.

The "Try It Out" did of course assume that you know roughly what you are doing when it comes to selecting data types for database columns. I don't have enough room to go into that in any detail here, but at the end of the chapter I'll provide you with pointers to online help to find out more about defining columns and other elements of SQL Server databases.

Designing tables is all well and good, as is the ability to add data to them. At some point, though, you are going to want to get data out. That's where *stored procedures* come in. You could create DataSets and use the designer to generate SQL code for you to grab data from the database, but it's good practice to store this SQL code in stored procedures;

they are faster to execute and more secure than embedding database code inside your application.

To create a stored procedure, just right-click on the stored procedures folder in the Database Explorer and select Add New Stored Procedure. The code editor will appear to let you key in the SQL for your stored procedure, as in Figure 16-18.

```
dbo.StoredProc...DATABASE1.MDF)   Database1DataSet.xsd   Form1.
   CREATE PROCEDURE dbo.StoredProcedure1
       /*
       (
       @parameter1 int = 5,
       @parameter2 datatype OUTPUT
       )
       */
   AS
       /* SET NOCOUNT ON */
       RETURN
```

Figure 16-18. *The code editor can be used to create stored procedures.*

As you can see, the code editor pops up with the template for a new stored procedure. You will need to know how to write SQL, though, to fill in the blanks.

You can use exactly the same process to create anything else you might need in a database, such as views and functions. Again, refer to the SQL Server Express online help referenced at the end of this chapter for more information on how to write the SQL statements for a stored procedure, as well as more info on just what views and functions are.

Writing Database Code

Let's move away from the visual tools for a moment and take a look at writing code to work with a database. Let's kick off with exploring how to move through rows from a database in code.

Try It Out: Navigating Through Rows in a Table

Start up a new console application. When the project is ready, add the Adventure Works database, just as you did in the first "Try It Out" earlier in this chapter. After you have the database in the project and you've selected the Contact, Employee, and EmployeeAddress tables, you'll start writing code.

Double-click on Module1.vb to open the code editor, ready to start writing code. When you added the data source to the project and created the DataSet, the VB Express IDE added in a few new classes for you. In fact, every box you see in the DataSet designer is a new class. These classes subclass standard ADO.NET classes in order to establish database connections, fire commands at the database, and of course retrieve and work with data. The beauty of the typed DataSets that the DataSet designer generates is that you don't have to worry about any of that stuff. Let's take a look.

The first thing you need to do is create a data adapter. *Data adapters* provide a conduit between the database and the DataSets and tables in your code. A data adapter is able to fire commands at the database to select data, and also handle any updates, inserts, and deletes for you. When you added the data source, the IDE actually generated all these SQL statements for you and created a customized data adapter for you to use:

```
Sub Main()
    Dim da As New _
    AdventureWorks_DataDataSetTableAdapters.EmployeeTableAdapter()

End Sub
```

Creating your data adapter then involves nothing more than creating an instance of a data adapter that the DataSet designer made for you. You'll find all the data adapters for this database living inside the `AdventureWorks_DataDataSetTableAdapters` namespace.

So, now you have a data adapter created, all you need to do now is grab data from the database. The generated code takes care of reading the `app.config` file to grab the connection string and connect to the database, and also takes care of issuing `Select` commands (the SQL commands that grab data) against the database. All you need to do is call one of the generated methods (`Fill()` or `GetData()`) to actually talk to the database and grab the data you want:

```
Sub Main()
    Dim da As New _
    AdventureWorks_DataDataSetTableAdapters.EmployeeTableAdapter()

    Dim table As New _
        AdventureWorks_DataDataSet.EmployeeDataTable()

    da.Fill(table)
End Sub
```

The first thing that happens is to create a new instance of the data table you want to work with, in this case the EmployeeDataTable(). In this database, all the tables live in the AdventureWorks_DataDataSet namespace.

After the table instance has been created, all that remains is to call the Fill() method on the data adapter. That fires off all the work of connecting to the database, issuing a query, grabbing the results, and then populating the data table itself.

The next step is to walk through the rows in the table:

```
Sub Main()
    Dim da As New _
    AdventureWorks_DataDataSetTableAdapters.EmployeeTableAdapter()

    Dim table As New _
        AdventureWorks_DataDataSet.EmployeeDataTable()

    da.Fill(table)
    For Each row As AdventureWorks_DataDataSet.EmployeeRow _
      In table.Rows

        Console.WriteLine("ID:{0}, {1}", row.EmployeeID, _
            row.LoginID)

    Next

    Console.ReadLine()

End Sub
```

That's all there is to it. Run the program now and you'll see the information in the table printed out to the console, just as in Figure 16-19.

Figure 16-19. *Run the application and you'll see data from all the rows written out.*

The table has a Rows collection, with each element in that collection being a row in the database. Because you are using a typed DataSet generated by the designer, you can walk through the rows and then use properties on each row to get at information inside it, like the EmployeeID and LoginID in this example.

You could, if you wanted, do away with the need for the DataSet designer completely and manually write code to do everything by hand, but why would you want to? The DataSet designer makes life so simple, and typed DataSets as you've just seen bring with them the added benefit of IntelliSense for column names and compile-time checking. If you are going to do database programming, always use a typed DataSet.

Save the application; we'll be coming back to it in a second.

You may have noticed when you built the DataSet in the designer that each data adapter gets two methods: GetData() and Fill(). In the example you just worked through, you used the Fill() method to populate a data table. So what exactly does GetData() do? The short answer is "exactly the same thing." Calling Fill() on a data adapter is the traditional way of doing things in .NET. The DataAdapter class itself, which the designer subclasses, has a Fill() method that when called invokes the Select statement embedded in the data adapter to grab data and put it somewhere (usually in a DataSet or table). GetData() on the other hand is a new method that will return a new DataTable to you. Which you use is really a matter of choice; obviously, though, GetData() cuts down on the need for you to create a new DataTable object first.

In the example you just worked through, you walked over the Rows collection to grab information from each row in a table. The humble DataRow (which EmployeeRow is a subclass of) is a very powerful object in its own right. You see, not only does it provide you with access to the data in a specific row, but it also tracks changes. You can find out from a DataRow if the row has been changed at all since it was last loaded, how it was changed, and even request the original data from the row in case you want to do a comparison.

That all sounds powerful enough, but terribly complex. It is, however, how the mighty DataAdapter works its magic. You see, you can call a method on a DataAdapter called Update() and pass in a data table with changes. The DataAdapter then walks through every row in the table looking for rows that have been changed. If the change is the result of an edit, the adapter can call an update command to update the original record in the database. If the change is because of a completely new row being added, the DataAdapter can spot that too, firing off an insert command to the database. Similarly, the DataAdapter can also spot rows that have been flagged as being deleted and call a delete command.

Let's take a brief look at all this in action and see how to update data in a table and get it put back into the database.

Try It Out: Updating Data

Load up the project you worked on in the preceding "Try It Out." You'll get rid of the code you wrote and replace it with some new code to demonstrate how to update data, but the data source you added for the Adventure Works database is going to come in handy once again.

Double-click on Module1.vb to bring up the code in the code editor, if it's not already on display. Delete all the code in the Main() function except the line that creates the data adapter. When you're finished, the function will look like this:

```
Sub Main()
    Dim da As New _
    AdventureWorks_DataDataSetTableAdapters.EmployeeTableAdapter()

End Sub
```

Let's use the GetData() method to see how that works, to grab a list of employees from the database:

```
Sub Main()
    Dim da As New _
    AdventureWorks_DataDataSetTableAdapters.EmployeeTableAdapter()

    Dim employees As AdventureWorks_DataDataSet.EmployeeDataTable = _
        da.GetData()

End Sub
```

As you can see here, you don't need to create an instance of the data table if you use the GetData() method; it returns a new fully populated table to you.

Now that you have your data, let's grab the first row from the database so that you can change it, and I'll show you how to use the row to find out its state:

```
Sub Main()
    Dim da As New _
    AdventureWorks_DataDataSetTableAdapters.EmployeeTableAdapter()

    Dim employees As AdventureWorks_DataDataSet.EmployeeDataTable = _
        da.GetData()

    Dim row As AdventureWorks_DataDataSet.EmployeeRow = employees(0)

End Sub
```

Something quite subtle is going on here. You could have used the Rows collection of the employees object to get at the row you want, but that would return to you an object of type DataRow. If you did that, you'd have to write code to cast that object to an EmployeeRow. The table classes generated by the DataSet designer have a default property that you can use as you have here. Just by treating the employees object as if it were an array, you get back the data row you want. After you get used to working this way, it's far more intuitive than diving down through collections and then subcollections and so on.

Now that you have the row you are going to update, let's find out what state it's in. Rows have a special property called RowState that returns an enum. This enum could be unchanged for a newly loaded record, modified for a record that was just changed, deleted if it's been deleted, or created for a new record:

```
Sub Main()
    Dim da As New _
    AdventureWorks_DataDataSetTableAdapters.EmployeeTableAdapter()

    Dim employees As AdventureWorks_DataDataSet.EmployeeDataTable = _
        da.GetData()

    Dim row As AdventureWorks_DataDataSet.EmployeeRow = employees(0)
    Console.WriteLine("Current row state: {0}", row.RowState)
End Sub
```

Before anything happens, you print out the row state just to see what happens.

To edit a row, you can't unfortunately just go changing property values. You need to tell the row what you are going to do to it. If you wanted to delete the row, for example, you'd just call its Delete() method. To make changes to the values in a row, you need to call BeginEdit(). When you're finished, either call EndEdit() to accept the changes, or CancelEdit() to throw them out. Incidentally, when we look at control binding in a little while, you'll be pleased to learn that bound controls do all these nasty method calls for you.

```
Sub Main()
    Dim da As New _
    AdventureWorks_DataDataSetTableAdapters.EmployeeTableAdapter()

    Dim employees As AdventureWorks_DataDataSet.EmployeeDataTable = _
        da.GetData()

    Dim row As AdventureWorks_DataDataSet.EmployeeRow = employees(0)
    Console.WriteLine("Current row state: {0}", row.RowState)
    row.BeginEdit()
    row.EndEdit()
End Sub
```

Between the BeginEdit() and EndEdit() calls, you can make your changes to the row:

```
Sub Main()
    Dim da As New _
    AdventureWorks_DataDataSetTableAdapters.EmployeeTableAdapter()

    Dim employees As AdventureWorks_DataDataSet.EmployeeDataTable = _
        da.GetData()

    Dim row As AdventureWorks_DataDataSet.EmployeeRow = employees(0)
    Console.WriteLine("Current row state: {0}", row.RowState)
    row.BeginEdit()
    row.LoginID = "Test"
    row.EndEdit()
End Sub
```

With the change to the row made, let's print out its new state. When a row changes (either being deleted, or edited, or even added), the table becomes aware of the change. You can call GetChanges() on the table itself to get an array of rows with changes back. Let's do just that:

```
Sub Main()
    Dim da As New _
    AdventureWorks_DataDataSetTableAdapters.EmployeeTableAdapter()

    Dim employees As AdventureWorks_DataDataSet.EmployeeDataTable = _
        da.GetData()

    Dim row As AdventureWorks_DataDataSet.EmployeeRow = employees(0)
    Console.WriteLine("Current row state: {0}", row.RowState)
    row.BeginEdit()
    row.LoginID = "Test"
    row.EndEdit()

    Console.WriteLine( _
        "Current row state: {0}" + vbCrLf + _
        "No. of rows changed:{1}", _
        row.RowState, employees.GetChanges().Rows.Count)
End Sub
```

The final step is to commit the changes to the database by using the data adapter you created at the top of the code. There are two stages to this. The first is to call Update() on the adapter. This will kick the adapter into life, looking through the rows for changes before calling the update command it generated silently when you built the DataSet. The second is to call AcceptChanges() on the table itself. The reason for this is that after the changes are written to the database, the rows that changed are still in your table and flagged as changed. Calling AcceptChanges() clears out all the changes, leaving you with just the current rows in the table and no more:

```
Sub Main()
    Dim da As New _
    AdventureWorks_DataDataSetTableAdapters.EmployeeTableAdapter()

    Dim employees As AdventureWorks_DataDataSet.EmployeeDataTable = _
        da.GetData()

    Dim row As AdventureWorks_DataDataSet.EmployeeRow = employees(0)
    Console.WriteLine("Current row state: {0}", row.RowState)
    row.BeginEdit()
    row.LoginID = "Test"
    row.EndEdit()

    Console.WriteLine( _
        "Current row state: {0}" + vbCrLf + _
        "No. of rows changed:{1}", _
        row.RowState, employees.GetChanges().Rows.Count)

    da.Update(employees)
    employees.AcceptChanges()
    Console.ReadLine()
End Sub
```

Run the program now to see the output in Figure 16-20.

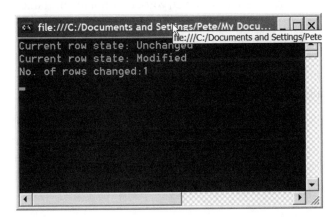

Figure 16-20. *Run the program to see the row state change and to update the database.*

If you use the Database Explorer now to show you the data in the Employees table, in the database you'll see your changed record right at the top.

So, to summarize, if you want to change a record, all you need to do is call `BeginEdit()` on the row in question, make your changes, and then call `EndEdit()`, `Update()` on the adapter and `AcceptChanges()` on the table. It seems convoluted I know, but you get used to it.

Alternately, to delete a row, call `Delete()` on the row in question and then `Update()` and `AcceptChanges()` just as if you were making an edit.

Adding a row is slightly different. Every table class created by the designer gets a `New...Row()` method, where the ellipsis (...) is replaced with the name of the table. For example, your `employees` object has a method called `NewEmployeeRow()`. This will return a new blank row for you to use. Simply set the properties on the row that you need and then call `AddEmployeeRow()` (or whatever your table is called) on the table object to store the row into the `Rows` collection.

There's a lot more you can do, including drilling down into the row itself to find out what changed, as well as validating the row, that unfortunately I don't have time to cover here. Feel free to explore the ADO.NET section in the online help for more information. For most cases, what I've covered here will be all you need to use. In fact, for most cases, it's more than you need to know because data binding can take care of much of the detail work for you.

___

So far we've used the DataSet pretty much out of the box. As you've seen, the DataSet designer automatically generates two methods to get data from the database, and implicitly produces the SQL code to update the database, delete records, and create new ones. It would be easy to presume that the DataSet designer is somewhat limiting, that it forces you down a path that's hard to deviate from. Nothing could be further from the truth. It's incredibly easy to change the default behavior of the produced DataSet, and almost trivial to extend it with even more functionality.

After the data connection wizard has produced the DataSet, you can configure the tables within it just by right-clicking in the designer view and selecting Configure from the pop-up menu. This will start the TableAdapter Configuration Wizard, as shown in Figure 16-21.

As you can see, this instantly displays the SQL code that's going to be used to grab data from the database. You can easily modify this either by typing new SQL code into the mini editor, or by clicking the Query Builder button to run the graphical query builder shown in Figure 16-22.

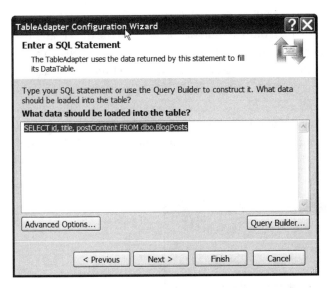

Figure 16-21. *You can easily access the TableAdapter Configuration Wizard by right-clicking on any table in the designer and selecting Configure.*

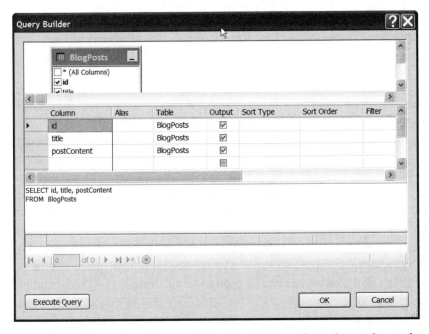

Figure 16-22. *The graphical query designer makes it a relatively painless task to develop quite complex queries.*

You can right-click in the upper pane of the graphical designer to add new tables, and then just click on columns to select which ones should be included in the query, and use the middle pane to specify the filter, sort, and search conditions. Of course you can also type code directly into the bottom pane if you so desire. When you're finished, to test the query just click the Execute Query button and you'll get a preview of the data that the query will pull back.

Back on the main wizard page, clicking the Advanced Options button brings up the dialog box that governs how the adapters that connect to the database work behind the scenes. You can see this in Figure 16-23.

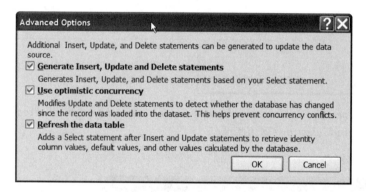

Figure 16-23. *The Advanced Options dialog box lets you control what happens behind the scenes.*

You can change whether or not the designer creates the Insert, Update, and Delete SQL statements, how the adapter handles concurrency (preventing one user of the application from overwriting another's work—not a big deal with SQL Express because it's designed for single users only, not multiple user systems). You can also force the adapter to refresh the data in the DataSet after an update. Neat, huh.

The one thing you can't do is set the DataSet to use stored procedures in the database. For that you need to drop back into the main designer view and right-click the table in question again.

The pop-up menu that appears when you right-click on a table lets you configure the data adapter, as I just showed you. It also enables you to add additional queries to the adapter. By default the designer creates two methods for you: one to Fill() a data table with data, and the other to run the same query but return a brand new data table for use. If you need to hit additional stored procedures in the database, or run additional queries, just right-click on the table adapter and choose Add Query.

The Query Configuration Wizard shown in Figure 16-24 lets you choose to access the database with SQL code, write a new stored procedure, or select an existing one.

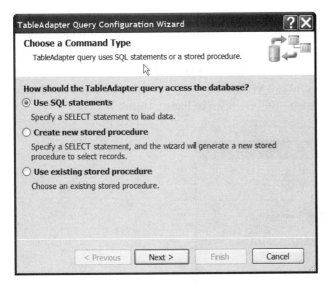

Figure 16-24. *The Query Configuration Wizard lets you add new queries into a table adapter and expose them as new methods that can be called in code.*

For example, choosing to reference an existing stored procedure takes you to a page to let you choose the stored procedure you want to call. Just select it from the drop-down list shown in Figure 16-25.

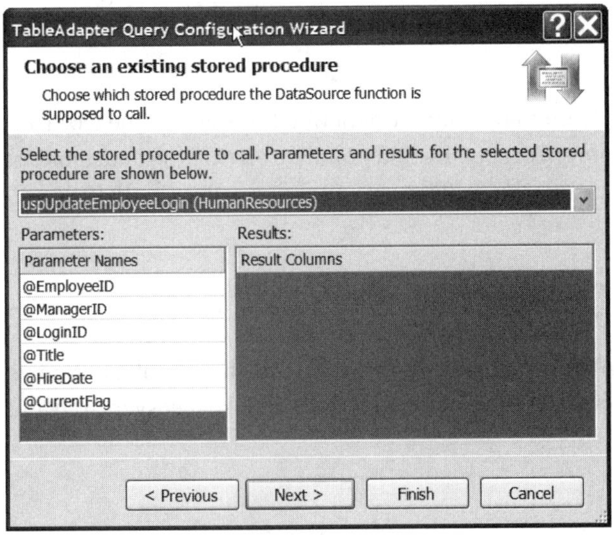

Figure 16-25. *You can easily reference existing stored procedures from the DataSet designer.*

When you choose a stored procedure, any parameters it expects will be shown, and these will ultimately become method parameters on a new method generated inside the data adapter. Just click Next to get to the next page, tell the wizard what kind of stored procedure this is (one that returns a bunch of a data, a stored procedure that returns a single record, or a stored procedure that updates the database and returns nothing), and finally specify a name for the methods to generate as shown in Figure 16-26.

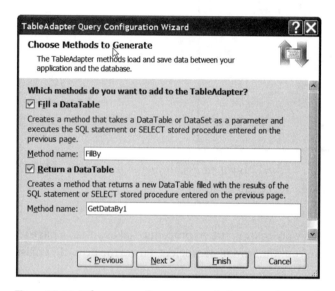

Figure 16-26. *When you reference an existing stored procedure in the designer, you get to set a name for the new method that will be added to the adapter.*

As with the GetData() and Fill() methods that are generated by default, the wizard will generate a method to run the stored procedure and populate an existing data table, as well as a method (the Get...() method) that will return a brand new DataTable to you.

An Overview of Data Binding

So far you've seen how easy it is to drop a grid onto a form "bound" to a database. You've also seen how to use the incredibly powerful DataSet designer to make it easy to grab and work with data in code.

Visual Basic 2005 Express lets you put those two concepts together (the DataSet and data binding) in a stunningly versatile way. Pretty much every single visual control in the Windows user interface controls toolbox can be data bound, making it easy to create applications that display data and let users edit it and work with it in whatever way they please. Best of all—it's really easy.

Rather than talk you through all the nitty-gritty details, let's dive straight into a nice "Try It Out" to see this stuff in action.

Try It Out: Data Binding

Start up a new Windows application and as before add the Adventure Works data source to the project. Also as before, add in at least the Employee table to the DataSet.

The first thing you need to do to bind controls on a form to the database is drop a special control onto the form called the BindingSource control. All the other controls you drop on will use this to get at the database. It's a nonvisual control, so when you add it to the form it appears underneath it, as shown in Figure 16-27.

Figure 16-27. *Adding a BindingSource control to the form is the first step in setting up bound controls.*

To make the BindingSource control work, you'll need to set two properties: DataSource and DataMember. DataSource just points the data source at our project's database. Click in it and then click the drop-down arrow to choose our project's data source, as shown in Figure 16-28.

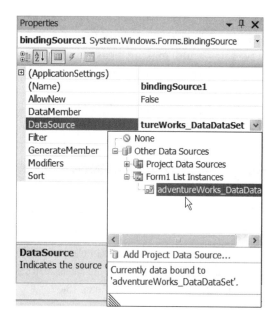

Figure 16-28. *Use the BindingSource's DataSource property to reference the database you want to bind to.*

The `DataMember` property identifies the individual table that you want to work with. Click in it and then use the drop-down list to select the Employee table.

Notice that as soon as you do this, the `AllowAddNew` property changes to `True`. Because the DataSet by default is configured to handle inserting new records into the database, the BindingSource control picks up on this and sets the property to `True` to indicate that at runtime it can be used to feed values from controls on the form into new records in the database.

After you have a BindingSource control set up, the next step is to drop a DataNavigator control onto the form. Go ahead and do this now and your form will look like mine in Figure 16-29.

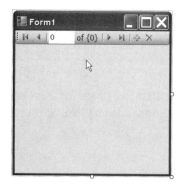

Figure 16-29. *Add a binding navigator to the form.*

This step isn't strictly required. You can set up bound controls on a form without this control, but the Binding-Navigator control adds so much functionality for free that it's worth using. The control is basically a toolbar that controls the BindingSource, letting you move from record to record in the DataSet's table, add new records, cancel changes, and so on. If you come from a Visual Basic 6 background, you'll have seen something similar for navigating through data. What's different is that the navigator is an extensible toolbar. You can easily add new buttons to it specific to your application. You can even select the elements that are already displayed inside it and hide them if necessary. It's a versatile control that you can customize to your heart's content.

After the navigator is on the form, you need to connect it to the BindingSource so that it knows what it's working with. You can do this with the `BindingSource` property. Simply click into the property and click the drop-down arrow to choose the BindingSource control we just set up.

Now add a text box, date time picker, and check box to the form, along with some labels, so that your form looks like the one in Figure 16-30.

Figure 16-30. *Set up some controls on the form like this.*

Don't worry about setting up the control names.

Select the first text box on the form and look through its properties. Right at the top of the list (if you have the properties sorted alphabetically), you'll find one called `DataBindings`. Expand this property and you'll see the properties shown in Figure 16-31.

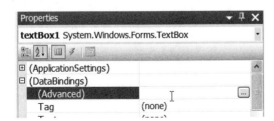

Figure 16-31. *The DataBindings property collection is your key to setting up bound controls.*

Click the Advanced property and then click the ellipsis button to bring up the Formatting and Advanced Binding dialog box in Figure 16-32.

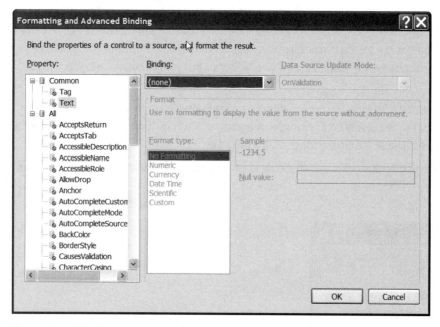

Figure 16-32. *The Formatting and Advanced Binding dialog is where you actually bind a control.*

Click in the Binding drop-down list and choose our BindingSource control and the LoginID field as shown in Figure 16-33.

You'll see instantly that you can now also specify events to fire on the control to validate the data inside it if the user makes changes. For now, just click the OK button to close the dialog and finish the binding.

Now walk through the same process to bind the other two controls. Bind the DateTimePicker control to the HireDate field, and bind the CheckBox to the SalariedFlag field.

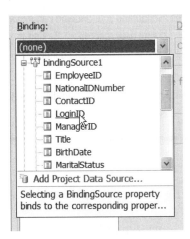

Figure 16-33. *Use the drop-down list to choose the field in the binding source that you want to bind a control to.*

That's all there is to it. Run the application now and you'll see your form appear like the one in Figure 16-34.

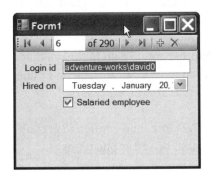

Figure 16-34. *When you're finished, you can run the application. It will have a vast amount of functionality, and you didn't even have to write a single line of code.*

Notice that the navigator automatically shows you the number of records available to you, and you can move through them by clicking on the VCR-like buttons on the control. You can create new records by clicking the New Record button (database constraints permitting, of course). You can change anything, and cancel changes with the Cancel button.

There's more to this, though. You'll find that if you explore the Formatting and Advanced Binding dialog that you can bind almost any property of any control to any field on the database. Have fun.

Summary

ADO.NET and database work in .NET is a massive subject, and I've had to make compromises in this chapter as to what I could cover. What I did cover are the basics of setting up a database, adding it to your project, and then of course using it both in code and through data binding of controls. There are whole books written on this subject, so if databases are something that fascinates you, you should definitely spend some time poring through the online help to find out more about the controls covered in this chapter. The Movie Collection starter kit application that ships with Visual Basic 2005 Express is also a great place to look for some good example code demonstrating the range of things you can do with databases and Visual Basic 2005.

It's also worthwhile reading up on the SQL Server Express online help to find all that that product can do. You can also find a lot of information on SQL Server Express online at the SQL Server Express site (http://msdn.microsoft.com/vstudio/express/sql/default.aspx).

For most of you, the ground we covered here should be more than enough to get you on the way to developing your own databases and database-driven applications.

CHAPTER 17

The Internet and Visual Basic

Call me weird, but I find talking to databases pretty cool. When I first came across them, the idea of being able to connect to some massive data source somewhere, extract volumes of information, and do with it as I wished seemed really quite neat. These days we all have access to a much bigger database than anyone could possibly have imagined just two decades ago: the Internet.

Visual Basic 2005 Express (and of course version 2 of the .NET Framework) ships with a bunch of tools that let you write programs that can actually go out on the Internet and do things. Perhaps you need a small application that will go out and get the next dates and times of your favorite TV shows. Perhaps you need to embed a web browser in your app and let your users view a mix of either local or remote web pages at runtime. Maybe you even need to have your program automatically exchange files with some remote server when it runs. All these things and more are possible with Visual Basic 2005 Express, and with very little effort. That's a key point, in fact. Doing the kind of Internet-enabled work that .NET makes simple was a huge nightmare for developers just a couple of years ago. Viva Microsoft.

Introducing the WebBrowser Control

So, to demonstrate a point, let's write our own custom web browser application. This would have taken a small team years of man effort in the past, but we'll have one knocked out in about 10 minutes. Now how's that for progress?

Try It Out: Building Your Own Web Browser

We're going to cheat of course. Visual Basic 2005 Express has a handy control called a WebBrowser control that handles everything to do with web pages without any effort on our part. Go ahead and start up a new Windows application project.

When the default form appears, drop a StatusStrip control onto the form, just as in Figure 17-1.

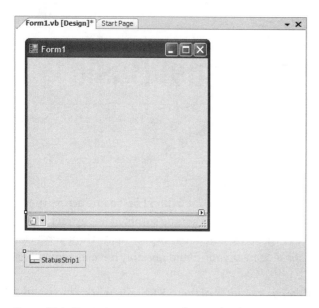

Figure 17-1. *Drop a status control onto the form.*

You'll use this control to display a progress bar as the web page loads. To do that, click on the drop-down arrow that's displayed on the status bar and choose ProgressBar from the list that appears. This will drop a progress bar onto the status bar, as you can see in Figure 17-2.

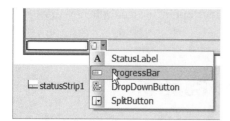

Figure 17-2. *Add a progress bar to the status bar by using the drop-down list inside the status bar.*

Don't worry about setting up the names of the status bar or its progress bar—we'll keep the app simple.

Next, if you take a look at the bottom of the list of Common Controls in the Toolbox, you'll see the WebBrowser control in Figure 17-3.

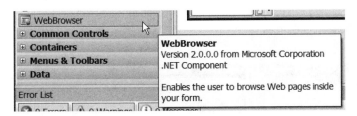

Figure 17-3. *The WebBrowser control lives at the bottom of the Common Controls collection in the Toolbox.*

Double-click the control to drop it onto the form. You won't actually see anything because by default the Web-Browser control docks within the window and takes up all available space. You will notice that the control has a smart tag like most of the new .NET controls, and the inside of the form will turn white (see Figure 17-4).

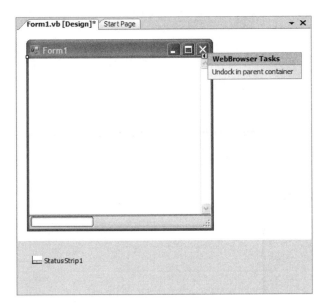

Figure 17-4. *Dropping the WebBrowser control onto the form doesn't really show anything special in design mode.*

Click on the WebBrowser inside the form and take a look at the properties. The properties that are of most interest to us live in the Behavior group of properties in the window, and control how the browser works—for example, whether the browser will have scroll bars, or whether it will accept the Microsoft Internet Explorer keyboard shortcuts, and so on. For now, just set the Url property to http://www.microsoft.com. This sets up the default website that will display in the browser when the application runs. You can see this in Figure 17-5, along with the other Behavior properties.

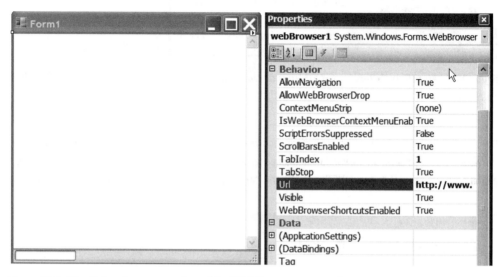

Figure 17-5. *The Behavior properties of the WebBrowser control*

Let's take a look at the events now. Click the Events button of the Properties window to switch to event view (see Figure 17-6).

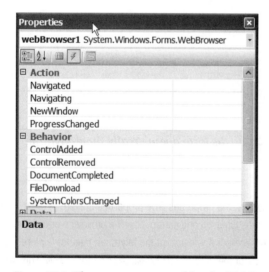

Figure 17-6. *The events supported by the WebBrowser control*

The event model of the WebBrowser control pretty much lets you hook into everything the control is doing, from navigating as a result of a click, to all stages of downloading and displaying a page. You can see them in the Action and Behavior groups of events.

Double-click the `ProgressChanged` property to drop into the code editor for that event. The Progress-Changed event, as its name suggests, fires to let you know the progress of an operation has changed. It's specifically geared to people who want to write code to update a progress bar. The `WebBrowserProgressChangedEventArgs` parameter e, for example, has two properties (`Maximum` and `Value`) that are specifically geared toward that task. So, your code gets real simple:

```
Private Sub WebBrowser1_ProgressChanged(ByVal sender As System.Object, _
    ByVal e As System.Windows.Forms.WebBrowserProgressChangedEventArgs) _
    Handles WebBrowser1.ProgressChanged

    ToolStripProgressBar1.Maximum = e.MaximumProgress
    ToolStripProgressBar1.Value = e.CurrentProgress

End Sub
```

Here you're just copying those two values out of the event parameter e and dumping them straight into your status bar's progress bar, and voilà—you have an updating status bar.

Well, almost.

The event will fire every time the browser does something in the progress of rendering a page, but it won't always fire when the page load is complete. So you should hook up the browser's DocumentCompleted event. Go back to the form editor, select the WebBrowser control, and then find the DocumentCompleted event in the event browser and double-click it to once again drop into the code window. Add the following highlighted lines to the DocumentCompleted event handler:

```
Private Sub WebBrowser1_DocumentCompleted(ByVal sender As System.Object, _
    ByVal e As System.Windows.Forms.WebBrowserDocumentCompletedEventArgs) _
    Handles WebBrowser1.DocumentCompleted

    ToolStripProgressBar1.Value = ToolStripProgressBar1.Maximum

End Sub
```

That's all there is to it—your simple browser app is complete. Run the program now and you'll not only see Microsoft's home page load, but the progress bar will update as well (see Figure 17-7).

Figure 17-7. *The WebBrowser control, once set up, takes care of almost everything.*

Feel free to click on links, and also to right-click on the browser to bring up the familiar Internet Explorer context menu that lets you navigate back and forward through pages, among other things.

Working with the WebBrowser Control

In the preceding example, you looked at the most obvious property of the control, the Url property, and also two of its events. There's a lot more that you can do to interact with the control through code, and surprisingly enough, for such a powerful control it's all very easy.

Take a look at the main methods that the control supports in Table 17-1, for example.

Table 17-1. *Methods of the WebBrowser Control*

Method	Description
GoBack()	Go back one page. Obviously, this works only if you've clicked on a link already.
GoForward()	Go forward one page. Works only if you've gone "back" from a page.
GoHome()	Go to IE's default home page.
GoSearch()	Go to IE's default search page.
Navigate()	Take a string URL to navigate to and go there.

The methods are all pretty simple to understand, so we're not going to dive into a full-blown "Try It Out." Feel free to experiment with them yourself.

Perhaps the most useful aspect of the control is that it's not limited to just web browsing. You can use the WebBrowser control to easily download files from the Internet, and even to build a fully functional FTP client right into your application. All you need to do is call Navigate with an FTP:// url. For example, if you call Navigate() with an address of ftp://ftp.gnu.org, you'll find yourself looking at the GNU FTP site, shown in Figure 17-8.

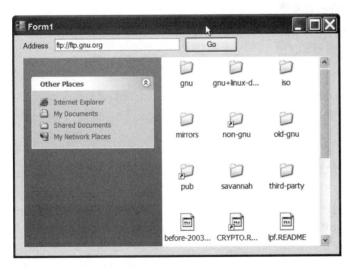

Figure 17-8. *Passing an FTP address to the WebBrowser control turns it into a neat FTP client.*

Double-clicking a directory here will take you into a separate FTP browser window from which you can drag and drop to download files, just as if you were working with an FTP site in the standard Windows Explorer way (see Figure 17-9).

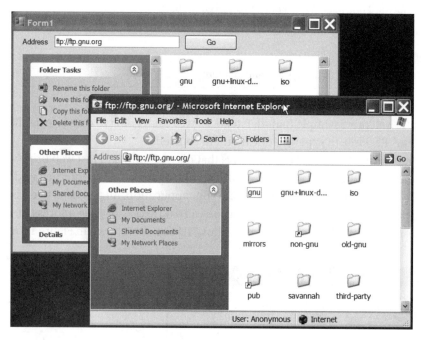

Figure 17-9. *Double-clicking an item opens up a standard Explorer window to browse and download the selected resource.*

Accessing the Web Through Code

Of course, you won't always want to display a WebBrowser control every time you want to do something on the Internet. Often it's quite handy just to be able to go out on the Internet and do something without the user seeing. For example, I wrote a program a while back that would automatically check for new videos on Microsoft's Channel 9 site and download them. Rather than display a WebBrowser control every time it did this, the code just downloaded the videos page and examined it to see whether there were new videos that I should get. If there were, the code would download them and just display a progress bar to me.

Listing that application as a "Try It Out" would take more pages than I'm allowed, but I can talk you through the general principle here. The root of the solution is a class in the .NET Framework called System.Net.WebClient. This gives you all the functionality of a browser, without the visual aspects, making it ideal for doing web-type stuff behind the scenes of the application's user interface. Let's take a look.

Try It Out: Using System.Net.WebClient

Let's write a really cool app. We're going to have the application extract data from Apress's page of forth-coming books. The titles of the books will then be listed in alphabetical order in a list box, and double-clicking an item will cause your default web browser to run and to display information on just that book in Apress's catalog. Hopefully by now you've begun to spot the trend whereby scary-sounding projects turn out surprisingly easy to do with .NET. This one is no exception.

Start up a brand new Windows Forms application; I named mine NewBooks. When the form editor appears, drop a Button control and a ListBox control onto the form. Also put a WebBrowser control on the form but set its Visible property to False. In design mode, your form should end up looking like the one in Figure 17-10.

Figure 17-10. *Arrange controls on your page like this. The control at the top left of the form is the WebBrowser control; set its Visible property to False so that it doesn't show at runtime.*

I know I said that we wouldn't be using a WebBrowser control in this example, and I've just made you add one to your form. Don't panic. The WebBrowser control can be used to open a real browser, and that's all we're going to use it for in this example.

Set up the names and properties of the controls on your page as shown in Table 17-2.

Table 17-2. *Properties of the Controls for Your Form*

Control	Property	Value
ListBox	Name	bookList
	Sorted	True
Button	Name	bookCheckButton
	Text	Check for books
WebBrowser	Name	browser

When you've finished laying out your form, double-click the Check for Books button to drop into the code editor for its Click event. Thinking about our goals, you'll need to grab the web page, extract the data, and then fill in the list box contents. So, the first thing to do is write the code to grab the web page itself.

You'll store the web page source in a string variable, and you'll write a separate function to use System.Net.WebClient to grab the web page source. So, add the following line of code to the click event handler:

```
Private Sub bookCheckButton_Click(ByVal sender As System.Object, _
    ByVal e As System.EventArgs) Handles bookCheckButton.Click

    Dim newBooksPage As String = _
        GetWebPage("http://www.apress.com/book/forthcoming.html")

End Sub
```

So, you call a function called GetWebPage and pass in the URL of the page you want. Let's write that function now. Directly underneath the click event handler, add this method, and after you're finished I'll talk you through how it works (you'll also need to add an Imports statement to the top of your class, as shown):

```
Imports System.Net
Public Class Form1

    Private Sub bookCheckButton_Click(ByVal sender As System.Object, _
        ByVal e As System.EventArgs) Handles bookCheckButton.Click

        Dim newBooksPage As String = _
            GetWebPage("http://www.apress.com/book/forthcoming.html")

    End Sub

    Private Function GetWebPage(ByVal url As String) As String

        Dim web As New WebClient()
        Return web.DownloadString(url)

    End Function

End Class
```

DownloadString() is one of a number of methods on the WebClient class that exist to download something from a remote server. In this case you're just telling WebClient that the resource you want to download (a web page) can be stored in a single string. All the code does is return whatever DownloadString() gives you.

Okay, at this point when the user clicks the button, you've managed to use WebClient to hit Apress's website and grab the page with all their forthcoming books on it. The next problem to tackle, of course, is extracting the book names and URLs for more information on them. First, you're going to need a place to store that information.

Go ahead and add a new class to the solution—call it Book.vb. This class is going to hold the book titles and URLs and also override ToString() so that you can add the objects straight into the list box. The code looks like this:

```
Public Class Book

    Public BookTitle As String
    Public BookURL As String

    Public Sub New(ByVal title As String, ByVal url As String)
        BookTitle = title
        BookURL = url
    End Sub

    Public Overrides Function ToString() As String
        Return BookTitle
    End Function

End Class
```

With the new Book class in place, you can focus on getting information out of the web page. For that you'll use a regular expression (or *regex* as it is more commonly known).

The first step is to create a Regex object. As I said in the sidebar, there isn't scope here to give an in-depth tutorial on regexes, but I will cover the basics of using them in .NET.

Add the following line of code into our click event handler, and an Imports statement to gain access to the regex classes:

```
Imports System.Net
Imports System.Text.RegularExpressions
Public Class Form1

    Private Sub bookCheckButton_Click(ByVal sender As System.Object, _
        ByVal e As System.EventArgs) Handles bookCheckButton.Click

        Dim newBooksPage As String = _
            GetWebPage("http://www.apress.com/book/forthcoming.html")
```

```
    ' Use a regex here to find all the book info
    Dim newBooksRegEx As Regex = _
            New Regex( _
            "<a href=""(/book/bookDisplay\.html\?bID=[0-9]+)"">([^<]+)</a>",

            RegexOptions.Singleline)

End Sub

Private Function GetWebPage(ByVal url As String) As String

    Dim web As New WebClient()
    Return web.DownloadString(url)

End Function
```

End Class

This creates a new Regex object, passing in two parameters: a string containing the regular expression itself, and the SingleLine option. The reason for the latter is that the data you get back from WebClient ends up as a single long line of text data, not multiple lines, so you need to tell the Regex object that you are going to work with a very big single line.

Now, although the regex itself (the string passed as the first option) looks horribly confusing, it's actually quite easy to follow. Regexes are interpreted character by character, from left to right. So that string says that you are going to look for the << character, followed by the a character, followed by a space, followed by h, then r, then e, then f, and so on. Basically, you specify in the regex the exact format of the actual HTML code that wraps each book on Apress's forthcoming books page. In addition, the regex contains parentheses to wrap up the parts of any match that contain the book's URL and title.

Now that you have created the regex itself, you can apply your string against it and grab the matches. Time for some more code:

```
    Private Sub bookCheckButton_Click(ByVal sender As System.Object, _
            ByVal e As System.EventArgs) Handles bookCheckButton.Click

    Dim newBooksPage As String = _
            GetWebPage("http://www.apress.com/book/forthcoming.html")
```

```
' Use a regex here to find all the book info
Dim newBooksRegEx As Regex = _
        New Regex( _
        "<a href=""(/book/bookDisplay\.html\?bID=[0-9]+)"">([^<]+)</a>",
    _
        RegexOptions.Singleline)


Dim books As MatchCollection = newBooksRegEx.Matches(newBooksPage)
For Each bookMatch As Match In books
    bookList.Items.Add( _
        New Book(bookMatch.Groups(2).Value, _
        bookMatch.Groups(1).Value))
Next

End Sub
```

Calling matches on the regex object and passing in a string (in this case the web page you downloaded) returns a `MatchCollection` object called books. You can iterate through this, pulling up each match that was found. The parentheses in the regex give match groups that you can use in the loop itself to extract the book's URL and title, and you can use those values to build an instance of your very own Book class. This gets added to the list box.

You're nearly done. The last piece of the puzzle is to use this information to pop open a browser when the user double-clicks on a book in the list. Head back to the visual form designer and select the ListBox control. Now, double-click the DoubleClick event in the event browser to drop into the list's double-click code, and start typing:

```
Private Sub bookList_DoubleClick(ByVal sender As System.Object, _
    ByVal e As System.EventArgs) Handles bookList.DoubleClick

    If bookList.SelectedIndex <> -1 Then
        Dim selectedBook As Book = CType(bookList.SelectedItem, Book)
        browser.Navigate("http://www.apress.com/" + _
                selectedBook.BookURL, True)

    End If

End Sub
```

AN ALTERNATE APPROACH TO DOWNLOADS

Just like files on your hard disk, Internet resources can be treated as streams. If you wanted more control over the download process, you could instead call `OpenStream()` on the web client. This would return a `Stream` object, which you could attach a reader to, just as if you were reading data from a file. From that point out, reading data from the remote server really does work the same as if you were reading data from a file on disk; just call `ReadToEnd()` on the `Reader` object and the net result would be a string representing the entire web page.

Given how simple `DownloadString()` is to use, you may be wondering why on earth anyone would want to use streams to download in the first place. The answer is that streams let you write a program independent of where the data comes from. Your app could just as well load and display a text file from disk as it could download a web page over the Internet. The actual code would be the same; only the method of obtaining a stream to read in the first place would change. Internet Explorer works this way, for example. You can click Open on Internet Explorer's File menu and enter either a filename or a web page to open. Presumably, behind the scenes, streams are used to treat both types of resources exactly the same way.

A WORD ON REGEXES (AND SPIDERS)

The solution that we're developing here is the genesis of something known as a spider. *Spiders* are small programs, usually without any user interface of note, that can go out on the Web and *repurpose* the information they find. In effect, spiders turn the whole World Wide Web into their user's own personal database on anything and everything. Spiders can do anything from grabbing stock quote information, to checking TV listing guides, to monitoring auctions on eBay. The sky is the limit with them, because their capabilities are constrained only by the amount of work that their developers are willing to put into them.

Spiders tend to use regexes, or regular expressions, to do most of their work because regexes are incredibly powerful tools when it comes to extracting tidbits of information from the mass of data that is the modern web page. However, regexes look hideous, and a complete discussion of how to use them, I'm afraid, deserves an entire book of its own and just doesn't fit into the scope of this one.

The basic format of a regex is simple. A *regex* is a string that contains characters that you want to match and special *meta characters* that tell the regex engine what to do. For example, parentheses are used to form *groups* of characters (something we use in the "Try It Out" to identify the URL of a book and its name). Square brackets are used to identify specific characters or character ranges, the most commonly used being `[0-9]` to mean numbers, and `[a-z]` meaning all lowercase letters of the alphabet. The symbols for plus sign, period, asterisk (`+ . *`) and question mark (`?`) also have special meanings and so must be preceded with a backslash (`\`) if you are interested in looking for those characters, rather than the regex engine interpreting them as special regex commands.

For more information on all this and much more, search the online help for regex. If you plan on doing a lot of Internet spider-type work, then I'd heartily recommend picking up Jeffrey Friedl's *Mastering Regular Expressions* book (O'Reilly Media, 2002).

The DoubleClick event fires on the list box whenever the user double-clicks it, whether it contains items or not. The first line of code then needs to make sure that the user did actually click an item, by checking that the ListBox's SelectedIndex property is not -1 (meaning nothing selected).

Providing that's all fine, the book is grabbed from the list, using the list's SelectedItem property. Finally, the magic. Remember that you set the WebBrowser control to not be visible. The reason for this is that you aren't going to use it. The WebBrowser control's Navigate() method can take two parameters. The first parameter is the URL to go to, and the second is a True or False indicator letting the control know whether it should open up a new browser. So, in this code you just pass True in here and you can get the WebBrowser control to run your system's default web browser and show the user the book page in question.

Run the program and you'll see a result much like mine in Figure 17-11.

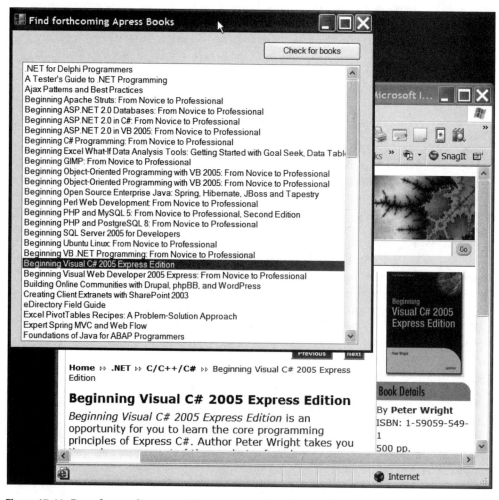

Figure 17-11. *Run the application. When you double-click an item in the list, a web browser appears, taking you directly to the page in question.*

As you can see, the WebClient can play a vital, incredibly useful role in many Internet applications. It's so easy to use that you'll often find that the actual code needed to work with it is minimal compared to everything else you need to make a full application.

Bear in mind that this solution is, of course, dependent on Apress never ever changing their website URL (www.apress.com). In a true production-grade application, you'd probably drag the base URL out into a configuration file, but the code was written to get a point across more than to be used as a valuable tool for years to come.

Handling Other Types of Data with WebClient

In the preceding "Try It Out," you saw a great example of how to download a web page into a string. A web page is, after all, just text, and strings are great for storing that. WebClient, though, can handle any kind of data, and can both upload it and download it. Table 17-3 lists the methods of WebClient.

Table 17-3. *Methods of System.Net.WebClient*

Method	Description
OpenRead()	Opens a stream for reading, just like opening a file stream
DownloadData()	Returns data from the remote web server as a byte array
DownloadFile()	Saves data from the remote web server as a file on your computer
DownloadString()	Downloads the file as a string from the remote server
OpenWrite()	Opens a connection to a remote server you want to send data to
UploadString()	Sends a string to the remote server
UploadData()	Takes a byte array to upload to the server
UploadFile()	Uploads a local file to the remote server

There are methods I haven't listed here. For every Upload and Download method, there is an alternate Async method that can be used to run on a separate thread. For example, DownloadDataAsync(), DownloadFileAsync(), UploadFileAsync(), and so on. The WebClient class raises a number of events to let you check on the status of these Async calls, and also handle the end result. For each Async call, there is a corresponding Completed event. For example, when a call to DownloadDataAsync() completes, the WebClient object will fire a DownloadDataCompleted event.

In the case of DownloadDataCompleted and DownloadStringCompleted, the actual data returned from the call is passed into the event handler. For example, here's an event handler for DownloadStringCompleted:

```
Public Sub OnDownloadStringCompleted(ByVal sender As Object, _
    ByVal e As DownloadStringCompletedEventArgs)
    Console.WriteLine(e.Result)
End Sub
```

As you can see, the actual string downloaded is held in the Result property of the DownloadStringCompletedEventArgs.

The DownloadDataCompleted event works in a similar way, but you need to cast the result to a byte array, because Result is declared as a generic Object type:

```
Public Sub OnDownloadDataCompleted(ByVal sender As Object, _
    ByVal e As DownloadDataCompletedEventArgs)

    Dim data() As Byte = CType(e.Result, Byte())

End Sub
```

What about the DownloadFileCompleted event? Both DownloadDataAsync() and DownloadStringAsync() need to return data, but DownloadFileAsync() just stores a file directly to your computer's hard disk, so what does the event give us? Actually, it gives you pretty much the same as the other two completed events. Both DownloadDataCompletedEventArgs and DownloadStringCompletedEventArgs are subclasses of AsyncCompletedEventArgs, which is the type of object passed to DownloadFileCompleted events. There are two important properties in this class that you should check in any kind of Async-completed event handler: Cancelled and Error.

Cancelled is a Boolean (true/false) value that you need to check to see whether the operation was cancelled. WebClient itself has a CancelAsync() method that can get called to cancel a download operation. When it's called, the download is cancelled, and the completed event is fired with Cancel set to True.

Error is actually an Exception object. So if Error is not Nothing, you can grab it and treat it just like a standard exception, raising it for other code to catch if you want to.

WebClient doesn't just fire off events when operations complete. It will also fire events to let you track the progress of an upload or download: DownloadProgressChanged() and UploadProgressChanged().

Both these events get a ProgressChangedEventArgs object passed to them that has a ProgressPercentage property attached. You can use this value directly to update a progress bar, or even just display a percentage complete value to the user.

Let's move away from the theory and put all this into practice, extending our previous "Try It Out" to work with asynchronous operations.

WHY ARE SO MANY CHANGES NECESSARY?

It's my fault—I admit it. If you take a look at the code we just developed, you'll notice that pretty much everything hangs off our button's Click event. The button's click event handler includes most of the code to download the page, then extract data from it, and then build the list box. That's three distinct operations! It's good practice to have your code structured so that it consists of methods that do just one thing and do it very well.

For example, we really should have a download method (got that one), a method to extract data from the page, and then another method to populate the list box. That's the refactoring that we are going to do right now. So, by moving to an asynchronous download model, we're not only improving the usability of the program for the user, but also improving the structure of our code.

Try It Out: Asynchronous WebClient Operations

Load up the NewBooks project you just worked on. We're going to have to refactor the code in the project quite a bit to work asynchronously.

The first thing you need to do is move all the code out of the Click event. When the button is clicked, you want just one thing to happen: the download.

Add in two new methods—GetBookDetailsFromWebPage() and AddBooksToListBox()—by using the code that was in the Click event. The new code looks like this:

```
Private Sub bookCheckButton_Click(ByVal sender As System.Object, _
    ByVal e As System.EventArgs) Handles bookCheckButton.Click

    GetWebPage("http://www.apress.com/book/forthcoming.html")

End Sub

Private Function GetBookDetailsFromWebPage(ByVal webPage As String) _
    As MatchCollection
    ' Use a regex here to find all the book info
    Dim newBooksRegEx As Regex = _
        New Regex( _
        "<a href=""(/book/bookDisplay\.html\?bID=[0-9]+)"">([^<]+)</a>", _
        RegexOptions.Singleline)

    Return newBooksRegEx.Matches(webPage)
```

```
    End Function

    Private Sub AddBooksToListBox(ByVal books As MatchCollection)

        For Each bookMatch As Match In books
            bookList.Items.Add( _
                New Book(bookMatch.Groups(2).Value, _
                bookMatch.Groups(1).Value))
        Next

    End Sub
```

Pay special attention to the method signatures here. GetBookDetailsFromWebPage() takes a string containing the web page source as a parameter. It runs the regex you had previously over that string and returns the MatchCollection.

The MatchCollection is then used as a parameter on the AddBooksToListBox() method, iterating over each item in the collection to build up your list box.

The eagle-eyed may also have noticed that we're no longer expecting a return value from our GetWebPage() method. The reason is that that method is no longer responsible for grabbing the web page source—it simply starts the process. You'll rewrite the entire GetWebPage() method from scratch so you can see how it works. First clear out all the code and change the function type to a subroutine, like this:

```
    Private Sub GetWebPage(ByVal url As String)

        Dim web As New WebClient()

    End Sub
```

You'll still need to create an instance of WebClient here, so I've left that line of code in. Because you'll be downloading the web page asynchronously, the first thing you need to do here is hook up the event handlers. Add the highlighted code shown here:

```
        private void GetWebPage(string url)
        {
            WebClient web = new WebClient();

        AddHandler web.DownloadStringCompleted, AddressOf DownloadComplete
        AddHandler web.DownloadProgressChanged, AddressOf ProgressChanged
        }
```

Next, you'll need two new methods to handle those events:

```
Private Sub GetWebPage(ByVal url As String)

    Dim web As New WebClient()
    AddHandler web.DownloadStringCompleted, AddressOf DownloadComplete
    AddHandler web.DownloadProgressChanged, AddressOf ProgressChanged

End Sub

Private Sub DownloadComplete(ByVal sender As Object, _
    ByVal e As DownloadStringCompletedEventArgs)

End Sub

Private Sub ProgressChanged(ByVal sender As Object, _
    ByVal e As DownloadProgressChangedEventArgs)

End Sub
```

Now, the final thing your GetWebPage() method needs to do is clear out anything already in the list box and start the download:

```
Private Sub GetWebPage(ByVal url As String)

    Dim web As New WebClient()
    AddHandler web.DownloadStringCompleted, AddressOf DownloadComplete
    AddHandler web.DownloadProgressChanged, AddressOf ProgressChanged

    bookList.Items.Clear()
    web.DownloadStringAsync(New Uri(url))

End Sub
```

Now here's a strange thing. When you call DownloadString(), you can just pass in the URL. However, DownloadStringAsync (as with all the other Async methods) expects a special object known as a Uri. You can create this on the fly, passing in your URL to its constructor.

You're finished with the GetWebPage() method. In fact, you're pretty much finished with all the big changes now. All you need to complete the app is to put some meaningful code into the two new event handlers. First, let's tackle ProgressChanged(). All you want to do here is copy your current download progress value into a progress bar. Of course, you don't have a progress bar on the form yet to work with, so head back into the form's design view and drop a progress bar at the bottom of the form, as in Figure 17-12.

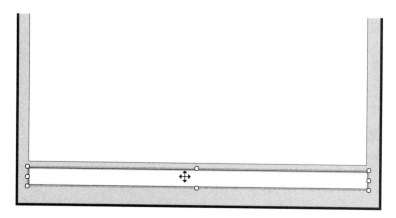

Figure 17-12. *Add a progress bar to the form.*

Name the progress bar downloadProgress and then hit F7 to jump back into the code. Find the ProgressChanged event handler and add a single line of code to it, as shown here:

```
Private Sub ProgressChanged(ByVal sender As Object, _
    ByVal e As DownloadProgressChangedEventArgs)

    downloadProgress.Value = e.ProgressPercentage

End Sub
```

Finally, let's code up the DownloadComplete() method. What you'll need to do here is make sure your progress bar shows 100 percent, and then check that the download operation was not cancelled. Assuming it wasn't, you can call your AddBooksToListBox() and GetBookDetailsFromWebPage() methods to finish the app:

```
Private Sub DownloadComplete(ByVal sender As Object, _
    ByVal e As DownloadStringCompletedEventArgs)

    downloadProgress.Value = 100
    If Not e.Cancelled Then
        Dim newBooksPage As String = e.Result
        AddBooksToListBox(GetBookDetailsFromWebPage(newBooksPage))
    End If

End Sub
```

And you're finished. After the download completes, this event fires and you can grab the downloaded string from the DownloadStringCompletedEventArgs passed into the handler. You can use that string to then call GetBookDetailsFromWebPage() (which you'll remember returns a MatchCollection), and pass the results straight into AddBooksToListBox() (which you'll remember expects a MatchCollection).

Run the application now and you'll see the screen shown in Figure 17-13.

Figure 17-13. *Run the application now and you'll get an updating progress bar while the page downloads on a separate thread.*

The app seems to work just as it did before, but behind the scenes you've got some key differences. First, your code structure is much better with each operation living in its own method and the click event handler for the button focusing on doing just one thing. Second, and probably more important for your users, is that if the connection to Apress's website is slow, they'll get feedback on the status of the download through the progress bar on the form because the download runs asynchronously.

Using Web Services

Although being able to access the Internet to download and upload stuff from an application is great fun, one of the biggest noises in the industry concerning .NET has to be web services. Prior to web services arriving, the World Wide Web was nothing more than a collection of disparate websites, some interactive, some not, that presented information to humans. Web services changes that, providing a way for people to share functionality as well as data, and at last making it easy for applications to be built from lots of different pieces all over the world.

Whole books have been written about web services and the intricacies of using them—Keith Ballinger's excellent tome .NET Web Services: Architecture and Implementation with .NET (Addison-Wesley Professional, 2003) being a prime example—but for our needs they are really very simple. Think of a web service as a class, with methods, that just happens to live on someone else's machine. Amazon.com, for example, provides web services that you can use to find out about the books they stock, providing you with the means to write applications that use parts of Amazon.com's code within them.

My good friend Walter Vijaykumar runs a fabulous website called WebserviceX.NET that hosts dozens and dozens of web services for anyone and everyone to use, covering everything from rendering text as Braille to finding numeric converters, and much more. He's kindly agreed for us to play with his site as we explore web services (thanks, Walter!).

So, let's get started. Launch a web browser (bet you didn't see that one coming) and point it at http://www.webservicex.net. After the page loads, you'll see a site much like that in Figure 17-14.

The site lists the top web services on the left side, and the most recent on the right. At the bottom of the page is a list of categories, so if you were after a service that could convert Celsius to Fahrenheit, for example, you'd click on the Value Manipulation / Unit Converter category. There's also a search box at the top right of the page. Clicking in this and keying in the word **Weather** produces the page shown in Figure 17-15.

There are three weather-related web services up at WebserviceX.NET, according to the results. To find out more about the service and get to the single most important page of the entire site, you'd just click one. For example, I clicked on USA Weather Forecast and got the page shown in Figure 17-16.

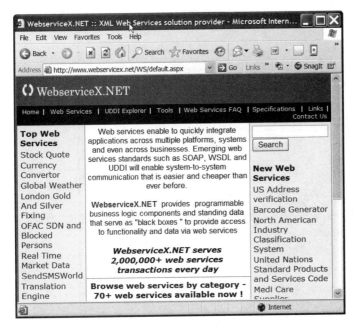

Figure 17-14. *The WebserviceX.NET home page*

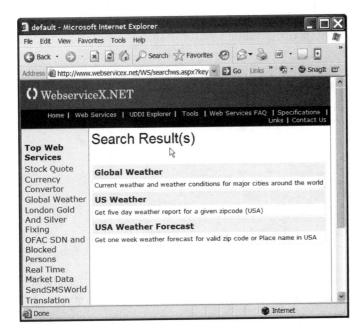

Figure 17-15. *You can also search for web services.*

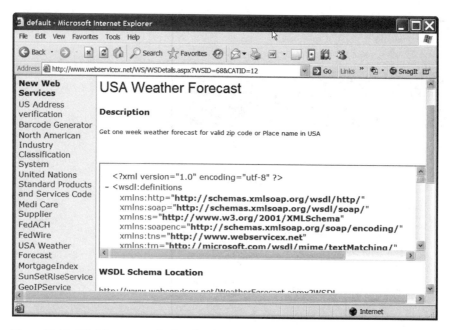

Figure 17-16. *Clicking on an individual web service takes you to its definition page.*

Why is this the most important page in the site? Well, the page shows you three important pieces of information: the web service definition, its location, and a description of the methods.

As I mentioned earlier, you can think of a web service as a class that lives on someone else's machine. Rather than having to have the source to the class on your own machine, you just need to know where the service lives, what it can do, and where it's described. Those three things are what this web page is all about.

WEBSERVICEX.NET AND THE SPIRIT OF EXPRESS

Aside from being useful for us to learn how to work with web services in Visual Basic 2005 Express, Walter's website really does exemplify everything Microsoft had in mind with the Express products. Here's a guy that in his spare time loves nothing more than to mess around with .NET code (personally, I prefer smashing Orcs and Trolls in online games), so he decided to set up a website to show off his efforts.

WebserviceX.NET is a collection of numerous web services written in C# that Walter uses not only to keep his coding skills up-to-date for fun, but also to make available to the world to use, for free. His site has become so popular that it gets around a million hits a day, and numerous businesses rely on his web services within their own critical applications.

Who said hobbyist coders can't make a difference?

The top of the page is taken up with a scrolling box showing you the Web Service Definition Language (WSDL). WSDL is the XML standard for describing a web service. It describes in excruciating detail every aspect of the web service, including the names of the methods it supports, the data types of any parameters to those methods, and so on. Take a look through it and you'll see that it's a pretty big document and quite confusing. The good news is that you don't have to be a WSDL expert to use a web service; understanding WSDL is something Visual Basic 2005 Express is quite happy doing on its own. If you decide you really want to know more about the WSDL format, you will find there are some great articles about all the deeper aspects of web services in the online help. Knowing that stuff, though, is most important if you intend to create your own web services, something that VB Express can't do.

The second item on the page is just a single line preceded by the heading WSDL Schema Location. In the case of the USA Weather Forecast web service, that location is `http://_www.webservicex.net/WeatherForecast.asmx?WSDL`. This innocuous, tiny piece of information is probably the single most important part of the page for you, because it provides the information you'll need to tell VB Express how to connect to the web service.

The bottom of the page shows the methods on the web service, the methods in the class if you like, that you can call. There are two here: `GetWeatherByPlaceName()` and `GetWeatherByZipCode()`. Clicking on either one of them takes you to yet another page, showing you the format of the method call itself, as you can see in Figure 17-17.

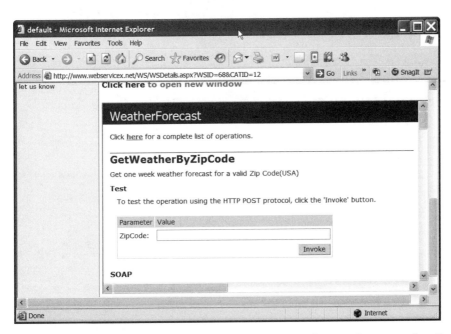

Figure 17-17. *Clicking on a method on the web service info page shows you detailed information about the method itself.*

Okay, so now you know how to find information about some web services, but how do you use them from VB Express? Well, the whole process is just as simple as working with a regular class. With a project loaded, you right-click on it in the Solution Explorer and choose Add Web Reference from the context menu that appears. You'll then be taken to a wizard to connect to the web service; this wizard looks like Figure 17-18.

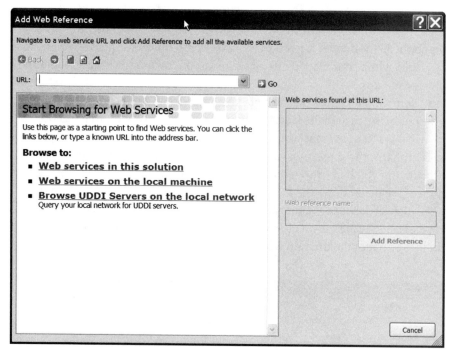

Figure 17-18. *Selecting Add Web Reference takes you to the Add Web Reference dialog.*

The first thing you need to do is enter the URL of the web service location. After that's done, the dialog changes to the one in Figure 17-19.

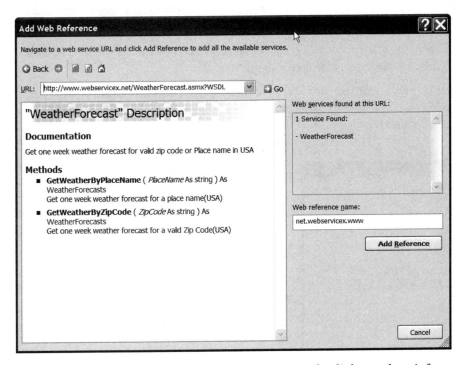

Figure 17-19. *Entering the URL of a web service changes the dialog to show information about it.*

All that remains is to enter a name for the class in the text box at the lower right of the dialog, and you're all set.

At this point, I think it makes sense to do this for real. Let's write a simple console application for calculating the exchange rate anywhere in the world.

Try It Out: Calling a Web Service

Start up a new console project and call it ExchangeRate. When the Solution Explorer appears, right-click the name of the project and choose Add Web Reference to display the Add Web Reference dialog.

Enter http://www.webservicex.net/CurrencyConvertor.asmx?WSDL as the URL of the service and click the Go button. The dialog changes to the one you just saw.

In the Web Reference Name dialog box, name the service WebServiceX and click the Add Reference button. The dialog vanishes and your Solution Explorer changes to show that you have a new web service reference in the project, as in Figure 17-20.

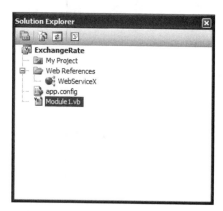

Figure 17-20. *Adding a web reference causes it to show up in the Solution Explorer.*

From this point on, you can write code and treat the web service just as if it were a typical class. Now, what you just did is add a reference to a web service. In real terms, that just creates a new namespace within your project. So if you named the project ExchangeRate, then you'll find the web service classes in ExchangeRate.WebServiceX. The first thing you need to do then is add an Imports clause to the code to Module1.vb:

```
Imports ExchangeRate.WebServiceX

Module Module1

    Sub Main()

    End Sub

End Module
```

Now you're ready to write code. The `CurrencyConvertor` service you are going to use has just one method, `ConversionRate()`. You pass in two enums that the service defines, representing the currency you want to convert from and the currency to convert to, and the method returns the exchange rate. Go ahead and add the code:

```
Imports ExchangeRate.WebServiceX

Module Module1

    Sub Main()

        Dim service As New CurrencyConvertor()
        Dim rate As Double

        rate = service.ConversionRate(Currency.GBP, Currency.USD)
        Console.WriteLine( _
                "The conversion rate from British Pounds to Dollars is {0}", _
                rate)
        Console.ReadLine()

    End Sub

End Module
```

If you run the program now, you'll see it display the conversion rate for British pounds to US dollars (Figure 17-21).

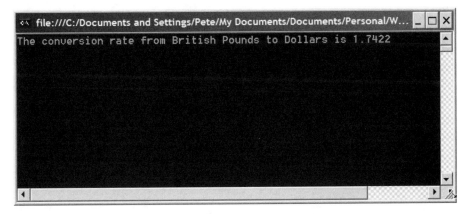

Figure 17-21. *Run the program, and the web service is used to find the exchange rate.*

The program seems trivial, doesn't it? Think about what it's doing for a second, though. We didn't write any code to find out exchange rates; we called a method on a web service. That web service is hosted on a computer in England and takes care of all the dirty business of looking up financial data and calculating an exchange rate between any two currencies. When we make the method call, VB Express behind the scenes connects to a web server in England, locates the web service we specified, sends data to it, gets data back, parses it into the correct format, and returns the result to you, just as if you'd called any method on a typical class.

It's also worth bearing in mind that we just used WebserviceX.NET here because it has a great selection of services and doesn't require us to register or jump through any hoops to use it. But you may be interested to learn that Google, eBay, and Amazon.com all provide extensive web services of their own. You need to go to their websites and register to use them, but after you are registered you have the complete power of the Google, eBay, and Amazon systems at your disposal to embed in your own code. In fact, the Movie Starter Kit application that ships with VB Express does just that, using Amazon.com's web services to locate movie information for you.

Summary

Visual Basic 2005 Express is far more than just a desktop development tool. Armed with the WebBrowser control, the classes in the `System.Net` namespace, and VB Express's excellent support for consuming remote web services, there is nothing stopping you from writing awesome applications that reach out far beyond the desktop and combine live data from sources all over the world.

CHAPTER 18
■ ■ ■

Threading

I cut my teeth programming games on the Commodore 64 back in the 80s. I remember vividly how cool it was when I discovered how to manage "interrupts" on that machine. The basic principle was simple: after a certain period of time, the computer had the ability to stop what it was doing and do something else, and then come back to what it was doing in the first place. This could happen hundreds or even thousands of times every second and give the impression that my humble 64 was doing two things at once. We'd use it to play a tune while at the same time keeping the graphics on-screen moving, and still responding to the player hammering a joystick.

Computers today still do the same thing. The difference between then and now is that modern chips from Intel and almost any operating system worth its salt are all designed from the ground up to do this. In fact, some of the newer dual-core and hyperthreading processors are designed to appear almost like two processors within the machine. Likewise, modern programming languages like VB make doing this kind of thing easy.

Microsoft Windows is designed to run more than one *process* (program) at once. In fact, even when it's running just one program, it's actually running a lot more than one. Just take a look at the Task Manager (press Ctrl+Alt+Del) to see a complete list of all the things running on your machine. These processes themselves are able to fire off small blocks of code to run concurrently with the main program, and these are called *threads*. What's happening behind the scenes is that the processor stops running one program and switches to the next, millions of times a second. If you have more than one physical processor in the machine, each processor does the same thing, making it seem like the computer is phenomenally powerful.

Threading, the act of getting more than one "thread" of code running at the same time, is wonderfully easy in Visual Basic 2005 Express, and in this chapter you'll see just how.

But before you dive into the code and see how to do it, maybe you're wondering just why you'd want to. The most common reason is user interface *responsiveness*. If your user interface has to load up a massive amount of data when the form loads, the chances are that the computer would seem to "hang." Windows may get to draw only a fraction of the user interface elements it needs before your code kicks in, chunking away so much that it prevents Windows from getting its own job done (making your user interface appear). In such instances, it's not uncommon for developers to load all that data in a separate thread. The user interface then comes into view very quickly, and the user is able to work with it, all while out of sight and out of mind a separate thread loads up all the data it needs for the program to work properly.

Timers

The simplest introduction to the principles behind multithreading is the *Timer control*. It's a dream to use, but technically it's not true multithreading. The event raised by the timer actually runs on the same thread as the main application. To use it, you just drop the timer onto a form, tell it when to fire, and then code in an event to respond to the timer going off. Unlike a cooking timer though, the .NET timer fires over and over at the same interval until you turn it off. Let's take a look.

Try It Out: The Timer Control

Start up a new Windows Forms application in Visual Basic 2005 Express. When the form editor appears, drop two Timer controls onto the form (you can find the Timer control on the Components tab of the Toolbox).

Select the first Timer control and take a look at its properties. Like many nonvisual controls, it doesn't have a great many of them (Figure 18-1).

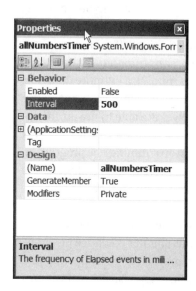

Figure 18-1. *The Timer control has very few properties associated with it.*

Only two properties are interesting: Interval and Enabled. The Interval property defines how often the timer fires its event, in thousandths of a second. So, setting a value of 500 causes the timer to fire every half a second. Go ahead and set the Name property to allNumbersTimer, and set the Interval property to

500. Set up the Name property of the second timer to evenNumbersTimer, and set its Interval to 800 (so it fires every 0.8 of a second).

Next, drop two lists and a button onto the form, as in Figure 18-2.

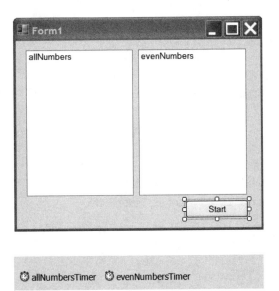

Figure 18-2. *Drop two lists onto the form—our timers will populate these at runtime.*

Name one of the list boxes allNumbers and name the other evenNumbers.

Now you'll write code into the two timers to populate both list boxes. Double-click on the allNumbersTimer to drop into the Timer control's Tick event. This is the event that fires every time the timer interval is reached. Just add a member variable into the class and fill in the Tick event so that it increments the variable and adds it to the list box, like this:

```
Public Class Form1

    Private _num As Integer = 0

    Private Sub allNumbersTimer_Tick(ByVal sender As System.Object, _
            ByVal e As System.EventArgs) Handles allNumbersTimer.Tick
        _num += 1
        allNumbers.Items.Add(_num)
    End Sub

End Class
```

Remember to put the _num variable outside of the method to make it a member of the class, and not the method.

Now do something similar for the evenNumbersTimer control. The variable and code are shown in bold here:

```
Public Class Form1

    Private _num As Integer = 0
    Private _evenNumber As Integer = 0

    Private Sub allNumbersTimer_Tick(ByVal sender As System.Object, _
        ByVal e As System.EventArgs) Handles allNumbersTimer.Tick
        _num += 1
        allNumbers.Items.Add(_num)
    End Sub

    Private Sub evenNumbersTimer_Tick(ByVal sender As System.Object, _
        ByVal e As System.EventArgs) Handles evenNumbersTimer.Tick
        _evenNumber += 2
        evenNumbers.Items.Add(_evenNumber)
    End Sub

End Class
```

You're finished. The first timer simply counts, incrementing a variable by 1 each time the timer fires, before adding the value into the first list box. The second timer, which you'll remember you set to a different interval, counts by 2, adding the number into the second list box.

The final step is to get that Start button working. Double-click it to drop into the code editor, and key in the following:

```
    Private Sub startButton_Click(ByVal sender As System.Object, _
        ByVal e As System.EventArgs) Handles startButton.Click
        allNumbersTimer.Enabled = Not allNumbersTimer.Enabled
        evenNumbersTimer.Enabled = Not evenNumbersTimer.Enabled
    End Sub
```

This code simply enables and disables the timers by reversing the value in the timers' Enabled property.

You're all set to run it now, so go ahead and run the application. Click the Start button when the form appears to start up the two timers, and then watch what happens (see Figure 18-3).

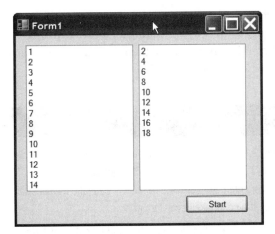

Figure 18-3. *When you run the program and click the Start button, the two lists will update at slightly different intervals, seemingly by themselves.*

Also, while the program is still running, try using the user interface; scroll the lists and select items in the lists. What you'll notice is that even though the program is still running, the timers don't affect the user interface at all. Even though the user interface is still updating, it still feels snappy, because the main thread is taking a break from time to time to process the code in your timer event handlers.

Timers, though, are usually used when the program needs to do something regularly. Perhaps you are writing an application that needs to check the status of a server from time to time to make sure it's still working. Or perhaps you need to display a clock in your application that updates in real time.

Tasks such as building a bunch of data behind the scenes, as our "Try It Out" application does, are best placed to use a dedicated thread that runs and runs until it's complete. That's where the BackgroundWorker control comes into play.

BackgroundWorker Control

The *BackgroundWorker control* provides you with an easy route into the full power of writing multithreaded programs. Behind the scenes, the control uses .NET's built-in support for multithreading—but between you and me, it's pretty confusing stuff. The BackgroundWorker control is a new addition to the .NET Framework that makes working with threads very simple indeed. For that reason, we won't even take a look at the behind-the-scenes way of doing things because there really isn't a need anymore. For the curious, take a look in the online help at the System.Threading namespace.

You'd use a BackgroundWorker control when you have a great deal of processing to do, or an operation that will simply take a long time to run (such as waiting for an email to arrive, for example). You just write your code into a standard method and then call it from the BackgroundWorker control's event model. This is all easiest to explain with a "Try It Out."

Try It Out: The BackgroundWorker Control

Let's write a simple program that calculates factorials. For those of you who, like me, flunked math, a *factorial* of a number is simply the sum of all numbers between 1 and itself. For example, the factorial of 3 is 6 (1 + 2 + 3). As you can imagine, calculating a factorial for a very high number (say, 10 million) can take a while. Calculating a bunch of factorials without really optimizing the code takes even longer.

Start up a new WinForms project (call it `CalcFactorials`), and drop some controls onto the default form in the project when it appears, so that it looks like mine in Figure 18-4.

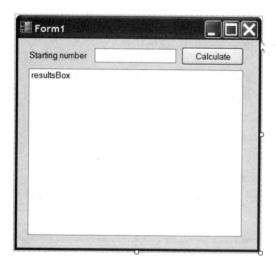

Figure 18-4. *Arrange controls on your form so that it looks like this.*

You can already see that I've set the name on the ListBox control to `resultsBox`. Do the same in your project, and also set the `Name` properties for the text box and command button to `startingNumber` and `calcButton`, respectively.

Next, double-click the Calculate button to drop into its click event handler. We'll put our code to calculate factorials in here. Go ahead and type it in:

```
Public Class Form1

    Private Sub calcButton_Click(ByVal sender As System.Object, _
        ByVal e As System.EventArgs) Handles calcButton.Click

        resultsBox.Items.Clear()

        Dim startingNum As Long = Long.Parse(startingNumber.Text)

        For currentNum As Long = startingNum To startingNum + 999
            Dim factorial As Long = 0
            For i As Long = 1 To currentNum
                factorial += i
            Next
            resultsBox.Items.Add( _
                String.Format("The factorial of {0} is {1}", _
                currentNum, factorial))
        Next

    End Sub

End Class
```

The code first clears out the list box, so if the user tries to calculate factorial after factorial, the list will clear out each time.

Next, the number entered into the text box is grabbed and used to create a For loop. The For loop contains the code to calculate the factorial for a number and all 999 numbers following it; so, the code calculates 1000 factorials starting at the number the user entered.

Run the program now and enter a starting number of 1000000 (1 million—six zeroes), and click the Calculate button. As soon as you do this, the For loop kicks in, calculating factorials. The problem is that the For loop is doing so much work that the application never gets a chance to redraw its display. The end result is a corrupted user interface, something I'm sure you've seen in one or two other Windows applications from time to time.

The BackgroundWorker control solves this little but deeply annoying program by letting us put that factorial code onto another thread.

When the program has finished doing its calculations, stop it.

Back in design mode, double-click the BackgroundWorker control to drop it onto the form. As with the Timer control, the BackgroundWorker is a nonvisual control so it appears underneath the form at design time, as in Figure 18-5.

Figure 18-5. *The BackgroundWorker control is a nonvisual control and appears beneath the form at design time.*

Leave the control name at its default of backgroundWorker1 and double-click it. You'll find yourself looking at the control's DoWork event handler.

When you run your program, it has just one thread, the user interface (UI) thread. When you run a Background-Worker control, you get a second thread. Now, a problem with multithreaded applications is that it's not easy for each thread to talk to another. In our program, for example, we have a need during the calculation process to add the factorials into the list box. The comment here tells us that we aren't going to be able to do that.

Now, if we were working with the normal behind-the-scenes .NET threading methods, we'd have to write some pretty nasty code to get one thread to update another. The BackgroundWorker control, though, gives us a really handy way to do things. It has a method called ReportProgress(). Calling this method, and passing data to it, causes another event on the control to fire. This event is called ProgressChanged, and I'm guessing from its name that Microsoft expected this method to be used to update progress bars on forms. What this means to us, though, is that this method does run on the same thread as the UI. So, by calling ReportProgress(), we can get an event on the main thread to fire, and thus update our UI.

Let's refactor the code we have into the BackgroundWorker events to see how all this works.

First, move all the code, except the first two lines, out of the command button handler and into the BackgroundWorker.DoWork event handler. Your source, with changes highlighted, will look like this:

```
Public Class Form1

    Private startingNum As Long

    Private Sub calcButton_Click(ByVal sender As System.Object, _
            ByVal e As System.EventArgs) Handles calcButton.Click

        resultsBox.Items.Clear()

        startingNum = Long.Parse(startingNumber.Text)

    End Sub

    Private Sub BackgroundWorker1_DoWork(ByVal sender As System.Object, _
        ByVal e As System.ComponentModel.DoWorkEventArgs) _
        Handles BackgroundWorker1.DoWork

        For currentNum As Long = startingNum To startingNum + 999
            Dim factorial As Long = 0
            For i As Long = 1 To currentNum
                factorial += i
            Next
            resultsBox.Items.Add( _
                String.Format("The factorial of {0} is {1}", _
                currentNum, factorial))
        Next

    End Sub
End Class
```

Notice also that I've made startingNum a member variable of the form, not a local anymore.

Next, let's add the code to the CalcButton's Click event to start the BackgroundWorker thread. Add the highlighted lines to the event handler:

```
Private Sub calcButton_Click(ByVal sender As System.Object, _
        ByVal e As System.EventArgs) Handles calcButton.Click

    resultsBox.Items.Clear()

    startingNum = Long.Parse(startingNumber.Text)
    BackgroundWorker1.WorkerReportsProgress = True
    BackgroundWorker1.RunWorkerAsync()

End Sub
```

Calling RunWorkerAsync() on the BackgroundWorker control starts the code in the DoWork event handler running on a separate thread. So, the code behind the calcButton just empties the list box, puts our starting number into a member variable, and then starts up the new thread.

All that remains is to fix the DoWork event handler so that it doesn't directly try to update the list box with the results, but instead fires the ReportProgress() method.

First, go back to the form editor. Click on the BackgroundWorker control and then look at the list of events that it supports in the Properties window. You can see these in Figure 18-6.

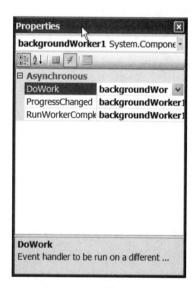

Figure 18-6. *The events supported by the BackgroundWorker control*

Double-click on the ProgressChanged event in the event list to drop back into the source editor for the BackgroundWorker's ProgressChanged event handler.

Let's add the code in here to update our list box:

```
Private Sub BackgroundWorker1_ProgressChanged( _
        ByVal sender As System.Object, _
        ByVal e As System.ComponentModel.ProgressChangedEventArgs) _
        Handles BackgroundWorker1.ProgressChanged

    resultsBox.Items.Add(e.UserState)

End Sub
```

Like many events, the ProgressChanged event gets a set of arguments passed to it as the second parameter, e. In the case of ProgressChangedEventArgs, there is a member called UserState. This is an object that can be passed to the event handler when the code calls ReportProgress(). In our case, we're just going to pass a string across so all the code here needs to do is add that string straight into the list box.

Go back up to the DoWork event handler and change the last line of code so that it calls ReportProgress() instead of trying to update the list box:

```
Private Sub BackgroundWorker1_DoWork(ByVal sender As System.Object, _
        ByVal e As System.ComponentModel.DoWorkEventArgs) _
        Handles BackgroundWorker1.DoWork

    For currentNum As Long = startingNum To startingNum + 999
        Dim factorial As Long = 0
        For i As Long = 1 To currentNum
            factorial += i
        Next
        BackgroundWorker1.ReportProgress( _
            0, String.Format("The factorial of {0} is {1}", _
            currentNum, factorial))
    Next

End Sub
```

ReportProgress() actually takes two parameters. The first is typically the percentage done. Remember, ReportProgress() and ProgressChanged were originally envisaged to provide you with a way to update a progress bar on the form, so it makes sense that the first parameter is the actual percentage complete. We won't bother with this, so our code just passes across 0 as the first parameter. The second parameter is the object that will eventually end up as ProgressChangedEventArgs.UserData, which in our case is a string.

Phew—that was a lot of typing. The end result, though, is really not all that different from the original code we had. Instead of our factorial calculating code being held in a single method, we now have it split across three.

The first part is fired when the user clicks the Calculate button. This grabs the number to start with and stores it in a member variable, and then starts the BackgroundWorker running. The second is the BackgroundWorker DoEvents handler, which calculates our factorials and holds the bulk of the code that was originally in the button's click handler. The third piece of code just updates the user interface of our application in a Progress-Changed event handler.

Run the program now. Notice how this time the user interface always redraws itself nicely and you're free to click around the list, selecting items and browsing, while the program goes about its business of calculating factorials.

Don't throw this program away just yet—we'll be "finessing" it a little more in the next section.

The biggest problem I find when working with threads is the guy sitting there using the program. You could write a wonderfully elegant multithreaded solution to keep everything snappy and responsive during a long-running operation, and then you get a phone call from an irate user asking why you didn't give him a way to cancel something. Users have no appreciation for what goes on behind the scenes.

The fact is, any time you are really going to want to use a thread, there's a good chance some user somewhere will want to cancel whatever it is your thread is doing. Perhaps it's taking too long for them (they have short attention spans). Perhaps they hit the wrong button and love your code, but really don't have the time to sit and wait for the first five million prime numbers to get calculated.

The BackgroundWorker control provides tools to let you cope with these annoyances.

Earlier when you saw the BackgroundWorker control's event list, you may have noticed that it supports three events. DoWork and ProgressChanged we used. The third event, RunWorkerCompleted, we didn't. The RunWorkerCompleted event is fired when the code in DoWork completes, either by natural causes or because it was cancelled. Working hand in hand with this are three properties: `CancellationPending`, `IsBusy`, and `WorkerSupportsCancellation`.

Setting the `WorkerSupportsCancellation` property to `True` enables you to cancel whatever the control is doing with a quick call to `CancelAsync()`. At any time you can check to see whether the control is still doing its thing with the `IsBusy` property, and see whether it is waiting to cancel by checking the `CancellationPending` property. Let's extend the earlier example to see all these things in action, and provide our users with a way to cancel the thread if they so desire.

Try It Out: Cancelling a Thread

Go back to the program you were just working on and take a look at the form editor once again. Click on the BackgroundWorker control and use the Properties window to set the SupportsCancellation property to True, just as in Figure 18-7.

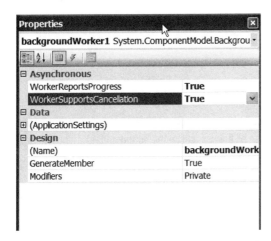

Figure 18-7. *Setting the SupportsCancellation property to True lets us write code to cancel background threads.*

Now bring up the event list of the control and double-click the RunWorkerCompleted event to get its handler stub into the code window. We won't write any code into the event just yet, but it's handy to have the event stub there in the code window so we don't go jumping around between designer and source editor throughout the example.

Now, go back up to the calcButton_click event. Let's add some code in there to change the text in the button to Cancel, and to enable us to actually cancel the worker if we need to. Make the following highlighted changes to the code:

```
Private Sub calcButton_Click(ByVal sender As System.Object, _
    ByVal e As System.EventArgs) Handles calcButton.Click


    If BackgroundWorker1.IsBusy Then
        BackgroundWorker1.CancelAsync()
```

```
        Else
            resultsBox.Items.Clear()

            startingNum = Long.Parse(startingNumber.Text)

            BackgroundWorker1.WorkerReportsProgress = True
            BackgroundWorker1.RunWorkerAsync()
            calcButton.Text = "Cancel"
        End If


    End Sub
```

When the button is clicked now, it first checks to see whether the thread is running. If it is, the code calls CancelAsync() to cancel it. Otherwise, the same code as before runs, but with an additional line to change the text of the button to Cancel. This means that as soon as the user clicks the button, the user instantly gets visual feedback for how to stop the long-running process from doing what it does.

Simply telling the BackgroundWorker to cancel is not enough. Our code in the DoWork handler needs to respond to the cancellation request by dropping out:

```
    Private Sub BackgroundWorker1_DoWork(ByVal sender As System.Object, _
        ByVal e As System.ComponentModel.DoWorkEventArgs) _
        Handles BackgroundWorker1.DoWork

        For currentNum As Long = startingNum To startingNum + 999

            If BackgroundWorker1.CancellationPending Then
                Return
            End If

            Dim factorial As Long = 0
            For i As Long = 1 To currentNum
                factorial += i
            Next
            BackgroundWorker1.ReportProgress( _
                0, String.Format("The factorial of {0} is {1}", _
                currentNum, factorial))
        Next


    End Sub
```

The first thing the loop does now is check whether a cancel request is pending. If it is, the code just returns, breaking out of the DoWork handler.

All that remains is to code up the RunWorkerCompleted() method, to put the text on the calcButton back the way it was:

```
Private Sub BackgroundWorker1_RunWorkerCompleted( _
    ByVal sender As System.Object, _
    ByVal e As System.ComponentModel.RunWorkerCompletedEventArgs) _
    Handles BackgroundWorker1.RunWorkerCompleted

    calcButton.Text = "Calculate"

End Sub
```

That's all there is to it. Run the program now to see it all in action.

Just to summarize what we did here, we enabled thread cancelling by setting the WorkerSupportsCancellation property to True on the control. Then to cancel the event, the code just calls CancelAsync() on the control, which in turn flips the CancellationPending flag on. Our code in DoWork just needs to check this flag to see whether it needs to exit early.

Race Conditions and Deadlocks

Computer programs are complex enough beasts when they are just doing one thing at a time. When you start to explore the world of threads, you end up with programs that do more than one thing at once, and life can get very complicated.

There are two specific conditions that you need to be aware of when you start working with multithreaded programs: race conditions and deadlocks.

A *race condition* occurs when two threads "race" for access to a resource. For example, you may have an object that's used in two threads. If one thread tries to change a value in the object while another tries to do the same thing, a race condition can occur. You can't guarantee which thread will get to the object first, and thus your code could end up with some nasty bugs.

To prevent this kind of thing from happening, Visual Basic has a special keyword called SyncLock. SyncLock is used to "lock" an object so that only the thread that locked it can work with it. For example:

```
SyncLock myEmployee
    myEmployee.IncreaseSalary( 10 )
End SyncLock
```

This locks the myEmployee object in order to increase its salary, preventing any other threads from also working with the object (perhaps to calculate the employee's bonus or tax) until the lock block has finished.

WHY WE DIDN'T USE A LOCK EARLIER

The example in the preceding "Try It Out" uses a shared variable, startingNum, to figure out which numbers we want to calculate factorials for. Now startingNum was initialized on the program's main thread, but read and worked with on the BackgroundWorker thread. It figures, then, that it should have been locked, but it wasn't. Why?

There are two reasons. First, locks can be used only with reference types (objects), and not value types (Integer, Boolean, Double, and so on). So a lock wouldn't have worked there because startingNum is a Long and not a reference type. Second, the order of things in our sample program guarantees that there won't be a locking problem. The value is set into the variable before the second thread is started. Had the value been changed while the thread was running, that could have caused all sorts of problems.

In general, whenever you need to access an object from a thread other than the main one (that is, a thread you created), you should lock it.

The opposite of a race condition is a *deadlock*. Whereas race conditions can cause your programs to do very strange things, deadlocks can cause them to just hang and do nothing for no apparent reason.

A deadlock occurs when two threads lock each other's resources. For example, one thread could lock an employee object and then wait for access to a department object. A second thread could have locked the department object and be waiting for the now locked employee object. The net result is that both threads stop dead in the water.

There is no magic keyword to prevent deadlocks from happening. You just need to be careful when writing your own code to make sure that you don't end up with a situation where a deadlock can occur.

Personally, I find the best way to achieve this is to use threads very sparingly indeed. If you have a desperate and clear need for a thread (to update the UI during a long-running operation, or to wait for something to happen while the main code continues), use them. Don't go nuts and drop threads all over the place, though, or you'll quickly end up in a huge mess of a program that is unbelievably difficult to debug.

Summary

The BackgroundWorker control and the Timer control provide you with a great deal of power when it comes to writing programs that seem to do more than one thing at once. Behind the scenes, the BackgroundWorker uses a bunch of .NET method calls to manage all the threading that quite frankly is pretty scary to get to grips with. The coolest part of the BackgroundWorker control is that we don't have to deal with that nasty stuff. Any time you want to fire up a new thread, just create an instance of the BackgroundWorker control (even in code), hook up the three events, and off you go.

CHAPTER 19

∎∎∎

Where to Now?

I can still clearly remember when I finished reading my first programming book. I had dutifully read all the pages, tried out all the examples, and done pretty much everything I had been told to do. Buoyed with my newfound knowledge, I sat down to write the next great killer application—and a strange thing happened. Well, more to the point, nothing happened. I didn't know where to start. I had no idea what I should do to begin my program. The book had shown me all the parts of the puzzle and had shown me how some of the bigger pieces fit together, but I lacked the experience to finish the jigsaw totally on my own.

That's where some of you are right now. Although we've certainly covered most of the cool features of Visual Basic 2005 Express, you may be wondering just where you go from here. When you put the book down, where can you turn for more help and advice? How can you start your first real program? Surely there's still more to learn?

The answer to that last question is an unequivocal yes! Programming is all about learning, constantly. Not a coding day will go by without you learning something new. As old as it makes me feel to say it, after 23 years of programming I still learn new stuff every day. Thankfully, though, the days of sitting in your den completely isolated from the rest of the world are over. There are plenty of resources out on the Internet, both official Microsoft ones and unofficial "fan" sites, to move you onward in your journey and to move you past the next hurdle: writing your first homegrown application.

Throughout this chapter then, I'll point you in the right direction, starting with some cool pieces of code from Microsoft known as starter kits, and moving all the way through to the great sites and blogs that you should definitely keep an eye on to learn more. By the end of the chapter, you'll definitely be in great shape to strike out on your own.

Starter Kits

The problem of not knowing exactly how to start writing your own programs is so common that Microsoft came up with a fantastic solution: *starter kits*. The idea behind starter kits is that "out of the box" you get a completely working program, documentation to help you understand what it does, and a set of code that you can then modify and tweak, effectively shaping it into the application you need.

Visual Basic 2005 Express ships with two starter kits: the Movie Collection starter kit and the Screen Saver starter kit. You can access them by simply starting a new project. The starter kits are shown at the end of the list of project templates, as shown in Figure 19-1.

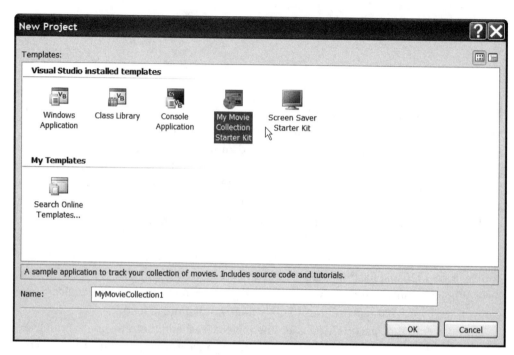

Figure 19-1. *You can access the starter kits just by clicking on Start New Project.*

When you choose a starter kit—for example, the Movie Collection starter kit—what happens is that VB Express creates a new project with a bunch of code and other resources (forms, images, and so on) inside. It also displays a web page telling you what the starter kit does and how to modify it. If you start a new project based on the Movie Collection starter kit, for example, VB Express will look like Figure 19-2.

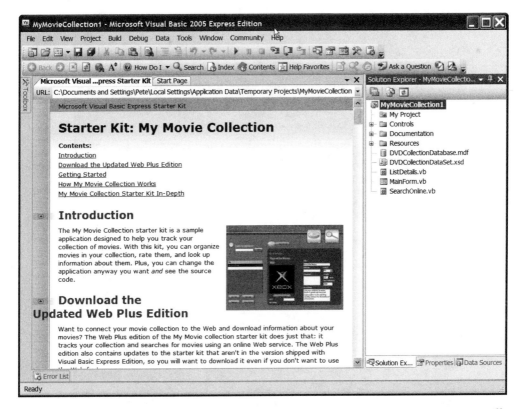

Figure 19-2. *Open the Movie Collection starter kit, and your development environment will look like this.*

There are more starter kits available beyond the basic two that ship with VB Express. If you point your browser at the Microsoft Express home page (`http://msdn.microsoft.com/vstudio/express`), you'll see a list of Express products on the left side of the page, as in Figure 19-3.

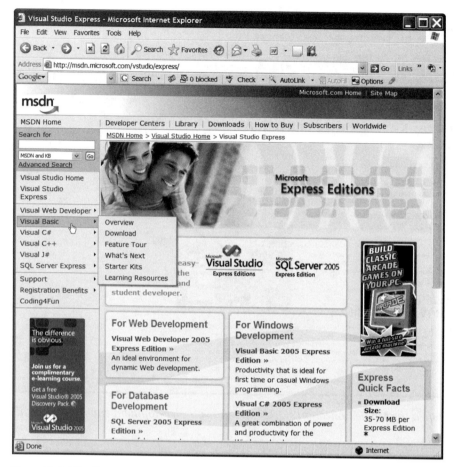

Figure 19-3. *The Express products home page*

By the way, notice on the left-hand navigation bar in Figure 19-3 that there's a Coding4Fun link. This is a great link for finding some neat snippets of code, articles, and challenges to improve your coding skills, and it's a wonderful resource for new developers.

You can find the starter kits simply by pointing at the product of your choice (our choice will naturally be Visual Basic) and then choosing Starter Kits from the menu that appears. As soon as you click the mouse, you'll be whizzed off to the Starter Kits page shown in Figure 19-4.

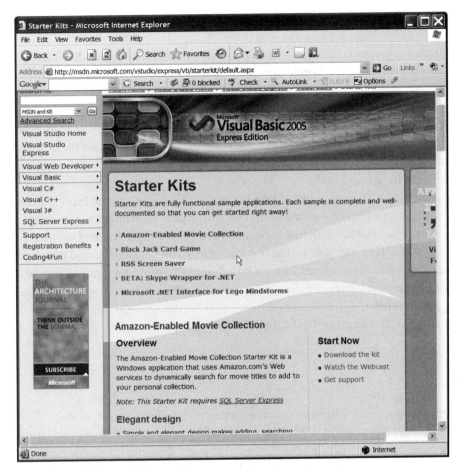

Figure 19-4. *The Starter Kits page for Visual Basic 2005 Express*

At the time of this writing, five starter kits are available for VB Express: the two that ship with the product, the Black Jack Card Game starter kit, the Skype Wrapper (which lets you build Voice over IP functionality into your applications), and an interface for the LEGO Mindstorms kits. Microsoft is promising more in the future, so keep a regular eye on this page.

The page does have links to download each of the starter kits, along with instructions on how to install them onto your machine. As I mentioned at the start, each kit comes with full instructions detailing not only what it does but also how to customize it, so why not dive in and have fun.

The Other Express Tools

Visiting the Express products home page in the preceding section brings us nicely onto the other Express products: SQL Server Express, Visual C++ Express, Visual J# Express, Visual C# Express, and Visual Web Developer Express.

If by now you are a die-hard Visual Basic 2005 fan, you may be wondering why I'm even bothering to mention the others. Well, two of them in particular should still be of interest to you. As you saw in Chapter 16, Visual Basic 2005 Express ships with SQL Server Express, so it's useful to know where that product lives should you want to explore SQL Server and databases in more detail.

Far more interesting, though, is Visual Web Developer Express. Of all the Express products, Visual Web Developer is the only one that supports more than one programming language (C# and Visual Basic). This tool is designed to let you build functional web-based applications with .NET, so now that you have cut your teeth on Visual Basic and Windows programming, Visual Web Developer Express is definitely the next tool that you should take a look at to turn your burgeoning Visual Basic coding skills toward the world of online application development.

Like Visual Basic 2005 Express, Visual Web Developer Express is a free download.

MSDN

All the Express products live within a section of Microsoft's website known as the Microsoft Developer Network (MSDN). This place should become your home away from home. The home page for MSDN is http://msdn.microsoft.com, and it's updated daily with new articles, video clips, code samples, and much more for .NET developers of all levels. You can access the full .NET Framework reference on the site; search for articles, code, and reference material on pretty much anything to do with programming; and even get involved in the community newsgroups and forums that Microsoft runs.

Now, I can't recommend these things highly enough. When I want to learn a new language fast, I turn to the forums. You'll find people there asking questions about almost everything that can be done with the language and tools, and you can use those questions either to guide your own study (I try to answer every unanswered question myself to further my own knowledge) or as a reference to find out the sorts of things that you can do. The MSDN community page can be found at http://msdn.microsoft.com/community/.

Blogs

Today, more and more people are getting involved in publishing blogs. In case you've never come across them before, a *blog* (it's short for web log) is an online journal in which people can write pretty much anything they want. There are blogs that cover people's daily lives, blogs targeted at products, and of course thousands of them targeted at programming and .NET.

You can read blogs just by visiting each one's web page, but a much better way to do things is to download a tool such as RSS Bandit. You see, blogs have things called *feeds* associated with them, and RSS Bandit can keep track of those feeds and automatically download new articles as they get posted. What's best is that RSS Bandit is actually written in .NET and grew out of a series of articles talking about how to develop such an application on MSDN. You can download RSS Bandit from its homepage at `http://www.rssbandit.org`.

As for the blogs themselves, you'll find a great selection at the Apress Ablog site at `http://blogs.apress.com/` (see Figure 19-5).

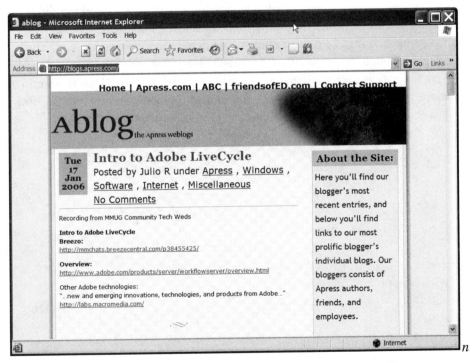

Figure 19-5. *The Ablog site, home to the blogs of Apress authors and staff*

The cool thing about blogs is that most blog authors also link to other people's blogs, so after you start reading one or two, you'll find links you'll want to follow even more. It then becomes even more important that you use a tool like RSS Bandit to keep track of everything.

There are also a ton of blogs listed at `http://msdn.microsoft.com/blogs`. These are blogs written by people employed by or very close to Microsoft. It's the word from the horse's mouth as far as .NET technical information is concerned.

I have a blog on the Ablog site, and I also have another less .NET-focused one at `http://peterwright.blogspot.com`.

Summary

I hope you've had fun working through this book. It was a lot of fun writing it. In this chapter I wanted to give you some pointers to online resources that can help you with the next step in your journey: creating your own applications.

Starter kits are a great stepping-stone to bigger things, giving you a working framework that you can tweak and play around with, but also giving you a full set of working code that you can explore and learn from. In addition, there are some great articles available on MSDN and through the world's newest publishing phenomenon, blogs.

Above all else, though, remember that you aren't alone. The community forums are there to serve not only as a reference but also as an interactive help line. Don't be afraid to post questions to the forums when you get stuck and you'll soon be on your way again.

Good luck, and be sure to drop me a line and let me know how you're doing.

Index

You Need the Companion eBook

Your purchase of this book entitles you to buy the companion PDF-version eBook for only $10. Take the weightless companion with you anywhere.

We believe this Apress title will prove so indispensable that you'll want to carry it with you everywhere, which is why we are offering the companion eBook (in PDF format) for $10 to customers who purchase this book now. Convenient and fully searchable, the PDF version of any content-rich, page-heavy Apress book makes a valuable addition to your programming library. You can easily find and copy code—or perform examples by quickly toggling between instructions and the application. Even simultaneously tackling a donut, diet soda, and complex code becomes simplified with hands-free eBooks!

Once you purchase your book, getting the $10 companion eBook is simple:

❶ Visit **www.apress.com/promo/tendollars/**.

❷ Complete a basic registration form to receive a randomly generated question about this title.

❸ Answer the question correctly in 60 seconds, and you will receive a promotional code to redeem for the $10.00 eBook.

2560 Ninth Street • Suite 219 • Berkeley, CA 94710

eBookshop

Offer valid through 03/07.

Apress®

Apress License Agreement (Single-User Products)

THIS IS A LEGAL AGREEMENT BETWEEN YOU, THE END USER, AND APRESS. BY OPENING THE SEALED CD PACKAGE, YOU ARE AGREEING TO BE BOUND BY THE TERMS OF THIS AGREEMENT. IF YOU DO NOT AGREE TO THE TERMS OF THIS AGREEMENT, PROMPTLY RETURN THE UNOPENED DISK PACKAGE AND THE ACCOMPANYING ITEMS (INCLUDING WRITTEN MATERIALS AND BINDERS AND OTHER CONTAINERS) TO THE PLACE YOU OBTAINED THEM FOR A FULL REFUND.

APRESS SOFTWARE LICENSE

1. GRANT OF LICENSE. Apress grants you the right to use one copy of the enclosed Microsoft software program collectively (the "SOFTWARE") on a single terminal connected to a single computer (e.g., with a single CPU). You may not network the SOFTWARE or otherwise use it on more than one computer or computer terminal at the same time.

2. COPYRIGHT. The SOFTWARE copyright is owned by Microsoft Corporation and is protected by United States copyright laws and international treaty provisions. The SOFTWARE contains licensed software programs, the use of which are governed by English language end user license agreements inside the licensed software programs. Therefore, you must treat each of the SOFTWARE programs like any other copyrighted material (e.g., a book or musical recording) except that you may either (a) make one copy of the SOFTWARE solely for backup or archival purposes, or (b) transfer the SOFTWARE to a single hard disk, provided you keep the original solely for backup or archival purposes. You may not copy the written material accompanying the SOFTWARE.

3. OTHER RESTRICTIONS. You may not rent or lease the SOFTWARE, but you may transfer the SOFTWARE and accompanying written materials on a permanent basis provided you retain no copies and the recipient agrees to the terms of this Agreement. You may not reverse engineer, decompile, or disassemble the SOFTWARE. If SOFTWARE is an update, any transfer must include the update and all prior versions. Distributors, dealers, and other resellers are prohibited from altering or opening the licensed SOFTWARE package.

4. By breaking the seal on the disc package, you agree to the terms and conditions printed in the Apress License Agreement. If you do not agree with the terms, simply return this book with the still-sealed CD package to the place of purchase for a refund.

DISCLAIMER OF WARRANTY

The program included in this book was supplied under a special license arrangement with Microsoft Corporation. For this reason Apress is responsible for the product warranty. If the media is defective, please return it to Apress which will arrange for its replacement. PLEASE DO NOT REUTRN IT TO OR CONTACT MICROSOFT CORPORATION FOR SOFTWARE SUPPORT. This product is provided for free, and no support is provided for by Apress or Microsoft Corporation. To the extent of any inconsistencies between this statement and the End User License Agreement which accompanies the program, this statement shall govern.

NO WARRANTIES. Apress disclaims all warranties, either express or implied, including, but not limited to, implied warranties of merchantability and fitness for a particular purpose, with respect to the SOFTWARE and the accompanying written materials. The software and any related documentation is provided "as is." You may have other rights, which vary from state to state.

NO LIABILITIES FOR CONSEQUENTIAL DAMAGES. In no event shall Apress be liable for any damages whatsoever (including, without limitation, damages from loss of business profits, business interruption, loss of business information, or other pecuniary loss) arising out of the use or inability to use this product, even if Apress has been advised of the possibility of such damages. Because some states do not allow the exclusion or limitation of liability for consequential or incidental damages, the above limitation may not apply to you.

U.S. GOVERNMENT RESTRICTED RIGHTS

The SOFTWARE and documentation are provided with RESTRICTED RIGHTS. Use, duplication, or disclosure by the Government is subject to restriction as set forth in subparagraph (c) (1) (ii) of The Rights in Technical Data and Computer Software clause at 52.227-7013. Contractor/manufacturer is Apress, 2560 Ninth Street, Suite 219, Berkeley, California, 94710.

This Agreement is governed by the laws of the State of California.

Should you have any questions concerning this Agreement, or if you wish to contact Apress for any reason, please write to Apress, 2560 Ninth Street, Suite 219, Berkeley, California, 94710.